The Polish Underground Army,
the Western Allies, and the
Failure of Strategic Unity
in World War II

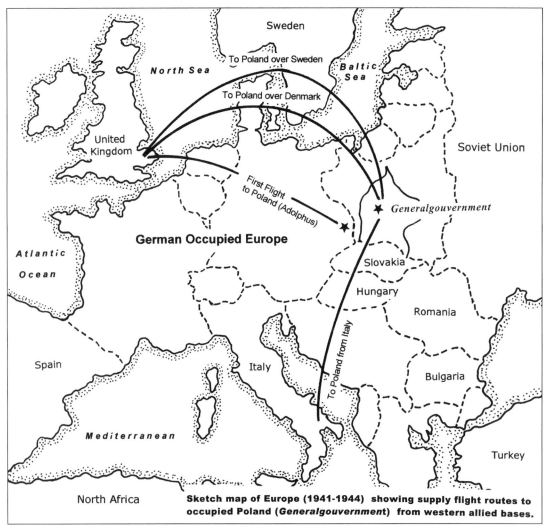

Sweden

North Sea

To Poland over Sweden

Baltic Sea

To Poland over Denmark

United Kingdom

Soviet Union

First Flight to Poland (Adolphus)

★ Generalgouvernement

German Occupied Europe

Atlantic Ocean

Slovakia

Hungary

Romania

Spain

Italy

To Poland from Italy

Bulgaria

Mediterranean

Turkey

North Africa

Sketch map of Europe (1941-1944) showing supply flight routes to occupied Poland (*Generalgouvernement*) from western allied bases.

GERALD H. KRAUSSE

The Polish Underground Army, the Western Allies, and the Failure of Strategic Unity in World War II

MICHAEL ALFRED PESZKE

Foreword by Piotr S. Wandycz

McFarland & Company, Inc., Publishers
Jefferson, North Carolina, and London

LIBRARY OF CONGRESS CATALOGUING-IN-PUBLICATION DATA

Peszke, Michael Alfred.
The Polish underground army, the Western Allies, and the failure of strategic unity in World War II / Michael Alfred Peszke ; foreword by Piotr S. Wandycz
p.   cm.
Includes bibliographical references and index.

ISBN 0-7864-2009-X (illustrated case binding : 50# alkaline paper)

1. World War, 1939–1945 — Poland.   2. Poland. Armia — History — World War, 1939–1945.
3. World War, 1939–1945 — Underground movements — Poland.   4. Strategy.
5. Poland — History — Occupation, 1939–1945.   6. Poland — History, Military — 20th century.
I. Title.
D765.P45   2005   940.54'12'0899185 — dc22   2004022362

British Library cataloguing data are available

On the cover: painting of Liberator Mk.VI of the Polish Air Force
Special Duties Squadron 1568, by Piotr Gorka; Polish Parachute Brigade Flag
(courtesy Polish Institute and General Sikorski Museum, London)

Manufactured in the United States of America

*McFarland & Company, Inc., Publishers
Box 611, Jefferson, North Carolina 28640
www.mcfarlandpub.com*

To my father, Lt. Col. Alfred Peszke, Polish Air Force,
whose life was dedicated to a free Poland
and whose love was lavished on his family;

and

my mother, Eugenia Halina Grebocka Peszke,
who took care of me throughout the
turbulent years of the Second World War.

Acknowledgments

The individuals and institutions that have helped, facilitated and supported the research that went into this book are too numerous to list, but there are some very specific individuals who went the extra mile to help out. I would like to express my appreciation to Mr. J. Galazka of the Pilsudski Institute of America, Mgr. Marcin Kwiecien of Jagellonian University, Mgr. Andrzej Suchcitz of the Polish Institute in London, Mrs. Diana Hall, Mr. Zbigniew Siemaszko, and finally Mr. T. Hughes, who did some spectacular research at the PRO. I would like to thank the libray staff of Central Connecticut State University for their gracious assistance throughout this project.

I thank Professor Piotr S. Wandycz, emeritus professor of history from Yale, and a renowned scholar of Polish history, for the foreword he wrote for this book. Thanks also go to artist Piotr Gorka for his painting, used on the cover of this book, of a Liberator Mk.VI of the Polish Air Force Special Duties Squadron 1568 depicted returning to its base in Italy after dropping supplies to the Polish Warsaw Uprising in August 1944. I also wish to thank Gerald H. Krausse, Ph.D., cartographer, who prepared the map appearing as a frontispiece facing the title page.

I am grateful to the Polonia Aid Foundation Trust that helped defray the costs of PRO research in London. Transcripts of Crown Records in the National Archives at Kew appear by permission of the Controller of Her Majesty's Stationery Office.

Quotations from *Memoirs of the Second World War* by Winston S. Churchill, copyright © 1959 by Houghton Mifflin Company, renewed 1987 by Lady Mary Soames, are reprinted by permission of Houghton Mifflin Company, all rights reserved.

Contents

Foreword

by PIOTR S. WANDYCZ

Bradford Durfee Professor of History Emeritus, Yale University

Poland's contribution to the Allied war effort is often minimized or glossed over in books dealing with the Second World War. And yet, in proportion to the size and population of their state, the Poles rendered great services in the war against the Axis powers. Before the outbreak of the war Polish cryptologists succeeded in breaking the German code and handed over the reconstructed Enigma machine to the French and the British. In the September 1939 campaign the Polish army, left to fight the Germans alone, inflicted heavy casualties on the Wehrmacht, particularly in armor and air force. According to some calculations, the Germans lost about 300 planes and close to 1,000 tanks. That the Western Allies drew no lesson from the Blitzkrieg was no fault of the Poles.

A Polish army was reconstituted in France in the form of two divisions (Grenadiers and Fusiliers), the Highland Brigade, and a small armored unit. Later, after the collapse of France, it was again recreated in Great Britain. Polish airmen played a conspicuous part in the Battle of Britain, the small Polish Navy performed valiantly, Polish troops — the First Armored Division of General Maczek, the Carpathian Brigade of General Kopanski and the Second Corps of General Anders — fought on virtually all western fronts, from Norway to Libya and from Italy to France, Belgium and the Netherlands. Polish soldiers in the Soviet-formed Berling army saw action in battles from Lenino to Berlin.

The home front, however, the struggle waged against the German occupier in Poland itself, was of special significance to the Poles. The British minister of Economic Warfare, Lord Selborne, realized this. He is cited in this book as writing: "To the Poles the war is in Poland and this is their last chance of fighting there." He referred to the Warsaw Uprising of 1944, which in a sense culminated the efforts of the Polish underground.

This book describes and analyzes the attempts of the Polish high command in Britain to integrate the Polish Home Army (i.e., the underground) into Western strategies. The interplay between these Polish efforts and British objectives is presented in detail and objectively.

Relying mainly on British and Polish archival documentation, Peszke unfolds this remarkable story, which really began in 1939 and went on until the end of the war. An eminent British historian of Special Operations Executive — with which the Polish side closely cooperated—called Sikorski's plans "grandiose" but not "absurd." Their implications were manifold. The plans involved assistance to the Home Army in the occupied country and required the use of planes for transportation of arms, munitions, paratroopers and highly trained personnel. The distance to be covered, and we must not forget the limited capacities of planes in World War II, raised tremendous problems. In some cases regarding military priorities—an offensive through the Balkans reaching into East Central Europe—the thinking of Sikorski and Churchill ran on parallel lines. In others, the Poles and the British did not see eye to eye and their priorities were different. No wonder, for the British were mainly concerned with their objectives and treated Polish goals as secondary. But there were also divisions among the British, and the author stresses Hugh Dalton's and Lord Selborne's understanding and empathy for the Polish position. One of the merits of this work is that we gain a good insight into British thinking and policies.

The Poles contributed to the Allied cause highly trained pilots who were forced to prove their valor and experience before the original Anglo-Polish agreement of 1940—humiliating to the Polish side—was replaced; the Polish squadrons, afterward even wings, were then recognized as autonomous units under Polish command. The final agreement on a separate Polish Air Force intervened only toward the end of the war in 1944.

In a strategy which foresaw major fighting on Polish soil, it was natural that paratroopers would occupy an important place. The Poles on British soil formed a unit of paratroopers which eventually reached the status of a brigade, commanded by General Sosabowski. The paratroopers, highly esteemed by the British, were according to explicit Anglo-Polish agreement to be used only for fighting in their homeland, and as the tragic Warsaw Uprising began the Poles entertained some vain hopes that they would not be used somewhere else. While sending them to Poland would demand means of transportation which the British insisted were not available, the Poles could not resist British pressure—there was a serious manpower shortage—to make the brigade participate in the disastrous operation at Arnhem. The brigade suffered very heavy losses, and General Sosabowski was forced to step down. It is clear that by having opposed the operation and having antagonized the British, Sosabowski became a convenient scapegoat. Cassandras are never popular.

If one thinks today of Arnhem and especially the Warsaw Uprising—to which the author devotes an important chapter—he cannot resist wondering about the realistic thinking or lack thereof shown by the Polish government in London and its high command, be it General Sikorski or General Sosnkowski. Perhaps the approach of Sikorski was too strongly influenced by the events of the First World War, when both Germany and Russia collapsed and the Polish legionaries and the POW (Secret Military Organization) fighters *within* the country were able to seize the initiative. One often speaks of generals fighting the previous war.

The author notes also Sikorski's overconfidence and his well-known personal vanity, but did the Polish military leaders really have a choice in the policies, military or diplomatic?

After the German attack on the Soviet Union in 1941, the Poles found themselves in a most peculiar situation within the Grand Alliance. They were to fight alongside the power which had treacherously and in collusion with Germany invaded and annexed half of their country in 1939, deported over a million of its citizens and murdered thousands of officers. Moscow showed no signs of willingness to make amends — on the contrary it firmly resisted giving up any of the annexed territories. Nor did Stalin abandon his objective of a postwar domination of East Central Europe, Poland included. Churchill, unlike Roosevelt, seemed to realize what was going on. Peszke cites the prime minister's remark at the Defence Committee section of the SOE: "Now that the Russians were advancing into Poland it was in our interest that Poland should be strong and well supported. Were she weak and overrun by the advancing Soviet armies, the result might hold great dangers in the future for the English-speaking peoples." But Churchill realized that Britain was the weakest of the Big Three and wartime exigencies often demanded glossing over differences with the Soviet Union.

This was bound to affect the plans of the Polish leaders whose voice was heard less and less in Allied counsels, which were strongly influenced by the Soviet Union. There were also unpleasant controversies between the Poles and the British concerning the use of planes, particularly in regard to aid to fighting Warsaw. But even if one recognizes some errors of judgment on the part of Polish leaders, they could not really avert the "defeat in victory," to borrow the title of the book by Ambassador Jan Ciechanowski.

Peszke presents this tragic story in a strictly chronological fashion, which makes perfectly good sense in view of the evolving international and military position of the Poles. The main outline of the story as well as certain aspects of it are well known, at least to the Polish reader. But as the author rightly points out, the question of seeking to integrate Polish wartime strategy into Western strategy, with all its ramifications, had not been fully tackled and needed to be presented in detail. Peszke concentrates on the Polish-British relationship, and treats the American aspect marginally. He is quite right because to America, and especially to President Roosevelt, Poland was of no real consequence. Peszke illustrates this fact by his account of Mikolajczyk's visit to Roosevelt in which the duplicity of the president was quite evident. The subsequent famous remark of Roosevelt at Yalta that Poland had been a source of trouble for 500 years was unfair and historically incorrect.

The last chapters of the book make particularly painful reading. The agony of Warsaw Uprising — irrespective of how one appraises it, and controversies do remain — is recalled once again, although from a different perspective. The author mentions the bitterness felt by Polish soldiers, airmen and sailors as VE Day was celebrated. This reviewer, then a junior artillery officer, remembers it well. Peszke ends his book with some remarks entitled "Discussion and Conclusion." They are valuable for one needs to approach "triumph and disaster" not only with understandable emotion. We must also try, as Kipling enjoins us, "to treat these two imposters just the same," and keep building once again for a better future.

Preface

Campaign: "A connected series of military operations
forming a distinct phase of a war."

"To the Poles the war is
in Poland"—Lord Selborne[1]

The five-year endeavor on the part of the Polish government to organize and nourish a clandestine secret army in occupied Poland and to integrate it into Western strategic planning easily falls into the Webster definition of a military campaign. It was
planned and had an ultimate goal, namely the establishment of a legitimate sovereign
authority in postwar Poland. The plan was to liberate as much Polish territory as possible through the effort of the Polish underground army, aided by supplies, trained specialists, and even parachute units and air components of the Polish forces from the
west. In the words of Mackenzie, the eminent historian of Britain's Special Operations
Executive (SOE), the Polish plan may have been "grandiose, but was not absurd."[2]

This, however, is not a history or even an outline of a history of the Polish clandestine military operations that were carried out in occupied Poland; it is not a history
of the Polish armed forces in exile, either. Definitive English-language studies of both
endeavors have yet to be published in Poland.[3]

While in the monograph I make a number of references to the activities of Polish land, air and naval forces in the West, it is merely to illustrate the size and relative
complexity of these forces in exile, which ultimately were intended to be moved to
Poland and which to some extent, tacit rather than explicit, were Poland's entrance fee
for consideration of their policy of seeking support, both diplomatic and military, from
the Western allies, primarily the British.

Finally, one more disclaimer—this is not a study of the many Polish staff plans
for an uprising in occupied Poland.[4] But this is the first attempt to synthesize the strategic thinking of the Polish commander in chief in exile in Paris and subsequently in
London. It attempts to document Polish efforts at obtaining Allied collaboration to aid
the Polish underground and attempts to create specialized forces to liaise with the
homeland. Clearly, the issue of staff planning for an uprising and staff planning for tying

in such efforts to Allied support were complementary. Polish plans for Western collaboration were dependent not only on Allied military support but ultimately on Allied political support, which in turn was affected by many international and national political dynamics. Many historians have already written on the different aspects of Polish governmental policy throughout the war.[5]

From a military vantage, the Poles did what they could to aid their British ally, and in some aspects Polish contributions were significant and even sincerely acknowledged at the time.[6]

As Britain's allies, the Polish forces formed in the West fought in many areas,[7] but the strategic arena for the Poles was obviously not the Middle East, the Italian peninsula or even France — it was Poland. This point was recognized by the British minister of Economic Warfare, Lord Selborne, who wrote in October 1943 to the British War Cabinet urging support for the Polish underground army: "To the Poles the war is in Poland and this is their last chance of fighting there."[8] This fight could only be waged by the Polish underground army or, as the Poles called it, the Home Army (*Armia Krajowa* or *AK*). The Poles strove to build it up, to arm it and furthermore to ensure that the only branches of the Polish armed forces in the West that could directly affect, support and intervene in occupied Poland, namely the Polish Air Force and the Polish Parachute Brigade, were trained, equipped and planned for use in Poland.

This was also recognized by the general officer commanding the Polish underground army, Gen. Stefan Rowecki who in September 1943 cabled the Polish military headquarters in London, "The [Polish] Air Force in the West is the only branch of the Polish Armed Forces that can contribute to the national uprising. All efforts should be dedicated to its growth. The Uprising cannot Fail."[9]

It would be a major error, however, to assume that the issue of air and parachute contracts with the occupied homeland was bruited only in 1943. In fact, this story began in 1939 and preoccupied the Poles throughout the war. Even the creation of the Polish clandestine state, under German occupation, was accomplished through an air link in September 1939.[10] Merrick wrote that "Poland had a fully operative underground network in place before the Germans had finished shooting."[11]

This complex history of effort and struggle is hardly known in the West. Some of this stems from the fact that the recounting of history is rarely espoused by the average citizen. Polish history suffers from very specific obstacles stemming from the Polish role in World War II and their diplomatic disagreement with the Soviets.

It is now some 60 years since the end of the Second World War. Passions have cooled and old enemies are now close allies in NATO; much of what is remembered or bruited is only vaguely relevant to the actual conflict or the causes of the war. The historical events that moved and afflicted so many have been covered by a patina of current irrelevance, such as movies masquerading as history, and have become mired in ethnocentric bias.

But the adage that the victor writes the history is very much the case when it comes to Poland and its history in the Second World War that, by whatever standard one cares to measure, the Poles lost. This tragic denouement was in spite of Poland being one of the three original allies and the first country to stand up to Germany in 1939. But in May 1945, when hostilities ceased, Poland was occupied by one of the two aggressors from 1939, namely the Soviet Union.[12] Clausewitz hypothesized what was intuitively known for centuries: that foreign policy and military confrontation are one and the same.[13] Therefore, while this is a primarily military historical study, the international and political situation compounded and affected Polish foreign policies and even Polish military options. The final result was a total defeat of all Polish plans, since Poland, in its war against Germany, had enjoyed at the very least symbolic support and sympathy, vis-à-vis the Soviets this was absolutely lacking.

Despite the Soviet Union's initial collusion with Germany in 1939 and its brutal aggression against Finland, all was forgotten as the Soviets fought the vaunted Germany army to a standstill at a time when the Western Powers were stalled.[14] This uncritical adulation was pervasive in the majority of the mass media of both the United Kingdom and the United States.[15] The Poles, in comparison, were counselled on how to be good democrats or castigated as fascistic warmongers. In Western societies still hurting from the prewar depression and with socialist movements enjoying strong support, the Soviet model seemed very attractive.[16]

The Poles became very much the victims of this mass media blitz as the Soviets and their many sympathizers were able to pervert Polish political goals and subsequently even Polish history, whenever it confronted the official Communist and hence Soviet party line. The partitions of Poland by the Germans and Soviets in 1939 were rationalized as merely an attempt by Stalin to protect the Ukrainan and Belorussian population from German occupation. The Katyn murders of Polish officers were dismissed as German propaganda and the Polish request for an International Red Cross investigation as an example of Polish political stupidity and Allied disloyalty.[17] The failure of the Soviets to allow Western Allied planes flying aid to the Warsaw insurgents in 1944 was blatantly ignored and the criminal act of arresting Polish underground leaders in Poland (March 1945) and trying them in Moscow only elicited comments about Soviet compassion since none were actually sentenced to death.

The Western acquiescence in Soviet occupation and political colonization of Poland resulted not only in a historical vacuum but also in ambiguity and ambivalence about Poland and its history. It is beyond doubt that many Britons were in fact quite ashamed of their passive role. Lord Ismay wrote, "Nobody can deny that the failure to secure freedom and independence for Poland has brought shame on the western Democracies."[18] But shame only lasts a short time and, as the saying goes, people move on.

The fact that the Poles, people of a minor country, even if an ally, were reluctant to accommodate what seemed to many a reasonable demand for a government "friendly" to the Soviets put the Polish government and its foreign policy on a collision course with much of Western public opinion. Thus, while in the first two years of the war the Poles were treated as gallant and even valuable allies, by 1945 they were perceived at best as tiresome relatives who had outstayed their welcome.

Since the Polish armed forces in the West were a political and diplomatic weapon of the Polish state and of the Polish government in exile, the forces opposed to Polish interest sought also to discredit the Polish military, then and later, whether by propagating myths or by silence. Thus, Polish military history of World War II is even more significant than the case for other countries directly influenced by political issues. That is the reason why in this monograph, whose focus is on military issues, political and foreign policy issues seem to intrude: they were major milestones that marked the highs and lows of Polish success and have left more lasting scars than the destruction of the war.

The tragic and dehumanizing experience of Poland during the last 50 years as a Soviet satellite and involuntary founding member of the Soviet-inspired and -controlled Warsaw Pact has succeeded in solidifying many misconceptions and has led to a distortion of the Polish experience during the Second World War.[19] In the United States, Poland in the Second World War is inevitably thought of as the locus of German concentration camps. This leaves an impression, intended or not, that somehow the Poles were implicated.[20]

Thus, after 50 years of being viewed through the Cold War prism as an enemy state with at best a distorted history of World War II, it is not surprising that knowledge of Polish contributions to the Allied coalition is fragmentary. The fact that there was a Polish grand design is unknown to even most Polish scholars, who for decades were unable to read or study Polish archives based in the United Kingdom and who were expected to parrot the Communist line that everything prior to 1939 in Poland and everything done by the Poles in exile was worthless and ideologically flawed.[21] In the English-speaking world this "blank page" of history is probably less true for military historians since many excellent monographs mention Polish contributions, often with words of high praise.[22] English-language studies of the Polish military are relatively rare, but can be found.[23]

The Polish government in exile began the process of recreating the Polish armed forces in France as early as October 1939 — in fact, even before Poland's defeat. The officer cadre of these forces were prewar, many going all the way back to 1919, hence there was a continuity of tradition and a consensus of war goals. Poland's foreign policy, its perception of friends and enemies, was also a continuation of prewar policies, and the same personalities who played a role in 1919–1939 were once again center stage. This continuation of policy, the challenges of various alliances, as well as military doctrine is emphasized in chapters I and II. We can see that the same countries played nearly identical roles vis-à-vis Poland in 1920, as enemies or friends.

The Polish staff and high command of this force based in London played a part in the Allied coalition but also attempted to develop its own long-term strategy. In retrospect, many have come to the erroneous conclusion that the Poles were completely unrealistic in all their plans and hopes, while many Poles have concluded that the British simply took advantage of them to have extra manpower. Both theses have a kernel of veracity, but such assumptions are simplistic given the complexities of the situation during the war. In February 1944, after Poland had been in fact delivered to the Soviet strategic area of interest, at a meeting of the Defence Committee section of the SOE, after the Tehran Conference, Churchill argued against Portal and for an extra allocation of planes for the Polish special duties flight: "Now that the Russians are advancing into Poland it is in our interest that Poland should be strong and well supported. Were she weak and overrun by the advancing Soviet armies, the result might hold great dangers in the future for the English-speaking peoples."[24] Thus Polish plans were not conceived in a complete political vacuum. On the other side, it has to be noted that Churchill schemed shamelessly with Stalin to move Polish troops out of the Soviet

Union in 1942 to buttress his anemic military strength in the Middle East.[25] Also, the British brutally coerced the Poles to have the Polish Parachute Brigade used in Northwest Europe, contrary to all prior agreements.[26]

Polish goals were well articulated and argued both in London and with the Combined Chiefs of Staffs in Washington. At times, primarily before the entrance of the Soviets on the side of the anti–German alliance, Poles enjoyed the wholehearted support of the British ally, but with time they were merely tolerated and later close to being derided. In the long run they were directly affected by the power of the Soviet Union on the only Polish ally with whom there was a formal treaty, the United Kingdom. The British lost power and influence during the war and Churchill as early as Tehran referred to the poor English donkey surrounded by the great Russian bear and the great American buffalo. Many called the grand coalition the alliance of the two and a half.[27]

The Big Three conference at Yalta sealed the fate of the constitutional Polish government in London, but in fact, as the Poles in the West argued, it also determined the fate of the country; Yalta apologists still insist that the agreements were fair but that the Soviets reneged. The many thousands of Poles who refused to go back to a Soviet-occupied country were now victimized by pejorative appellations as closet fascists, anti–Semites and vagabond shirkers who refused to participate in the labor of rebuilding their homeland, while allegedly pining for their huge estates.

In a world weary of war, where many, both intellectuals as well as proletariat, were leaning to the new secular religion of egalitarianism and who had for many years been expected to celebrate the contributions of the Soviets, the Polish cause was at best tiresome, but too often painted in the most outrageous terms. The United States ambassador in Moscow described the Polish government in London (in January 1944) in the following words: "predominantly a group of aristocrats looking to Americans and British to restore their position in Poland and landed properties and feudalistic system."[28] At Yalta, Roosevelt interrupted a Churchillian attempt to persuade Stalin to a fig-leaf compromise, by stating: "The Polish question has been giving the world a headache over a period of five centuries."[29]

Many prominent Americans had a strange disdain for all East Europeans, so much at odds with their so-often bruited commitment to human rights and democratic principles. Many viewed the future axis of Soviet and American collaboration as mankind's best hope. The same American statesmen who wished to see an end to the British Empire as well as French and Dutch colonial rule were paradoxically sympathetic to Soviet policy of subjugating neighbors to Soviet control.[30] Hopkins assured Stalin in 1945 that the United States did not share Churchill's policies and that the question of Poland was of no special interest to the United States, which saw no desire for any particular kind of government in that country.[31] Hopkins assured Stalin there would be no disagreement over Poland but that claims against Polish interest must not offend Western opinion or the six million voting Polish-Americans.[32]

This monograph develops the Polish strategy for supporting and arming the Polish underground army right from the beginning in France in October 1939, to the bitter end of April 1945. But even more important, the monograph traces the attempts by Gen. Wladyslaw Sikorski and his successor, General Kazimierz Sosnkowski, to integrate the Polish Home Army into Western strategy.

For the Poles, it was obvious that sovereignty could be achieved only by a defeat of Germany and some attempt to keep the Soviets out of Poland, either by promoting the Balkan route or at least so strengthening the Polish clandestine forces that they would be centers of Polish autonomy in the sea of Soviet armies. This long-term strategic goal could be accomplished only through a combination of factors: the implementation of the Churchillian Balkan strategy, which initially strove to inveigle the Turks to the Allied side,[33] and the Polish plans to subvert Romania and Hungary to the Allied side.[34] Churchill's plans were rebuffed by the Turks, defeated by the Germans in the Aegean and scoffed at by the Americans.[35] But as long as they persisted there was also some indirect hope for the Poles.

From the very beginning, Sikorski looked to the Balkan strategy for the eventual victory over Germany. Even before France's defeat, Polish military evacuees were routed to the French mandate of Syria to form what was hoped to be a corps, but became merely an independent autonomous infantry brigade, the Carpathian Brigade. Sikorski hoped for a grand alliance of the various Balkan and Danubian countries, based on the old traditional alliance of Poland and Romania, and that of Poland and Hungary. (It was unfortunate that Poland's good relations and political efforts with those neighbors were confounded by their own enmity over Transylvania.) If successful, this would have resulted in a well-armed clandestine force in occupied Poland aiding allied armies through the "soft underbelly of Europe." Sikorski's strategic eventuality was very much shared by Churchill, though there appear to be no archival documents to prove that this was discussed by the two statesmen. Given the close and quite informal relationship that the two enjoyed it is at least quite plausible that Sikorski was encouraged in his plans by either direct or indirect communications from Downing Street.

Churchill's strategic concept was fatally impacted when Allied troops were moved out of Italy to invade southern France in August 1944. But as late as 1945 he still urged Field Marshal Alexander to plan a strike into Austria from Italy.

This strategic approach came to an end in August 1944, when Churchill reluctantly acceded to American pressure for the withdrawal of a number of divisions from the Italian campaign for the invasion of southern France (Operation Dragoon).[36]

This five-year struggle was carried out at the diplomatic level and also by developing an independent mode of moving arms to Poland (the Polish special duties flight) and training a potential praetorian guard to hold such autonomous centers in Poland, namely the independent Parachute Brigade. Thus, the monograph gives considerable attention to these Polish services and formations. Polish requirements were constantly at odds with both British political goals and British military needs. This became particularly true for the allocation of long-range aircraft and Polish multiengined crews and the eventual use of the Polish Parachute Brigade.

The rest of the Polish military in exile was hoped to be a reserve to be moved to Poland, a logistical exercise which the Poles realized required British assistance and collaboration. Finally the Polish Government exerted all efforts to have the Polish clandestine forces, the Armia Krajowa (AK), declared Allied combatants and thus be legitimized by the Western powers before the eyes of both Germans and Soviets, who both sought their destruction.

The Interwar Period, 1919–1939

It has been well argued that the Second World War was merely a continuation of the Great War of 1914–1918. With the exception of the defunct Austro-Hungarian Empire, all the other major powers of that conflict, whether seemingly victorious or temporarily vanquished, were either seeking to consolidate their positions achieved at the Paris Peace Treaty, or plotting to undo their mandates.[1]

This was also true for Poland which found its historic place in the concert of free nations as a result of the collapse of the three partitioning powers.[2] Poland, before its independence had even been internationally recognized, had to wage one major war against the Russians and a draining series of border conflicts with Germany. This struggle to assure viable boundaries resulted in bitter and open enmity of the Germans, encouraged in their attitude by the British, and a deep-rooted hostility of the Soviets.[3]

Following the Polish victory over the Soviets in 1920, capped by the victory at Warsaw in August 1920[4] the Polish Army was significantly and adversely affected by a combination of factors all having one common denominator, namely the lack of capital investment, general worldwide economic malaise and inadequate industrial infrastructure in Poland. This economic blight, a direct result of the exploitive policies of the three partitioning powers, was capped by the fact that Poland was the battlefield of the four-year struggle between the Central Powers (Germany and Austria-Hungary) and Tsarist Russia.* In the West, peace was achieved on November 11, 1918, but for Poland it was only the beginning of protracted discussions and negotiations in Paris. Poland's interests were inevitably a pawn in the great game of international diplomacy.[5]

Poland's interwar policy was based on the French Alliance, signed on February 19, 1921, in Paris by Marshal Pilsudski and the French president, Millerand. This was augmented by a treaty with the Romanians of March 3, 1921. After the signing of the Polish-French Alliance in 1921, France gave Poland considerable credits and also sold much World War I surplus war material, not only much of it quite worthless but all with economic conditions.[6] The Polish obligation under the Polish-French military treaty

---

Poland embarked on her independence in 1918 with industrial output at 20 percent of the 1913 production. The loss of Polish industry in that period was estimated at 73 billion French francs. Furthermore, the worldwide crisis of 1929 hit Poland severely with every fourth Polish worker being unemployed. Poland's per capita annual income of 610 zlotys compared to the Western average of 2,490 zlotys.

was that Poland maintain a standing army of 30 infantry divisions. This commitment was scrupulously maintained to September 1939. The French in turn undertook the reciprocal obligation of going to war against Germany if Poland was attacked.[7] The British viewed this French policy with a jaundiced eye.[8]

The alliance with France, coupled to the victorious Polish Army, was a credible deterrent to the hostility of the disarmed Weimar Republic.[9] In turn the Germans looked to the Soviets to remedy their own strategic situation by the signing of the Rapallo Treaty in 1922.[10]

But the bloom began to fade quickly on the French alliance. The French always pined for their pre–1914 relationship with the Russians, since Poland was a poor substitute for an Eastern counterweight to Germany. The French also looked to Britain for support, sensing that their bloodied country was unable to stand up to Germany and certainly not against Germany and Italy together. The British in turn worked to integrate Germany back into the family of European nations, as a bulwark against Communism, and even at Poland's expense.[11]

Between 1924 and 1932 the French did everything to keep in step with the British and to arrive at an accommodation with Germany. In this they were strongly encouraged by the British, where the Foreign Office minuted in 1931 that "sooner or later it will be necessary to force a settlement on Poland."[12] In December 1932 at Geneva the five powers, France, Italy, UK, Germany and the USA, endorsed the proposition that Germany had an equality of right to re-arm while the British made it clear that they had little interest in "Mitteleuropa" and envisioned that legitimate German grievances in the east would need to be corrected to ensure peace and stability in Europe. As Hitler began his rearmament, the British made many diplomatic overtures to show him that there was good will.[13]

Poland felt betrayed by the French when the Treaty of Locarno (1925) regularized German western boundaries but failed to do so for the east.[14] But what is not well known that the French, as a price for British support, agreed that were Germany to attack Poland, the French response would be conditional on a vote in the League of Nations condemning German aggression. Poland protested, but to little avail. The alliance, if not dead, was significantly weakened in the eyes of all parties.

In addition, complicating the international problems which faced the Poles was their own internal political situation where numerous political parties, with very unique idiosyncratic agendas, constantly battled each other and led to executive anarchy.[15] All these factors inexorably led to the coup d'état by Pilsudski in 1926.[16]

The Poles have always insisted that when Hitler came to power, they offered France an alliance in a preventive war against Germany. Whether this Polish diplomatic initiative actually took place is one of the most controversial disputes of prewar international diplomacy since the French have always categorically denied that it took place, arguing that there are no Polish or French archives to prove this alleged Pilsudski overture. But if Pilsudski did in fact take such an initiative it is highly unlikely that, having spent all his life in conspiracies, a paper trail would have been left. It is, however, very plausible that Hitler either believed that such Polish initiatives had taken place or was concerned that they might.[17]

Paradoxically it was Hitler's rise to power that led to the nonaggression declaration between Germany and Poland on January 26, 1934. Also, it is not clear whether Hitler wanted to buy time, or whether he in fact hoped to have Poland as a loyal satellite in his projected war against Communism.

The chronology of events is that the Poles turned to Germany and asked an open-ended question: since Germany had withdrawn from the League of Nations, the Polish government wished to know whether there were other steps in Polish-German relations to compensate for this loss of security. The nonaggression declaration quickly followed.

It is paradoxical that Poland became the focus of intense criticism by the same countries that had signed the Locarno Treaty and exerted pressure on Poland to accommodate to German revisionism to undo the alleged inequities of the Versailles treaty. In December 1938, three months after the Munich conference which is now synonymous with appeasement, the French signed a nonaggression treaty with Germany which in fact was Locarno to the tenth degree as far as Germany was concerned.[18]

Concurrently, after a 12-year period of very hostile relations with the Soviet Union, where the boundary was porous for the movement of agents of both sides, Poland signed a Treaty of Non-Aggression with its huge eastern neighbor on July 25, 1932. This treaty formally accepted the Polish-Soviet boundary negotiated by both sides in the Peace Treaty of Riga of March 18, 1921, and it was in force on September 17, 1939.

In 1936, the German entry into the demilitarized zone west of the Rhine contrary to the provisions of the Versailles treaty forced the French and even the British to face the reality of the German threat. As a result of this crisis, the French invited Pilsudski's successor, Edward Smigly-Rydz, to France which led to a new and very significant military rearmament loan, negotiated at Rambouillet in September 1936. This was a significant infusion of two billion francs over a four-year period and required judicious management.[19]

The Last Months of Peace and Britain's Guarantee to Poland

The German march into Prague on March 15, 1939, after the promising but humiliating agreements reached at Munich the prior year, finally led the British to make a decision to support Poland and Romania.[20] This was the famous and very controversial guarantee of Poland's sovereignty on March 30, 1939. Chamberlain's government had agonized about the best policy to contain Germany and the only options were either the Soviet Union and the despised Bolsheviks or Poland — a much weaker partner. The British military assessed the situation as follows.

"The value of Poland lay not in the capacity of her army to launch an offensive against Germany, which was virtually non-existent, but in her capacity to absorb German divisions. Above all she must not be allowed to supplement them by subordinating her foreign policy to Hitler's, or to allow them free reign in the west by maintaining an attitude of benevolent neutrality." Furthermore, the British chiefs stated, "It was better to fight with Poland as an ally than without her."[21]

It is fair to say that Polish public opinion would never have stood for any policy which might have been historically analogous to the first and second partitions, and that the Polish armed forces would have fought in the most unfavorable circumstances. The same attitude of unyielding determination influenced and guided Polish foreign policy. But the British could not rationally come to such a conclusion and wished to preclude the Polish armed forces from enhancing German military potential. Hitler immediately renounced the Polish-German declaration on April 28, 1939. His rationale was that: "This agreement contained one single exception which was in practice conceded to Poland. It was laid down that the pacts of mutual assistance already entered into by Poland [this applied to the pact with France] should not be affected by this agreement."

Hitler proceeded to argue that the British initiatives guaranteeing Poland's sovereignty infringed on the Polish-German declaration.[22]

The only parsimonious explanation of British foreign policy characterized by its unwillingness to advance a loan, with no plans to come to Poland's military aid or even to implement its promises of aerial attacks, is in fact that the British wished to ensure that the Polish armed forces would not be at the side of the Germans.

Polish Plans for Clandestine Activity

The Poles had a long history of clandestine activities. For years such activity had been directed at the Soviet Union, namely the highly secret and controversial "Prometheus" policy. This was initiated by Pilsudski with the hope that the many nationalist and ethnic groups enslaved by the Soviet Union would be encouraged to gain independence and hence weaken the monolithic eastern neighbor.[23]

But furthermore, Pilsudski and his close adherents had spent considerable time in various clandestine organizations, the last and best organized being the Polska Organizacia Wojskowa and the many guerrilla groups that had operated against the Germans in the disputed territories of Silesia. The next step to formulating plans for clandestine activity in case of war was a natural and logical development leading to a specialized and ultra-secret section — Ekspozytura nr. 2 — based in the already highly secret Section II (Intelligence) of the Polish Staff. The goal of the section was the destruction of military communications and arsenals, and the formation of diversionary groups specializing in sabotage. In the early years of independence much of this was in fact directed at Russia, but in 1938 plans were also formulated for action in western Poland in event of German aggression. Over 200 such secret patrols were formed and deployed in September 1939.[24] Since these plans were secret, the details are often hard to tease out due to the obvious need-to-know rule of all secret agencies. Therefore, individual reminiscences, valuable as they are, may in fact be rather one-dimensional.

When in 1939 the Poles were reorienting their plans to face the Germans, Dabrowski, one of the senior officers of this clandestine group, commented that it had taken the Poles years to develop a secret network of agents in the East and it was impossible to duplicate this in the west, particularly given the highly developed area of the West compared to the East.[25] Even so, the following regions were picked as having crucial strategic importance: Lomza, Mlawa, Torun, Poznan, Lodz, Krakow and a total of 900 trained cadre were to be left in place. These men were in the majority reserve officers, with a documented integrity of character and known for their patriotism. In conjunction with this plan, 300 underground storage bunkers were constructed and stored with dynamite, grenades, 450 pistols plus other diversionary equipment. The actual fate of these provisions is not known. There were some serious snafus, e.g. military equipment sent in the last days of the peace to a diversionary unit were requisitioned by a regular army commander at the train depot for the use of their own units. The Free City of Danzig had a Polish post office which was defended by one of these clandestine groups.[26]

This effort was to be complemented by diversionary parachute attacks, primarily aimed at German troops concentrations and rail movements in East Prussia.

Parachute units began to undertake training in 1937 in Legionowo (near Warsaw) with about a hundred volunteers from many branches of the army. The training included knowledge of folding a parachute, 15 drops from a tower, followed by jumps from a static balloon and then from a plane. In September 1938 (the traditional month for army maneuvers after the harvest was gathered), the course focused on training the parachutists in diversionary tactics and techniques. This exercise was organized into sections of 24 parachutists in three squads, consisting respectively of communications, engineers and supporting infantry. These units were equipped with light machine guns and hand grenades, and the engineers carried simulated explosive equipment while the communications specialists had carrier pigeons and wireless sets and generators as well as batteries. The section was transported on two LOT Airlines Fokkers to Lwow and then took part in the military maneuvers.

The diversionary part of the exercise went well, although the wireless sets did not perform adequately; but the overall satisfactory estimate of the performance of the parachute diversionary units led to the formal creation in May 1939 of the Wojskowy Osrodek Spadochronowy in Bydgoszcz as an extension of the IV (Torun) Air Regiment (WOS Army Parachute Center). The officers in charge of training were Gorecki and Sigenfeld (engineers) and Malinowski (communications). The new Polish MORS submachine gun was added to the equipment of the parachute units. In June 1939, the WOS began the training of the first group of 40 officers and 40 noncommissioned officers, all volunteers. Parachutes were Polish-made American Irvings. In mid–August, the WOS put on an exhibition maneuver, where the parachute unit attacked a major rail connection, while the other side consisted of a battalion of engineers of rail repair section. The maneuver was successful and led to the beginning of the second tour of training and the writing of staff instructions on preventing such diversionary tactics against the Poles.[27]

Preparations for War

During the summer of 1939, politicians and diplomats of the Western states, including those of Poland's allies, strove mightily and with increasing guile, if not duplicity, to avert war. The Poles in turn were clearly concerned that the final result of this peace-seeking process would in fact be another version of Munich with Poland being now asked to pay the price of "peace in our time." With that concern the Poles made it as clear as possible that any German infringement of the status of the Free City of Danzig would be a cassus belli for Poland. This was not endorsed by the French or British until the last days of peace but was eventually agreed to in the Polish-British Treaty of Mutual Assistance of August 25, 1939.

Military discussions began to be held by Polish staff representatives with their French and British counterparts. This was the first step in the long and at times warm and also too frequently bitter and frustrating collaboration between the Polish military and its Western allies.

The first of these meetings occurred in Paris on May 16, 1939, in which the Poles were represented by the minister of Military Affairs, General Kasprzycki, while the French side was led by Generals Gamelin and Georges. The French representatives were worried that the onset of war would be an invasion of France by combined German and Italian forces and wanted the Poles to be prepared to attack Germany.

In the event of a German attack on Poland, Gamelin assured the Poles that the French Army would develop an offensive by the 15th day of the war. However, air operations by the French were to be initiated immediately. This meeting was followed by a special subcommittee on air matters. The Poles were represented by Colonel Karpinski of Poland's military aviation and the French by General Vuillemin, chief of staff of the French Air Force. The French agreed in principle to move five bomber squadrons to Polish bases for shuttle bombing of German targets. In fact, very preliminary steps in this direction were implemented.[28] The joint commission agreed to undertake immediate negotiations on all the essentials involved with such plans, such as radio communications, logistical support and preparation of bases on Polish territory and their maintenance. Following these talks, the Polish staff then delegated General Kossowski to Paris, accompanied by experts in the area of ground, air and naval matters whose task was to promote the acquisition of war materiel vital to Polish war needs.

On May 19, 1939, Gamelin signed the military protocol but made its implementation conditioned on the signing of the political protocol which the French foreign office postponed till September 4, 1939. The most likely explanation is that the Polish demand that any German operations against Danzig were to be considered as "cassus belli" was not acceptable to the French. But the French again followed the British in declaring war against the Germans, by September 4, and the political protocol was signed on that day since it was obvious that the Germans were attacking the Polish state and not just seeking a putsch in Danzig.[29] In other words, even with Gamelin's caveat of an offensive 15 days after September 3, the French forces should have launched significant attacks against Germany, while French air offensive should have started on September 4.

In his postwar memoirs, Sir Edmund Ironside commented: "The French had lied to the Poles in saying they are going to attack. There is no idea of it."[30]

In turn, on May 24, 1939, the British naval and air force representatives met with their Polish colleagues, but these talks were merely informative. The British refused to consider the move of any British surface ships to the Baltic. It was in these talks that the idea of moving the major Polish surface ships to the United Kingdom was first bruited.

In addition, General Stachiewicz, Polish chief of staff, also had talks with the British military representative, General Clayton, and on July 19, the British chief of the General Staff, General Ironside, arrived in Warsaw and held a number of meetings in which he was forthcoming in promise of aid but restrained in any commitment of British military actions except for the immediate imposition of a blockade by the Royal Navy and operations by the Royal Air Force. It is interesting what the British military attaché to Poland, Lt. Col. Edward Roland Sword, wrote in his diaries when discussing Ironside's mission to Poland. "He tells me his task, which consisted largely in trying to obtain a guarantee from the Poles that they will not precipitate a war through a corporal blowing up a bridge."[31]

In view of these joint talks at the highest levels of the military, the argument advanced by the Poles throughout the war, that in fact it was a coalition effort, can be validated. But in all of this the one concrete and substantial support, namely a British loan for purchase of military equipment, was not forthcoming. There was a major split in the British government on this point. The Foreign Office actually, perhaps weakly, did argue for such loans, but the Treasury was categorically opposed and stood its ground. It is interesting what Ironside cabled London from Warsaw in July 1939. Describing the Polish efforts at preparing for the war as "little short of prodigious," Ironside went on to say, "We ought not to make so many conditions to our financial aid. That one of the ways of convincing Hitler that we are serious is by granting this monetary aid to Poland. That the Poles are strong enough to resist."[32] Also during these staff talks, the Poles gave a copy of a reconstructed Enigma machine to both their French and British allies.[33]

The Polish Army had already been on a partial mobilization since March 1939 but during the summer months the intensity of preparations heightened. The field armies were assigned their sectors, staffs were mobilized and field fortifications expeditiously constructed, particularly in the densely populated region of Silesia.[34] Secret bases were planned and constructed.

Polish Army dispositions, often criticized, have a logical explanation when both Polish military strategy and Polish political fears are taken into consideration. Polish strategy was basically to be the morass into which German armies would be drawn while the French attacked in the west; hence armies were positioned close to the German border so that the Germans would have to develop their resources in moving into Poland rather than just driving in. There was also a serious political concern that if the Germans drove in to western Poland without a fight, and then agreed to arbitration, the Western democracies might be tempted to pursue the Munich road of appeasement. The Polish Foreign Ministry was sensitive to the fact that many in the United Kingdom were sympathetic to German revisionist claims, particularly the conservative elements who feared Soviet Communism and saw in Germany a strong shield against Soviet Marxist encroachment. These conservative groups were of the opinion that the Germans should be allowed their rightful place in the concert of the European nations, and allowed to exercise a controlling influence in central and eastern Europe. It was even to lead to Hitler's overthrow.[35]

British Assistance to Poland in September 1939

The British were already thinking of helping the Poles develop guerrilla forces and their primary aim was to sabotage Polish rail lines and oil fields so that when (!) captured by the Germans they would not be available to aid the German economy. This all evolved from a visit to London in late June 1939 by General L. Rayski, deputy minister of Military Affairs. His primary reason for traveling to London was to negotiate the purchase of military material that was to be obtained after the hoped-for positive conclusion of negotiations for a loan.[36] The promised supplies, meager at best, failed to even arrive in Poland, but the British expressed an interest in diversions behind German lines in Poland.

As a result, two Polish II Bureau officers went to London — Stanislaw Wlodzimierz Pawel Gano (head of the Technical Section of the II Bureau) and technical expert Mieczyslaw Frankowski. Eventually the Polish staff delegated Charaszkiewicz to continue talks with the British. Charaszkiewicz wrote in his report that the topics were (1) general methodology of diversionary activities, e.g. recruitment, training, communications, storage of diversionary equipment, (2) general principles of partisan work, and (3) demonstrating to the British the actual parameters of Polish equipment. The following were excluded from discussions: (1) discussions of operational plans, (2) political issues, and (3) any discussion of joint operations.[37] Charaszkiewicz's contacts in London were Col. Holland and Lt. Col. Colin Gubbins as well as various specialists in diversionary equipment such as engineers and electrical, mechanical and chemical experts.

Colonel Gubbins, who was to be associated with British clandestine activities and always had warm and loyal relations with the Poles, was seconded by the British War Office MI R, a section dedicated to fomenting psychological and material sabotage. Colonel Gubbins was then specifically charged with liaison with the Polish clandestine forces. This was prior to the formation of SOE.[38] Colonel Gubbins and his small group of modern-day buccaneers was the total British military effort to support their new ally.

The British were particularly interested in preparing for guerrilla activity in Poland with special attention to the area of Lwow to Krakow (i.e., railroad communications for oil from Boryslaw to the west). It again needs to be commented that the MI R mission to Romania that same year had instructions to sabotage the oil fields at Ploesti. Two years later, Britain's first mission to their new Soviet ally also was supposed to ensure that the Caucasus oil fields did not fall into German hands intact.[39]

Charaszkiewicz writes that the Polish equipment far surpassed the British except for special boring machines to facilitate the dynamiting and destruction of railroads. The Poles were offered such an item which was to be then reproduced in Poland, but it came too late.[40]

But even the journey of Gubbins and his colleagues showed the lack of urgency of British aid to Poland. Gubbins departed from London with specific War Office instructions to inspire confidence among the Poles. They traveled by train through France, a journey of 36 hours since priority was being given to French troop movements. A quick trip aboard the HMS *Shropshire* from Marseilles found them in Alexandria on the eve of the German attack. An imperial flying boat was chartered and the RAF persuaded to provide two flying boats which got them as far as Piraeus when, hearing of the German invasion of Poland, the RAF crew refused to go farther. The Polish ambassador in Athens arranged for a flight on a Polish LOT Airlines Lockheed returning from Haifa and staging to Bucharest. Thus this totality of British aid to Poland was able to proceed. After a stop at Bucharest, the British passengers were disembarked at Cernauti and then went by taxis arranged by Polish consuls.[41] Finally they arrived in Poland to join up with the British head of the Military Mission, headed by the enigmatic and heroic Gen. Adrian Carton de Wiart.[42]

The German Invasion, September 1, 1939

On August 23 the Soviets and Germans signed the Molotov-Ribbentrop Pact.[43] What is paradoxical is that two days later the British signed the treaty of mutual assistance with the Poles (see Appendix I). Was this the final step of ensuring that the Poles would fight against the Germans?

The archival evidence that proves that the Polish General Staff predicted the date of the German attack are the mobilization orders for Poland's aviation. On August 26, mobilization orders for ground components of combat units were issued and these were moved to secret bases. On August 31, the majority of the combat units were flown out to secret bases. Thus no aviation units were destroyed on the ground as has often been written. On August 30, Poland declared general mobilization but the British and French ambassadors protested that such a move on Poland's part would be perceived as a provocative act and might make it harder for the Western parliaments to honor their treaty obligation. The general mobilization was rescinded. It is a sad commentary on the way that history is written that some Western politicians condemned Poland for failure to order a timely mobilization.

During the summer of 1939, all shipping offices were moved from Gdynia to Warsaw. In August, all merchant marine and fishing fleets were placed on a state of alert and Polish transports were diverted from Polish ports, delayed in their sailing for Poland or if in Polish waters expedited in departure. On August 28, all Polish flag carriers were ordered to stay out of the Baltic and to obey only coded orders from Warsaw.[44] On August 30, 1939, the Polish Destroyer Division received instructions and weighed anchor to sail for the United Kingdom.[45]

Thus Beck's attempt to navigate between the Scylla and Charybdis of German and Soviet enmity and enticement for satellite status came to an end as he listened to the siren songs of the Western powers and their guarantees.* The overwhelming number of Poles, with the exception of a small group of Communists who saw Poland's refuge in alliance with the Soviet Union, decades after the tragic events, see no alternatives to Polish policy.

The German attack was carried out on September 1.[46] Three agonizingly long (for the Poles) days later, the British and French governments, after having issued a joint

---

*His own epitaph was that he made German aggression against Poland into a world war. This sounds hollow given the horrible destruction visited on Poland. See Beck, Final Report.

ultimatum to Germany to cease offensive operations against Poland (which was ignored), declared war.[47] For Hitler, the actual declaration was an unpleasant surprise since the prior pacifist tendencies of the Western democracies impeached their credibility.

The Poles strove to make the Germans develop their primary attack right on the Polish boundary, then to fall back to force the Germans to regroup for a move and to fight once again. It was hoped that when the French attacked on the 15th day of the war, as called for by the military convention, the Poles would counterattack with their reserve army group — Army Prusy.

It is this part of the Polish strategy that is so completely unappreciated in the West. Since the Western Allies had no intention of coming to Poland's help, it has been conveniently ignored that the prewar military task called for a joint effort on land and in the air. The general attitude in the West to Polish plans and efforts is based on the final outcome, and since the outcome was not only tragic but, until the French debacle of 1940, humiliating and devastating, then the majority opinion held that Polish dispositions had to be inherently flawed and incompetent.

This strategy of a defensive retreat, always strong enough to force the opponent to deploy but always fluid enough to escape the encirclement, was Smigly-Rydz's plan. As the German offensive unfolded and Polish forces were pressed ever further back east, a decision was made to make a final stand with their backs to the Romanian border — the Romanian beachhead. Romania had agreements guaranteeing transit of war materiel from the port of Constance to Poland. Ships with supplies from the West were already sailing for Constance.

In the early hours of September 17, the Soviets invaded Poland, breaking their Non-Aggression Treaty which they had only recently reiterated as binding. In the late hours of that fateful day, the Polish Government crossed the boundary into Romania, and Smigly-Rydz gave up on his last-ditch attempt to form a defensive perimeter on the Romanian boundary. Polish forces were ordered to cross to neutral countries, primarily Hungary and Romania but some units also moved over to Lithuania and even Latvia. The Soviet invaders faced only skeleton units of the Korpus Ochrony Pogranicza (KOP) and had no problem sweeping through what was in most situations symbolic resistance. But a number of KOP battalions did mount up a heroic stand. When overwhelmed, the Polish officers and noncommissioned officers were in most instances murdered on the spot. The situation was confused by the fact that Smigly-Rydz gave orders for Polish troops not to fight the Soviets unless attacked.

As the Polish forces evacuated to Romania and Hungary, the tragic battle and the bloody defense of Warsaw ensued. Warsaw was repeatedly battered by German heavy artillery, and bombed by German planes in what later became known as carpet bombing. Incendiaries were also dropped and many historic buildings burned down. This included the Royal Castle and many irreplaceable cultural artifacts of the Polish nation.

The Germans have always been convinced that it was their air and ground bombardment that led to the surrender of Warsaw. In time it probably would have been the cause, but the cause for the capitulation has to be sought in a more heroic deed. On September 26, a Polish plane, interned by the Romanians, was surreptitiously taken over by Stanislaw Riess, a test pilot for the PZL (Polskie Zaklady Lotnicze). On the pretense of flying within Romania, he flew a passenger, Major Galinat, the personal emissary of Marshal Smigly-Rydz to the GOC of Warsaw. Landing in Mokotow, which was a piece of no-man's land between Polish and German positions on the outskirts of Warsaw, the emissary, Major Galinat, was disembarked, and conveyed two orders from Smigly-Rydz: one for the city to capitulate to save further loss of life and property, and the second to form a Polish clandestine military organization.

In fact, this had already been bruited at the highest level of the Warsaw Command since Lt. Gen. Michael Karasiewicz-Tokarzewski had proposed such an organization and the orders from Smigly-Rydz finalized the plans. This was Smigly-Rydz's last executive order. When an artillery cannonade intensified and masked the noise of the engine, Riess took off and landed in neutral Lithuania.[48]

One day after Warsaw capitulated, the fortress of Modlin also surrendered. The Polish peninsula of Hel, which also contained the naval port of Hel, fought till October 1. On October 4, General Kleeberg and his decimated divisions fought the last symbolic battle at Kock.

But isolated resistance continued. As the clandestine forces were being formed, vestiges of uniformed units, often relatively quite cohesive, persisted. The best known and one that passed into Polish legend was Major Dobrzanski's (Hubal) cavalry regiment that was only wiped out by an ambush toward the end of April 1940.[49]

Brief Analysis of September 1939

The September campaign is still a topic which excites passion or relative disinterest if not disdain. One of the more patronizing praises uttered has been that the Poles went to war with an army that was good by First World War standards. In fact, the Poles went to war with a fine army, as good as most in September 1939. They were up against an army which was better than all the other armies put together.

It is a truism that the Poles lost the war before it was started. The long exposed boundaries devoid of any natural barriers, and the exposed bulge of the Poznan salient with the absolutely indefensible Pomeranian corridor surrounded on both sides by German territory guaranteed a German advantage. Even the Silesian region which, until the German annexation of the remnants of the Czech state, was protected by the Carpathian mountains in the south, was a vulnerable region. For the German command, the problem was as to how far east to carry out the classic pincer with troops moving from the East Prussian region and those from Czech provinces. It would appear that the Germans initially planned a very conservative operation expecting to eliminate the Polish Army west of the Vistula. The constraint for the Germans was their concern that a two-front war was a possibility and that their armies needed to get the job done quickly, without becoming trapped in the far eastern reaches of Poland, and to be available as soon as possible to face the French.

For the Poles, the strategy was exactly the reciprocal: victory could come only as part of a coalition effort. This demanded the sacrifice of many Polish lives, the loss of much Polish territory by the drawing in of the German forces into Poland, the tying in of as many German divisions as possible so that there would be as few as possible facing the French. The Poles strove to make the Germans develop their primary attack right on the Polish boundary, then to fall back, forcing the Germans to regroup for a move and to fight once again. It was hoped that when the French attacked on the 15th day of the war as called for by the military convention, the Poles would counterattack with their reserve army group, Army Prusy. It is this part of the Polish strategy that is so completely unappreciated in the West. Since the Western Allies had no intention of implementing their guarantees, Poland's disposition has been critiqued on the basis of the final and tragic outcome.

Finally, the passivity of the Western Allies in September was easier to explain if the root cause of Poland's defeat could be laid to Polish incompetence. Therefore, the ready acceptance of various myths, such as the destruction of aviation on the first day, the frequent allusions to irresponsible cavalry charges, the bad military dispositions.

In September 1939, the Germans defeated the Poles within two weeks and mopped up the remnants in the next three. But the campaign would have undoubtedly lasted longer without the Soviet invasion in the East. In May and June 1940, the Germans defeated the combined armies of France, Belgium, Holland and a sizeable and very well-equipped British Expeditionary Corps in less than six weeks.[50] While against Poland they enjoyed the surprise of new tactics, that should not have been the case in France.[51] But the most vital difference is that against the Poles the Germans had a thousand kilometer boundary devoid of natural barriers; the French had the Maginot Line and the Germans broke through the Ardennes on a very narrow front. Against the Poles in September, the Germans sustained approximately 15,000 casualties, while in 1940 about 27,000. The German successes against the Soviets in the first months of their offensive in 1941 were spectacular. As the old British soldier said, "You haven't been to war until you've fought the Germans."[52]

Kennedy, who based his monograph on German records, cites Rundstedt as saying after the war that the September 1939 campaign had significantly eroded the Wermacht's capacity for operations. The bulk of the German armed forces had to be committed to overcome the Poles, and expenditure in ammunition, gasoline, and materiel was such as to preclude concurrent German operations on a similar scale in the west or elsewhere.[53]

The official German history of the Second World War has two very pertinent points. "The inadequacy of Polish political judgment was reflected in the belief of effective support from Britain and France." The German historians acknowledge that the "decisive factor was the political and military starting position which it has to be admitted could not have been greatly improved."[54]

The German historians furthermore write, "The Wermacht which had gone to war willingly if not enthusiastically relying on political leadership and its seeming justified demands against Poland, had created the prerequisites of an occupation policy that run counter to international law, an occupation policy which it often watched helplessly and which attracted to it an odium of shared responsibility."[55] Hitler gambled and won.[56]

All of Polish Silesia, the whole of the historic provinces known as Wielkopolska, which included Poznan, and Polish Pomerania including Gdynia, were incorporated into the German Reich and most of their non–German populations expelled into the new German colony of Generalgouvernment based on Cracow and Warsaw. In this region, some basic Polish social structures were allowed to continue though under very strict German control. But in the East, under Soviet occupation, Poland became a chaotic killing field. The Soviets encouraged ethnic strife and pitted Poles against Ukrainans, Ukrainans against Poles and the Jews against both groups. With all civilized and civilian Polish administration eradicated, and all the Polish police either murdered on the spot or sent to the Soviet gulags, the rest of the citizenry became the objects of more or less officially sanctioned banditry as all social conventions were willfully destroyed.[57]

On September 6, 1939, a bare three days after the British declared war, Polish warships sailed from a British port on the North Sea and began operations alongside the Royal Navy which were to go on to May 1945.

On September 9, *ORP Blyskawica* was detached to escort a British freighter, *SS Lassell*, with military supplies for Poland through Galatz or possibly Tulcea in Romania. The voyage was called off at Gibraltar due to the deteriorating Polish situation.

On September 15, the French government placed a military compound in Coetquidan at the disposal of the Polish military authorities in France to base and train the Polish infantry division, whose formation was agreed to in prewar negotiations. There were already about 15,000 volunteers from the Polish diaspora in France for such service.

The first of the Polish ground forces in the West was being formed, shortly to be transformed into the forces in exile.

The Fight Continues:
October 1939 through June 1940

The Constitution Is Preserved

On September 9, 1939, the French ambassador to Poland, Noel, suggested that in the event of a breakdown of Polish defenses, consideration be given to the Polish government moving its residence to France. Two days later, the Polish foreign minister, Beck, formally asked the French government through Noel whether the French would agree to give the Poles a *droit de residence,* on the same precedent as given the Belgians in 1914. An affirmative reply was received.

The invasion by the Soviets in the early hours of September 17 found the Polish government in Kuty, near the Romanian border. The Polish-Romanian treaty obliged both countries to aid each other in the event of an unprovoked attack by the Soviets on either signatory and the Soviet attack (in spite of an existing treaty of nonaggression between the Polish Republic and the Soviet Union) seemed to be the trigger for its activation. Given the circumstances and realities, the Polish government formally released the Romanians from their treaty obligation but requested a *droit de passage* for the Polish government, the Polish High Command and the Polish military through Romania to France. The Romanians forthwith granted the Polish government and the Polish president the right of passage in an unofficial capacity, but expressed reservations about the military.

The actual reality was less benign since all in the Polish government, including the president, were interned. The Romanians were under pressure and significant diplomatic duress from both the Germans and the Soviets. The Polish military, consistent with prevailing international law, were interned though the Romanians were quite helpful in being inefficient in guarding the Poles who escaped in thousands for France.*

It was inevitable that given this leadership vacuum a completely new governance had to be created in allied France. Articles 13 and 24 of the Polish Constitution of 1935 provided that in an emergency and event of war the Polish President could appoint a successor.[1] President Moscicki availed himself of this constitutional prerogative and

---

*On September 21, the prime minister of Romania, Armand Calinescu, was assassinated by members of the fascistic and pro–German Iron Guard.

expressed a wish that General Kazimierz Sosnkowski be his successor. But Sosnkowski, when last heard of, was still fighting in Poland and there was no guarantee that he would avoid capture, not be killed or be able to get to France. So after very intense negotiations in which the French and their favorite Pole, the Francophile Sikorski, were involved, the nomination went to Wladyslaw Raczkiewicz.[2] During this short period of functional interregnum, the Polish ambassador in Paris, Juliusz Lukasiewicz, was the liaison between the interned Polish president and the French government and was ably assisted by the Polish ambassador to the Court of Saint James's, Edward Raczynski.[3]

President Raczkiewicz asked General Wladyslaw Sikorski to form a coalition government; Sikorski agreed with a significant caveat, namely the so-called Paris Convention that the president would agree not to act unilaterally but to consult the cabinet. When finally Sosnkowski managed to escape to France, with a very enhanced reputation for his last-ditch stand in Southeast Poland, Raczkiewicz offered to resign and to appoint him as president following the stated wishes of Moscicki. Sosnkowski refused, arguing that one more change in the high office would not be politically desirable from the Polish *raison d'etre*.[4] But President Raczkiewicz, exercising his recently acquired constitutional prerogatives, appointed General K. Sosnkowski as his designated successor which given that Sosnkowski was a Pilsudski adherent, while Sikorski was a disgruntled anti–Pilsudskite, caused immediate and long-term acrimony within Polish ranks. Furthermore, Sikorski felt that Raczkiewicz by taking this step broke the spirit if not the law of the Paris convention. The political animosity based on past experiences prevailed throughout the war. Raczkiewicz however, after obtaining Smigly-Rydz's formal resignation, appointed Sikorski, already prime minister, to the post of commander in chief. Finally Sikorski also occupied the post of minister of Military Affairs, which was a cabinet position.[5] Thus all the executive functions of the Polish government in exile were now centered in one individual.

On September 29, 1939, Sikorski made it clear that the formation of a Polish army at the side of the French ally was his highest priority, and this was repeated in his formal speech to the Polish government and the National Council (*Rada Narodowa*) on January 23, 1940. "The recreation of the Polish Army in its greatest size is the most important and essential goal of the Government," and also on March 5, 1940, "The main goal should be the main effort of all our diplomatic missions and of our propaganda. We have to reach every Polish community in exile, move it and inspire it to fight for a free Poland."[6]

On November 7, 1939 the Polish General Staff was formed and its first chief was Col. Alexander Kedzior. The naval structure of command was essentially identical to the prewar, with Rear Adm. Jerzy Swirski in command. The Military Aviation, in January 1940 renamed the Polish Air Force, (*Polskie Sily Lotnicze*) continued for a while to be commanded by Gen. Jozef Zajac. Except for the position of the commander in chief and the two deputy ministers for Military Affairs, Generals Marian Kukiel and Izydor Modelski, the other military posts were retained by prewar senior officers.

The exiles, and the leadership of the clandestine military and civil authorities in occupied Poland, regardless of their own political biases, were overwhelmingly loyal to the Polish government formed in Paris. The only exception to this was the small number of adherents of the Communist Party, who followed the Soviet-dictated policy and till 1941 condemned the war against Germany as a capitalist venture. A number of political parties, such as the National Democrats and the Peasant Party, which participated in the Polish coalition government in Paris, protected the existence of their unique partisan groups.

Polish Evacuees in Hungary and Romania

The numbers and composition of the Polish forces evacuated to the two neighboring countries of Hungary and Romania was the direct result of a number of congruent factors. The defeat of the Polish armies at their main projected line of Vistula led to a strategic decision of moving all forces to the southeast and anchoring the last redoubt on the Romanian boundary.

Thus the government, the commander in chief and his staff as well as many rear echelon formations and training centers were within miles of the boundary.

The definitive decision to order a move was, in fact, issued by the commander in chief through a still-functioning chain of command after the Soviets moved into Poland.

It was established in October 1939 that about 85,000 Polish military had crossed into neutral countries and been formally interned. Forty thousand were in Hungary and close to 30,000 in Romania, including 9,276 personnel of Poland's Military Aviation.[7] Close to 15,000 went into Lithuania and Latvia, again including a significant number of aviation personnel from the V Air Regiment of Lida.

About 140 planes of Poland's Military Aviation also flew into internment. These included 54 fighters, 27 Los bombers, 31 Karas light bombers and numerous training and sport club planes. Polish planes were all requisitioned by the Romanians and used in their war against the Soviets in 1941–1944.[8]

Hungary had the most ground forces combat units, the most significant in quality and quantity being the 10th Motorized Cavalry Brigade (commanded by Col. S. Maczek) which had fought a great retreat action in Poland and became the precursor of the Polish Armored Division in the United Kingdom.[9]

Except for the aviation personnel who were all front-line combat personnel, the interned included many officers, many of senior rank who had functioned in administrative posts in eastern Poland.

There was one group of great value evacuated to Romania of which there was little resonance, for obvious reasons, namely the officers of the Polish Intelligence Section (Section II of the General Staff), who were to play a vital role in the future coalition effort. Of all the prewar collaboration achieved by the Poles with their Western Allies, the best results and highest degree of goodwill was among the three intelligence services. Sikorski was convinced that the Allies would defeat the Germans in a matter of months and in the beginning directed the Polish II Bureau to activities that would continue the prewar Promethean movement and the penetration of the Soviets. As a result the Polish intelligence officers established close links with many agencies in South East Europe and particularly in Budapest, and attempted to renew contacts with the Japanese.[10]

The 15,000 Poles who were interned in the Baltic countries had a much more difficult task in escaping. The Soviets and Germans placed a very effective embargo on shipping from these countries to Sweden. Ships were stopped and Poles attempting to escape were removed and taken to German or Soviet prisons. The air route to Sweden was available for some individual officers, usually of importance, but not for the thousands of lower-echelon personnel. Finally in 1940, as the Soviets took over the Baltic republics, all the interned Poles were moved to Soviet camps, but since this took place after the mass murders of the Poles at places like Katyn and Staobielsk, all survived and were released in 1941 under the terms of the Soviet "amnesty" negotiated by Sikorski (see Chapter 4).

The Polish Underground Movement Is Formed

It needs to be remembered that in the first stages of the German occupation, many clandestine military groups were formed which espoused both political and ideological goals for a future resurrected and liberated country, coupled with military resistance. But the first of any significance, then and later, was, in fact, the child of the Sanacjia, created by the orders of Marshal Smigly-Rydz through the chief of the II Bureau, Colonel Smolenski, given on September 17 just prior to the forced evacuation to Romania. In turn, Smolenski ordered Major Charaszkiewicz, who followed the descending ladder of command by instructing Major Galinat to expedite the departure of previously recruited officers for occupied Poland to initiate diversionary activities.[11]

Smolenski furthermore ordered that Edmund Galinat would be the man in charge of the political aspects of diversion. (Clearly this was felt in the circumstances to be a strictly military business.) When Galinat flew into Warsaw on September 26, he in turn accepted the seniority of Tokarzewski (see Chapter 1).[12]

This led to the formation of *Sluzba Zwyciestwu Polski,* or SZP (Service for Poland's Victory), which combined political and military aims but its clearly prewar provenance and association with Pilsudski adherents did not sit well with Sikorski, who promptly separated the political from the military leadership. These changes were political but not illogical. Sikorski undoubtedly wished to ensure that his own political vision would prevail in postwar Poland. Hence, Sikorski changed the name of the military secret organization to *Zwiazek Walki Zbrojnej* (Association for Armed Struggle). But the same cadre of officers continued to work in the clandestine organization, and their own traditional loyalties were minimally affected by the political issues taking place in exile.

Sikorski, to ensure his control of the underground, appointed Gen. Kazimierz Sosnkowski in Paris to the post of general officer commanding of the *Zwiazek Walki Zbrojnej,* and then broke up the local commands in Poland by seconding Tokarzewski to the Soviet zone of occupation and appointing Col. Stefan Rowecki (shortly promoted to general) to command in the German zone of occupation. Tokarzewski was soon arrested by the Soviets who failed to penetrate his disguise. Unlike many, Tokarzewski survived, and lived to fight another day when released in 1941 (see Chapter 4).

For ease of understanding, the clandestine military organization will be called Armia Krajowa (Home Army) or AK for short, even though its official name appeared much later in February 1942. This is to emphasize the fact that is the focus of this monograph, that the Polish military struggle in Poland was part of the overall coalition war against Germany. The Polish Home Army (A.K.) owed its allegiance to the Polish government in the West and was completely loyal to the Polish commander in chief in exile and was aided by supplies from the West.

After the German attack on the Soviets (summer 1941) the Communists formed their own partisan units and supplied them by air from their Russian territory. (This is discussed further in Chapter V.)

On the civilian and political side, Sikorski formed a subcommittee of the cabinet for home affairs, *Komitet Ministrow dla Spraw Kraju* (the Minister's Committee for Home Affairs) and also created the post of a government delegate (*Delegat Rzadu)* in Poland with the formal rank of vice prime minister. The first person appointed to this post was Ratajski, a prominent member of the Polish "Stronictwo Pracy."

General Sosnkowski, minister for Polish Affairs and in overall command of the military struggle in Poland, directed his first efforts at implementing a courier route from France to Poland and the assessment of the best way to provide the embryonic underground military groups in Poland with appropriate equipment and support. The problem of radio communication was also high on the list of priorities and this was solved expeditiously.

On November 28, 1939, Sikorski issued an order to the general officer commanding the Polish Air Force in Paris, General Zajac, to begin organizing an air liaison with occupied Poland.[13] Presumably following that order, Polish authorities in December 1939 (while still in France) contacted the British regarding technical assistance in flying couriers to Poland.[14] The Polish State Airlines (Lot) had managed to evacuate a number of their civilian planes (Lockheed Super-Electras) to the West and it was planned to modify them for use as courier planes to Poland. Other smaller planes able to actually land in Poland were also considered, such as the Percival Gull. The Poles also attempted to buy back two Polish RWD-15s sold privately in Romania. One of these was, in fact, able to undergo long flights since it was specially modified for Stanislaw Karpinski's attempt to fly solo to New Zealand. For whatever reason, the new owners refused to part with the planes. The problem was that a plane with the requisite range to reach Poland from the West necessitated a well-prepared air field. A small plane able to land on a rough field would lack the range. Serious consideration was also given to a large float plane since such a plane might have the range and could theoretically land on a lake, of which there were many in Poland. Later in the war, in the summer of 1941, the British proposed using a captured German four-engined long-range Focke-Wulf Condor for flights to occupied Poland.[15] This plane had the range for flights to Poland and back, and being German it may have confused both the Germans and the neutral Swedes over whose territories all the flights from the UK were planned.

But in late 1939 and early 1940, the realistic view prevailed that it was easier to have Polish couriers travel through neutral Italy and then the Danubian Countries and then to cross the boundary over the Carpathian mountains than to have a plane fly that long distance from France or possibly the Middle East. But supplies could not be carried by couriers who were smuggled in various ways across the Polish-Hungarian boundary. The issue of supplies to the clandestine groups was a problem and remained an issue throughout the war.

The British in their own memos portrayed their ambivalence about Polish initiatives. A representative of the FO wrote, "we should not show ourselves too forthcoming in our answers."[16] In March 1940, General Sosnkowski again attempted to negotiate with the British regarding air liaison with Poland. Again the British FO, while expressing sympathy, wrote: "a somewhat nebulous but avowedly urgent Polish project of November 1939." But the FO recommended a "lean to negative."[17]

During this first phase of contacts between Polish authorities in France and the occupied homeland, the overland route gave good results as far as couriers were concerned and in early 1940 Polish radio communications began to function between the occupied homeland and Polish Military Headquarters in France.

After France's capitulation in June 1940 and when Italy became a belligerent by attacking France and declaring war on Britain, the situation became very difficult. The reality of Germany's extending its direct hegemony over the Balkans further compounded the problems and the overland route became ever more time consuming and dangerous. But it continued to be the primary route for agents going from Poland to the West until 1943. In the summer of 1944, a number of agents were extracted from Poland by planes operating from Italy. The Poles continued to enjoy good relations with the Hungarians and Budapest was a major Polish courier and radio link with occupied Poland.

The peregrinations of the first courier of the Polish General Staff from the United Kingdom are illustrative of the problem created by Italy's joining the Axis. Col. Emil Fieldorf volunteered for assignment to the AK. On July 17, 1940, he was dispatched by sea from the United Kingdom to North Africa. Hence he assumed the name of *Nil* (i.e., Nile). He then traveled to Istanbul, from thence to Bucharest, to Budapest and to Warsaw, a journey of 51 days![18]

During the winter months (1939–1940) two mid-level Polish officers, Majors Kalenkiewicz and Gorski, who were friends and shared an intense patriotism, began to write profuse memoranda to their superiors about the need to create a Polish parachute force for supporting the clandestine activity in occupied Poland. This enthusiasm finally elicited caustic remarks from senior staffers about their unrealistic approach to the realities of the Polish situation in France and the need to preserve the Polish civilian population from German retribution at least until there was a chance for a final victorious revolt.

Gorski had been involved with the prewar Polish parachute training center in Bydgoszcz, and was undoubtedly frustrated about the fact that the effort to develop and train Polish parachute diversionary forces had not been at all utilized in September.[19]

The Polish Forces Are Created in the West

Negotiations for Polish armed forces in France in event of war with Germany had been bruited as early as 1925. This topic was again discussed and agreement reached in the Polish-French military talks in May 1939 in Paris. The Poles and the French were aware that there were many hundreds of thousands of Polish immigrant industrial workers in France and Belgium. Most of these remained Polish citizens and were subject to Polish law regarding compulsory conscription, or call-up from the automatic reserve status which followed the obligatory military service.

The French agreed in principle that the Polish authorities had the right to enforce their law, but apart from allowing voluntary service, the French placed a number of civilian occupations in a protected, exempt status, such as coal miners and agricultural workers, two areas in which the majority of the Polish migrants were employed. Even with these caveats from the French it was thought that there would be a pool of about 120,000 Polish citizens who would be eligible for service in the Polish armed forces.

Recruitment began on September 3, with the French placing the camp at Coetquidan in Brittany at Polish disposal.

But the core of the future armed forces were the professional cadres interned in Romania and Hungary. The British and French governments assisted the Poles in their evacuation plans, which were carried out by all means and a variety of routes.

Forty percent of the 43,000 were evacuated by the land route through Yugoslavia and the still-neutral Italy, and 60 percent by sea from the Romanian port of Constance or the Greek port of Piraeus directly to France. Among the chartered ships utilized in the evacuation were Polish liners that had been kept out of the Baltic prior to the first of September, including the old Polish liner SS *Warszawa*, relegated prior to the war to the Levantine route.

The Polish staff planned on having a total of 180,000 men available for service in the West, and proposed the formation of two army corps of two infantry divisions each, and of one armored division. The military agreement signed by the Polish and French authorities on January 4, 1940, confirmed Polish aspirations. The First Corps was to be ready for action in April 1940. The Second Corps was to reach ready status in August 1940. The French made it clear that there was absolutely no chance of the armored division being equipped prior to late 1941.

As an ally, the Polish government was extended many considerations, yet in the area of the military the enthusiasm was muted. Neither the French nor the British were aggressive in rearming the Poles. Many in the French staffs urged that Polish units be formed at the level of battalions and integrated in French regiments since they were convinced that Polish military leadership had failed in September 1939. The reluctance of the French to encourage a serious growth and centralization of the Polish armed forces in France may in fact be partially understood in this context of the French hope that negotiations would terminate the unfortunate and unhappy martial interlude. The presence of centralized and well-equipped Polish units committed to regaining full sovereignty and territorial integrity may not have been compatible with French plans for negotiated peace and a compromise at clearly Polish expense.

The Western democracies were undoubtedly very passive in their conduct of the war, which quickly became known as the sitzkrieg or phony war. The only anti–German strategy that was articulated was an economic blockade enforced by Royal Navy warships, a plan which had paid significant dividends during the Great War.[20]

Sikorski's War Strategy

From the very beginning, Sikorski looked to the Balkan strategy for the eventual victory over Germany. He hoped for a grand alliance of the various Balkan and Danubian countries based on the old traditional alliance of Poland and Romania, and that of Poland and Hungary. (It was unfortunate that Poland's good relations and political efforts with those neighbors were confounded by their own enmity over Transylvania.) This was to be complemented by Turkish interests in that region which the British were courting assiduously.[21] It is also worth keeping in mind that until June 1940, that is throughout the period of the phony war, Italy continued to be a neutral and nonbelligerent power and continued to have friendly and diplomatic relations with the Polish government in France.

Historically, Poland and Italy had very warm relations until 1939, and the Polish minister of Foreign Affairs, Jozef Beck, looked to the Polish-Italian alliance as anchoring the extreme ends of a Middle European alliance which would act as a counter to German and Soviet expansion. The British in 1940 still courted the Italians and attempted to keep them in a neutral and thus pro–Allied situation. Following the occupation of Warsaw by the Germans in September 1939, the Italian Embassy in that city continued to function though under a different name, and the Italian diplomats, as well as the Italian royal family and the Vatican, were able to alleviate some of the most cruel excesses of the German occupation in the early part of the war.[22]

It was with that in mind that, early in April 1940, Sikorski began to divert some Polish evacuees from the Balkans to Syria and appointed Col. Stanislaw Kopanski to take command of this formation which was ultimately to be of corps strength. By the summer of 1940, Poles in Syria had over 5,000 officers and men and this led to the formation of the Carpathian Brigade.

Military Aviation

Since the issue of air assistance as a form of maintaining communications and flying in supplies is so paramount to this monograph, much detail will be given to the history of its phoenix-like recreation in the West.

The Poles believed that they had enough personnel for forming at least 15 and perhaps as many as 20 squadrons, distributed between the United Kingdom and France.[23]

But that was the Polish plan; the reality was so different. In the first year of the war, till October 1940, the Polish aviators were the proverbial Cinderella of the Polish military, unwanted and disparaged as far as the Western Allies were concerned. While the Polish Navy was actively engaged in operations from British ports as early as September 1939, and even Polish land forces were being organized and trained in France and Syria, albeit at a snail's pace, close to 9,000 air and ground crews of the Polish Military Aviation who had been evacuated to Romania on September 17, the day the Soviets struck, sat in French camps and vegetated.

As the Polish aviation personnel arrived in France through a variety of clandestine ways from Romania,[24] they were processed and housed at the old Olympic village near Lyons. Nothing was happening and the actual living conditions in the bitter winter of 1939-40 were far from acceptable.

The January 4, 1940, agreement signed by the Polish and French Governments stipulated that Polish air units would be formed and would be an independent *Forces*

Aeriennes Polonaise. But in spite of the agreements the French showed even less enthusiasm in forming Polish aviation units than in forming large (divisional size) Polish ground units. In the meanwhile, the highly skilled Polish air crews, the superb mechanics, sat on their hands, ruminated and, as many young people do, blamed their elders for their troubles. Some of that blame was justified, some was not; some was realistic, some imagined. They had fought hard in September 1939, even gained limited successes, but the French did not seem to care and wanted to teach the Poles how to fly obsolescent planes and to keep as far as possible from the front line. Concerns about their families in Poland and inactivity led to bitterness. This might have been the reason for such strenuous efforts on the part of the Polish aviation authorities in France to move a lion's share of the aviation personnel to Britain where the Polish Navy was active and even appreciated.

Partly because of this, the Polish Air Force Inspectorate in Paris argued for a British partnership. The familiarity of prewar Polish personnel with British equipment, which had been manufactured in Poland under license agreements with British firms, was given as the main reason. What probably was left unsaid and was more persuasive was the fame of the Royal Air Force and its obvious technical and administrative superiority over the French L'Armee de l'Air. By January 1940, the Poles also were clearly disappointed and frustrated at the slow progress in the formation of Polish air units in France.[25] While Polish naval units were already functioning effectively out of British harbors and participating in Allied maritime operations in the North Sea and in the English Channel, Polish air personnel in France were waiting not just for equipment but for even the most basic training and familiarization with French equipment.

In many instances, Polish units received planes that the French considered unfit for their own pilots, let alone combat (e.g., the CR 714 Cyclone). But for the Poles this was better than no planes at all.[26]

The dynamics of inactivity changed due to the Soviet invasion of Finland. In December 1939, the Soviets, in their classic ploy, recognized a small renegade group of Finnish Communists as the Finnish People's Government and gave it their assistance by invading Finland. All the time, of course, denying that they were invading a sovereign country!

The Russian invasion was condemned by the League of Nations on December 14, 1939, its last heroic act. The Soviets were expelled from the organization and all member countries were asked to give the Finns assistance. Most promised, though the farther away they were, the more enthusiastic their call for aid; the closer, such as Sweden or Norway, the more muted and restrained. But assistance to Finland also gave the possibility of exerting control over the valuable Swedish iron ore and thus enhancing the rather limp economic blockade by which the Western Powers hoped to win the war. The French called for army landings at Petsamo and even planned long-range bombing raids against Baku in the Caucuses to deprive the Germans of oil.

This French policy initiative appears so inexplicable that it deserves a short attempt at clarification. It can be understood in the context of the history of the Third Republic which emerged from the Second Empire in 1870 which was fractured by many social and political forces. The monarchists and Catholics abhorred the anticlerical republic. The radicals and left-wing parties hated the republic as representative of the bourgeois and peasantry. The bloody civil war in Spain between ideological forces that were fermenting in France led to the perception that Communism was at the gates of France. Each ideological side was concerned. The left wing saw the victory of the Franco groups as a dire warning, and the same dire consequences were the conclusion of the right-wing groups who saw Franco's victory as a close thing. The Munich agreement, strangely enough, finished off the radical, left-wing Front Populaire. Daladier formed the new government with the right wing in power, and shortly broke the back of a general labor strike and established a reputation with the right wing. Daladier in retrospect appears to have been far more committed to fighting Communism (but not necessarily the Soviet Union) than Germany. Daladier jumped at the opportunity in 1939 as a result of the Molotov-Ribbentropp pact, to outlaw the French Communist Party and arrested many Communist legislators. This policy did not gain continued parliamentary confidence and when the Finns asked for an armistice in March 1940 he was voted out of office and replaced by Raynaud, a man of the right, who was opposed to the appeasement of Germany and had favored a Soviet alliance. In March 1940, however, he continued the anti–Soviet military preparations begun by his predecessor.[27]

There were specific consequences of the Finnish situation regarding the Polish Air Force. The Finnish situation offered the possibility of aiding the Finns, and of possibly enhancing the blockade on Swedish iron and even Russian oil. In this new situation, suddenly the Poles, de facto at war with the Soviets because of the invasion on September 17, were to be encouraged. A Polish fighter wing was formed from the various three-plane flights that had been grudgingly formed, and a brigade-sized unit was carved out of the two infantry divisions in the final stages of training. The French even urged that the Polish warships, based in the United Kingdom, be allowed to operate in the North and Arctic seas to support the Finns.

The Finns fought a good fight but were eventually forced to an armistice and the plans for Western military aid came to nothing. But the Polish wing (shortly renamed *I/145 Grouppe de Chasse Polonaise de Varsovie*) formed to aid the Finns was in existence and could not, nor would be, disbanded.[28]

Negotiations Regarding Moving Aviation Personnel to the UK

The initial negotiations between the Poles and the British regarding the transfer of the Polish aviation personnel to the United Kingdom were started in late October 1939, and were both protracted and highly unsatisfactory for the Poles.

The British while uttering diplomatic pleasantries about how honored they were to have the Poles wish to form units alongside the Royal Air Force, were very loath to take more than a small token percentage of the Polish airmen to the United Kingdom. On October 25, 1939, in a memorandum to Polish authorities in France, the British presented their conditions; the most egregious was that the Poles to be transferred to Great Britain would have to be enrolled in the RAF as volunteer reserve, and take an oath of allegiance to the king. Demeaning also were the conditions that Poles not wear their own national insignia and that all officers be enrolled in the lowest rank of pilot officer with promotions made on basis of function and at the discretion of the RAF officers in command.

The British reasons for their unhelpful stand were numerous: the British lacked suitable accommodation (highly dubious), the Poles had insufficient command of English (very true), and alleged problems of a constitutional nature since foreign troops could not be stationed on British soil. This last was clearly a bogus issue since the Polish Navy was already based in Britain and after the collapse of France, the British House of Commons quickly took appropriate legislative action.

What was most likely the case is that the British were worried about the morale of the Polish air crews and they had reasonable cause to be concerned about their fluency in English. Also their British military mission had given a very erroneous and poor assessment of the performance of Polish aviation,[29] which had been amplified by an idiosyncratic if not bigoted report by a so-called RAF expert on Polish matters.[30]

Instead of a great asset, which eventually the Poles turned out to be, the two allied governments saw in the Polish fliers a burden which had to be shared. In protracted negotiations between the Poles and the British and French and also between the French and British this *burden* was finally split as a 50-50 division, assuming that the Poles accepted British conditions. For reasons which even 60 years later defy any rational explanation, the Poles accepted the British conditions. Keep in mind that this agreement was signed on June 11, 1940, well after the Norwegian Campaign, in which Polish warships and the Polish Podhalanska Brigade had distinguished itself.

The contrast between the Polish and British naval agreements and the air force one is like night and day. The naval treaty accepted as its keystone the absolute sovereignty of Polish ships and of Polish personnel. Polish warships sailed under the Polish flag, were commanded by Polish officers, and were responsible to the Polish Ministry of Military Affairs through the naval headquarters. To facilitate communications, the British assigned to each Polish warship a Royal Navy signals officers. There were no provisions that Polish commanding officers or appointments had to be cleared with the British Admiralty. The British Admiralty undertook to provide for the financial support of the Polish fleet and personnel until the end of hostilities and to provide facilities in London for the Polish Naval Headquarters. This move was effected in June 1940.

Thus 2,500 Polish air personnel were slowly moved to RAF Eastchurch where the humiliation was different from that in France. But as the evacuation of Poles from the Balkans continued, the number of aviation personnel grew well above 5,000, going to about 8,000, and the debate between the Western Allies became acrimonious; were the Poles to be divided half and half or was 2,500 the maximum that the British were prepared to accept? The Poles insisted that the agreement spelled out a 50-percent division and the British Foreign Office agreed.[31] But these close to puerile discussions became moot as France fell.

Few of the Poles who volunteered for transfer to the United Kingdom and were accepted by a mixed Polish and British commission realized the conditions. Some refused to take the oath of allegiance and were shipped back to France, but there was a certain level of official Polish pressure on the Poles at Eastchurch to accept these conditions for the good of the country.

Thus a beginning was made for the formation of two Polish light bomber squadrons in the UK. The Polish inspector for the Poles who went to Britain was General Kalkus.

When the rest of the Polish Air Force personnel arrived in the United Kingdom in June 1940, after the capitulation of France, the agreement was modified. The oath of allegiance to the king was discontinued and Polish military discipline, law, and custom, including the wearing of Polish decorations and insignia, was now permitted. However, British regulations took precedence over Polish military regulations if the two were in conflict. The Polish staff was permitted to form a Polish Air Force Inspectorate with the right of inspection of Polish air units, but no right to command.[32]

There has to be a question of why the Polish Navy was able to negotiate such a perfectly reasonable and equitable agreement while Sikorski and Zajac in Paris failed to preserve even a scintilla of Polish autonomy in the case of the first air force agreement. Were the Admiralty officials and Churchill, who was already first lord of the Admiralty, so much more accommodating to Polish aspirations, or was the performance of the Polish warships in those early days of the war sufficiently impressive to allay the British insularity? Was the negotiating skill of the British-educated and highly anglicized Polish ambassador to the Court of Saint James's — Count Edward Raczynski — so much better than that of Sikorski and Zajac? Were the British Air Ministry representatives so patronizing and disinterested in the Polish contribution to their air effort?

But by the end of April 1940, the Poles had managed to create the following forces. In the United Kingdom, the Poles had centralized all their naval personnel, which totaled 1,347 officers and sailors, as well as 2,315 officers and others of their air force where two bomber squadrons were in the process of formation.

French Syria had 4,038 officers and men in the soon-to-be-famous Carpathian Brigade. In Metropolitan France the Polish Armed Forces had 41,992 officers and men in two infantry divisions and one armored brigade, and another 25,301 officers and men in various training centers.

The Polish Air Force in France had 7,235 officers and airmen, and in addition to the fighter units two reconnaissance squadrons and one bomber squadron were being formed.

Poles in the Norwegian Campaign

Norway was a great prize, both for the Allies as well as the Germans. The Germans wanted to protect this route, to enlarge their opening into the Atlantic, to minimize the British maritime blockade, and to surround Sweden. The British wished to prevent German access to the iron and if possible to benefit from it themselves.[33] The Norwegians hoped to remain neutral. The Poles desperately wanted to fight either Germans or Soviets since both were cruel oppressors and occupiers.

But in April 1940, the pace accelerated dramatically as the Germans, sensing that the British might place their troops in Norway, implemented very successful combined ground, air and naval operations. The first step in Denmark was simple beyond expectation. A German squad arrived hidden in a barge, as if a Trojan horse, in Copenhagen harbor and the troops disembarked while the Danish Foreign Office was given the ultimatum of either the destruction of Copenhagen or the country being placed under German protection. The second alternative was accepted by the Danes, who had been beaten by the Germans earlier in the century and who were being offered a continued independent existence with their own government, armed forces, legislature, and the continuation of their monarchy.

The invasion of Norway was more bloody for all sides. The Germans were aided by a small group of pro–German senior officers and politicians led by Quisling, whose name was to become a synonym for treacherous collaboration. Some Norwegian units fought hard, some were given confusing instructions and some were pro–German and anti–British. The Germans moved their troops into Norway by ship and by air transport. But the British and French also reacted quickly to move their forces to confront the Germans.[34]

One of the first harbingers of this invasion occurred on April 8, 1940, when *Orzel* (under the command of Kapitan Marynarki Jan Grudzinski) was on her fifth patrol near the south shore of Norway and observed a ship at the entrance to Oslofjord. The ship turned out to be *Rio de Janeiro* out of Hamburg and according to the Deutscher Lloyd registered as a 9,800-ton passenger vessel. The sunken ship was one of the armada of German vessels that sailed into Norwegian ports without declaration of war.[35]

Before the Podhalanska Brigade landed in Norway, other Polish warships participated in naval operations. The destroyer squadron — ORP *Burza* (*Storm*), ORP *Blyskawica* (*Lightning*), and ORP *Grom* (*Thunder*) — battled in the icy waters of the Norwegian fiords at the side of the Royal Navy. The Polish destroyers were engaged in operations between Narvik and Lofoten islands, at times actually transporting allied units, providing them with escort and anti-aircraft fire protection.

The German navy suffered a series of crippling defeats at the hands of the Allies, but the German air force maintained significant air superiority and *Grom* was hit by bombs and sunk. On April 14, 1940, an Allied expeditionary force disembarked in Norway with the goal of capturing the strategic port of Narvik, already in German hands. This force consisted of three battalions of the British 24th Guards Brigade, five battalions of French troops (three Alpine Chasseurs and two Foreign Legion), and four battalions of the Polish Podhalanska Brigade. In ground troops the Poles numbered one-third of the Narvik Allied Expeditionary Force, and the proportion of the Polish contribution increased as the British brigade was withdrawn and moved to Bodo.

During the period when Allied units had been fighting in Norway, the following events had already occurred on the continent of Europe: the Belgians had capitulated, Holland had been overrun, and the British had evacuated from the beaches of Dunkirk on June 3.

The decision to abandon Norway was tragic, and led to the overthrow of the Chamberlain government and the formation of the British coalition government, chaired, at the strong pressure of the British Labour Party, by Winston Churchill, a maverick conservative.

Poles in the French Campaign

The phony war had come to an abrupt end on May 10, 1940, when the Germans, taking no heed of the proclamations of neutrality by Holland and Belgium, invaded these countries in a modified von Schlieffen maneuver and went on to defeat the combined Dutch, Belgian, French and British armies in less than six weeks.

The French Campaign may historically be divided into two parts. The first part begins on May 10, with the German breakthrough out of the Ardennes and terminates with the evacuation of the British and French troops hemmed into the perimeter around the English Channel ports of Dunkirk, Boulogne, and Calais. Polish ground troops did not participate in this phase of the Battle of France. The second phase began on June 5, with the German attack on French positions at the Somme and Aisne, and concluded with the French asking for an armistice, as the Germans reached the River Gironde on June 22.

It is close to ironic that now the French, who had dragged their feet in every respect, turned to the Poles and asked for assistance from the Polish clandestine groups to take some burden off the hard-pressed French forces.[36]

The only major cohesive Polish aviation unit was the Groupe de Chasse Polonaise de Varsovie 1/145. This consisted of 35 pilots and about 130 ground crew. None of the other planned aviation units were ready by May but well over 100 Polish fighter pilots fought in the skies of France, flying a motley collection of various French planes, many obsolescent.[37] Many of these pilots were organized in small three-plane flights, called the chimney flights, formed and stationed to provide defense for French industrial regions. The Polish fighters achieved over 50 documented victories.

In addition to the 8,000 Polish airmen in France there were also nearly 1,500 Polish air personnel in northern Africa. Numerous Polish aviation personnel were also seconded to French combat units.

The impending military and political French debacle came as a shock to Poles, who admired French culture and in the French Army, honed in the bloody battles of World War I, saw the acme of elan and military doctrine. It was particularly stunning for that Francophile, Sikorski. He not only continued to express the strongest words of support for the French and for their new commander in chief, General Weygand, who replaced Gamelin, but categorically castigated as a defeatist anyone who wanted to make plans based on the worst-case scenario. For that lack of reality he has been strongly criticized, and even Kukiel, one of his closest friends, admitted that Sikorski's convictions of the final French victory were obstinately held.[38]

On June 11, Weygand advised his government that the situation was catastrophic and that armistice talks should be initiated, but on June 13, Weygand appealed to Sikorski for all Polish troops to be thrown into the battle. On June 13, Paris was declared an open city.*

The Polish government evacuated to the Bordeaux region at Libourne but still was kept in the dark about French intentions. Sikorski arrived in Libourne on June 17. As the Polish government was preparing the text of an appeal to Churchill, the latter coincidentally invited Sikorski for consultations. It was quickly agreed that the Polish president and certain members of the government board the British cruiser HMS *Arethuse*. Sikorski on June 18 was picked up by an RAF plane and flown to London to contact

*There was a strange disconnect in Weygand's thinking. As a military man he wanted to fight as long as possible, but as a statesman he wanted the French government to ask for peace terms to protect the country and to ensure that it was not the French Army that had capitulated, as happened in Belgium.

Churchill. General Sosnkowski was now left in charge of the military. Meanwhile on June 17, the French initiated talks with the Germans through their embassy in Spain. Petain had now replaced Raynaud as prime minister and the overtures to Germany were contrary to the Polish-French Agreement which precluded either signatory from initiating political talks with the enemy without prior initial consultation.[39]

Churchill met with Sikorski in Downing Street and the witness to this meeting, Raczynski, describes the meeting as full of melodramatics. Sikorski posed one question to Churchill: did Britain intend to fight? Allegedly with tears in eyes, Churchill responded, to the death or to victory. Sikorski then asked for British help in evacuating the Poles from France, which was immediately implemented with great efficiency. On June 19, Sikorski made his famous BBC speech to all Poles in France, and urged Poland to continue the fight in the underground and in exile. After making his speech, Sikorski flew back to France and arrived June 20 in Libourne; he left orders for evacuation and flew back to the United Kingdom, taking Sosnkowski and a small number of staff officers with him.

Prior to flying off to the United Kingdom, Sosnkowski sent a message to Poland, giving General Rowecki in occupied Poland sole and total command of the whole Polish clandestine military organization.

The final evacuation was left to generals Kukiel, Modelski and Burkhardt. The Polish government and military staffs in Libourne, unable to obtain French help in facilitating the evacuation, were delighted to be informed that British shipping would be available for the transport of all Polish military and civilian personnel from France to the United Kingdom.

The Evacuation from France

Sikorski's successful trip to London did little to undo the chaos of the situation facing the Polish units, training centers and aviation units scattered all over France. The French, for their part, were perplexed at the idea of the Poles evacuating to the United Kingdom since it was their conviction that the British would also capitulate in a short time. The majority of the Poles were just not aware of the extent of the catastrophe suffered by their French ally, and many just not aware of the order from Sikorski. For Maj. Gen. Bronislaw Duch, the general officer commanding of the Polish Grenadier Division, which was deeply embroiled in heavy fighting, Sikorski's orders posed a dilemma since they contradicted his loyalty to his French Army superior. Thus the grenadier division continued to hold the front line and to fight until after the armistice went into effect. By then it was too late to disentangle the division, which was surrounded by German forces, and all its officers and men were taken prisoners of war.

Those Polish units which were in the rear, or in early stages of formation and thus not committed piecemeal to battle as well as some training centers were evacuated, as long as they had access to radio communication with Polish headquarters and organic transport. The Podhalanska Brigade, saved from its fruitless victory at Narvik, was sacrificed by Polish idealism and Allied stupidity bordering on duplicity. It was disembarked in Brittany to reinforce the nonexistent stronghold. Most of the brigade was lost as was the Fourth Infantry division which in the early stages of formation was also moved north to reinforce the nonexistent front.

The last Polish unit to embark for the United Kingdom was the Second Battalion of the Armored Brigade which, detached for rearguard action from its main training center, was able to break away and reached St. Jean de Luz on June 24, two days after the armistice had gone into effect. As the Poles were embarking, the last units set up a defensive perimeter, as much from the Germans, only a few miles away, as from the hostile French administration, which, not unreasonably, saw the Polish action as incompatible with the terms of the armistice.*

Forty thousand Poles had fought in the Battle of France and all were lost. Only 19,000 officers and men of the Polish armed forces were evacuated to the United Kingdom from France in June 1940. Of this number, 5,600 were transported on Polish merchant ships. This number of evacuees to Britain represented only 23 percent of the Polish forces in France in the summer of 1940.

Again due to good luck and good communications, the majority of the Polish Air Force personnel were saved, though many did evacuate by plane or ship to North Africa.

The following Polish ships participated in the evacuation: the liners *Batory* and *Sobieski*, m/s *Lechistan*, s/s *Chorzow*, s/s *Kmicic*, s/s *Wilno*, and two Polish fishing trawlers, *Korab* and *Delfin*. These Polish ships transported 5,600 men to the United Kingdom. In this Allied operation, code named Aerial, a total of 191,870 men were evacuated to the United Kingdom. The British numbered 144,171; Polish, 24,352; French, 18,246; Czechoslovakians, 4,939; and Belgians, 163.[40]

The Polish Brigade in French Syria was, however, saved. The commanding officer of the Carpathian Brigade, General Kopanski, had clear orders to move to British Palestine if the French commander obeyed the French government's call for an armistice. His unit, well centralized and cohesive, was on a full alert and in spite of some French recalcitrance the move was expedited.

There were positive aspects to the French debacle. The Poles had suffered an absolute military catastrophe in 1939 and developed an inferiority complex that was aided and abetted by the French and encouraged by those Polish politicians who had suffered both real and imaginary persecutions at the hands of Poland's ruling Sanacja prior to the war. In 1940, the defeat of a much larger and better-prepared French Army and the precipitate evacuation of the British Expeditionary Corps put the situation in a different perspective. The 1939 campaign was now seen in a perspective which improved the morale of the personnel of the Polish armed forces. Also, the evacuation to Britain was arranged by Polish officers; the men traveled as organized units in uniform under Polish command and in many instances on Polish ships.

The defeat of the French appeared to make the Germans invincible and masters of the continent. This had an immediate and very deleterious effect in the occupied homeland. The persecution of all things Polish increased, with seemingly the Germans

---

*There is a story, possibly apocryphal, that an evacuating Polish unit short of gasoline asked the French townspeople for gasoline. This was refused. The Polish commanding officer allegedly told the French mayor that thtey were about to witness a fight which would place their town in history books. The Poles were about to dig in and fight to the death. Gasoline was quickly supplied.

and Soviets competing with each other to see who could exterminate Polish culture and the Polish community more effectively. By all objective standards and with a 50-year retrospective, the first prize has to go to the Soviets. It appears that this was the time when Soviet and German representatives met in occupied Krakow and decided the fate of the Polish officers in Soviet captivity. One can only speculate that the Germans did not wish the Soviets to have the kernel of a Polish army since they were already thinking of the final defeat of Communism. The Soviets were not about to cross their powerful and seemingly invincible ally.

As a result of the French capitulation, it was obvious that the war would now be prolonged. Sosnkowski sent a message to the occupied homeland that efforts at an uprising would also have to be postponed and that patience would have to be the key word. Finally, Sikorski confirmed the appointment of General Rowecki to the post of general officer commanding the Polish underground army but Sosnkowski remained as minister for Home Affairs.

The French interval in the Polish struggle was over.

June 1940 through June 1941

Settling Down in the United Kingdom

When the Polish government and the remnants of its forces, saved from the French debacle, arrived in the United Kingdom they had been preceded by the small Polish Navy and its naval headquarters, as well as by a small group of Polish Air Force personnel who were based in Eastchurch. The arrival of the nearly 20,000 additional Polish military allegedly presented the British with a constitutional dilemma. This is hard to understand, since the Polish Navy, including its land-based training and headquarters, was in the United Kingdom without exciting a constitutional dilemma or crisis.[1]

The realities of the possibility of an imminent German invasion led remarkably quickly to the signing of a Polish-British military agreement and enabling legislature in the House of Commons. Given the fact that the British were facing great peril it is surprising how much time was given to Polish requests to negotiate a land forces agreement and to renegotiate the past air force agreement. General Sikorski now attempted with only a modicum of success to undo the damage of the June 1940 air force agreement. His goal was a comprehensive military treaty which would be compatible with Polish interests and analogous to the agreements signed with the French in January 1940 and the Polish-UK naval agreement of November 1939. He succeeded regarding the Polish ground forces but only very partially in regard to the air force since the British Air Ministry balked.

Churchill, in one of his internal memos to Lord Ismay, as early as June 26, 1940, wrote: "In principle we ought to make the most of the Poles. They should be assembled, made comfortable and re-equipped as soon as possible."[2] The British Polish Forces Committee on July 1, 1940, discussed and accepted the Polish positions that the Polish ground forces would be an autonomous allied force while the Polish Air Force would be symbolically autonomous and no longer part of the Royal Air Force Volunteer Reserve.[3]

The British Air Ministry and its chiefs were not happy with the "sudden" decision of the Polish government to press for a Polish Air Force separate from the RAF. The British memos confirm that close to 10,000 Polish air personnel were now in the United Kingdom and quaintly differentiate the original group who were enrolled in the RAFVR as the British Poles, while the evacuees from France are in turn described as French Poles.[4] In its July 3 internal memo the air ministry position is as follows: "There is going to be intense political pressure by General Sikorski to form a Polish Air Force

The President of Poland, Wladyslaw Raczkiewicz, being greeted by King George VI (in uniform) on arrival in London, June 1940, after France's capitulation.

Legion entirely under Polish control; The Army apparently has agreed to allow the formation of a wholly Polish Army and we shall find it difficult to resist pressure from them to be allowed to form their own Air Force." The memo finishes with this expression of Air Ministry policy, which in fact was implemented in substance: "I am sure our policy must be to resist this pressure and to insist upon any Polish squadrons which we form here being incorporated in the Air Force (i.e., RAF) and working under direct Air Force control."

The Polish negotiations for an autonomous Polish Air Force were strongly and successfully confronted by the British Air Ministry, which while conceding minor cosmetic points prevailed on maintaining substantive RAF prerogatives. The points conceded were to dispense with enrollment in the RAFVR and the oath of allegiance to the British monarch, and the Poles were now allowed to wear Polish insignia and Polish decorations according to the Polish set of priorities[5] and fly the Polish flag on bases where Poles were stationed. But the British prevailed on having complete operational control over Polish squadrons and even for a time had RAF officers in command of the Polish fighter squadrons. It was agreed that Polish personnel would not serve outside of the European theater of operations.[6]

The memo concluded that in addition to the current two Polish (Fairey Battle) bomber squadrons two further bomber and two fighter squadrons would be formed and that some Poles would be sent to ferrying duties and some to the Army Cooperation units.[7] The Polish Army Cooperation Squadron was stipulated to be under Polish control and assigned to the Polish ground troops in Scotland.[8]

Administrative Background

Special military conventions signed between the Polish government and the host (the government of the United Kingdom), regulated the administrative and disciplinary aspects of the garrisoning of the Polish armed forces.[9]

The Polish government was located in London (as were the governments of many German-occupied countries) and maintained embassies in most countries, the most important being London, Washington, Lisbon, Madrid, Stockholm, Ottawa, Ankara, Tokyo, Geneva and Budapest.[10]

The Polish Military Headquarters were also in London, at the Rubens Hotel on Buckingham Palace Road. In addition to the London headquarters, Sikorski, who always dreamed of taking a field command and leading his troops personally, had a field HQ in Gask, Scotland. During this time, Gen. Wladyslaw Sikorski still held the positions of prime minister, commander in chief, and minister for Military Affairs.

Sikorski's War Aims and Strategic Mission of the Polish Armed Forces

Sikorski's outline for Poland's war aims was that Poland was to be reinstituted in its 1939 boundaries but with the elimination of the East Prussia enclave and the incorporation of the so-called Free City of Danzig into Poland.

Sikorski hoped to achieve these aims by the active participation of the armed forces at the side of the British ally, which was to be an entry fee for the Poles to take part in allied planning of the war and the postwar European settlement. Until the time when the Soviets came into the war, this policy bore fruit and seemed successful.

To achieve these policy goals, five specific albeit complementary aspects were undertaken:

1. the creation of a Polish-controlled system of radio communications with Poland, utilizing its own secret cipher codes;
2. the development of a Polish-controlled system of dropping couriers;
3. the recruitment and training of such couriers in parachute techniques;
4. the development of Polish land and air forces for concentration in Poland to strengthen the Polish underground army;
5. finally tying in the Polish underground army to the Western strategic and military goals.

Many of these goals had been in the works even in France. But neither the French nor the British were all that energized by Polish plans and in fact at times were close to being negative. The political climate had now changed.

The Polish president visited the Polish 309 Army Cooperation Squadron based in Scotland in 1941.

The Polish armed forces were officially divided into the underground army in occupied Poland and the forces in exile at the side of the British ally. The ultimate purpose of the underground army (the name of Home Army —*Armia Krajowa*— was only given in February 1942) was to guarantee that in the most expeditious moment an armed rising would take place which would establish de facto and not just de jure control of Polish territory in the name of the Polish government. But the most immediate goal was to gather intelligence and to promote the morale of the Polish nation, suffering from brutal German repression. This was done in many ways, by the publication of underground papers, selective sabotage, and by the trial and highly publicized execution of selected oppressors who were most guilty of inhuman treatment of the Polish citizens.

The task of the Polish military in exile was in some ways both simpler and more difficult. It was to be a support base for the Polish underground by training cadres for those elements of the armed forces which could not be developed or trained in German-occupied Poland, such as the air force, the navy, and certain specialized components of the land forces as armored units, engineers, etc. It was to be a highly visible force whose active part at the side of the Western Allies would address the basic motif of the Polish forces and government in exile: "We do not beg for freedom, we fight for freedom." Finally, it was intended that at the most appropriate moment the forces were to be moved to Poland to reinforce the Home Army.

The formal signing of the Polish-British Military Agreement, August 5, 1940. From the left: Count Edward Raczynski, Polish ambassador to the Court of Saint James's, General Wladyslaw Sikorski, Polish prime minister and commander-in-chief, Winston S. Churchill, and August Zaleski, Polish foreign minister. (Courtesy of the Polish Institute and Sikorski Museum, London.)

Gen. W. Sikorski, the Polish prime minister and commander in chief, was of the opinion that the only strategy which would ensure the liberation of Poland by the Western Allies, and hopefully with the participation of Polish troops, was the Balkan route. The Poles had good relations with the Romanians and Bulgarians and very warm relations with the Hungarians. The Balkan strategy was also espoused by Churchill who worked hard to get the Turks to his side and argued the concept of the "soft underbelly" of Europe until the invasion of southern France in August 1944.[11]

The events of the summer of 1940 were momentous indeed. The major Polish continental ally had capitulated while their island hosts were facing a strangulating naval submarine blockade and were in the process of fighting for their existence over the skies of south England. The military problems facing the British, caused by the capitulation of France and the entry of Italy on the side of the Axis powers, made manpower a most pressing issue. Churchill also exerted all his efforts to inveigle both the Soviet Union and the United States into the grand coalition against Germany. From the very first contact between Sikorski and Churchill the first of these issues was broached and efforts made to get the Poles to accommodate with the Soviets to arrange for the release of the many hundreds of thousands of Polish prisoners in Soviet captivity. This possibility of adding to the Polish military was not foreign to Sikorski, who already in France asked the Polish staff to work up a series of optional ideas in the event of either a German attack on the Soviets or the Soviets joining the British in an anti–German alliance. These ideas were then rather awkwardly formulated through a Polish journalist, Litauer, who had strong left-wing sympathies and was suspected by many as a Soviet agent.[12] The Polish staff plans were contingent on various international scenarios with the most likely being a prediction of a German attack on the Soviets.

On June 29, 1940, Sikorski formed a new section in the Polish General Staff. Colonel Smolenski (Section VI) would be liaison with the Polish underground now commanded exclusively by Maj. Gen. Stefan Rowecki, based in German-occupied Poland.

But the war went on. The Polish armed forces were now after their second lost campaign. The Poles from the very first were absolutely committed to being full participants in the struggle against Germany. The Polish Navy had been operating out of British ports since 1939; the Polish fighter squadrons became active partners in the defense of the British Isles; the Polish bomber squadrons were also entering combat operations in attacks on German ports and invasion barge concentrations. From Sikorski down to the last soldier, the Poles were determined to be counted on to fulfill their allied obligation and to be taken seriously by allies, neutrals, and the enemy. There was an initial period of despondency, accentuated by the dismal Scottish climate, the quality of life in unheated tents and barracks, strange and different food, and worry about loved ones back in Poland. Many of the rank and file were either recruited from the Polish migration in prewar France and used to French food, including wine with meals; even those from Poland had got accustomed to such a diet. This led to some isolated and short-lived discipline problems in the ground forces. But the Poles quickly adjusted and began to pride themselves on their appellation — *Sikorski's Tourists.*

Battle of Britain

The evacuation from France was shortly followed by the aerial battle known as the Battle of Britain. The German U-boat offensive had not yet reached its acme, but the German preparations for invasion in occupied France were obvious and the preliminary step was going to be a German air offensive to establish air superiority over the English Channel. The German navy had taken such a beating at the hands of the Royal Navy in the Norwegian waters, (in spite of German air superiority in that campaign) that the head of the Kriegsmarine, Admiral Raeder, made it clear that he could not guarantee a successful invasion and the safety of the German land troops without full German air supremacy over the English Channel.

In this situation, the British now realized the value of the Polish fighter pilots, though there was considerable and persistent concern, partially justified, about the English-language skills of the Poles, since all RAF fighter units were directed by ground control.

In the air struggle over southern England and the city of London, two Polish fighter squadrons took part: the 302nd Poznanski and 303rd Kosciuszko. But there were also many Polish pilots in RAF squadrons. By the end of the Battle of Britain, 154 Polish fighter pilots fought over British skies either in the two all–Polish squadrons or in various RAF units.[13]

The Poles were a success. They were visited by the king and queen, by the Duke of Kent, by Mr. Churchill, by Air Marshal Douglas Sholto and the minister for Air, Archibald Sinclair.[14] They were also visited by one of the original members of Kosciuszko squadron, the American Colonel C. Cooper.[15]

Particularly effective was the fact that this battle took place over London and the south counties, and millions of Britons followed the battle during the day, scanning the skies for the contrails of the enemy and of the attacking fighters. Then in the evening they listened to the BBC and in the morning read about what they had seen. One of the messages received by the 303rd was from the BBC: "The BBC sends warm greeting to the famous 303rd Polish Squadron with lively congratulations upon its magnificent record and all the best wishes for the future. You use the air for your gallant exploits and we for telling the world of them. FW Ogilvie, Director-General Broadcasting House. London, 20th September, 1940."[16]

But the most important aspect of the Polish participation in the aerial battle was the infusion of well over a hundred experienced pilots when the British resources were strained. Thanks to a very imaginative and energetic program of the British aircraft industry, decentralized and ably directed by Lord Beaverbrook, the RAF was not short of serviceable planes, but very short of experienced pilots. A good comment on this is the reference in Churchill's memoirs to the fact on his second trip to France (June 13, 1940), after obviously failing to encourage the French not to give up, he made only two conditions: one is very well known, about the French Navy being protected from a takeover by the Germans; but the second one referred to the four hundred German pilots in captivity in France, many shot down by British pilots. Churchill insisted that they all ought to be turned over to the British. They were not, but the stakes of the war depended on such relatively small numbers.[17]

Less glamorous, but more onerous and much bloodier, was the bomber offensive which began to develop in the late 1940s and accentuated in intensity during 1941. In this, the four Polish bomber squadrons, initially equipped with the outdated, single-engined Fairey Battle, but having converted to the two-engined Wellington, were full participants. The Polish part in this bomber offensive was important to the extent that it further negated Polish attempts to move crews to the special duties operations which the Poles arduously sought to develop.

The success of the Poles in the Battle of Britain and also their sacrifice in the bomber squadrons, began to bear some fruit in 1941. The British Air Ministry, formally upholding the revised (August 1940) agreement began to accommodate the Poles, creating a mini–Polish fighter command staff with the first Polish Fighter Command liaison being Colonel Pawlikowski, the 1939 commander of the fighter brigade, as part of its own fighter command headquarters. Polish officers were also assigned to ground control and technical operations in various RAF commands. During 1941, Polish liaison officers were appointed to various RAF commands and to all bases where Poles were stationed.

The RAF authorities in their projected planning had reserved the numbers 300 through 309 for Polish squadrons since they assumed that there would be available air crews for only nine squadrons. But the Polish air strength still grew in 1941. By the end of 1940, all the bomber squadrons that the Poles were going to have on their establishment, namely 300, 301, 304 and 305, were fully operational, but additional fighter squadrons continued to be formed: 315 (Deblinski), 316 (Warszawski) and 317 (Wilenski), which joined the existing Polish o. de b. of 302 (Poznanski), 303 (Kosciuszko), 306 (Torunski), 307 night fighter (Lwowski), and 308 (Krakowski). Number 309 went to the Polish Army Cooperation Squadron in Scotland.*

All fighter squadrons were flying either the Hurricane or the Spitfire, the exception being the 307 night fighter equipped with the Bolton Paul Defiant[18] (a one-engine, two-crew plane) and shortly converting to the two-engined Beaufighter. As further Polish fighter squadrons entered operations, a number began to be grouped in all Polish wings. The first commanding officer of the Polish wing was Major Urbanowicz, shortly succeeded by Colonel Rolski.[19]

Having won a strategic victory in the Battle of Britain, the RAF Fighter Command began to undertake offensive operations over German-occupied France.[20] On August 14, 1941, the First Polish Fighter Wing, commanded by Major Janus and consisting of three Polish squadrons, 306, 308 and 315, carried out a sweep around St. Omar-Burge. The Polish wing intercepted a formation of approximately 25 ME-109s and in the ensuing dogfight the Poles shot down 15 German planes and lost four of their own. This was the beginning of aggressive air interdiction into German airspace.

Polish Intelligence Services

But the Polish dowry to the Allied cause was much more than the small number of superb fighter pilots and 20,000 fighting men. Their major contribution to the British and Allied war effort was again in the field of intelligence, just as in the summer of 1939 it had been the Enigma Machine. The Poles had a superb intelligence network based in France, North Africa and Switzerland; France was also home to the Bruno decrypting station. By 1944, the Polish (offensive) intelligence network had 420 agents outside of occupied Poland, based in Lisbon, Stockholm, Berne, Madrid, Budapest, Istanbul, Vichy France, North Africa and in occupied Holland, Denmark and Belgium.[21]

The Poles placed their Section II at the disposal of the British but as a quid pro quo requested and obtained (at that time without any reservations), the right to use their own ciphers, without British oversight, which they had developed in France. The Poles were the only allied country that was given this unique status, though as the war progressed it was challenged by some agencies of the British government. Due to support from members of the British SOE, the Poles kept their ciphers to the end of hostilities.[22]

While the British and Polish intelligence services collaborated, there were areas of

---

*It will be noted that all Polish fighter squadrons were named after cities in Poland, with the exception of 315, which was named after the Polish Air Force officer's academy.

rivalry and even of suspicion. The two most prominent divisive issues concerned the wife of the Polish military attaché to Berlin prior to the war, Madam Szymanska, who was resident in Switzerland and maintained a covert contact with Admiral Canaris and Die Schwarze Kapelle. She became a target of Polish defensive intelligence. The other was the glamorous Krystyna Skarbek — Countess Gizycka (known by the British as Countess Christine Granville), who actually worked for British intelligence out of Budapest, and maintained contact with a fringe clandestine group in Poland — the Musketeers. Sikorski was adamant about the British breaking off all contacts with her.[23]

The full story of this is lost in conspiracy theories and buried or in destroyed archives, but Sikorski was concerned lest some fringe group add to his political and diplomatic problems by appearing to negotiate with the Germans. He also was close to frantic about the fact that Marshal Smigly-Rydz had escaped from Romania to Hungary in December 1939 and attempted to establish contacts with the Polish underground, which culminated in October 1941 with his escape from Hungary to occupied Poland.[24] This presented Sikorski with the proverbial "ghost" coming for dinner since he perceived it as a potential challenge to not only his absolute control of the military, but also as a possible strong political opposition to his own policy of accommodating and negotiating with the Soviets.

Polish Military Radio Network*

This is as good a place as any to give a succinct account of the Polish radio communication network which evolved over a number of years. There were three independent radio systems: the military one, which is the focus of this study, and two civilian ones, serving the needs of the Polish foreign service and the Polish Ministry of Home Affairs. This last one in fact became close to a monopoly of the major coalition partner, namely Mr. Mikojaczyk's Peasant Party.

In France in the spring of 1940, the Polish military had two long-range wireless transmitters and receivers: Regina, serving the II Section (Intelligence), and Angers on behalf of contacts with occupied Poland.[25]

On evacuation to Britain, the military transmitters worked on behalf of the Polish HQ (i.e., VI Section for liaison with Poland) and also for communication with other Polish units in exile. It also served the needs of the London-based Ministry of Defence and its security section (later in the war renamed the Ministry of Military Affairs.)

The locations of these Polish radio stations and their establishment varied. But as the war continued the importance and hence the number of stations and personnel increased. The initial unit serving the needs of the Polish military was based at Dower House in Stanmore. Then the responsibilities were divided, with Barnes Lodge working on behalf of the Polish HQ and assisted by Connington, while Boxmoor took over all radio intelligence working for the II Section (Intelligence) of the Polish staff. This radio surveillance station monitoring German and Russian radio communications also collaborated with Bletchley Park. In August 1944, the complexity of these communi-

---

*I am indebted and grateful to Zbigniew S. Siemaszko for most of the details pertaining to this section of Polish radio operations in World War II.

cations led to the creation of the Batalion Lacznosci Sztabu NW (Signals Battalion of the commander in chief). It was based at Dower House in Stanmore, near London. But some sections dealing with Section VI (contact with the underground) and espionage were in London at 13 Upper Belgrave and Wilton Streets, a short walk from the Rubens Hotel, the site of the Polish Military Headquarters. A supporting base was in Scotland at Polmont in Stirlingshire, which trained radio operators for parachuting to Poland and also supplied new cadres for the London-based company. At its height it had eight officers and 114 of other ranks.[26] This company also provided a detached section for the central radio system for the commander in chief and these were based at Chipperfield Lodge and at Kings Langley. By July 1944, the company had 23 transmitting stations in the United Kingdom. These came either from Hallicrafter RCA or from Polish production.

In occupied Poland, the Home Army possessed 57 radio stations, 10 restricted for air liaison. Most of these stations used the Polish radio sets manufactured in England by Polish engineers at the Anglo-Polish Radio Wireless Research and Manufacturing Company in Stanmore. Eight hundred of these radio sets were dropped in Poland by August 1944. Pierre Lorain writes, "The Polish series was certainly one of the most brilliantly designed in the domain of clandestine transmissions. ... between 1941 and 1944 ten models were manufactured in substantial quantities. It was not until 1943 that the British specialists produced sets of equal and perhaps superior quality."[27]

Independently of the work being done by Polish engineers in the United Kingdom, there was a parallel effort in occupied Poland where radios were built on the basis of a set developed prior to September 1939. This had been intended for use by Polish intelligence services, most likely in German territories, and had in fact been captured by the Germans but then stolen by the Poles from the German-controlled electronics factory, Ava. The Polish engineer was Heftman. The set was used to establish contact with Budapest on March 1940.

The reverse radio contact from the United Kingdom to Poland first took place on September 18, 1940.

The radio system serving the Polish HQ also had the following transmitting and receiving radio links: Aza in France, Team and Sara in the Middle East, Barbara in Hungary and Stanislawa in Sweden.

The Polish Intelligence Service (II Section of the staff) also had its own system and codes. These were based in the Middle East, Switzerland, the Iberian Peninsula, Algiers and 12 in France!

The major Polish ground units had their own radio systems, e.g., Szkot with the First Corps in Scotland, Jan with the First Armored, Feliks with the Parachute Brigade and Wicek with the Polish Corps in the Middle East. The 2 Corps in Italy finally got its own independent radio system in the middle of 1944, called Wladek.

All these Polish systems communicated with each other as the need arose. Finally, the Ministry of Military Defense had six stations of its own system with its own ciphers.

In 1944, the Polish radio at Barnes Lodge communicated with 95 other stations with an average of 81 telegrams per day. One of the paradoxes is that the headquarters of the 2 Corps depended on other radio systems for so long, until the summer of 1944. In fact, it appears that the corps depended either on the intelligence network or Baza

11 (Mewa). To give further support for contacts with Poland, in 1943 a second major station was formed in Brindisi, Italy. It was in relatively close proximity to the base of the Polish Special Duties flight once that was moved to Italy.

Needless to say the British were often very unhappy about the ability of the various Polish units and command systems to communicate with each other and in their own cipher. It is an intriguing thought whether the British cracked or attempted to crack the Polish ciphers at Bletchley Park.

In the weeks preceding D-Day, the British requested the Poles to share all their transmissions before forwarding. This was complied with and the Poles resumed their secret transmissions after the Normandy landings were no longer a secret and their primacy no longer in doubt.*

This unique and completely autonomous radio system pertained only to Polish ground units and also to the Polish HQ. This was not the case for the Polish Air Force or the Polish Navy, which lacked any similar independence in communications and were completely tied to the British system. Polish Air Force personnel and Polish squadrons were so interspersed with the Royal Air Force that individuals and even squadrons were nearly operationally interchangeable. This was also true for the Polish warships which in combat operations depended exclusively on British signals. Only in port during breaks between operations did the Polish naval command have any administrative jurisdiction about promotions and changes in crew.

Finally, there were two Polish-language radio services, one officially run by the BBC and one by the Polish government. There was a third, English-based radio system, which purported to be broadcasting from occupied Poland, called Swit, and which took the masquerade so far as to occasionally not transmit, at times to start late or finish early, with apologies extended to their listeners as being due to causes outside of their control, but leaving the impression that the Germans were close to locating the Poles.[28]

Polish Units in Scotland and Recruitment Efforts

While the Polish General Staff laid long-term plans, the host country faced a direct peril, the possibility of a German invasion which could come by sea and air. The impressive success of the German paratroopers in Crete was still to come (spring 1941) but the Germans had already demonstrated their proficiency in the capture of the Belgian forts considered impregnable from ground attack. Hence the task which the Poles in the United Kingdom faced was not only to bring order to their units, to retrain the men with British equipment, but also to achieve prompt combat readiness.

Scotland, while not considered the primary invasion point was vulnerable to small

---

It is a rule of thumb in intelligence work that any change in a pattern of communications augurs a major new developement. In 1939, the Poles were able to support their human intelligence about the impending German aggression by the fact that the Germans changed their code. One has to assume that the sudden silence of the Polish communications in a code which the Germans never cracked might have alerted the Germans to the impending landings in France. But the fact is that the Germans expected an invasion and the secret to be kept as long as possible was its location.

diversionary attacks from enemy paratroops and even from the sea. As early as July 1940 a battalion of the Polish First Infantry Brigade Group began its anti-invasion duties near Glasgow. By August 1940, within two months of the evacuation of the Polish forces from France, the Polish ground units were going through an intense process of retraining, reorganization, and redeployment. While the numbers were small, they still represented a force sufficiently combat trained, and in most instances combat experienced, to be given responsibility for a defensive perimeter north of Edinburgh.

In the unique situation faced by the Poles and by their British hosts, still in expectation of a German assault, the organizational idiosyncrasies were of secondary importance. Having said that, the changes in units reflected the ambitions of the Poles to have a motorized corps, although confronted by a serious shortage of manpower. The Polish ground forces were also assigned a Polish Army Cooperation Squadron, 309, formed on November 23, 1940, at Renfrew, flying the outdated Lysander. When the Royal Air Force disbanded the Army Cooperation Command as a result of experiences gleaned in North Africa, the Polish squadron was equipped with Mustangs and assigned to the 133rd Polish Wing.

The Polish corps may not have been capable of resisting a full-scale German offensive, but it was clearly well able to defend against even a major German airborne landing and had the mobility to respond to situations of an emergency nature. The grandiose title of a corps was self-evident; but it was a praetorian guard compared to the British Home Guard, which was still armed with shotguns and walking sticks.

Because of the danger confronting the British it was decided to form cadre brigades where the relative excess of Polish junior officers was placed. Junior officers without a functional assignment were, without prejudice to their rank, made into ordinary riflemen. Four such cadre brigades were formed and motorized, each equivalent to a rifle company.

The history of one is directly relevant to the topic of this monograph. It was also hoped that as recruitment of volunteers from Polish migrants in Canada, the United States, and South America developed, the cadre brigades would lose this unique character, and indeed could be fleshed out to become regular brigade-sized units of the Polish Army. There were some pragmatic and immediate results of this plan. The First Polish Army Corps was strengthened with a number of mobile, independent, company-sized units of skilled, highly motivated and experienced troops. Putting the officers in such cadre units enabled the Polish High Command to undertake immediate and aggressive steps to retrain the officers as well as giving them very concrete and practical tasks which took their minds off their obvious concern about the future of the war, the fate of their country, and of their families left behind in Poland.

There were two other ways that the excess of Polish officers was utilized. About 200 who volunteered and were suitable by British standards went on contract to the West African Rifles.[29] A smaller number crewed British armored trains which patrolled regions where there was a danger of German parachute incursions.[30]

The Polish authorities were at this time still not quite clear how many more Poles would manage to escape to Britain from Vichy France. It is, in retrospect, obvious that hopes for large numbers of volunteers from the Polish immigrants living in Canada and the United States were unfounded. The Polish staff decided that it would be the 4th

Cadre Rifle Brigade (commanded by Col. Stanislaw Sosabowski) which would be shipped to Canada to provide senior noncommissioned and junior officer material. But even as these plans were being made, the cadre brigade embarked on anti-invasion training in collaboration with territorial units of the British Home Guard.

The hopes and expectations that large numbers of Polish migrants living in Canada and the United States would flock to the Polish colors to express their patriotic zeal, as did their forebears in 1917, failed to materialize. It was a different era and a different generation from 1917. The Canadian and American Polonia gave generously of its money and in later years attempted to lobby on behalf of the Polish cause, but was reluctant to send its young men to be slaughtered on a foreign continent on behalf of values which it no longer completely endorsed or shared. Fewer than 500 volunteered.[31] The Canadian mission of the 4th Cadre Brigade was cancelled. But its heroic history was only to begin.

The first phase of the growth of Polish armed forces in exile came to a practical stop in the autumn of 1940. An additional increment was the evacuation of 2,000 airmen from French North Africa in July 1940 while another 3,288 officers and men were transported from Romania and Hungary to Palestine, reinforcing the Carpathian Brigade. Poles who had been stranded in France continued to attempt to escape to Britain but many thousands were caught by the Spanish police and were interned in horrible and deplorable conditions by the Spaniards. The infamous Spanish camp of Miranda is in tragic contrast to the hospitality and humaneness shown the Poles by the Romanians and Hungarians.

Polish Feluccas

Some of this evacuation was expedited by a very unique Polish naval component, the feluccas of the Polish Gibraltar naval mission.

In March 1941, a young Polish naval officer, Marian Kadulski, was seconded to Gibraltar to organize clandestine sea evacuation from Metropolitan France and its North African territories. Eventually he was joined by two other officers, Buchowski and Michalkiewicz. Not to antagonize Franco, Spain's dictator, the British specifically forbade any operations out of Spain. Kadulski purchased a small number of fishing feluccas and began to conduct clandestine operations inserting Polish and eventually British and French agents in North Africa and southern France as well as evacuating stranded Poles and occasionally returning agents.[32] These operations also supported the Polish-run intelligence agency Agency Africa, headed by Slowikowski.[33] As is so often the case, the administrative hierarchy was complicated. Kadulski was directly responsible to the Polish mission in Lisbon, which in itself was a hotbed of clandestine activities, both Allied and German.[34] His colleagues were seconded by the Polish Navy to SOE in the area, commanded by the famous Capt. F. H. Slocum, RN. All three Polish officers received high British awards for their work, Kadulski and Buchowski the Distinguished Service Order and Michalkiewicz the Distinguished Service Cross.

While hundreds of Poles were extracted, the awards were undoubtedly for the clandestine activities so ably done by the Poles.

First Staff Plans on Behalf of the Homeland

Polish plans for intelligence gathering and for sabotage were enthusiastically endorsed by the British, who had in the months just after the Dunkirk evacuation initiated their policy of "setting Europe ablaze."[35] Though as Foot writes, for about 18 months after the creation of the Special Operations Executive, "the twigs of early resistance were still too damp outside of Poland, which the SOE could hardly reach, to do more than smolder."[36]

But the Poles wanted more than to just be a vital source of intelligence gathering, they wanted help in making the embers break out in flames at an appropriate time.

The correspondence between the Poles and British for Poles to be seconded to the highly secret British training base at Inverlochy began as early as August 12, 1940.[37] On October 10, 1940, the Polish prime minister and commander in chief, Gen. Wladyslaw Sikorski, issued a highly secret order to his closest military advisors — the Officer in Charge for liaison with the Polish Home Army (General Kazimierz Sosnkowski), as well as the chief of staff and inspector general of the Polish Air Force. This document spelled out political, diplomatic and military goals. The goal for the Polish armed forces in exile was to mobilize the greatest number of troops for an airlift to Poland in order to buttress and strengthen a Polish uprising. This was to include both air units as well as ground forces.[38] In December 1940, Sikorski, in his correspondence with Sir Archibald Sinclair, requested British assistance in the formation of a Polish parachute brigade. In his memorandum, which dealt primarily with various aspects of the Polish Air Force in the United Kingdom, such as training, technical and administrative branches, Sikorski went on to write: "Finally, I should like to call another and no less important matter to your attention, i.e. the preparation of Polish parachute units. These units will be destined to land on a Polish territory in order to take command of the general rising anticipated for the final phase of the war."[39]

It was also in October 1940 that General Sikorski re-created the III Section of the staff, with Colonel Marecki as its head.[40] The section was called "planning" but it had two specific charges. It was to be the forum for planning all contingencies associated with the proposed general uprising in Poland and with the detailed plans for the formation, training and eventual deployment of the Polish parachute forces.[41] The function of the VI Section was to be executive as well as liaison with the British SOE.

This began the long and sisyphian task of planning a major uprising (Burza) and also working out a strategy for its success by involving the Western Allies. The plan was, as the British historian Mackenzie wrote, "grandiose" but as he qualified his assessment, "not absurd."[42]

It is not the focus of this study to analyze all the different plans and contingencies worked up by the Oddzial III. But the following parameters are important to be kept in mind. The plan did not envision an armed struggle against the Soviets, but in a worst-case scenario it did gave the option of the AK going into a clandestine posture. It was not conceptualized as an armed uprising against the German forces, but only as a plan to capture as much territory in the central regions of Warsaw, Lublin, and Kielce from a disintegrating enemy. The plan to some extent was based on the experience of November 1918 when the completely demoralized German forces allowed themselves to be disarmed by barely armed members of the Polish Polska Organizacjia Wojskowa (POW).

Finally, all the Polish plans were based on significant Western Allied assistance, particularly in the first phase which required total air transport commitment and in the second phase which called for naval and shipborne landing near Kolobrzeg. Thus Polish naval officers participated in these staff discussions.

Within weeks of the cancellation of the plans to move the 4th Cadre Brigade to Canada, the chief of staff to General Sikorski, Col. Tadeusz Klimecki, alerted its commanding officer, Colonel Sosabowski, to the fact that the British were interested in training Poles in diversionary activities and were prepared to make their training centers available to Polish volunteers. It is unclear whether Klimecki picked Sosabowski's unit because it consisted of young, intelligent and dedicated officers, or whether Sosabowski persuaded Klimecki that the 4th Cadre Brigade was ideal for the job. But the final planning negotiations were carried out by the representatives of the Polish staff and SOE, namely Colonel Marecki and Perkins, respectively.

As is the case with successful projects, many claimed to have been the originators of the idea. Based on the available archival material, it is most likely that the idea came from the British, namely Gubbins of the SOE, with input from Perkins. Sosabowski's memoirs, which suggest that he thought of this and carried out all the plans for training, have to be discounted.[43] Furthermore it was not the only Polish unit that was considered for parachute training, since two battalions of infantry from the Scottish-based First Corps were also supposed to undergo such training since this was in line with Sikorski's concept that all forces in exile were to be moved to Poland, by air if necessary.

Independently, facilities at Inverlochy and Ringway were also opened up to the Poles. Sosabowski had gathered a group of highly motivated and patriotic officers in his cadre brigade and inspired them to be the elite unit of the Polish Army in exile. They rose to his challenge.

All Polish volunteers for courier duty to Poland as well as the cadre of the 4th Cadre (Parachute) Brigade went to Ringway and to Inverlochy Castle. At the brigade headquarters in Largo House, Polish engineers constructed a parachute training tower for free falls. The 4th Cadre Rifle Brigade was to be the center for training for diversionary activity.

The parachute training was done at Ringway, where the Poles had established a strong presence with two prewar Polish officers and instructors from the Bydgoszcz parachute center, Captains Gorski and Gebolys. These Polish officers were very important in the creation of Polish parachute units. The British archives endorse this view: "they [i.e., the Poles] have a number of first class parachute jumping instructors, and they are prepared to provide a full instructional administrative staff for Ringway."[44] Inverlochy Castle (Secret Station No. 38) near Fort William in Scotland was the center of British commando training as well as at Audley End and Saffron Walden. The Poles collaborated closely with various British officers, including Col. Terry Roper-Caldbeck, Major Mackus, Lt. Colonel Evans and Maj. Angus Kennedy. The Poles established their own small training groups, initially headed by Capt. Franciszek Koprowski and shortly succeeded by Maj. J. Hartman. Except for the parachute training at Ringway, done under British command, the various sabotage and clandestine courses were run by the Poles and were based eventually in a number of different centers, both in Scotland (Chalfont and Latimer) and also in England at Inchmery.

In November 1940, a bare six months after the Poles arrived in the United Kingdom, the British officers were well satisfied with the progress of the Poles and reported, "Poles keen as mustard, best chaps that had ever been there," but this was coupled with concern that the Poles were too ambitious and were trying to run full courses at Inverlochy and Ringway to eventually train two battalions.[45]

All Polish volunteers for courier duty to Poland also went to Ringway and to Inverlochy Castle for training.

This was a success which complemented the development of the radio network, and now needed the creation of a system of delivering the recruited couriers, officers trained in clandestine activities, and supplies to Poland.[46]

Polish Parachute Brigade Created

Thus was the parachute brigade conceived and brought to fruition on September 23, 1941, when General Sikorski visited the cadre unit and observed maneuvers. The exercise, codenamed Mielec, involved capturing a hypothetical landing strip in Poland and providing cover for the landing of other ground forces and of Polish combat fighter squadrons. Planes of the Polish 309th squadron also took part. On that same day, General Sikorski renamed the Fourth Cadre Brigade the First Parachute Brigade (*Pierwsza Brygada Spadochronowa*) and took it out of the order of battle of the First Polish Army Corps and placed it directly under the command of the Polish staff in London.

First Polish Call for an Independent Liaison Flight

While the Polish-British collaboration in the area of parachute training was smooth and satisfactory, substantive difficulties arose when it came to the establishment of a Polish-controlled system of dropping couriers and supplies in Poland. This problem was not one between the Poles and the British, but more of a jurisdictional dispute between the British Ministry of Economic Warfare and the air ministry, which had scant sympathy for anything which distracted from their main mission — the bomber offensive.

It is often forgotten how short of suitable planes and experienced crews the RAF was in the early years of the war. The shortage of crews and planes was such that even by the end of the war, the RAF had only two squadrons of four-engined special duties aircraft based in the United Kingdom.

The first unit operating on behalf of the SOE was Flight 419/1419, formed in August 1940, based at North Weald and flying the Lysanders. In October, two Whitleys were added and the flight became the nucleus of RAF Squadron 138 and moved to Tempsford. It then took on Halifaxes and the Stirlings. RAF Squadron 161 was formed in February 1941 from the King's Flight and also equipped with Whitleys, then Halifaxes and Stirlings.[47]

The air ministry endorsed its staff's views that all efforts should be on the bomber offensive against German targets. The life expectancy of bomber crews was about one in four survival for completion of a 30-mission tour, and the gallows humor in bomber units, British and Polish, was that they were "dead men on leave." The RAF did not even have any four-engined bomber units until late 1941 and the range of Wellingtons was limited, Berlin being as far as the British could bomb. Supplies to France could be flown by the one-engined Lysander, Norway could be reached by the famous Shetland Express of Norwegian and Scottish fishing trawlers, but Poland was beyond the ready reach of any planes until the four-engined Halifax became available. Efforts were made to fly the Whitley, but its slow speed and horrible flying characteristics were anathema to crews. Furthermore, bearing in mind the northern latitudes of Britain, the nights in summer were too short for the planes to fly to and back under the cover of darkness. It was impossible for the planes to fly the direct route and they had to be detoured over Denmark and southern Sweden and hence over the Baltic, which added considerable distance and resulting time.

These were the background facts when early in February 1941, the Polish prime minister, Sikorski, requested that the British Air Ministry second experienced Polish crews from the Polish Bomber Squadrons of the RAF Bomber Command to train in special duties for flights to Poland.[48]

It is assumed that the reason for this clarion call came because of the fiasco of the first mission to Poland, flown in February 1941, codenamed Adolphus. An RAF crew flew a Polish team and lost their way and dropped them over Germany and not German-occupied Poland. The couriers managed to make their way to the Polish Generalgouvernment area, but all supplies were lost including shortwave radios for air-to-ground contact. Furthermore, the Poles were bent out of shape (pun not intended) because they had practiced jumping out of modified Whitleys with a trap-door exit in the bottom of the fuselage while the plane used on the mission was the old bomber model and the courier carrying supplies had to squeeze through a small door in the side of the fuselage. The couriers often remarked that when fully kitted out for the parachute drop, they looked like the Michelin Man. Getting out of the door of the plane with the slipstream was a major effort.

Since the flight took 11 hours, the Royal Air Force took the position that such flights to Poland were impractical and the clandestine organization would need to use radio beacons for targeting future drops. The Polish AK already had a small section of pre-war air force officers, and their position was that such a request showed a complete lack of understanding of the problems confronting underground forces. Such a radio beacon was too bulky to be moved easily and if the RAF plane could home in on it, so could the Germans.[49] The Polish AK and the London-based VI Section officers were able to work out a system where general decisions regarding a planned mission were coded by the playing of certain songs on the Polish radio while the final reception "committee" directed the drop and wind direction by the use of the old-fashioned battery-powered lamps that formed an arrow. However, radio voice mail communication between the plane and reception committee was possible and implemented. Thus, about 100 kilometers short of the reception zone the plane would begin transmission, and then the ground radio would respond, giving last-minute weather (especially wind) conditions. Once the plane engines were audible, the ground lights would be switched on.

The Poles used every diplomatic and other artifice to persuade the British authorities to form a Polish flight.[50] Eventually, with support from Dalton and Gubbins, the Poles were given permission to form a three-plane section as part of the RAF 138 Wing and a small section seconded with a resulting first successful flight on November 7, 1941. (Also see below in Chapter 4.)

Polish Staff Plans to Move Polish
Combat Squadrons to Poland

But landing a Polish parachute brigade was merely a prelude to transferring elements of the Polish Air Force from the United Kingdom to Poland. The Polish Air Force Inspectorate and the Polish General Staff began to work on this project. This was to be fourth leg of the project.

In December 1941, Odzial VI of the commander in chief's staff initiated the discussion for preliminary planning to give the Polish underground army air support. This comprehensive outline of strategic and tactical goals included the first articulated plan for moving Polish combat squadrons to Poland: Plan Uzycia i Organizcji Lotnictwa oraz Wojsk Desantowych na Korzysc Kraju (Plan for the use and organization of Air and Airborne Forces on behalf of the Homeland).[51]

The plan's main points concerned practical as well as doctrinal issues. The plan stated a major principle: that the role of air power, as the only service capable of bringing needed supplies and manpower to Poland, as well as giving needed air cover to the projected uprising, was so vital that any decision regarding the timing of the future insurrection should be conditioned on its active participation. The staff asked a question (rhetorical?) whether an uprising should even be started without securing air support (see Chapter 7).

The memorandum proposed the following targets vital to achieving the strategic goals. The capture of a number of major airfields by AK units, which would need to be supported by air drops from the West. Following such local success, Polish fighter squadrons from the West were to fly to Poland and begin close Air-Support operations from bases controlled by insurgents. To accomplish this ambitious and imaginative plan, the staff stated that 450 four-engined planes would need to be dedicated to this task, so that 150 craft could operate daily for the first five crucial days of operations. The plan also went into details of communication needs and asked for a study of suitable areas where local control could be wrested from the Germans. This plan was written after the German attack on the Soviets and all Polish territory was now exclusively under German control.[52] To use a popular expression, the plan was quite a stretch.

But when the SOE archives in the PRO for Poland were opened in 1995, lo and behold, the files showed that this plan had actually been proposed back in 1940 by the British. Was the Polish plan a clone? Or did both staffs independently come up with a close to analogous idea? The British plan for an insurrection in Poland was clearly to

King George VI and his wife, Queen Elizabeth visited Polish troops in Scotland in March 1941. General Sikorski, the official host, is at left. (Courtesy of the Polish Institute and Sikorski Museum, London.)

cause as much problems for the Germans in occupied Poland as possible. It was also probably written before the Polish government asserted itself in London and imposed its control over all clandestine activity in the homeland. The British plan was called "*Description of a Descent Region and of its work during the Descent.*"[53]

By the end of 1941, the Polish forces had created a training cadre of a parachute unit but lacked even a vestige of air transport capability, which even the Royal Air Force did not posses in required numbers. One point dealt with the criticism of the air

Another view of the Royal visitors, with the King (saluting), General Sikorski (at right), and General Sir Alan Brooke, the British Chief of the Imperial General Staff, behind the Queen. Sir Alan was later promoted to Field Marshal. (Courtesy of the Polish Institute and Sikorski Museum, London.)

treaty signed by the Poles and the British in 1940, which was referred to euphemistically as "unfortunate," and stated that it had to be modified so that the Polish Air Staffs would be created and have the potential for autonomous functioning. The internal memorandum urged that the Polish Air Force be allocated more manpower, so that it could become autonomous by developing its own supporting services. The plan was forwarded to the Polish Air Force Inspectorate for detailed implementation.

The proposal that elicited outrage from the Polish Air Staff was the suggestion for the decentralization of Polish fighter squadrons once they had arrived in Poland. This was contrary to all RAF doctrine and the Polish Air Staff was strongly influenced by the prestige of the RAF, which had won the Battle of Britain due to its centralized control system. The senior Polish Air Force officers who reviewed the memorandum were uninhibited in their opposition and scrawled "Nie, Nie, Nie, Nie" on the margins of the drafts.

But it needs to be commented that the Battle of Britain was won by a centrally commanded force, directed to a narrow and highly predictable area of operations where radar played a crucial role. But in the plans for Poland, the Polish squadrons would have lacked established airfields, and at that time there were still no movable radar facilities; therefore the suggestion for decentralization was not that outrageous given the circumstances of a projected operation from primitive air fields.

Mr. and Mrs. Churchill were also guests of the Polish forces in Scotland. (Courtesy of the Polish Institute and Sikorski Museum, London.)

The plan also emphasized the crucial aspect of the growth of the Polish Air Staff and the goal of 12 fighter and four dive bomber squadrons which could be achieved by dissolving two bomber squadrons. The memorandum addressed the reality that the Poles would depend on their British allies for air transport, but would need to be independent in the provision of actual local support.

The conclusion was still rather optimistic since it gave 1942 as the year in which the Polish Air Force could be capable of independent operations. But it also acknowledged that the lack of British air transport made any such operations unlikely before the end of 1943 at best. The memorandum discussed a number of options and accepted that without the airborne forces it would require six transport planes to give logistical support to each fighter squadron. Mechanics and other ground support personnel were to come from specialized units of the AK supports for each squadron. This would still have required a total of 72 planes which the Poles neither possessed nor had the trained crews and mechanics to support. The memorandum had a number of sketch maps illustrating the distances to Poland from such regions as the United Kingdom (920 miles); the Middle East (1,366 miles); the Caucasus (1,040 miles); northern France (790 miles); very intriguing for 1941, south Norway (710 miles); and northern Turkey (1,070

Prime Minister and Mrs. Churchill visit Polish forces in 1941. (Courtesy of the Polish Institute and Sikorski Museum, London.)

miles). The staffs were of the opinion that the United Kingdom's bases gave the best promise for anchoring the operation.

The political underpinning of the proposed plan is obvious since it stated that while in the then-current political configuration Germany remained Poland's number one enemy, the uprising had to be timed so the Poles by their efforts, and not the Allies by their negotiations, would establish Polish sovereignty and boundaries. This is an open-ended statement which, given the projected distances, suggests that the Polish staff was considering all possible contingencies, such as a British invasion of Norway or the Turks coming in on the side of the Allies, an eventuality strongly worked for by Churchill.

The memorandum described the areas to be captured by the AK as complexes of air bases which would become centers of resistance and which would contain at least one base suitable for handling big transports.

The staff stated that in certain unexpected situations the fighter squadrons might have to fly to Poland and would have to be equipped with long-range drop tanks. The staff opined that Polish mechanics would be capable and required to make these modifications.

This was the first and in fact most comprehensive and even imaginative plan for addressing a number of contingencies that could develop on Polish territory.

Queen Elizabeth and King George VI meeting Polish troops in Scotland in early 1941. (Courtesy of the Polish Institute and Sikorski Museum, London.)

Summary of the First Year in the United Kingdom

The first year on British soil was in every respect a Polish success story. Thanks to the efforts of its air crews, sailors, and the Carpathian Brigade in beleaguered Tobruk, the Poles had paid their dues to the British and Allied side. Polish political fortunes were also blooming, and Sikorski enjoyed wide acclaim in British circles.

In 1940, the British were concerned about constitutional issues of stationing foreign troops on British soil. In early 1941, King George VI and his wife, Queen Elizabeth, visited Polish forces in Scotland, and spent a night in a castle "guarded" by Polish Army units.

Dalton, who was the first minister in charge of subversive activities, was in those early years very sympathetic to the Poles. In his diary he wrote on January 15, 1941, of meeting with Eden: "I speak of the Belgian Government and Pierlot's refusal to broaden it, of the Poles and Sikorski's predominance over all the rest."[54] Dalton visited the Poles in Scotland and exhorted them. "I tell them that on the day of victory, Poland as the first nation to stand up to Hitler, while others have been groveling on their bellies should ride in the van of the victory march."[55] This is so ironic given what did happen at the Victory Parade in 1946. In February 1941, Dalton wrote to Churchill and gave him a brief summary of the various positive outcomes and difficulties encountered in dealing with the Poles. Dalton also urged that Churchill make some significant state-ment on behalf of the Polish effort and contribution to the common cause. The letter concludes with a hand-written note: "We have spent Christmas with General [i.e., Sikorski] and his troops in Scotland; a moving experience."[56]

These were not isolated statements at that time. Perhaps the most persuasive is Churchill's address to the Polish nation to celebrate the Polish National Day of May 3rd in 1941, which was undoubtedly due to the diplomatic prompting of Dalton.[57]

Two senior Polish generals and one admiral were awarded the British Order of the Bath, Knight Commanders, Military Division, for the excellence of their commands. They were Maj. Gen. Stanislaw Ujejski, inspector general of the Polish Air Force; Lt. Gen. Marian Kukiel, commander of the Polish First Corps; and Rear Adm. Jerzy Swirski, commandant of the Polish Navy.

The Poles could be satisfied. They had paid their dues to the alliance and were appreciated. Their strategy was congruous to that of Churchill, namely the Balkan route. Their first, albeit hesitant, contacts with their occupied homeland had been achieved.

However the Poles had failed, and never did succeed, in developing a direct access for their Polish uprising plans with the British Chief of Staffs or their Joint Planning Committee. The British insisted that everything relating to the Polish underground be liaised with and through the British SOE.

One of the junior Polish officers allowed himself a comment that the British refused to see Polish plans as anything more than diversionary activities and insisted on chan-neling everything through Gubbins, whom he rather unfairly characterized as a wannabe (to use a current American slang expression) Lawrence of Arabia without the latter's charisma.

It would seem that some Polish officers believed that the SOE was a barrier between the Poles and the British staff. They urged that Sikorski take up this issue directly with Churchill.

In late 1941, one of the Polish officers (Kalenkiewicz) who was a very active pro-ponent of a Polish uprising and its support by combined Polish and Allied forces was parachuted to Poland. Prior to his flight he was invited for lunch by a British officer of the SOE who urged him to be cautious in his reports to the Poles in occupied Poland. The SOE officers, and to be fair all the British staffs, were always quite punctilious and loyal in warning the Poles when they perceived Polish enthusiasm as running away from British reality or British policy.[58]

4

July 1941 through December 1942

Germany Invades the Soviet Union

The invasion of the Soviet Union by its short-lived, opportunistic ally, did not come as a surprise to those in the know, and in the United Kingdom was very much hoped for. No matter how desirable an event, few really thought that Hitler would be capable of something so strategically stupid.[1] There is enough archival evidence that Stalin did not think this would happen, or at least not in 1941 with the British bruised but very far from defeated. All the warnings which were conveyed to the Soviets by the Western Allies (including intelligence material from Polish sources) were dismissed as attempts by the West to cause a rift in the German-Soviet alliance.[2] In Poland there was nearly universal hope that the events of 1917–1918 would repeat themselves, and that the two oppressors would be so bloodied and exhausted that the Western democracies would dictate peace.

The German attack of June 22, 1941, turned out to be the single most determining event of the war in Europe. It was also the most seminal event for the Polish cause and began to have an immediate negative impact on Polish diplomacy and Polish strategic thinking. The Polish government began to be in an ever-growing mode of reacting to events rather than attempting to shape foreign policy.

It had very far-reaching changes in the occupied homeland. The Poles were not unhappy at the fact that both their oppressors were now at war with each other. The expeditious expulsion of the Soviets and their Communist minions and sympathizers was welcome. These Communist agents and their sympathizers had in less than two years of occupation through their brutal and chaotic regime led to the complete destruction of the Polish civic community in eastern Poland and the eradication of most social and civic leadership. The Poles who had occupied even minor positions, such as village post office managers, railroad or firefighter employees and certainly all police officers, had been murdered on the spot or deported to Soviet gulags. Those that remained had either been cowed and intimidated, or were opportunistically collaborative with the new social future.

The Polish experience under German rule was horrible but with the exception of the eastern regions, there was no anarchy or local ethnic strife. In German-occupied Poland, it was clear as to who was the enemy. In the Soviet zone, the ethnic and even in some isolated cases political sympathies were always a fault line of potential treachery.[3]

With time a new plague descended on the Poles in those unhappy regions, namely the scourge of the Communist partisans supplied by air from the Soviet Union and commanded by Red Army officers, completely uncaring of the consequences to the local population of their activities.[4]

These Communist-led partisan groups were composed of tragic remnants of escaped or hiding Jews, as well as of many escaped Soviet prisoners or Soviet soldiers lost during the Soviet withdrawal in the summer of 1941. These groups were absolutely uncaring of the local population and were expected to live off the land. That this led to further bitter and bloody ethnic strife was of no concern to the Soviet government whose philosophy was that in a revolution, the current systems had to be completely destroyed to be rebuilt in the new Marxist ideology.

But there was another significant political change. Until the Soviets were attacked, the official Communist position was that the Germans were fighting the capitalists and thus, on the right side of the inevitable revolution. Now the Communists were eager to do their share.

As one of Poland's partitioning powers became an overnight ally of the British, the diffident if not ridiculed Communists, who had in many instances espoused the Stalinist posture of condemning the capitalist war, were now able to be patriots as well as advocates of the anti–Nazi war. Churchill in his postwar memoirs summarized it well:

> Up to the moment when the Soviet Government was set upon by Hitler they seemed to care for nobody but themselves. Afterwards this mood naturally became more marked. Hitherto they had watched with stony composure the destruction of the front in France in 1940, and our vain efforts in 1941 to create a front in the Balkans. They had given important economic aid to Nazi Germany and had helped them in more minor ways. Now, having been deceived and taken by surprise, they were themselves under the flaming German sword. Their first impulse and lasting policy was to demand all possible succor from Great Britain and her Empire, the possible partition of which between Stalin and Hitler had for the last eight months beguiled Soviet minds from the progress of German concentrations in the East. They did not hesitate to appeal in urgent and strident terms to harassed and struggling Britain to send them the munitions on which we were counting, above all, even in the summer of 1941 they clamored for British landings in Europe, regardless of risk and cost, to establish a second front. The British communists, who had hitherto done their worst which was not much, in our factories, and had denounced the "capitalist and imperialist war" turned about again overnight and began to scrawl the slogan, "Second Front Now," upon the walls and hoardings.[5]

This citation gives the perspective to the events as they were but regrettably Churchill wrote and articulated these views only well after the war, and after the so-called "iron curtain" had fallen over Europe. In these wartime years, few dared to make such comments.

The possibility of an alliance and of ending the de jure war against the Soviets was not merely an important Polish diplomatic option but it also had major humanitarian and military aspects. It allowed for the release of perhaps a million and half Poles being held captive in horrible circumstances in the Soviet Union; it also gave the promise of an influx of many hundreds of thousands of military personnel to the Polish armed forces. All reports from 1939 suggested that close to 300,000 Polish military had been taken prisoner of war by the Soviets. In late summer 1941, the unthinkable was still not appreciated — that there had been the most grievous genocide committed on Polish officers and noncommissioned officers and other ranks.

But the other fundamental issue had to do with a restoration of diplomatic relations and acceptance of the Soviet-Polish Treaty of 1921. For the British, the issues had different priorities but revolved around the same problem: the release of Polish military for the fight against Germany and the quickest and most expeditious resolution of the dilemma of diplomatic relations between Britain's old ally, de facto and de jure, and now Britain's most important ally — the Soviet Union.

Churchill wrote in his memoirs after the war:

> The British Government were in a dilemma from the beginning. We had gone to war with Germany as the direct result of our guarantee to Poland. We had a strong obligation to support the interest of our first ally. At this stage in the struggle we could not admit the legality of the Russian occupation of Polish territory in 1939. In this summer of 1941, less than two weeks after the appearance of Russia on our side in the struggle against Germany, we could not force our new and sorely threatened ally to abandon, even on paper, regions on her frontiers which she had regarded for generations as vital to her security. There was no way out.[6]

The Polish Government and the Soviets Resume Diplomatic Relations

As a result of the discussion held in London between General Sikorski and the Soviet ambassador to Britain, Mr. Maiski, a political agreement was signed on July 30, 1941, which stipulated that all previous Soviet-German agreements concerning the partition of Poland had lost their validity and were null and void. The British eagerly brokered this agreement which led to the Polish government and the Soviet Union establishing diplomatic relations and to the Soviet commitment that a Polish Army would be formed on Soviet territory, accountable to the Polish government.[7]

There were a number of points that were contentious and were not settled, particularly issues of boundary and of the citizenship of Poles. The Soviets took the position that since there were elections in Poland (under Soviet control) and since the results of the vote were the usual 99.9 percent majority to accede to the Soviet Union, then only Polish nationals, and only by a special dispensation of the Soviet Presidium, would be allowed to join the Polish Army. To add insult to injury, the Soviets offered to give Polish nationals an "amnesty" prior to their release but only after the Soviet authorities were satisfied of their Polish nationality! This determination was to be made by Soviet bureaucrats whose attitude to Poles varied from benign indifference to outright hostility.

Sikorski was motivated by his vision that the Polish forces had to be strengthened and was led by Eden to believe that his negotiating options were not unlimited. Furthermore he was genuinely concerned by the desperate plight of the Poles in the Soviet Union. Sikorski sought British help in guaranteeing the Polish rights vis-à-vis the Soviet Union. The British had always resisted any guarantee of the Polish-Soviet boundary and in fact had supported a boundary based on their concept of an ethnographic resolution to the Polish question, the so-called Curzon line. Their policy position was that territories which had a Polish majority were to be in Poland; but those where the Poles were in a minority, regardless of the wishes of the local denizens, Ukrainans, Jews, Byelorussians, were to be in the Soviet Union.

To assure himself of British support, Sikorski requested a statement from the British foreign secretary on the boundary issue. Sir Anthony Eden in a House of Commons statement disavowed British approval of any changes in boundaries made after September 1, 1939. The positive impact of this policy position statement was immediately undercut by a clarification in a Parliamentary debate in which Eden stated that Britain had never guaranteed any specific Polish boundary.[8] The agreement, hailed by the British as a great step to allied unity and future European collaboration, was questionable from a Polish constitutional viewpoint since the Polish foreign minister, Mr. Zaleski, was kept at arm's length from the negotiations and the Polish president refused to countersign the agreement. In reality, it was a British deal which included General Sikorski. As a result, Mr. Zaleski resigned as did General Sosnkowski, the minister for Home Affairs. This staged the future Polish struggle for a viable, realistic and honorable policy toward the Soviet Union.

The SOE archives, which acknowledge that this organization also had significant connections to Polish intelligence services and their own British agents in Poland, have this interesting comment: "Since the visit of Sikorski to Russia we have received several telegrams from Poland protesting against Sikorski's promise to collaborate with Russia after the war."[9] The close to two-year occupation of eastern Poland by the Soviets had eroded any empathy for that totalitarian regime. This unanimous stance of the Polish underground was to completely influence the Polish policies in London.

Interestingly the first "official" Polish representative to Moscow was Jozef Retinger, the man whom Churchill dispatched to find Sikorski in France in June 1940.[10]

The signing of the agreement allowed Sikorski to dispatch a military mission headed by Gen. Zygmunt Szyszko-Bohusz to Moscow in August 1941. General Sikorski nominated General W. Anders as the Polish commanding officer in the Soviet Union.

The actual history of the formation, disposition, provisioning and the final evacuation of the Polish Army in the Soviet Union is fundamental to understanding the history of the Polish endeavor in World War II. It is a history of Polish hopes and aspirations, of Allied exploitation, of Soviet duplicity leading relentlessly to a Polish political and strategic debacle. To understand the seemingly contradictory issues which followed on each other in a relatively short period of time, the following facts are important.

The policies of the Polish government and its representatives (General Anders) in the Soviet Union were not always identical and in fact at times were nearly contradictory. Sikorski pragmatically worked toward a genuine understanding with the Soviets based on mutual respect and noninterference. The released Poles in the Soviet Union were imbued with intense hatred for the Soviets for their oppression and their stupid brutality. They continued to be, even after release, cognizant of the duplicity of the Soviets and haunted by the thousands of their missing comrades!

The authors of *Destiny Can Wait* wrote:

> With some outstanding exceptions the Polish prisoners of war in the German oflags and stalags were dealt with according to the international conventions. But the Poles captured by the Russians were in the great majority of cases treated as political offenders — guilty of Polish patriotism, of holding Western ideas, of not being Communists, and so on. Most of them were sent to penal servitude in the Arctic tundra or in the sub–Arctic wastes of Siberia, where they laboured under such frightful treatment that the death rate was appalling.[11]

Furthermore the policy of the Soviet Union as symbolized by Stalin underwent a change between 1941 and 1942, after the Soviets successfully survived the winter of 1941-42. In fact, in 1941 the Soviets granted some negotiating points to the Poles in areas which were not fundamental to their perception that the boundary changes effected in 1939 were permanent. After 1942, their posture began changing. All Poles, military or civilian, who had been residents of territories incorporated into the Soviet Union were now consistently ruled to be Soviet citizens with no recourse to the Polish consulates.

Soviet policy toward the Poles was undoubtedly Machiavellian and skillfully pragmatic and influenced by their long-range policies for Eastern Europe and constantly tuned by their perception of their own military strength and their importance to the Western Allies. Their policies were aided by skillful propaganda and its success on the fertile ground of admiration for Soviet military heroism at a time when the Western Allies had only failures.[12] As Stalin realized that his behavior did not elicit any rebukes or negative consequences but rather extravagant adulation, while the Poles who, opposing his policies, were condemned, Soviet policy became aggressive and brutally disdainful.

Thousands of Poles in Soviet Captivity Released

But to go back to the early days of the restored ties, Polish optimism was high. The Polish estimates were that between September 1939 and the invasion of the Soviet Union by the Germans in June 1941 over a million Polish citizens had been deported to the Soviet Union. It was estimated that over 100,000 were prewar Polish reservists or active duty personnel, while 150,000 Polish citizens were thought to have been inducted into the armed forces of the Soviet Union. It was expected that nearly a quarter million men might be available for service in the Polish Army.

The British were only a trifle less optimistic. But their own agenda is also quite obvious. On November 9, 1941, the chief of the Imperial Staff noted that "It is believed that the total number of Poles who might eventually become available in Russia is 120,000–150,00." A memo dated November 19, 1941, notes that India would be a good place to concentrate the Polish troops to rehabilitate them from the "harsh treatment they have received before the Polish-Russian Pact." Finally, the following is a vital citation to the British perception of the importance and the subsidiary role that the British envisaged for the Poles: "I should like to stress the importance which I attach, for military reasons, to the evacuation of as many Poles as possible. We want 10,000 in this country, 2,000 in the Middle east to bring the Polish Forces now in existence. The successful withdrawal of the remainder — I believe that something like 150,000 are involved — would be a great contribution of good fighting men to our cause."[13]

On the other hand, the Soviets initially claimed that there were only a mere 30,000 Polish (male) citizens in the Soviet Union. Yet on October 31, 1939, Molotov had proudly proclaimed to the Supreme Soviet that 300,000 Polish military had been taken prisoner.[14] By all accounts, 46,000 prisoners were released to German control. Forty-one thousand were documented as dying in Soviet control, 25,000 were released to Polish authorities after being granted an "amnesty," and about 100,000 (including the 15,000 Polish officers murdered at places such as Katyn) were missing! Whenever approached by the Poles the Soviets claimed ignorance of the whereabouts of the officers. They asserted that they had no knowledge of the whereabouts of the many thousands of Polish officers who had been captured in eastern Poland in 1939, and whose existence in Soviet camps was documented by correspondence with their families through 1940.

In spite of these difficulties, by November 1941 the Polish forces in the Soviet Union numbered about 40,000 men, many of whom had not been in the prewar Polish military. It was noted that 60 percent of them did not have boots. The food rations were kept to the original Soviet estimate that only 30,000 Poles were available. In addition to the Polish soldiers, numerous Polish women (wives, widows, and single) had gathered around these Polish oases in the land of Communism. There were also hundreds of children. The Poles faced a winter of starvation, cold and sickness since there was inadequate clothing and food and no medicines.

In the Soviet Union, Thousands of Polish Officers Missing

In the background was the continued specter of the missing Polish officers. At this point, General W. Sikorski made his decision to travel to the Soviet Union to inspect the Polish troops and meet with Stalin. On his way, Sikorski visited Tobruk, besieged by combined German and Italian forces, and visited the Polish Carpathian Brigade, which was part of the defensive garrison. This episode well illustrates the bravery and complete abnegation of personal concern and ability to tolerate considerable discomfort on the part of General Sikorski, who always thrived on contacts with the fighting man.

On December 3, 1941, Sikorski and Stalin met to discuss the overall political situation and the specifics of the Polish camps in the Soviet Union. Stalin made overtures to Sikorski to discuss the territorial dispute between Poland and the Soviets. Sikorski categorically refused to negotiate, holding firm to the idea that the Sikorski-Maiski agreement had declared all Soviet-German pacts as null and void and further discussions were moot. On the other hand, Sikorski demanded to know what had happened to his many officers missing in the Soviet Union and received the ingenuous reply that all Poles had been released and that the officers must have all escaped. Sikorski riposted, "to where?" The reply was "to Mongolia." But the Polish prime minister and commander in chief was able to get a satisfactory increase of the top limit of the Polish forces in the Soviet Union, which was now agreed at being 96,000 officers and men formed into six infantry divisions.

Sikorski also obtained Stalin's agreement to the evacuation of all air force personnel and sufficient numbers to bring the Polish land forces in the United Kingdom to strength (25,000 was agreed upon as the number to be evacuated), and to have Stalin relocate the Polish camps in the Asian provinces of the Uzbek Soviet Socialist Republic. The food portions were also increased.

In the Soviet Union during the spring of 1942, the situation of the Poles, military and civilian, continued to deteriorate. Malaria, hepatitis and vitamin deficiency diseases were so prevalent and the physical health of the men so poor that between April and August of 1942 over 4,000 Polish soldiers died of debilitating disease. That was about 10 percent of the total establishment, a loss which would not be even approximated by the most bloody battles, such as the storming of Monte Cassino and at Falaise. At any time over a third of all soldiers were unable to perform their duties because of sickness.

In addition to the hardships the troops were concerned about the situation of their families, often also deported to the Soviet Union and still not reunited. Equipment was short of establishment since the three infantry divisions (Soviet style) only had 8,651 rifles and 16 artillery pieces for the 44,000 men.

By March 1942, the strength of the Polish Army in the Soviet Union reached about 67,500 officers and men. In addition to the military personnel there were thousands of Polish civilians living on the periphery of the Polish camps and existing on the food portions of the military. Thus when the Soviets cut the food portions to 26,000, starvation faced the Poles. At this time, General Sikorski was on his second visit to the United States. General Anders protested the cut in food and requested and was granted a visit with Stalin. This was also at the time of Churchill's first visit to Moscow. In addition to the talks between Stalin and Churchill and between Anders and Stalin, the Polish commander also met with Churchill and senior British generals.[15]

Anders' meeting with Stalin resulted in a number of agreements which had far-reaching consequences. Stalin did agree to raise the number of Polish food rations to 44,000 and gave Anders permission to evacuate the balance to the Middle East. But the other side of the coin was that the strength of the Polish Army was now fixed at 44,000 and all new recruitment was stopped after Churchill was safely on his way. The Soviet position was that Anders was at full strength.

Churchill, who must have been involved in the outcome of the discussions, cabled Sikorski in the United States that the balance of the Poles should be evacuated to Palestine. Churchill thus solicited Sikorski's agreement and consent to the proposition that all Polish troops remain in the Middle East and only small numbers of indispensable replacement be transported to the United Kingdom. Sikorski replied that a minimum of 14,000 were needed to address the needs of the armored division, the parachute brigade and the air and naval forces.

The Bomber Offensive and Irreplaceable Polish Crew Losses

While the Poles were attempting to salvage their countrymen from the Soviet hell, and also working to reconstruct an army and a viable foreign policy, the war in the west did not ameliorate. The British were now involved in two major struggles, against U-boats and the disguised long-range armed raiders which preyed on Allied ships and the inherently flawed bomber offensive against German industrial targets. The U-boat menace threatened the very existence of the British Isles and Churchill wrote, "The only thing that ever really frightened me during the war was the U-boat peril."[16]

The bomber offensive was also being carried on with all-out intensity. But the results were disappointing and even Churchill noted that "air photographs show how little damage was being done. It also appeared that the crews knew this, and were discouraged by the poor results of so much hazard."[17] Sikorski had became aware of this bloodletting early in 1941 and was painfully conscious of the lack of reserves in the Polish Air Force. In February 1941, he initiated efforts to second experienced Polish crews for duty in supplying Poland. This was a difficult time to plan a new strategy given the realities of crew shortages in the Royal Air Force. The four Polish bomber squadrons were vital to the British effort. Sikorski wrote to Sir Charles Portal in the British Air Ministry on July 22, 1941:

> My Dear Sir Charles,
>   The Polish Air Force have of late been taking a considerable part in action and are the object of my particular concern. I would be very grateful if you shared my observations with regard to the Polish Bomber Squadrons. The Bomber Squadrons have as yet not attained their full strength. The average strength of a squadron is not more than 12 crews which is considerably below the establishment. During their long period of operational activity they suffered considerable losses and in spite of a great effort the 18th OTU is incapable of training a number of crews sufficient to replace the current losses and complete establishments. Numerically, the question appears as follows. Up to July 10th, the Polish Bomber Squadrons have performed 133 operation flights engaging 727 aircraft. The losses including killed, missing and wounded were 139 men. During the same period only 120 flying personnel were trained. In view of the difficulties and time required for training of bomber crews, I would suggest that the operational activity of the bomber squadrons should be diminished until their full establishments are completed. I will be very grateful to you for giving the matter your kind consideration.
>   Yours Very Sincerely,
>   Sikorski[18]

Sir Charles Portal must have communicated with the Bomber Command Chief, Air Marshal Sir Richard Peirse, because on July 30, 1941, the latter confirms the inadequate number of aircraft in the OTU but finishes with this point:

> With regard to Sikorski's last point. I am very much averse to taking the Polish Squadrons off operations or attempting to reduce their present effort. Apart from the fact that we all want the operational effort we can get just now, it would have a depressing effect on the very keen Polish crews and in any case their new crews have to graduate through shorter and more simple operations.

There were at that time four operational Polish bomber squadrons, flying the two-engined Wellington bomber. The 18th OTU at Bramcote was a nearly all–Polish operation. But it is touching to see the concern of the Royal Air Force marshal about the possible depressing effect on the Polish crews were they not to be allowed to fly and lose their lives on the clearly flawed operations.

Sikorski acknowledged the letter but expressed his continued concern, stating: "I am aware of their keen fighting spirit which will never allow them to admit that they are worn out, especially at a moment when air operations are so important to the final issue of the war."

The British archives document a continued exchange of letters between Portal and Peirse and the projection that by October 12, 1941, there would be another 40 Polish crews available and Peirse's disagreement about the state of the Polish crews while admitting that "the casualties together with the failure of the Squadrons to raise their strength — they have in fact wasted — is having a depressing effect."

Portal cuts through this semantic nonsense and writes that whatever is the correct name for the situation, "We all remember from the last war the enormous importance attached to the full breakfast table, and I really cannot wonder at general Sikorski becoming uneasy."

On August 31, 1941, the British Air Ministry communicated to Sikorski that pending further output of trained crews the Polish bomber effort would be reduced. The important part of this poorly known historical fact, one which both the Poles and the British have not publicized, is not merely the great effort of the Polish bomber crews, who spoke of themselves as "dead men on leave," but that it was in this context of the all-out bomber offensive that the Poles were trying to create their special duties flight for missions to Poland.

Veteran Polish Crews Seconded to Special Duties

The first Polish overture in the direction of developing a Polish-controlled capacity to air drop supplies to Poland came in 1940, but the situation was complicated, not merely by shortage of aircraft, but lack of suitable aircraft and by fact that the chief of bomber command had little sympathy with clandestine activities of any sort and was short of experienced crews for his bomber offensive.

The liaison flights presented a new challenge, particularly for the navigators but even for the pilots and air gunners. All crews when approaching the drop zone had to reduce height and then operated by visual navigation, identifying landmarks. The route was over the North Sea, Denmark, and crossing the Polish Baltic shore between Gdansk and Kolobrzeg. The distance was approximately 1,600 kilometers each way.

But with great perseverance, in October 1941, the Poles were able to second the first of their veteran crews that completed their tour to the Royal Air Force Special Duties Squadron.[19] This crew, commanded by Col. Roman Rudkowski (who had just given up command of Squadron 301 after completing his tour) with Capt. Stanislaw Krol as navigator, flew the first mission on November 7, 1941. The actual mission was completed but adverse winds forced the plane to land in southern Sweden where the crew, after a short internment, was returned to the United Kingdom. Two more Polish crews joined the RAF 138 and made their first flights to Poland on December 27, 1941, and January 8, 1942.

The Polish archives have a dramatic account of the December 27, 1941, mission. This was to be the third flight to Poland; the first was an all–RAF crew that failed to find the drop zone; the second was an all–Polish crew that could not make it back due to shortage of gasoline. This third flight was ordered by the RAF Air Ministry with concurrence by Gubbins. Why the RAF authorities were so adamant on insisting on this flight is not clear. The Poles stated that their reception committee could not be arranged prior to the 28th and, perhaps even more pragmatic, that their plane was not ready for such a flight. The VI Section requested the mission be postponed until both parameters were met. In turn, Gubbins stated that the air ministry was adamant on the flight because it had waited for a long time for suitable weather conditions; Gubbins added that in view of the general reluctance of the air ministry, its current positive attitude should be embraced. In view of the pressure of the British SOE, the Polish Head of Section VI stated that he would reserve his final decision until the last moment when the weather conditions were again updated and the plane in a satisfactory state. The Polish BBC radio gave the agreed-on tune to alert the Polish reception committee. The Polish couriers to be dropped agreed that they would rather fly that night and be dropped in a general region if the reception committee was not in place rather than postpone the flight.

Hours before the departure Rudkowski, after repeated insistence, was finally allowed access to the "Polish" plane and its Polish crew and found that the automatic pilot ("George") was not functioning and that antifreezing precautions had been carried out poorly. The weather communiqué was also unfavorable. As an experienced combat commander Rudkowski (who had completed 30 operational bombing missions and had commanded a Polish bomber squadron) stated that the mission should be postponed. The British SOE delegate (an army officer) overruled the Polish objections. At this point the Polish Section VI representative — Captain Jazwinski (also an army officer) demanded to be able to contact the Polish HQ. The British found that there was not enough time to accommodate the Polish request. Furthermore they insisted that the head of Section VI had agreed to the mission if the plane was ready and in the RAF's opinion the plane was ready. In turn, the skipper of the Polish crew, Sergeant Pieniazek, received orders from Rudkowski that were the weather conditions to deteriorate from the forecast (about 50/50) then the plane should abort the mission.

The mission took close to 12 hours and the couriers were dropped over a wood and two were caught in trees. Now it was a Polish navigator who made an error in identifying the drop zone and as a result the containers were lost and two of the Poles killed in a firefight while crossing the boundary between Germany and the occupied territory of Poland. On returning, the Polish flight engineer stated that the Halifax had a malfunctioning gyroscope , that the automatic pilot did not work and that the engines were not synchronized.[20] Another issue was the fact that the Polish crew was given leaflets to be dropped over Poland. This was contrary to Polish policy which wished to keep these clandestine flights as secret as possible. The leaflets were dumped in the North Sea.[21]

One can only speculate that the British decision may have had something to do with the fact that the British wished to make their presence and interest in Poland known now that the Soviets were at war.

Rowecki cabled London that he could not understand why the mission had been sent one day ahead of schedule and why a mistake had been made in navigation.[22]

The general Polish feeling is best described by the Polish aide-memoire to the air ministry in February 1942: "The best men have been appointed and the best available aircraft, the Halifax, have been supplied for their job. These men, picked from Polish Bomber squadrons, have been attached to 138 Squadron where they have found themselves among strangers who are not in a position to appreciate their value."

The memoir bluntly stated that the British ground personnel were not responsive and that automatic pilots malfunctioned causing severe and unnecessary stress on flights which often took over 12 hours. It stated that routine maintenance performed by British ground crews was inferior to that of Polish mechanics who served with exclusively Polish squadrons. The Polish crews seconded to the RAF 138 Squadron complained that they were asked to fly long missions to Norway and Austria but that flights to Poland were cancelled. In fact, a complete Polish crew commanded by Captain Voelnagel was lost on a flight to Austria (April 1942) which had been authorized even when all bomber operations over the continent were suspended by bad weather.

The Poles requested that three Halifax aircraft be exclusively at Polish disposal and that Polish mechanics be transferred to service the aircraft. They also expressed the hope that as soon as possible American Liberators would be made available. Finally, they urged that a Polish flight be formed under Polish command.[23]

The British had a different view of the problem and a memo to the chief of air staff, dated February 2, 1942, alleged the following:

> No. 138 Squadron comprises British, Polish, and Czech air crews. This arrangement adversely affects the general operational flexibility since the Squadron Commander is unable to make the maximum effort where it is most needed at any time. The Squadron, Station, Group and I myself consider that a much greater output would be possible if British crews only were employed. This mixture of nationalities has been felt none the less by the Poles themselves, but in view of their strong desire to have a separate unit the Polish Inspectorate have encouraged Polish crews in No. 138 Squadron to pay direct allegiance to and make direct contact with their own Headquarters rather than to consider themselves normal squadron crews. British crews in No. 138 Squadron have successfully completed operations on behalf of the Czechs, French, Norwegians, Dutch, Belgians and in Denmark. Although the Czech crews have been in the Squadron, all successful Czech operations have been completed by British pilots. The same could readily be done for Poland if the Poles were willing. This would entail posting all foreign crews away from No. 138 Squadron to vacancies in normal Bomber Squadrons.

The alternative of raising a Polish flight would be most uneconomical for the following reasons:

(1) Flights to Poland are limited to the long hours of darkness i.e. about 5½ months of the year.

(2) Owing to the rare occasions when flights to are possible in the winter months, there is a large wastage of man-power and aircraft potential if the crews and aircraft cannot be used for special operations in other European Countries.

The RAF officer also attempted to rebut Polish criticism and pointed out that automatic pilots were a luxury, not a necessity, and that the flight to Poland of a Halifax without an automatic pilot took place at the most pressing insistence of the Polish HQ. This alleged fact is not documented by any evidence and contrary to Polish archives. The RAF memorandum also commented with some depreciation that "the Poles, unlike all other nationals whose operations are co-ordinated by SOE, retain under their control, certain detailed information of their operations until the actual day of the flight." This last-minute Polish briefing, in the words of the RAF officer, "causes last minute lack of composure." However, it was left unsaid who was losing composure and Polish sources hint strongly that the British resented the last-minute briefing of Polish staff officers given to Polish crews in Polish. The report confirmed that the Halifax plane had a range limited to west of the Vistula.[24]

There must have been a fair amount of correspondence on this subject between the various British ministries and undoubtedly demarche on the part of Sikorski with Dalton if not even with Portal and Churchill. The Poles did find an ally in the minister of Economic Warfare (Dalton) who on February 12, 1942, wrote to Sir Archibald Sinclair, minister for Air:

I have for some time been on the point of taking up with you again the question of flights to Poland, but, as the whole problem of aircraft facilities for S.O.E. has been under active discussion between your officers and mine, I have not done so. Now, however, General Sikorski tells me that he has once again approached you directly on the Polish aspect of the question, I, therefore, send my views on this subject, as my officers have, as you know, been very intimately concerned in these arrangements and have kept me constantly informed of their progress. I can appreciate quite clearly the Polish standpoint. Their case is that they were promised, early last year, that the winter of 1941/42 would see the establishment of regular flights from here to Poland in order to transport the staff officers, money and material so badly needed by their secret army at home to enable them to continue their struggle, which is paying a handsome dividend at present, against the Germans. Actually, this promise has only been fulfilled to the extent of three flights (all of which have been successful) in place of the minimum twelve which, after negotiations with your Ministry, they had been led, with reason, to expect. Equally I can understand the point of view your officers, as explained to me by my own staff and by your A.C.A.S. (I). I realise the shortage of aircraft and I realise also that, not unreasonably, your staff is unwilling to hand over the entire conduct of such flights to the Poles, or to accept Polish interference in the operational arrangements of 138 Squadron (in which the Halifaxes used by the Polish flights are now incorporated), since they consider this a purely Air Force responsibility.

Dalton's recommendation and conclusion:

> I feel the only solution of this most complex problem is to allow the Poles, within the limits imposed by you and by me, in our respective spheres to run their own show for a trial period, to see whether they can make a success of it. I cannot help feeling that, if we do not do this, both you and I will be badgered by the Poles, who will blame us for the ineffectiveness of our support, and, on the other, by your 138 Squadron, who will complain of the continual trouble that the Poles are creating within squadron.
>
> A solution which suggests itself to me is that, of the Halifaxes now on the strength of 138 Squadron since its recent increase, two or three should be set aside for the primary use of Poles and Czechs, and attached to a Halifax station. Reluctant as I am to place any limitation on the employment of the Halifaxes, I consider the relative value of the secret organization in Poland and Czechoslovakia is sufficiently great, compared with activities in other parts of Europe, to justify this allotment, the more so as I am assured by both governments that, if for any reason flights to Poland or Czechoslovakia are impossible, these aircraft and their allied crews would be made available for such long range flights to other countries as I may require.[25]

The Halifax was clearly not up to the job, and the Poles now pressed for taking delivery of the heavy four-engined Liberator from the United States.

In the new minister of Economic Warfare, Lord Selborne, the Poles continued to find support for their strategic plans. Lord Selborne wrote a long memorandum to Sir Archibald Sinclair, minister for Air, outlining the Polish government's irritation and then stating his position in a very sympathetic manner. This was dated August 17, 1942:

> I should be very grateful if you could lend your personal help to clear up serious difficulties that have arisen between the Air Ministry and our Polish Allies. The cause of this friction is, I understand, twofold:
>
> (1) The Air Ministry refuse to allow officers from Polish headquarters to accompany their operational parties to Tempsford aerodrome.
> (2) The Air Ministry has refused to provide the Poles with three Polish crews to form a reserve for the three Halifax aircraft already manned by Polish personnel.

Lord Selborne continued:

> The matter is really important, and very serious, because these very difficult dropping operations in Poland (which are playing a vital part in the attack on German communications) cannot be successfully accomplished unless there is complete mutual confidence between the R.A.F., S.O.E., and the Poles. I attach the greatest importance to this Polish work. During the last operational season the Polish crews were conspicuously successful and on one occasion only (which was partly our fault) failed to find the reception area. As communications between the reception committee and Polish G.H.Q. may go on until the last moment, we think the presence of a responsible Polish Staff officer at the time of emplaning is an operational necessity. Apart from this, the exclusion of these officers is a humiliation which the Poles can hardly be expected to accept in view of their contribution of fourteen squadrons now fighting with the R.A.F.

General Sikorski feels so strongly on the point that he has instructed his Chief of Staff to tell me that he cannot go on under present conditions.

In regard to the 100% reserve crews requested by the Poles, this also is supported by S.O.E. If we do lose a Polish crew on a trip, it would take a very long time to obtain and train another one in four-engined bomber work. If we were to lose two crews, we should be in a very bad way indeed.[26]

Shortly, the route over Denmark became too dangerous when the Germans reinforced the Danish area with extra artillery and fighter forces. Squadron 138 lost eight planes out of 16 plane missions, two of them with Polish crews. The new route was now extended and encroached on neutral Sweden. It was safer but 200 kilometers longer and the flights took 16 hours. This not only placed a great stress on the crews but also limited such expeditions to the winter months when nights were long.

The last flight to Poland in the winter of 1941–42 took place on the night of April 8, 1942. That was only the night-drop mission to Poland. The flights took over 11 hours and could occur only when the night was at least 12 hours in duration. But the above exchange had some positive effect and a memo dated September 1942 goes a long way to pour oil on troubled waters and to acknowledge that the Poles were not the cause of "lack of composure." It noted, "During this first moon period the Polish Section were restricted to four days work, in which time we have been fortunately able to take advantage of two days of fine weather." The report states that during these two days, when nights began to stretch to over 10 hours, but avoiding full moon and requiring good weather, a difficult triad to achieve, 21 trained operators, two political couriers, significant amounts of money in dollar notes, gold, and German money, five wireless sets capable of transmitting back to the UK, and 10 receiving sets were delivered to Poland. Further, 15 containers carrying a total of two tons of sabotage material were also dropped. The SOE report praised the cooperation between the Polish VI Bureau, and 138 Squadron, concluding, "The success of this moon's operations are due in the main to the organisation of which has been set up inside Poland, and the extreme keeness of the VI Bureau in London. This section [i.e., SOE] has done little except to carry out commissions to the two above mentioned bodies."[27]

Let it be added that in fact RAF Squadron 138 did little to facilitate the Polish missions since all four missions were carried out by Polish crews and codenamed Rheumatism, Smallpox, Chickenpox and Measles.

But the next flight (No. 13) only took place on the night of October 1. It was once again a Polish crew, as were 30 of the other 35 missions flown to Poland before operations were discontinued from the United Kingdom in October 1943. These were resumed from Italy in April 1944,[28] a lacuna of six months. In April 1943, the Polish presence in Squadron 138 was given some autonomy by the formation of a Polish flight as an extra third flight in the RAF unit with more Polish crews and their own Polish mechanics.

Sikorski's Planning Conference in London, April 1942

In April 1942, General Sikorski called a meeting of the senior Polish military advisors in London to discuss the future structure and disposition of the Polish armed forces. The most important senior officers were Lt. Gen. Wladyslaw Anders, who flew in from the Soviet Union; Lt. Gen. Jozef Zajac (general officer commanding the Polish Forces, Middle East); Lt. Gen. Marian Kukiel (general officer commanding the First Polish Army Corps in Scotland); Maj. Gen. Tadeusz Klimecki (chief of staff); Maj. Gen. Stanislaw Ujejski (inspector general of the air force); and Adm. Jerzy Swirski (commandant of the Polish Navy). In addition, a number of other senior generals also attended, including Maj. Gen. Stanislaw Sosabowski (general officer commanding Polish Parachute Brigade) and Maj. Gen. Stanislaw Kopanski (general officer commanding the Polish Carpathian Division, which had been moved from Libya to Palestine and was being fleshed out to division size by increments from the Soviet Union).

The agenda was the future growth and distribution of the Polish armed forces. The actual conference took two days and was punctuated by a meeting of Sikorski with Churchill and his advisors. General Kukiel and the Polish chief of staff both argued that as much as possible, all Polish troops should be concentrated in the United Kingdom. General Ujejski strongly argued the need for more replacements for his bloodied squadrons and concurred that the United Kingdom offered the best location for such training. General Anders urged, and was supported by Zajac, that all Poles should be concentrated in the Middle East, including the air force, since it was the Balkan route that offered the Poles the best and quickest route to their homeland. This option also allowed the easiest return to the Soviet Union if the political developments became propitious. Sikorski dismissed the second option and offered his own option, which was probably a compromise between his political and diplomatic hopes for continued cooperation with the Soviets and the reality of the recent Churchillian message about shortage of transportation. He supported the transfer of about 14,000 men to the United Kingdom, and expressed his hope to have a Polish army in the Soviet Union, as well as a corps in the Middle East. General Kukiel argued (in fact, predicted) that it would be from the United Kingdom that the invasion of Europe would be undertaken and that it behooved the Poles to be at the focus of military operations and not at the sideline. Anders countered the argument by stating that to move Polish troops to the United Kingdom would guarantee that the Soviets would stop all further recruitment to the Polish forces. (The Soviets stopped all such recruitment anyway and Anders was aware of that by the time of the London meeting.) After meeting with Churchill and other British leaders, Sikorski reworked his proposal and now requested only 8,000 men for transfer to the United Kingdom. The proposed allocation of 5,500 to the First Army Corps in Scotland, 1,500 to the air force and 1,000 to the navy was pitifully small and quite inadequate. Admiral Swirski stated that such a small increment would not allow him to commission two new fleet destroyers that the British had offered. General Ujejski argued that a minimum of 4,000 men of good health and education were required just to support the current needs of the Polish Air Force, to say nothing of future growth. He further advised that for the Polish Air Force to develop into an autonomous and independent air arm would require 30,000 men.

Further discussion became concrete, namely the o. de b. of the First Polish Army Corps and of the Polish Parachute Brigade.

Two options were offered: 1) a corps of one armored division (consisting of a brigade of tanks and one of infantry) plus supporting services; 2) an armored division plus a brigade of infantry. Both options included the development of the parachute brigade. The increment of 5,500 met neither option but the second option was even less practical. The final recommendation was that the increment would be added to the existing major units of the First Polish Army Corps: the First Infantry Brigade, the 10th Motorized Cavalry Brigade and the 6th Armored (renamed from Tank Brigade).

After further debate, a decision was also made that the parachute brigade would be fleshed out to become an autonomous fighting unit, though an argument had been made to keep it as a cadre training unit for specialized liaison with Poland. The conference also recommended that the Carpathian Division in the Middle East be enlarged to three brigades with extra supporting services so that it would become the nucleus of a corps.

Most Polish plans were thwarted by both the continued lack of manpower and British unwillingness or inability to provide shipping. The reality was that in the spring of 1942 the British were desperately short of transport ships and of manpower but were able to find the means to ship Australians back to Australia. It is also a fact that the two Polish transports working with the British (M.S. *Batory* and M.S. *Sobieski*) had the potential to transport about 5,000 men between them on each mission. The Poles could have made an argument that Polish ships were aiding the Allied cause and hence should be available for missions which enhanced Polish policies. In fact, a year later the Polish 2 Army Corps was partially moved from Egypt to Italy on Polish ships. The fundamental fact which dictated the ultimate Polish dispositions was the British shortage of personnel in the Middle East and their reluctance to move divisions based in the United Kingdom which were intended for the eventual invasion of the continent. The British chief of the Imperial General Staff, Alanbrooke, wrote in his diaries that: "Any forces in the Middle East this summer will be a Godsend to us."[29]

When the future of the parachute brigade was brought up for discussion, Gen. Gustaw Paszkiewicz, general officer commanding Third Infantry Brigade Group in Scotland, uttered the prophetic words that if the brigade were brought up to full strength, the British would use it for their own purposes. He furthermore suggested that it was better to leave it at a strength of about 400 officers and 300 of other ranks to serve as a cadre unit for courier and clandestine operations in Poland. In turn, Sosabowski replied that a cadre unit did not represent a combat-efficient unit and added that were men to be found, the English would undoubtedly provide the equipment. Again, ironically prophetic, the final decision reached by Sikorski was to develop the unit to full strength by transfer of men from the Middle East out of the Soviet Union.[30]

Sikorski's Strategic Policy Updated

On May 1, 1942, Sikorski thus articulated Polish military goals in his instructions to Lt. Gen. Wladyslaw Anders, the Polish general officer commanding in the Soviet Union:

> There are three factors on the Allied side which will be decisive for the final outcome of the war. They are:

— Soviet Armed Forces.
— Allied Armed Forces (in particular those of Great Britain and the United States, and at their side, a portion of the Polish Armed Forces).
— The subjugated countries of Europe.

Sikorski outlined a rather optimistic view of the Polish case but did articulate his policy quite well:

> Our war effort, carried on unceasingly and with increased intensity, has but one aim: Poland, Poland only, a Poland which might be sounder, safer and stronger than the Poland which so resolutely started to fight against the barbarian aggression of our secular enemy.

And,

> Our present position is infinitely better. However, let us not forget at what cost it has been achieved, by Polish blood, suffering and labour. Which is the shortest way to Poland? From Russia, the Middle east or Great Britain? Nobody can answer this now. However, what matters most is that at least a portion of the Polish Armed Forces, staying outside Poland, should reinforce the Home Army with modern weapons, in order that the latter may become a center of order and authority and enable us, in the most efficient way, to take hold of East Prussia, Gdansk and the German part of Upper Silesia, removing the Germans from those provinces. In this decisive historical moment only accomplished facts will count.
>
> The Polish Armed Forces must be posted on the existing and future war fronts in such a way that they would be able, in any case, to reach Poland within the shortest possible time. We do not refuse to allow participation of Polish Armed Forces in the war.
>
> On the contrary. Heretofore, the Polish soldiers have fought on all the war fronts. However, I have neither the right nor the intention to risk a concentration of the whole or a major part of the Polish Armed Forces on one theater of war, where a possible misfortune could bring about their excessive, if not complete, destruction.[31]

In his very long instructions to Anders, the Polish commander in chief and premier touched on many general, specific, political and organizational matters. The theme was one of entreaty to Anders and his men to hang tough in the very difficult and cruel environment of the Soviet Union. While Sikorski was attempting to formulate Polish goals, Churchill and his military advisors were hard at work in springing the Poles from a very accommodating and obliging Stalin. The British shortage of men bordered on desperate in the Middle East, as is evident from the communication of June 22, 1942, between Major General Regulski to the Polish chief of staff, Major Klimecki, in London: "The War Office has inquired of me several times what has happened about the further evacuation of our troops from the USSR to Palestine; it appears, beyond any doubt, from these enquiries, that the English are greatly interested in the further stage of this evacuation and that they are anxious for it being speeded up."[32]

What deserves emphasis from the instructions to Anders is that Sikorski clearly looked ahead to the struggle in Poland where the Polish Forces would become a "center of order and authority." Sikorski in his discourse states that in the United Kingdom certain combat units will be formed including "one Parachute Brigade as an advance guard to Poland."

Politically the Polish government was still committed to a policy of having a Polish army in the Soviet Union, and even as late as May 1942 Sikorski cabled General Anders instructions and the Polish government's express wishes. The following quotes are particularly relevant: "I strongly desire that you should grasp my intentions regarding the Polish Armed Forces, and because of that I am briefly summing up my views in writing, to enable you to see my opinions on the general military situation and the plans for the organization, disposition and use of the Polish Armed Forces arising from it."

Sikorski continued in this vein: "I have full understanding of the feelings of the soldiers in Russia under your command, General, especially after the last evacuation. I appeal, nevertheless, to their patriotism and their trained will, which has so well stood the test. They should remain in absolute discipline in a post so important for Poland."

General Sikorski enclosed an official message from the Polish Government which stated:

> The Polish Cabinet reaffirms that it would be in accordance with Polish interests and with the policy that found expression in the Agreement concluded with the Soviet Government of 30 July 1941 to leave on Soviet territory part of the Polish Armed Forces which would subsequently fight on the Eastern front side by side with the Soviet Army.[33]

That was the official position of the Polish Government, of the Polish commander in chief, but it was undermined by the British and eroded by the feelings of the Poles in the Soviet Union.

Evacuation of Polish Troops from the Soviet Union

The Poles in the Soviet Union just wanted out and grasped at any excuse to get out, and in this one goal were aided and abetted by the Soviets, who also wanted the Poles out. There is a very old Polish proverb: man proposes but God disposes; and in this instance, the British were the ultimate disposers of Polish fortunes. Sikorski's plans for a Polish army to be left in the Soviet Union were thwarted by the bitterness of the Poles in the Soviet Union and British guile in engineering the evacuation from a very obliging and accommodating Stalin. The British were short of troops and were faced with tremendous problems in the Middle East. The final decision about the evacuation was made by Churchill and Stalin which completely bypassed the Polish constitutional government in London. On July, 1942, Churchill wrote to Stalin about the difficulties in the North Atlantic and Arctic Sea convoys and the need to beat Rommell in North Africa. He then referred to the Polish forces still in the Soviet Union:

> I am sure it would be in our common interest, Premier Stalin, to have the three divisions of Poles you so kindly offered join their compatriots in Palestine, where we can arm them fully. These would play a most important part in future

fighting, as well as keeping the Turks in good heart by the sense of growing numbers to the southward. Hope this project of yours, which we greatly value, will not fall to the ground on account of the Poles wanting to bring with the troops a considerable mass of their women and children, who are largely dependent on the rations of the Polish soldiers. The feeding of these dependents will be a considerable burden to us. We think it well worthwhile bearing that burden for the sake of forming this Polish army, which will be used faithfully for our common advantage. We are very hard up for food ourselves in the Levant area but there is enough in India if we can bring it from there. If we do not get the Poles, we should have to fill their places by drawing on the preparations now going forward on a vast scale for the Anglo-American mass invasion of the continent.[34]

This offer was most likely made by Molotov to Churchill while the Russian commissar was in London in July 1942. It is very obvious that Stalin was happy to do Mr. Churchill this favor. The need of the British for troops in that region can be better understood if it is kept in mind that on February 15, 1942, the Japanese captured Singapore, which Churchill described as "the worst disaster and capitulation in British history." The British victory at El Alamein took place only in October 1942. The final evacuation of all Polish forces from the Soviet Union occurred in August 1942 and highlighted the fact that Churchill and Stalin disposed of Polish troops with some possibly ingenuous complicity on the part of General Anders. It did, however, build a legend of Anders as a man who saved 112,000 men, women and children from Soviet extermination and made Anders more than just a senior general, but a man who led an exodus.

The Soviets in their message to General Anders authorizing the evacuation and offering their assistance in the transport of Poles (arranged in the most expeditious manner) stated that they were granting the Polish commander's request to evacuate from the Soviet Union. The Soviet position has insisted that the Poles wished to leave because of their unwillingness to fight the Germans.

The British were still faced with the possibility of a German breakthrough into the northern Iraq oil-producing region, either from Turkey or from the Soviet Caucasus; and General Wilson, the British commander of the Polish Air Force, was delighted to place the Polish forces in a region where they could add military muscle to his defense as well as to begin the retraining with British equipment. Churchill wrote, "The Levant-Caspian front is almost bare. If General Auchinleck wins the Battle of Egypt we could no doubt build up a force of perhaps eight divisions which with the four Polish divisions when trained, would play a strong part in delaying a German southward advance."[35]

The reality was that the Poles had a lot of men who were just not fit for military service since their hardships had led to chronic health problems and since the Soviets had selectively released only the elderly from their work battalions. That available manpower eroded to barely 45,000 officers and men. General Sikorski's hopes were thwarted.

It would be tiresome to elaborate all the various proposals and counterproposals that were made and studied and dismissed either by the British or the Polish side. The British staffs for logistical reasons wanted the Poles to be modeled exactly on the British establishment, while the Poles wanted to project as large a force as possible. The British argued that the Poles lacked not only the requisite manpower but even the numbers of skilled men for such an ambitious undertaking. Churchill minuted the following memorandum to General Ismay and broke through the impasse:

> I regard the equipment of the Polish Corps as of first importance and urgency in view of the cannibalisation of British divisions and the withdrawal of the Australians and South Africans from the Eighth Army. Let a scheme be prepared showing dates by which the various divisions can be equipped with rifles, 25-pounders, anti-tank and anti-aircraft mortars and machine guns, and Bren gun carriers; also tanks. It is not necessary to adhere to exactly British standards. These can be attained later. Let me have the earliest dates when these fine troops will have the minimum equipment to acquire substantial fighting value. Let me have forecasts for January 31, February 28, March 21.[36]

Generally, however, equipment and food were available, and health improved; and in spite of the at-times rigorous nature of the country in which the Poles were based and to which they were not acclimatized, training proceeded well. In 1943, when General Patton visited the Polish troops, he described them as "the best looking troops, including the British and American, that I have ever seen."[37]

Polish Parachute Brigade and Its Intended Mission

The Poles treasured their parachute brigade and placed hopes on its future role way beyond its potential, let alone actual, capabilities. They also continued to press the British for an ultimate commitment to facilitating air transport to Poland. The parachute brigade was to be the vanguard for Poland. At the same time, the Polish commander in chief hoped to have the First Polish Army Corps in Scotland used as a major Polish contribution in the foreseen operations in northwest Europe. The British were more realistic and did not see how the shortage of personnel could be undone to allow the Poles to play their part.

On August 21, 1942, the British accepted the cadre unit as a full-fledged parachute brigade and placed it under Lt. Gen. Frederick Browning, the commanding general of the British Airborne Corps. In September 1942, the first contingent of 300 Poles arrived from the Soviet Union. Further increments followed, including some of the men from the Third Infantry Brigade Group who had already received parachute training.

The Polish High Command was adamant about the ultimate mission of the unit. In a letter to Gen. Sir Bernard Paget, Sikorski wrote:

> With reference to our correspondence of August 21,1942, concerning the organization of the Polish Army in Great Britain, I would like to inform you that having thoroughly considered on the spot both our needs and our potentials, I believe that a number of alterations should be introduced into the plan of organization of our Army Corps. At the outset I wish to confirm the main and accepted points: 1) Employment of the Polish units in offensive actions in the Continent. 2) Stipulate that the Parachute Brigade only be used for liaison with Poland and for support of an armed movement in Poland.[38]

In their quarterly progress reports on Allied forces in the United Kingdom, the British followed the progress of this unit. Their comments were very laudatory:

> September 30, 1941. The Poles have for some time been working at preliminary instruction and exercises for the parachute unit which they hope to train. They have their own training ground and are competent to make a very show of it.
>
> June 30, 1942. Parachutists were dropped from Whitley Bombers on the rear of a system of beach defenses which were holding up an imaginary sea landing. A wind of 30–40 mph was blowing at the time, and the fact that there were no casualties among the men dropped, testifies to the excellence of their preliminary training.
>
> September 30, 1943. The Polish Parachute Brigade organized in four battalions with supporting arms has been reinforced and is now composed of the best material and is about 2,500 men strong. It is reserved in the hands of the Polish Commander-in-Chief for operations in Poland.[39]

By and large, all Allied quarterly reports on Polish units, air, naval or land, were positive, though the comments on the parachute brigade are particularly glowing. Such was not the case for all of the other allied countries' armed forces. These were not mass media release publicity bites but critical staff assessments. While the British praised the accomplishments of the Polish Parachute Brigade and acknowledged its ultimate goal, "reserved for operations in Poland," there is evidence that as early as May 1942 they considered this to be impossible. There is a draft of a memo to have been sent to General Sikorski, but no evidence in the British or Polish archives that it was delivered:

> We have been reluctantly forced to the conclusion that the physical problem of transporting materials for secret armies in Eastern Europe is insuperable. I hope, however, that in September [1942] it will be possible to resume, on an increasing scale, the dropping of a limited number of personnel [Staff officers for the secret Army and Air Force] and stores for diversionary activities. The Chiefs of Staff are fully alive to your desire that preparation should be made for a Polish airborne force to be despatched to Poland when a general rising takes place. This question has been fully considered and the conclusion has been reached, with regret, that the despatch of such a force is not a practical possibility in the foreseeable future, bearing in mind, amongst other factors, the long distance involved and the severe shortage of suitable aircraft and gliders.[40]

In August 1942, General Sikorski sent the following message to Sir Bernard Paget, the British commander of Home Forces, from his field quarters in Gask, Scotland:

> Having examined on the spot both our needs and our possibilities, I believe that a number of alterations should be introduced into the plan of organization of our Army Corps. At the outset I wish to confirm the main and accepted points: employment of Polish units in offensive action on the continent; stipulation to use the Parachute Brigade only for liaison with Poland and for supporting an armed movement in Poland; preparation to form further Polish armed forces on the continent from reserves of personnel existing over there—as shown in the letter to Lord Selborne, No. 4685/XIV/2/42, dated 25.8.42. Consequently, in fulfillment of these principles it is my intention to bring into battle on the

continent the whole of the Polish Corps as an operational formation under its own command.[41]

Sikorski developed this point further, spelling out in detail the current numbers of military personnel being transported to the United Kingdom and addressed various details. It is obvious that the British had not absolutely agreed to the inclusion of the Polish First Army Corps in operations on the Continent. But that possibility was also not excluded, as later correspondence suggests. They certainly accepted the existence of the First Army Corps as an administrative entity. Sikorski also spelled out that the personnel on the Continent would come from the Poles still living in France and that de Gaulle had agreed to the Poles recruiting in France. There were also many thousands of Poles interned in Switzerland since the whole of the Second Infantry Division had crossed the Swiss boundary in June 1940 from France after the French armistice. Finally, Sikorski again argued that the parachute brigade would guarantee the support of an insurrection in Poland. This point was accepted by the British though the question of how the parachute brigade would be transported to Poland was never clarified.

The Silent and Unseen: Polish Couriers to Poland

It was from the ranks of the 4th Cadre Brigade that many of the first Silent and Unseen (Cichociemni) officers were recruited for parachuting into Poland. But in addition, many other junior and even very senior officers (including generals) were recruited from many different branches of the Polish armed forces for service in occupied Poland. They were hand picked with the primary purpose of enhancing the administrative, technical and staff work of the Polish Secret Army (the Home Army), and in a number of isolated instances were to actually lead combat units. In this latter group were officers seconded to the operation called Wachlarz, which was an attempt to demonstrate to the British ally that the Poles were capable of organizing active sabotage behind the German front lines on behalf of the Soviet Union. This was a high visibility political demonstration.[42]

Later in the war, General Bor-Komorowski specifically requested the following spectrum of specialists to be sent to Poland. He outlined the need for 17 staff officers, 68 communications personnel, 40 air force, 15 intelligence, and experts in sabotage (30) armored forces (15) and even four naval officers.[43] It is worth emphasizing for the sake of objective historical analysis that while the Poles in the West were planning to have a parachute brigade ready for transport to Poland, the AK authorities were trying to fill their specific personnel needs and the parachute brigade did not figure on their wish list.

The kernel of Wachlarz occurred on September 29, 1941, when Sikorski requested two sections of his general staff, the III and VI, to begin preparing extensive plans for active intervention on behalf of the Soviet Union. In October 1941, the Soviet General Zukow, representing the Soviet General Staff, arrived in London for talks with the British, but also met with Polish staff around issues of Polish anti–German sabotage on behalf of the Soviets. To actualize such a major diversionary activity Polish Headquarters in London decided that officers from the UK cognizant of and sympathetic to the policy aims of the Polish government needed to be placed in command. Approximately half of the officers in command of this operation, which extended over thousands of square miles in the hinterlands of pre–1939 Poland and extended east into Belorussian, Lithuanian and Ukrainian territories, came from the ranks of cichociemni. There were no Polish indigenous populations to act as a base of material or moral support for these units.

Wachlarz operated throughout 1942 and early 1943 with somewhat disappointing results. Some of it was the lack of sufficient war materiel, which was partially due to the necessity of moving all supplies from central Poland through German-occupied and -controlled territory. Also, the initial blush of Soviet collaboration in this effort quickly evaporated because it became more important to the Soviets to emphasize the Soviet nature of the marchlands. The general officer commanding the AK telegraphed the Polish London Headquarters on February 11, 1943 (that is, after the German defeat at Stalingrad), that his organization would be able to carry out massive sabotage of German rail and communication links in areas behind the German front lines. This was, in part, a response to Sikorski's requests that the Poles demonstrate their capability for such active sabotage. The offer was coupled with certain desiderata such as increased drops of military equipment and the necessity of increasing the range of air operations to drops east of Wilno. This last was an impossible request due to the limitations of the planes available at the time. However, some of these proposals were based on the possibility that such air drops could originate in the Soviet Union.

On February 26, 1943, the Polish ambassador to Moscow, Mr. Tadeusz Romer, was called to see Stalin and in the all-night conference offered the Soviets a reactivation of the Polish diversionary activity behind German lines. It is not clear whether this was in any way coupled with a request to use Soviet air bases for the supply of necessary military supplies. The ideal situation would have been shuttle runs, with a small number of Polish planes dropping specialized equipment from British bases, landing in the Soviet Union, and on the way back dropping captured German equipment, which was, in fact, in standard use by the AK. Stalin rejected the Polish proposal as placing the local population at too high a risk. In reality, by this time the Soviets had caught their second breath and were developing their own clandestine activities in western Russia and even in the old pre–1939 Polish territories.

By the end of the war, a total of 2,412 officers and senior noncommissioned officers had volunteered for such service in Poland and 346 were actually dropped.[44] Thus by planning or perhaps by pure chance the brigade became the only parachute training unit for the Polish Army. But there were other skills which the cichociemni needed to learn. Sabotage and explosives training was provided at Inverlochy Castle; physical training at Garramowr; counterintelligence at Glasgow; communications at Dundee and Auchtertool and later Polmont. In later years, when the Polish Special Duty Flight moved to Italy, the training was done completely near Brindisi. This became known as Base 11 and its commanding officer was Colonel Jazwinski.

Until 1944, when three Mosty (Wildhorn) operations were carried out from Italy, and some personnel extracted, all couriers returning from Poland had to undergo a very dangerous and time-consuming journey through occupied territories. That so many did make it is a tribute to the personal courage and the administrative efficiency of the Polish system. A number of these couriers deserve special mention. Capt. Jozef Zabielski was the first of the paratroopers to return over the land route. He was vital in teaching new volunteers the rigors of living under German occupation. Jan Karski, on his third and last mission in November 1942, alerted the West to the tragic plight of the Jews in occupied Poland.[45] He wrote a short book on the Clandestine State and after the war settled in the United States where he was highly respected for his wartime efforts on behalf of the Polish Jews under German occupation.[46] George "Jur" Lerski was parachuted to Poland in February 1943. His story is the most exciting regarding the actual preparation, flight and his work in occupied Poland. He then made his way through Germany, Belgium, France, and Spain to Gibraltar, reporting on the vehemently negative position of the underground toward any territorial compromise.[47] Jan Nowak made his way to the United Kingdom through the good graces of a Swedish coal ship to Sweden and then to the United Kingdom. He was again sent to Poland on the eve of the Warsaw Uprising by the third and last Mosty operation.

The life of a soldier in the Polish underground was indeed a test of character. The Polish airman, soldier or sailor, even in the heat of battle and of suffering, was surrounded by his comrades. He was commanded, he was fed, and if wounded he would be treated; if killed, he would be given a soldier's burial; if captured by the Germans, by and large, he was treated correctly according to the Geneva conventions. The soldier of the AK was always on his own and since he or she used a pseudonym even loved ones were kept in ignorance, though they often suspected with pride the activities of their sons and daughters, husbands, wives and parents. The organization was based on small concentric circles so that an arrest and a breach could be quickly localized. But treachery was always feared. The Polish underground counterintelligence services had relatively little problem identifying the so-called volksdeutch who after the German occupation of Poland claimed German ethnicity. Bu the highest titre of suspicion was attached to individuals who were suspected of left-wing leanings. Foot wrote of the collaborators: "All over Europe they were the bane of honest men and women. Even in Norway there were some; even in Poland they were not absolutely unknown, though rare; in France they pullulated; in Holland there were more than enough."[48]

By and large the Poles trusted each other, but few were able to resist torture. Thus, the iron rule was never to say more to anyone than was necessary. Life was a jungle in which the individual walked on his own. To be wounded might mean to be abandoned, to be captured was worse than death. To be killed meant to be buried in a nameless grave. The Germans reacted to the Polish clandestine groups with their typical efficiency. But in spite of all the street arrests, the torture and the intimidation, the underground grew. The men who, in the West, volunteered for such service were indeed heroes.

Staff Work on Moving Polish Air Units to Poland

At the same time as the events were unfolding between Sikorski and Churchill, and between Sikorski and Anders and, more importantly for the Polish future, between Churchill and Stalin, the everyday lives of staffs went on. The main effort was directed at determining the manner in which the Poles could be moved to Poland and the manner in which the Polish Home Army could be assisted and also tied into the strategy of the Western Powers. The formal reply to the 1941 memorandum initiated by the commander in chief staff from the Polish Air Force Inspectorate was written by Lt. Col. Bohuszewicz on June 20, 1942. "Uwagi do Planu Wsparcia Powstania Przez Lotnictwo"[49] (comments to the Plan for Air Support of the Uprising). Where the staff of the commander in chief were basing their future options on the configuration of the most optimistic events, the air force inspectorate was coldly realistic. Its report was short and to the point. Firstly it pointed out that the Polish Air Force in the United Kingdom was in diametrically different circumstances from the Polish land forces since it lacked its own autonomous administrative staffs and its logistical and quartermaster support services. It pointed out that the agreement of 1940 was not merely unfortunate but it was disastrous for the long-term growth of the Polish Air Force Service since it was completely under RAF operational and even to some extent administrative control. It pointed out that many prewar senior Polish air officers were in active combat service and could not be seconded to Polish staffs or to the re-created Polish Staff College without British permission. In the circumstances of the exigencies of the bomber offensive the British were loath to grant such Polish initiatives, unless the officers had completed their entire tour of operations. Given the high casualties, there was a significant loss of such accomplished officers. The Polish memorandum emphasized that the first step had to be a revision of the agreement so that the Polish Air Force could develop its own staffs. It also stated that the Polish government had to ask the United Kingdom for air transport assistance and, failing that, the Poles needed to resign from any plans to support the AK by air from the United Kingdom.

The air force inspectorate also commented that the then current equipment of the Polish squadrons did not lend itself for operations in Poland, since the Spitfire needed a long start and the light bombers required asphalt or concrete landing fields. The staff officer, with great civil courage, concluded that the major problem that precluded realistic progress in most of these areas was the failure of the Polish commander in chief to implement the directive of February 1942 for securing an agreement of the British Air Ministry to support the Polish underground by the Polish Air Force. The memorandum referred to the need to replenish the personnel of the bloodied Polish bomber squadrons, the imperative to form support units, and concluded with a detailed analysis of the communication needs in case Polish squadrons were moved to Poland. The problem of communication was vital, and while the radio communication between "Polish" London and the homeland was solved thanks to some excellent work by Polish specialists, the problem of radio communication between arriving planes and the ground (in Poland), and subsequently how to control combat squadrons within Poland, was never completely solved. Failing the support of the British ally to implement all Polish postulates the Polish Home Army commander should be advised that there was no hope for direct air assistance.

Sikorski Appeals to Roosevelt for American Liberators

In December 1942, General Sikorski flew on this third visit to the United States via Canada. His purpose was a mixture of politics as well as networking with the United

General Wladyslaw Sikorski decorates Polish airmen "somewhere" in the UK. The Polish Air Force was the crown jewel of the Polish Armed Forces in World War II. The youth of the officers is striking. (Courtesy of the Polish Institute and Sikorski Museum, London).

States government and its agencies, particularly the American chiefs of staff, for help in tying in the Polish AK to Allied strategic plans. The British were at best cool to having Polish plans for an uprising on the agenda of their own chiefs of staff and quite opposed for this to be on the agenda of the Combined Chiefs of Staffs in Washington. They made it crystal clear, and the Americans accepted the British position, that Poland (and the rest of continental Europe) were in the area of British strategic interest.

Sikorski's trip began in a serious international climate since the Soviets were allegedly threatening to sign a cease-fire with the Germans, and Churchill was allegedly so worried that he wished to do whatever it took (at other people's expense) to ensure that they continued to fight. Polish boundary revisions were one of the Soviet demands and in this context Sikorski wanted to get Roosevelt's support to preclude such territorial banter. Furthermore, Sikorski wanted to have a Polish representative in Washington on the Combined Chiefs of Staff. His efforts were less than successful but were not a complete failure, and Mitkiewicz became the Polish assignee to the Combined Chiefs of Staff and the genial Colonel Marecki, head of Section III (Planning), was given an audience by American staffs.[50] Sikorski argued the merits of the Balkan strategy and Marecki discoursed on the need to tie in the Polish AK with Allied planning and the importance of such a well-armed uprising on German morale and its logistical systems.

The Americans were polite but restrained and informally made it clear that the Poles "belonged" to the British, while the British representative, Field Marshal Sir John Dill, was cool and remarked that the Poles were ignoring the Eastern Front (i.e., the Russians).

From a purely public relations point of view, the Sikorski trip was at least not a failure. Roosevelt accepted the Polish principle that in wartime territorial changes should not be made (though by the end of 1943 at Tehran he did not keep faith) and was sympathetic to Polish requests for Liberators.

The Poles now embarked on a concerted effort to obtain American-built long-range Liberators. In this venture, they were supported by the British, albeit with the stipulation that any consignment of these planes to the Poles should not come out of the British assignment. Sikorski was looking for a total of 12 such long-range planes, and the British stated that they would endorse the acquisition of six such planes directly from the United States. There is an internal memo dated June 23, 1942, which clarifies the British position: "We should support the Poles in the acquisition of the six Liberators in addition to our own allocation and that we should instruct our representative to emphasize to the American authorities the importance we attach to those Polish operations."[51]

At the same time the internal memorandum made it clear that the Poles could not expect to get six Liberators and still keep their six Halifaxes. On December 9, 1942, the British Chiefs of Staff were alerted that the Poles had approached the Americans directly for a supply of Liberators. This was very much what had been proposed by the British but the United States Chiefs of Staff turned down the request for the following reasons:

> [We] cannot take action on this request without jeopardizing basic agreements in which the U.S. and Great Britain have accepted definite responsibilities for the provision of aircraft within the various theatres of operations. In accordance with these agreements Poland is within a British theatre of operations and responsibility. In view of the unfulfilled demands in its own theatres and areas of responsibility the U.S. has no Liberators available for additional commitments. Your request therefore has been referred to the British COS for consideration in connection with possible allocation from British sources."[52]

During that period of time, there was a number of exchanges between the British Air Ministry in London and its representatives in Washington at Combined Chiefs of Staff (RAFDEL), as well as between the Poles and the British. When the British realized that there would be no planes for the Poles from the United States outside of their own allocation, then they urged that the matter be dropped. But on January 8, 1943, Roosevelt, after his talks with Sikorski, wrote directly to Churchill and endorsed the Polish plan and suggested that the planes be made available from the British allotment. This contact between Sikorski and Roosevelt took place during the Polish leader's third and final visit to the United States in December 1942. His final paragraph is worth quoting:

> I feel, however, that his [Sikorski's] proposal has a great deal of merit, and I told him, therefore, that I would refer the matter to you, with the request that

you give it all possible consideration. It was my thought (which I did not, however, convey to him) that you might perhaps be able to spare him six out of the total of 398 B-24's allocated from U.S. production under the recent Arnold-Evill-McCain-Patterson agreement.[53]

In spite of British official reluctance to become too involved in Polish clandestine affairs outside of intelligence gathering, in spite of the real difficulties associated with the long distances and shortages of suitable planes, flights were carried out, supplies, couriers as well as military personnel flown in. But it was a drop in the bucket of the needs, and the Poles continued to inopportune their allies.

Polish Combat Squadrons

Selborne refers in his aide de memoire of August 1942 to the 14 Polish squadrons. Four of these were fully committed to the bomber offensive. The acme of Polish bomber operations occurred in 1942 and was commented on by the British Air minister, Sir Archibald Sinclair, in his message to General Sikorski:

> Polish crews to the number of 101 took part in the large scale operations in Cologne and Ruhr. The Royal Air Force has learned to admire the valor, tenacity and efficiency of their Polish Allies. In these operations again they here show how admirable is their contribution in support of our common cause to the destruction of the war power of the enemy. We are grateful to you and to Poland for these redoubtable squadrons.[54]

Shortly after that all-out effort, a number of major changes took place. The 301 Squadron was disbanded and existed merely as a symbolic presence since the appellation was unofficially given to the Polish Special Duties Flight. The 304 Squadron was assigned in May 1942 to the Royal Air Coastal Command and began operations aimed at destroying German U-boats. Finally, Squadron 305 was reequipped with the two-engined Mosquito and assigned to the 2nd Tactical Command. This fantastic wood-built plane was an incremental advance in every respect, speed, endurance and bomb-carrying capacity. It served the Royal Air Force as a bomber, pathfinder, reconnaissance and even fighter plane. It fulfilled all roles without rivals. Even now, when seen in the Royal Air Force Museum at Hendon, it looks as sleek as any modern jet.

The other Polish squadrons with the exception of 307 (two-engined night fighter), were all single-engined day fighter units. The Poles had distinguished themselves in the Battle of Britain, but fought either as individual squadrons or in small 12-plane squadrons.

But in 1941 the Poles formed their first fighter wing, which was followed shortly by a second one. The squadrons rotated, but it was a great step forward from the prior year, when Polish pilots were close to distrusted and the RAF insisted that its officers had to command since the Poles were such an unknown quality.

The fortunes of war had also changed. RAF Fighter Command, having kept its supremacy over the skies of Britain, began to undertake aggressive sweeps over the Channel into German-occupied France. Also, the bomber command undertook day bombing runs of targets in France, concentrating on rail and port facilities. Fighter squadrons provided escort for such missions.

On August 14, 1941, the First Polish Fighter Wing, consisting of the 306, 308 and 315 Polish squadrons, while led by Major Janus, was carrying out a sweep around St. Omar-Burges. The Poles made contact with a number of German fighter planes milling around one of their own bases. In the ensuing air battle the Poles shot down 15 German planes and lost four of their own.

This was a prelude to their great success which took place during the Dieppe landings. The Allied probe, directed at testing German coastal defences in Dieppe (August 1942), gave the Polish fighter units their next laurels. Five Polish squadrons, 302 (Poznanksi), 303 (Kosciuszko), 306 (Torunski), 308 (Krakowski), and 317 (Wilenski) fought as one Polish-commanded (Maj. Stefan Janus) operational wing. The commanding officers of 303, Zumbach, and 317, Skalski, together worked out a trap for the Germans. The 317 (Wilenski) Squadron played the part of inexperienced pilots who had difficulty in keeping formation and were generally unaware. This proved a tempting bait for the Germans, who descended on the Poles, to be in turn attacked by Zumbach and the Kosciuszko fliers from above. In the otherwise disastrous landings, the Poles flew 224 missions and shot down 16 German planes which was 18 percent of all enemy craft destroyed, for the loss of two Polish pilots.

Major Janus was awarded the British Distinguished Service Cross and four Distinguished Flying Crosses went to two other pilots, while Zumbach and Skalski received bars to their previous awards. Within weeks, RAF Station Northolt became a Polish command, and the first Polish base commander was the 1939 Poznan Wing leader, Col. Mieczyslaw Mumler.

A spectacular victory.[55]

January 1943 through November 1943

First Polish Staff Officers Parachuted to Poland

In January 1943, the first cadre of Polish Air Force officers was parachuted into Poland, headed by Col. Roman Rudkowski, who had completed a full tour of 30 bomber combat missions and had also flown the first air drop missions to Poland. He became the head of the Air Force Section of the AK staff and was extracted in May 1944 in the second of the three Mosty (wildhorn) operations.

The instructions given to the Polish Air Force officers being parachuted into Poland were to acquaint the Polish underground staff with the capabilities of the Polish Air Force as well as its limitations. The most important message was that Polish plans had not been approved by the British and their full realization could take place only after acceptance and approval by the British. Rudkowski and his colleagues were also given instructions to develop plans to utilize all captured German equipment, including planes, for immediate use by arriving Polish squadrons. Finally, the cadre was to function as a Polish Air Force staff in the AK to augment the small group of prewar aviation officers, the most notable being Colonels Bernard Adamecki and Adam Kurowski.[1] What needs to be emphasized is that the instructions to the air force officers made it clear that the transfer of Polish air units from the West would occur only after complete German military collapse or surrender unless the British were more forthcoming with their logistical support.

Lt. Jur Lerski, who was parachuted into Poland in February 1943, writes that prior to his mission he met with Sikorski, who had just returned from his third (and last) trip to the United States, and received the following instructions for the commander of the Polish Home Army:

> Assure him we are doing our best to increase, as he requires, the supply of weapons and ammunition from the air. For this purpose I have just secured in Washington the delivery of a squadron of American Liberators to replace the smaller and slower British Halifaxes. The First Polish Airborne Brigade is being trained in Scotland to parachute in support of the forthcoming Uprising at home.[2]

There can be no question but that Sikorski made such requests, and that he strongly worked for their accomplishment, but it is also true that his hopes often outran the reality. If that was the only criticism that could be directed at Sikorski, then it would be nearly understandable that given the Polish situation people in leadership positions had to put the best face on difficult issues. But there is a more serious problem here, namely that he wanted the leadership of the AK to be impressed by his negotiating and diplomatic skills and in fact may have seriously prejudiced rational decision making by the clandestine organization.

On March 15, 1943, the commander in chief expedited Capt. Jan Gorski, a very distinguished officer who had been working with the embryonic Polish Parachute Brigade at the British training center — Ringway. He carried a short and succinct order:

> Captain Jan Gorski is to be seconded to the Air Force section of the Home Army Staff and is to advise the Home Army Commander regarding the extent of the changes which have occurred in the Polish Air Force in the United Kingdom; and to acquaint the Home Staff with the new proposed plans for Air Force support of the Uprising. Because of his personal background he is to develop plans locally for the parachuting of the Polish Para Brigade to capture a base or complex of air bases.[3]

It would appear in hindsight that the air force cadre had the task of being realistic while the task assigned to Captain Gorski by his orders was much more optimistic and verging on the improbable.

These very optimistic assessments and the unfortunately less than completely accurate presentation of facts emanating from Sikorski must have made an impact on the leadership of the Polish underground. It needs a reminder that these views were sent to Poland on Sikorski's "watch." This point is important since his successor has been a lightning rod for much criticism around the issues of transparency about Polish capabilities in the West.

It was conceivable that Polish fighter squadrons might have been able to fly a one-way trip to bases in Poland, secured by Polish AK personnel. Such personnel would have had to be able to provide basic mechanical services. That was feasible. The Poles had no transport planes so any hope of parachuting the Polish Parachute Brigade without extensive British support was out of the question.

To address the problem of communication and air force personnel shortages, the Poles embarked on a pragmatic solution to this need. In June 1943, the Polish staff organized a course for 50 army officers and 120 noncommissioned officers of the land army at the Polish Center of Communications in Scotland. After training they were to be parachuted into Poland to work on behalf of the communication needs of the Polish Air Force.[4]

International Background

On January 16, 1943, the Soviets communicated to the Polish ambassador in Moscow, Adam Romer, who had just replaced Kot, that the agreement of December 1, 1941, governing the right to claim Polish citizenship by individuals who had lived in the Polish prewar territories that had been incorporated into the Soviet republics, was rescinded. It was under the proviso of this agreement that the Poles were able to muster their land forces and which allowed a small number of their families to be allowed to leave the Soviet Union in 1942. This agreement was very specific and by Soviet interpretation pertained only to those prewar Polish citizens who could verify their Polish ethnicity and nationality to the satisfaction of the Soviet functionaries. Prewar Polish citizens of non–Polish ethnicity, such as Jews, had from the beginning been precluded from this agreement. Now even Poles, who had the misfortune to have been residents of territories incorporated into the Soviet Union in 1939, were in the eyes of the Soviets forever Soviet citizens. This immediately closed any possibility of the Poles recruiting any further men for their evacuated forces.

The Soviets had by January 1943 survived a second major German offensive and were now slowly grinding down the trapped German armies at Stalingrad. The whole world was in awe of the splendid courage of the Soviet soldier, and of the willpower to endure the greatest privations. The Soviets had also become quite reassured that their callous and intimidating behavior toward the Poles elicited remarks of criticism only in the Polish reaction or at best pleas for maintaining Allied solidarity.

In retrospect, many political scientists are convinced that Stalin was attempting to provoke the Polish government into breaking off diplomatic relations. Stenton, as well as any historian, outlines the cascade of anti–Polish propaganda that was being orchestrated in Moscow which played up the historical perception that Poland was a land of feudal landowners and of anti–Semites. "Soviet ill will and Zionist antipathy made the Polish question repulsively propagandistic even on the pages of the British newspapers."[5] Shortly after the great Soviet victory at Stalingrad, the Soviets proclaimed that the Baltic States and part of Romania (Bessarabia) were integral parts of the Soviet Union. In March 1943, Poland's Eastern territories were added to this list.

The Poles in London were attacked as being "quislings" and their position as contrary to the spirit of the Atlantic Charter. Shortly after, the Union of Patriots surfaced in Moscow. There was no response from the British government or the appropriate agencies of the BBC radio. The official directive was that there should be "no further reference to Polish-Soviet controversy."[6] The head of the Polish section of the BBC opined that unless steps were taken in the UK to counteract this propaganda, then the "Soviet suggestion that they [i.e. the Polish government] were a quasi-fascist rump would be widely accepted."[7] This slowly became the perception if not an actual creed of the left-wing and pro–Soviet groups in the West.

But the break came in a different manner and was implemented by the Soviets.

Katyn

On April 12, 1943, the German radio announced that a mass grave of Polish officers had been discovered near Smolensk in Soviet territories now under German occupation. The very first announcement identified some of the names of the officers who had been missing since 1940 and about whom Sikorski and other Polish diplomats had made repeated interventions. The Polish government asked for an impartial investigation by the International Red Cross. Stalin professed to be so insulted by the Polish request for an impartial International Red Cross investigation that he broke diplomatic relations with the Polish government. The Western Powers were also very disconcerted and in many cases offended at the politically incorrect and gauche step of the Poles in asking for an investigation of the cause of death of thousands of Polish officers.

If the liberal West really believed that this atrocity was one of the many perpetrated by the Germans, then why all the umbrage? Stenton gives a good account of the machinations on the part of the official British circles to square the circle. Credit must be given that the official BBC radio did not accept the Soviet excuses but it convoluted itself to avoid blaming the Soviets. It is however obvious that at the highest circles of the British government and its various agencies the issue was beyond debate.[8] But as Stenton writes, "Stalin's decision to use Katyn against the Poles made it the defining instance of his policy; the British response was the harbinger of theirs."[9]

Churchill clearly did not believe the Stalin version but argued with Sikorski that as the soldiers were dead there was nothing that anybody could do about it. After the war, Churchill wrote:

> Eventually in September, 1943, the region of Katyn was occupied by the Russians. After the recapture of Smolensk a committee composed exclusively of Russians was appointed to inquire about the fate of the Poles of Katyn. Their report, issued in January, 1944, claims that the three camps were not evacuated in time, owing to the rapidity of German advance, and that the Polish prisoners fell into German hands and were later slaughtered by them. This version to be believed involves acceptance of the fact that nearly 15,000 Polish officers and men, of whom there was no record since the spring of 1940, passed into German hands in July, 1941, and were later destroyed by the Germans without one single person escaping and reporting, either to the Russian authorities or to the Polish Consul in Russia or to the underground Movement in Poland. When we remember the confusion caused by the German advance, that the guards of the camps must have fled as the invaders came nearer, and all the contacts afterwards during this period of Russo-Polish co-operation, the belief seems an act of faith.[10]

Sikorski's plans of a foreign policy based on a good neighbor relationship with the Soviet Union were destroyed. The British supported Polish hopes and were behind efforts to resume diplomatic ties, but the conditions now made by the Soviets meant the complete dismantling of the Polish government. This predicted the future course.[11]

The Polish troops in the Middle East were restive. They had always been convinced that their officers had been murdered, because of their own experiences of the brutal life in the Soviet concentration camps. Many had left some members of their family behind. The overwhelming majority hailed from the eastern Polish provinces, the Kresy, Lwow, and the disputed regions of Polish Lithuania, the old Duchy of Lithuania. They were painfully aware that the Soviets were claiming their lands and that their allies, the British, were at best disinterested, at worst in favor of Soviet claims. Anders himself kept an iron grip on his troops and had their overwhelming loyalty. The unasked question which haunted the Polish staff in London and must have perturbed the British was where goes Anders and his troops?

Sikorski's Inspection of Polish Forces in the Middle East and His Accident

Concerned about the situation and particularly worried about the attitude of the independent Anders, Sikorski flew off to the Middle East to visit the Polish Army. Sikorski put the best face on the evacuation of the Polish troops from the Soviet Union and on the behind-the-scenes maneuvering which moved the Polish troops to Persia. What Sikorski did know was that Anders jumped at the chance of getting his survivors out of the Soviet Union, and apparently did not even wait for orders from Sikorski when the opportunity offered itself thanks to Churchill's military needs in the Middle East and Stalin's largesse.

This was Sikorski's fifth major trip of the war. He did not return. The accident occurred on his return from the inspection which by every account was reassuring to Sikorski and had a positive effect on the morale of the Polish troops.

In the late hours of July 4, 1943, the American-built B-24 (Liberator —# AL523) assigned to an RAF unit (Squadron 511) for ferrying VIPs, piloted by a Czech (Edward Prchal) in RAF service, crashed within minutes of taking off from the Gibraltar field. It plunged at full speed into the sea, in full sight of many spectators. All aboard, with the exception of the pilot, were killed. Gen. Wladyslaw Sikorski's body was found and his uniform is still exhibited at the Polish Institute in London, in the museum section named after him — the Sikorski Museum.[12]

Maj. Gen. Tadeusz Klimecki, the Polish chief of staff, and Col. Andrzej Marecki, chief of operations of the Polish Army, were also killed, as was General Sikorski's only daughter, Mrs. Zofia Lesniowska, the general's personal secretary, and Lt. Jozef Ponikiewski, his adjutant. General Sikorski had also been accompanied by an Englishman, one of those men whose integrity gave the world the concept that an Englishman's word is his bond. Maj. Victor Cazalet, member of Parliament, was the British government's liaison with Sikorski. Known for his strong Polish sympathies, he was also becoming a well-known, albeit discrete, critic of Churchill's pro–Soviet policies.

The Polish destroyer ORP *Orkan*, was ordered to Gibraltar to pick up Sikorski's body for transport to the United Kingdom. The funeral took place at the Roman Catholic Cathedral of Westminster in London and was attended by both Churchill and Eden, and of course the complete Polish cabinet and president. The Polish armed forces provided the guard of honor, with Polish units being brought down from Scotland for the funeral. The British provided a battalion of Coldstream Guards for ceremonial duties. In the middle of the war, it was a day of pomp and circumstance. General Sikorski was then buried at the Polish military cemetery in Newark, England.[13]

Churchill, as usual, rose to the occasion and wrote a magnificent eulogy.

> At the invitation of the President and Government of Poland, who are our guests in London, I speak these words to Poles all over the world; to the Armed Forces of Poland in Britain and the Middle East; to Poles in exile in many

countries; to Poles in German prison camps and Poles forced to labour for the enemy; and in particular to the inhabitants of Poland itself, who are enduring with unlimited fortitude the worst that any enemy of unexampled brutality can do to them.

I mourn with you the tragic loss of your Prime Minister and Commander-in-Chief, General Sikorski. I knew him well. He was a true statesman, a true soldier, a true comrade, a true ally, and above all a true Pole.

He is gone; but if he were here at my side I think he would wish me to say this and I say it from my heart. Soldiers must die, but by their death they nourish the nation that gave them birth. Sikorski is dead, but it is in this sense that you must think of your dead Prime Minister and Commander-in-Chief. Remember that he strove for the unity of all Poles, the unity of in a single aim the defeat and punishment of the German despoilers of Poland, he strove too, unceasingly, for that larger unity of all the European peoples, for the closest collaboration in the common struggle with Poland's Allies in the West and in the East. He knew that in such partnership lies the surest hope of Poland's speedy liberation and greatness. His efforts and your sacrifices shall not be in vain. Be worthy of his example. Prepare yourselves to die for Poland — for many of you to whom I speak must die, as many of us must die, and as he died, for his country, and the common cause. In the farewell to your dear leader let us mingle renewed loyalties. We shall not forget him. I shall not forget you. My own thoughts are with you and will be with you always."[14]

This eloquent and moving speech heartened the Poles who had been reeling under the barrage of anti–Polish editorials, and questions in Parliament.[15]

The Royal Air Force, as is policy, convened a court of inquiry on July 7, 1943, by the order of Air Marshal Sir John C. Slessor KCB DSO MC. The president was Group Capt. J. G. Elton DFC. It included Wing Commander A. W. Kay and Squadron Leader D. M. Wellings DFC. A Polish Air Force officer, Major S. Dudzinski, was invited to be present as an observer without the right to ask questions.[16]

Shortly, the Polish ambassador in London received a cover letter from the Air Ministry: "I have the honour to submit to your excellency the draft of Air Ministry Press Communiqué which the Air Ministry is anxious to issue immediately on the approval of the Polish authority."

The actual, proposed, press communiqué that was enclosed read as follows:

> The report of the Court of Inquiry which has been investigating the cause of the Liberator accident on July 4, 1943, in which General Sikorski lost his life, has now been received. The findings of the Court and the observations of the officers whose duty is to review and comment on these findings have been considered, and it is apparent that the accident was due to jamming of elevator controls shortly after take off with the result that the aircraft became uncontrollable.
>
> After most careful examination of all available evidence, including that of the pilot, it has not been possible to determine how the jamming occurred but it has been established that there was no sabotage.
>
> It is also clear that the captain of the aircraft, who is a pilot of great experience and exceptional ability, was in no way to blame.
>
> An officer of the Polish Air Force attended throughout the proceedings.[17]

The statement that the cause was not determined, but that sabotage was ruled out, was inherently illogical. The Polish government refused to endorse the communiqué, stating its objections, but the report was released anyway.

That was the first and final word of the British. The Poles were in a bind and caught up in the dilemma of either acceding to what was most obviously a whitewash, or appearing to challenge their British hosts and impute their integrity. Given the recent experience with the news of the Katyn massacre, this was a sensitive problem. But the Polish government, through the Ministry of the Interior, delegated a Polish engineer to investigate the report. Mr. T. Ullman questioned the conclusion of the court of inquiry.

Independently, the Polish Air Force also appointed a commission to look at the evidence and the report and came to the following conclusion: that the pilot's testimony (that the cause of the accident was due to the blocking of the rudder control) could not be verified, because not all parts of the plane had been recovered. With the available materials and testimony, it was impossible to establish the cause of the accident, a frequent finding in the investigation of plane crashes.

Following this seeming impasse, the Polish minister of Justice empanelled a three-man commission which was chaired by the state procurator, Dr. Tadeusz Cyprian. The commission came up with the following points:

- The available materials and testimony did not answer the questions of the cause of the accident.
- Since it was impossible to establish that sabotage occurred, the cause had to remain as due to unknown factors.
- All parts of the plane would need to be recovered and examined by experts to establish the cause of the blocking of the rudder.
- The three-man commission concluded that it shared the opinion of the Polish Air Force Inspector's Commission regarding the Royal Air Force court conclusion as too categorical on the basis of available material.

But why were the British so cavalier and so hurried and atypically so illogical? Conspiracy theories still abound. Who was to blame and who had the most to benefit? It is quite paradoxical that Poland's enemy number one was never seriously considered as the cause of the tragedy, assuming that it was not an accident, which it may have been. The German propaganda that had stirred problems over Katyn got into high gear and blamed the British. The British discreetly blamed the Polish officers of the Intelligence Department, long at odds with Sikorski over his pro–Soviet policy.

The fact that the accident or sabotage occurred on a British airfield, where there were no Polish air force or intelligence officers, makes the British innuendo ridiculous. The fact that their enquiry came to such an illogical and very strange conclusion certainly adds credence to the possibility that the British knew they had something to hide. But it may not have been the British government but Soviet agents such as Philby who were based locally.[18] It is also possible that the British suspected the Soviets, since they undoubtedly knew that the Soviets had been responsible for Katyn but given the pattern of strange accommodation to Stalin's demands it is not at all implausible that Churchill would have turned the other cheek at the loss of a Polish ally and a British critic (Victor Cazalet) of his policy.

In any murder investigation the issue is potential motive. Who had the most to gain by removing Sikorski from the international political equation? If, in fact, the British thought Sikorski was a strong leader who would command the loyalty of the exiled Poles, then in the troublesome future that was apparent to all, Sikorski would also be most inconvenient. Contrary to what British commentators have stated, a strong Polish leader was not in the British interest at this time. One may ask whether Sikorski was, in fact, a strong Polish leader. Had the accident occurred prior to his visit to the Middle East, then theoretically the enmity of those opposed to his pro–Soviet policies may be entertained, but at this time, Sikorski was in the middle of a major course correction. Which way would it have gone is of course the big question. Mitkiewicz writes that on Sikorski's last trip to the United States the Polish prime minister was so disgusted that he even blurted out the thought that he should reconcile with Stalin and move his government to the Soviet Union. But that was before Katyn.[19] Stalin may have been interested in Sikorski's servility in 1941 but not in 1943.

Was this also a Soviet way of assuring a change and major reshuffle of the Polish government? Certainly that was the consequence of the tragedy. The post of Prime Minister went to Stanislaw Mikolajczyk, while General Sosnkowski became the C.-in-C.

But there was another victim in this accident: Victor Cazalet. He was a very influential member of the British Parliament, and was very pro–Polish and thus nearly by definition, very anti–Soviet. In the winter of 1941–1942, when the British were negotiating a treaty arrangement with the Soviets, the question of boundaries and territorial changes since 1939 was a matter of great import. Understandably the Poles were adamant in their position that the Riga Treaty boundaries and the integrity of Lithuania as an independent country be spelled out. The Soviets clearly wished to have their 1939 and 1940 gains acknowledged by the British. The British hoped to regularize their new allied relationship and performed diplomatic acrobatics. Their policies may be excused only if they had strong reasons to worry about a separate peace agreement between Stalin and Hitler.

It appears that Cazalet led a very successful opposition to the government's policy and finally the issue of boundary changes was omitted.[20] It is, in fact, quite plausible to aver that Cazalet in the British House of Commons presented a greater threat to Soviet policies than Sikorski.

There was another Polish tragedy in this same period. The general officer commanding of the AK, Maj. Gen. Stefan Rowecki, was betrayed in late June 1944 by a Polish traitor, Ludwik Kalkstein, and held till 1944 when he was murdered.[21] He was replaced by Maj. Gen. Tadeusz Komorowski, who used the pseudonym of Bor.[22]

Churchill, shortly after the accident and death of General Sikorski, wrote:

> The time has come to bring the Polish troops from Persia into the Mediterranean theatre. Politically, this is highly desirable, as the men wish to fight, and once engaged will worry less about their own affairs which are tragic. The whole corps should be moved from Persia to Port Said and Alexandria. The intention is to use them immediately.[23]

The numbers of evacuated Poles from the Soviet Union continued to erode due to attrition by illness, and after moving to Palestine due to desertions of Polish Jews.[24]

Polish Initiatives at the Combined Chiefs of Staff

But the war continued and the work of the staffs also proceeded. The continued efforts were to make coherent plans of the organizational standards of the Polish First (Scotland) and 2 Army Corps (Middle East) and to integrate the Polish AK into the strategy of the Western Allied Powers. The Polish representative was Colonel L. Mitkiewicz, ably aided by the elegant and British-educated count, Capt. Stefan Zamoyski.

On June 30, 1943, before General Sikorski's accident, the Poles presented a brief to the Allies, which began as follows: "The Military Forces of Poland, today, consist of the Polish Armed Forces in the United Kingdom, an army in the Middle East and a secret military organization in Poland. The Secret Military Organization is the principle component of the Polish Military Forces at the disposal of the Polish Commander-in-Chief."

The memorandum further outlined the actual composition of the Polish Armed Forces in the UK and the Middle East but specifically underscored the importance of the Polish Home Army to Allied strategy.

> Immediately after the occupation of Poland, a secret army had been formed in the country which was centered in the Warsaw, Cracow, Lodz and Lublin area. This army was in contact with the Polish government in London and under the command of General Sikorski. Liaison was maintained by radio and by a Polish flight of a British squadron. Men, particularly officers, small arms, signal equipment and demolition material had been flown in to them. General Sikorski considered this secret army as the main force of Poland since it was situated in the country and supported by the people. The intention was to coordinate action by this secret army with that of the Polish forces abroad and with Allied plans. It was important that the closest liaison be maintained with this army since its tie with the Polish General Staff had to be strengthened, and the interests of the Allies in its well being and operations demonstrated. Unless the ties were close, there was danger of an ill-timed movement started without direct coordination with Allied Command. The geographical situation of this army was immensely valuable. It separated the main German forces on the eastern front from their bases in the Reich and was in a position to cut their lines of communication should Germany wish to draw forces from the East for action in the West. General Sikorski's conception was to seize control of central Poland with the secret army, then to reinforce it by the transfer of Polish air forces and the Polish Parachute Brigade from the United Kingdom. Later, if possible, Polish Land Forces would be added. All these plans required the use of considerable air transport, and further, it was essential that they should be coordinated with and form part of the Allied offensive in Europe. In addition to severing German concentrations between the Eastern front and the Reich, the secret army would engage considerable German forces and a very important area in Europe would be under Allied control.[25]

This enunciation of Polish strategy found no favor in Washington. It was around that very time that the British chiefs developed their directive regarding Polish forces. It would seem that Sikorski either never saw it or had no opportunity to respond to it. This directive, dated July 14, 1943, affirmed most points that had been previously urged by the Poles. It agreed that the Polish First Armored Division would participate in the Northwest Europe operations, and that the "ultimate aim will be to concentrate the Polish Forces in Poland. The time when this object can be achieved will depend in particular upon the establishment of communications and opening of supply routes." The directive also acknowledged that the "The Polish Parachute Brigade will be reserved for direct action in Poland, but the moment and method of this employment must be governed by the availability of aircraft." This is important in that as late as July 1943 the British still acknowledged the primary mission and role of the Polish Parachute Brigade. This was to change in the summer of 1944, as we will see later.

This should have been a sufficient warning to the Polish command and perhaps it may have still been timely for the Polish staff to keep the parachute brigade at a cadre level for sabotage activity in Poland and for the training of officers for drops into Poland. A good model for this was the independent Parachute Grenadier Company that was recruited and formed for implementing the Bardsea Plan (see Chapter 6).

If that language was not enough, the statement regarding the arming of the Polish underground army should have been the final warning and should have led to a major revision of the 1942 Polish strategic plans formulated at the London conference of the Polish generals. In alluding to the arming of the Polish secret army, the directive used the term "desirability" instead of necessity:

> The desirability of preparing the Secret Army in Poland for action co-ordinated with the military operations of the Allies is recognized and the very effective sabotage carried out by that Army fully appreciated. It is therefore of great importance that this Army should be supplied with largest possible quantity of equipment before large scale operations on the continent begin. The quantity that will be delivered will only be limited by the availability from time to time of suitable aircraft. SOE will continue to act as coordinating authority and agent to whom the Polish General Staff should refer all matters in connection with sabotage and organization of resistance and secret armies. In order to assist in planning the future operations of these Polish Forces SOE will produce as soon as possible an estimate of the amount of equipment which it is hoped to set aside over a period for transport to Poland as opportunity offers.[26]

This was a irremediable defeat of the Polish strategy. First of all, the statement is clear that supplies will be flown in as opportunity allows. War is not carried out by logistics as opportunity allows. Secondly, and perhaps even more telling, was the defeat of the Polish principle that Polish underground activity was not just an SOE activity, but a Polish autonomous operation. The Poles had always gone on record that their underground secret army was "the principal component at the disposal of the Polish Commander-in-Chief," while the British essentially saw it as part of the overall sabotage work being carried out by the SOE.

The seeds of Polish failure and defeat were sown since it was obvious that in spite of polite platitudes, the Allied Combined Chiefs of Staff and the British viewed Polish activities as best confined to sabotage and intelligence gathering. The proverbial bottom line was that the Poles could either accommodate their underground work to the dictates of the SOE, or, as a British air marshal would say a bare year later, "stew in their own juice."

But the Poles still had great hopes that this very disappointing turn of events would be redressed. On September 17, 1943, at the 119th meeting of the Combined Chiefs of Staff, the Polish representative, Colonel L. Mitkiewicz, presented the following memorandum to the Allied Staff:

> The Polish General Staff deem the recognition by the Combined Chiefs of Staff of the plan for the immediate preparation of the Secret Army in Poland as vitally important to the overall war effort. Poland occupies a central position in the region defined in the West by Germany proper, in the North by the Baltic Sea, in the East by the German EAST-WALL and the Black Sea, and in the South by the Mediterranean. In consequence of the development of Allied operations in Southern Europe the whole of the above determined area has acquired preeminent strategic significance.
>
> While these territories are held by the enemy, there remains a strong potential resistance which requires only means and direction for timely activation. The countries of this German hegemony are to a greater or lesser degree preparing for open military revolt. With adequate assistance they could undoubtedly precipitate the fall of the German European defenses. These forces would at the same time provide for Allied military security against chaos and organized movements, either from within the Reich or from elements of the Wehrmacht dispersed throughout Europe.
>
> In this area Poland has retained an advanced military organization operating under the orders of the Polish General Staff in London. Recent military progress both in Eastern Europe and in the Mediterranean area brings forward a demand for determining strategic responsibility with regard to the territory of Poland. In active operations the Polish Armed Forces in the United Kingdom will probably be employed under a joint Anglo-American Command. The purpose and employment of the Secret Army in Poland are of primary strategic interest to the Allies, engaged in military operations against Germany.
>
> In accordance with the requirements of coordinated leadership, the Polish General Staff, therefore, consider it essential that the entire Polish Armed Forces should be placed under a common Allied Command, and the area of Poland should be considered one of joint strategic responsibility.
>
> Equipment is flown from the United Kingdom for the maintenance of subversive activities, sabotage, and intelligence conducted by the Secret Army.
>
> It has now become essential to intensify considerably the scale of these activities. Moreover, it is necessary to transfer to Poland a sufficient quantity of arms for the seizure, at the given signal, of certain points of subsequent reception for the bulk of combat equipment.
>
> The performance of this task requires 500 operational flights to Poland before April 1944. The execution of 300 flights has been agreed upon by the British Joint Staff. In order to cover the remaining 200 flights and for reasons of increasing liaison requirements, the Polish General Staff recommend the establishment of a Special Squadron of 18–20 B-24 bombers.
>
> The success of the general rising of the Secret Army will be conditioned upon the supply of sufficient combat equipment to the points previously captured and secured by the initial insurgent groups. The development of the operation will mainly depend upon the extent of equipment and reinforcement supplied from abroad.

The insurrection should occur when the bulk of the German forces are fully engaged, and when the rears are demoralized by facing an apparently hopeless struggle. The German High Command will then be incapable of directing and coordinating action against an organized rising on its own rear and on hostile soil.

The determination of a propitious opportunity for the rising by the Secret Army will be difficult.

It will, however, become inevitable in order to prevent the rising from being occasioned by an uncontrollable flow of events. Nor should this decision under any circumstance delay the preparation or influence the execution of the plan.

Timely preparation and assistance will assure the direction of the military effort of Poland in conformance with Allied intentions.

The concern of the Polish staff was that events in Poland might have a life of their own and not be controlled by staff decisions. This came to pass in August 1944 when the city of Warsaw took up arms, but the immediate response came on September 23, 1943. Generals Redman and Deane, on behalf of the Combined Secretariat, wrote:

The Combined Chiefs of Staff have given careful consideration to the paper which you submitted to them at their meeting on 2nd July, 1943, and we have been directed to forward you their comments.

The Combined Chiefs of Staff appreciate the great importance that is attached by the Polish Commander-in-Chief to the role envisaged by him for the Polish Secret Army. The operation requirements of active theaters, however, are heavy; the Secret Army could not openly take an active part against the Axis until direct land or sea communications were immediately in prospect; there is also a lack of suitable aircraft for the delivery of large quantities of supplies to Poland.

For these reasons the Combined Chiefs of Staff are unable at the present time to see their way to the allocation of the equipment required for the Polish Secret Army.

The supplies requested from U.S. and British sources for sabotage and intelligence activities in Poland have been approved, and the appropriate authorities have been so informed.

The shortage of heavy bomber aircraft continues and the Combined Chiefs of Staff regret therefore that at present it is not possible to allocate such aircraft to the Polish Government for delivery to Poland of supplies for sabotage and subversive activities. At the same time they are most anxious to render what help may be possible. With this in view one squadron and eventually two squadrons of U.S. heavy bombers, which are not operational for full daylight combat, will be organized to operate from the UK under Commanding General of the Eight Air Force for the support of sabotage and intelligence activities by Polish and other underground groups in Europe. Instructions have been issued to the Commanding General, European Theater of Operations, to this effect. These aircraft will be in addition to those aircraft sorties now being found under British arrangements.

signed H. Redman and JR Deane for the Combined Secretariat.[27]

The Polish Underground Articulates Its Own Plans

On September 10, 1943, the general officer commanding of the Armia Krajowa (Bor-Komorowski) cabled London and articulated his perception of the impending challenge facing his command and his conviction of the importance of air power. It also reflected a less-than-adequate knowledge of the realities of the Polish political situation and inadequate knowledge of the capabilities of the allied Royal Air Force and of the Polish Air Force.

Some of the misperception of the actual potential of the Polish Air Force was based on the success of the Polish pilots and the effective propaganda of the first years of the war. The message can be summarized as follows. Bor-Komorowski accepted that the situation in which the Polish squadrons might have to operate while participating in the national uprising would be dramatically different from their well-established and well-protected bases in the UK. He saw the participation of the air force as carrying a great risk, but commented that the whole nature of the projected uprising was a serious risk if it were to accomplish its goals. The telegram made the exhortation that all effort in the West should be concentrated on the air force since it was the only way that the forces in exile would be able to play any part in the first and thus the most crucial phase of the uprising. The telegram concluded that neither time nor place could be guaranteed since both would be conditioned on the nature of the unfolding military events outside of Polish control. The date of 1943 was mentioned as a possibility and Bor-Komorowski urged that the Polish Air Force be ready immediately. The main postulate of the proposed plan was: the uprising cannot fail.[28]

The telegram then listed 40 priority bombing targets and described the current situation in regard to communications between Poland and the United Kingdom. It was an excellent and thoughtful analysis of the situation from the vantage point of a dedicated and gallant officer whose every day under German occupation was a high-risk gamble.

There was one flaw: the Polish Air Force in the West was not able to undertake such an independent action. Even if Poland was conceived as being in the Western area of political and strategic interest, it is quite problematical that the Western Powers could have moved an air transport fleet across the continent to Poland, unless Germany was completely disarmed.

A New Commander in Chief Takes Over Planning

Sosnkowski, having succeeded Sikorski in July 1943 as the Polish commander in chief, wrote to Sir Alan Brooke on September 20, 1943, after the first British directive for Polish forces was promulgated. Sosnkowski's letter addressed many issues, including the importance of "avoiding dispersion" of Polish forces and the principle that as much as possible the Polish corps in the Middle East be used as one major formation under Polish command, while the First Polish Corps in the United Kingdom be fleshed out in the near future and also used as a single major Polish formation.

But the most serious point raised by Sosnkowski was the specific wording of the original directive regarding the Polish underground army. Sosnkowski wrote:

I would like to give my support to the opinion already expressed by the Polish Command concerning the necessity of leaving at the beginning of para 5. the sentence "it is considered necessary" and not only "desirable" that the Polish Secret Army be prepared for operations coordinated with those of the Allies, as the adequate equipment of this Army in war materials is one of the fundamental conditions for starting the rising. I trust that the execution of this plan will be a practical proposition in the nearest future, considering the present Allied possibilities in the air.

As a result of conferences between representatives of the British and the Polish General Staffs [on March 27, 1943, between Colonel Marecki and General Ismay, and on April 7, 1943, between Colonel Marecki and General Kennedy] the principle was established that all matters concerning diversive activities and intelligence work in Poland, as well as questions of supply for the Secret Army operations will be dealt with in direct talks between the British and the Polish Staffs. It seems to me that this just principle ought to find its expression in a modification of the second part of par. 5. of the "Directive" in the following manner:

The SOE shall continue to act as coordinating authority and as a body, whom the Polish General Staff should consult in all matters connected with the current diversive action and with the supplying of the Secret Army with armaments and equipment necessary to start the rising. Operational matters coordination of the rising with Allied Operations will subjected to mutual consultation between the Polish General Staff and the Imperial General Staff.

I should therefore be grateful for kindly expressing your opinion about these suggestions.

General Sosnkowski[29]

An internal British memo (September 28, 1943) comments that two recommendations arrived in Washington for the Combined Chiefs of Staff (267/3) on September 17, 1943: 1) that an increased measure of support for the Polish underground was desirable, and that 2) it was not proposed to go so far as to equip the secret army for military purposes. The memo continues that since the Poles in London did not seem aware of point 2) then they should be informed as soon as possible, preferably in Washington through the Combined Chiefs of Staff, so that "they can concentrate their energies on sabotage, para-military and intelligence work."[30]

On October 3, 1943, another internal War Office memo addressed the disputed point forthrightly:

With regard to General Sosnkowski's letter to the C.I.G.S. and the draft reply, I think this covers completely all the points which we would wish to raise and I have no comments upon it. With regard to the more general point raised, both in General Sosnkowski's letter and in J.S.M. 1198, I feel that the time is fast approaching when we must tell the Poles firmly and without ambiguity, what the fate of their main plan for the support of the Secret Army is to be.

As I understand it, as a result of CCS 267/3 dated 17th September, the Combined Chiefs have already turned down the plan as it stands. If this is so, then the quicker the Poles are told so, the better. I have written to Hollis [General Sir Leslie Hollis, assistant secretary to the War Cabinet and the Chiefs of Staff Committee] to this effect and attach a copy of my letter to him. I should obviously have sent you a copy and apologise for not doing so before.

I think it is clear that the plan, as at present proposed, is impracticable. We have held long discussions with Polish H.Q. on the subject, pointing out, among others things, that the conception of maintaining by air an Air Force inside Poland seems quite impossible.

In their reply to our comments, the Poles made the following points:

There were two hypotheses upon which the Secret Army might be ordered to rise:

(i) In the event of a general German crack-up.

In this case it seems to me that we should have won the war already, and there would therefore be no military necessity to support a Secret Army.

(ii) In the event of Allied penetration into Central Europe.

It seems highly unlikely since the Poles made it clear that by 'Allied' they meant British and/or American Forces, not Russian.

They still consider the maintenance of an Air Force inside Poland to be essential.

In order to try and tie the situation up finally, I was proposing to put forward to the J.P.S. a paper, asking for strategical direction regarding the action required from resistance groups in Czecho-Slovakia, Poland and Hungary. The root of the trouble seems to be that we have never really decided how we wish to use these people in the final phases, and moreover, these three countries do not fall within any of the operational theaters, and therefore there is no one below the Chiefs of Staffs to whom we can look for detailed directives.

> signed, Barry
>
>> ps. Since dictating the above, I have spoken with Price of the Chiefs of Staff Secretariat. He does not feel that they could take action on my letter attached, and suggests that I raise the whole problem in the paper for the J.P.S. to which I have referred above.[31]

The letter from Sir Alan Brooke stipulated to prior agreements about the advantage of using the Polish corps (i.e., the First Motorized Corps, in 1943 consisting of only one armored division and some training elements), as one major tactical unit once it was brought up to full establishment; it then addressed Sosnkowski's concerns about the word "desirability" versus "necessity."

> At the time that the Chiefs of Staff Committee approved the "Directive Governing the Future Employment of the Polish Land Forces," the question of using the word "necessity" in place of "desirability" with reference to preparing the Polish Secret Army, was fully examined. I should like to make it plain that in using the word 'desirability', as was finally decided by the Committee, they did not in any way minimize the importance that would have been implied by the use of the alternative word. You will, however, have learned from my letter dated October 7th, how it is at present unavoidable that the scale of effort which can be applied to the equipping of the Secret Army must remain limited. I am not therefore in favour of altering the terms of the Directive, which might imply an overriding priority for this work, unco-ordinated with the successive developments of the war.[32]

Brooke then went on to reemphasize the role of SOE in the organization and coordination of the activities of the underground Forces of the German occupied countries, concluding with this: "I and my staff are, of course, always at your disposal for such consultations as are necessary, but I should be very reluctant to interfere with the responsibilities which have been laid upon SOE in this respect, which they are undoubtedly best fitted to discharge."

In retrospect, we now know that the Polish plans for tying in the Polish underground to Allied military planning came to naught. But as can be seen from the above correspondence the situation was sufficiently fluid that the Polish General Staff continued to make the best-case option plans. In this endeavor, the Poles were supported by the minister of Economic Warfare, Lord Selborne, who thus took up the Polish cause writing the following memorandum on October 21, 1943:

> The season during which the night is long enough to infiltrate men and equipment to Poland by air from the U.K. extends from September to April. In August last General Sosnkowski pressed us for acceptance of a programme of 600 successful sorties during the coming season, i.e., 75 a month. We said this was impossible, but that we hoped to achieve 300 successful operations, i.e., 35–40 a month. General Sosnkowski now says that he never accepted this figure. In effect we were only able to achieve 16 operations in September and so far only 7 in October. The reason for this failure is the increase in the German night fighter force in N.W. Germany. During September we lost 6 aircraft in 22 sorties and in October, 1 out of 8. These losses compelled the Air Ministry to route S.O.E. aircraft on a more northerly course. The effect of this is so to increase the mileage that the aircraft can only reach the N.W. corner of Poland, whereas General Sosnkowski wants his equipment delivered all over Poland, and has a large number of men standing by to receive them.

Lord Selborne then suggested that the Polish flight be moved to Italy, that these planes be earmarked for use to Poland and not be part of a pool of planes for use in the Balkans, since both the secretary of state for Air and CIGS had stated that they are "primarily at their disposal." Selborne concluded:

> In the circumstances, I do not propose to ask for an increased allotment of aircraft for S.O.E. work now but I shall feel bound to ask shortly for more aircraft for 1944 and the claims of Poland will occupy a prominent place in my case.
>
> I confess to great sympathy with the Polish standpoint. They braved Hitler in 1939 on Britain's guaranteed support. They have been crucified. They have not winced. Alone among our occupied Allies they have no Quisling. They have incurred considerable casualties in very successfully attacking German communications to Russia at our request. They have an organized army of 250,000 in Poland which only needs equipment. To be told that Britain cannot afford them more than 6 aircraft is a bit hard.
>
> The case for increased assistance to Poland rests less on strategy than on Polish morale, to which I attach great importance. I also think that the very difficult role we may later have to play with them in regard to their Eastern frontier may perhaps be facilitated if we succeed in making some response to the appeal which General Sosnkowski has addressed to me. To the Poles the war is in Poland and this is their last chance of fighting there."[33]

As part of the S.O.E.-endorsed effort, it was agreed that the RAF Bomber Command would use its crews between bombing missions to carry out aid to the Poles. This was a result of the intercession made by Sosnkowski in October 1943 that the number of missions was below what had been promised. The promise made was that until the Poles got well established in Italy there would be a nine sorties a month from the United Kingdom. Selborne further commented that in expectation of the nine sorties 24 Polish couriers had been gathered and reception committees in Poland prepared.

Suddenly the commander in chief of Bomber command placed a veto on all such flights. There was a clear second priority for such supply missions which tended to be cancelled when more important targets and weather were in synchrony. There was also an allegation, completely unfounded, that the Polish clandestine groups had been infiltrated by the Germans. How much of this was due to disinformation from Communist agents, how much due to the fact that a real crisis in the Dutch underground was unthinkingly associated with the Poles, and finally how much was an excuse to buy time on the part of the RAF Bomber Command is still not completely clarified. Selborne again came to the Polish rescue.

> I feel, and I am sure you will agree, that we have a very heavy responsibility towards the Poles concerning the Reception Committees. The Polish heroes composing them have to tramp or bicycle long miles from their homes to the rendezvous and there exist in hiding amid the rigors of a Polish winter. This is bad enough when they are buoyed up by the hope of a successful operation but, as night succeeds night and disappointment continues, the strongest may be forgiven if their will to continue resistance becomes impaired. The plan on which these Committees work cannot be switched or cancelled at a moment's notice in the way that orders to an air force with full base facilities at its disposal can be varied.
>
> In the circumstances, is it really fair for C.-in-C. Bomber Command to force us to tell the Poles that the route from the United Kingdom is so dangerous that it cannot be contemplated by Bomber Command? If we add to such a statement an excuse that we are not satisfied with the integrity of their organisation in Poland until an enquiry into the matter has been concluded, in spite of all the evidence that exists of the splendid work the Resistance Groups in Poland are doing, then I feel we shall indeed have placed ourselves in a most humiliating and unenviable position and one which we shall really have no answer whatever to the resulting Polish outburst.

Selborne's intercession was of little avail since the bomber command had its own priorities and its crews had, in fact, little chance to find very difficult targets in Poland. Bomber command's whole strategy depended on the small group of superbly trained and experienced crews of the pathfinders, whose gallant crews marked out the bombing zones with multicolored incendiary bombs and then gave direction to the incoming waves of bombers. The navigational skills of the average bomber command crew were very primitive. Polish crews were no whit better in astral navigation but knew the Polish countryside and topography and could follow the contours of rivers, lakes, etc., so that the small hamlets or woods sheltering the reception committees were found. For an Allied crew a Polish wood was one of many, but to a Polish crew a wood, copse, or hamlet was a place well-known, loved and familiar. But as we read in the previous chapter, even Polish navigators could get confused at night when the visibility was less than perfect.

The Polish Air Force Inspector Responds to the AK

On October 16, 1943, Gen. Mateusz Izycki, who had succeeded Ujejski as the new inspector of the Polish Air Force, requested the authorization of the Polish commander in chief (which was given) to reply to the telegram of the AK which placed such high expectations on the support of the Polish aviation units in the impending uprising.

Izycki's reply consisted of four bullet statements: that due to the lack of presence of allies on the continent, support of the uprising by air units from the United Kingdom was impossible; that a select group of air force officers would be dispatched to Poland to clarify the situation; that instructions regarding German equipment would be transmitted to Poland; and a request for more details about a number of other airfields located on Polish territory.[34]

If one stipulates that the British were willing to give the Poles the resources requested, and the Polish squadrons flown to operate out of ill-prepared and possibly poorly defended bases, then it seems certain that the Luftwaffe would still have had the superiority to destroy the Poles, unless the whole German military strength was so demoralized as to be incapable of fighting.

Therefore the hypothetical plan was based on the supposition of a complete German military collapse, and the imperative to establish Polish constitutional government control over Polish central territories. It was, in fact, as much anti–Soviet as anti–German. Given the climate of pro–Soviet policies in the West it was, in retrospect, a non-starter, but in mid–1943 hope was all that the Poles had.

By October 20, 1943, the Polish Air Force Inspectorate had fleshed out its original short cable.[35] Once again the inspectorate revisited many of the same points that had been made in the prior cables, such as the lack of autonomy and insufficient staffs above wing level and complete dependence on British support services, such as radar, meteorological reports, reconnaissance, supplies, logistics. Only in the area of medical support was there relative Polish autonomy since the Poles had their own hospitals, doctors, dentists and, in Edinburgh, even their own medical school.[36]

The report also repeated that Polish tactical groups did not have their own staffs and certainly no independent communication system. The Poles were working hard to remedy their dependence on the RAF infrastructure. Seventy-six officers and 751 personnel of other ranks had been assigned to signals and communications. Poles were now also being trained as armorers and for meteorological services. By now, all Polish squadrons had their own photo section. In all of this the Poles received very sympathetic support and understanding from the air ministry.

Izycki also emphasized that the drastic personnel shortages not only prevented the expansion of the Polish Air Force, but that the bloody losses in the bomber offensive had forced the dissolution of one of the four bomber squadrons. The report concluded that the British were also struggling with personnel shortages and were unlikely to be in a situation to give any concrete assistance. The air force inspector advised the homeland that plans were in progress on the creation of a Polish Independent Tactical Air Group, comprising eight fighter squadrons, four ground support squadrons and all serviced by Polish personnel and commanded by a Polish tactical staff. It was presumed that such an independent air group would be in a position to undertake independent air operations. But as always the Polish air inspector cautioned that all such endeavors would require not only British permission for the growth of the Polish Air Force but the authorization of the Polish commander in chief to move the necessary numbers of personnel from the ground forces to the air force, acquisition of suitable equipment and the retraining of crews in new roles. Finally, it would require the air ministry to guarantee the availability of sufficient numbers of transport planes to move the quartermaster services and supplies to Poland.

It is vital to note that the Polish Air Force inspector concluded that air support for the Polish Uprising could occur only with the full concurrence and support of the Allies, which to date had not been received.

Attrition and Downsizing in the Polish Air Force

The losses in the bomber squadrons and the fact that there were no replacements forced major changes. One of the squadrons (304) was so decimated that it was transferred in May 1942 to the coastal command, where its below-level establishment, often only six crews, was not such a problem as in bomber command. This squadron, short of established personnel, was moved to coastal command to minimize losses which could not be replaced. Yet by war's end it lost another 106 aircrew but did sink two German U-boats: U-441 and U-321. It also won the RAF Coastal Command first prize for navigation. The Polish Navy was very seriously interested in this squadron and even made rather persistent endeavors, but unavailing efforts, to have it placed under its domain.

Of the three remaining bomber squadrons, 301 was disbanded completely in April 1943 and 305 moved to the Tactical Air Force and reequipped with Mosquitoes in September 1943. In fact, the British Air Ministry strongly urged that the remaining 300 also be reequipped with Mosquitoes and assigned to Tactical Air Command. But for prestige reasons, the Poles wanted to have a bomber squadron, one equipped with four-engined heavies — the Lancaster.

The Polish Air Force in the United Kingdom had a principle that there should be at least one Polish squadron in every British RAF Command. This was not done for public relations reasons, but to insure that the Poles had "hands-on" experience in all aspects of the air force. In addition, there were small Polish mini-command structures in every RAF Command (except bomber) and in most RAF groups in which Polish squadrons served. So while RAF Bomber Command refused a Polish request for a small mini staff (as was the case for fighter, training, tactical and even coastal) it encouraged a Polish staff presence in RAF Group 1 of bomber command.

The overwhelming majority of the Polish flying personnel were prewar professional cadres, most of whom had graduated from various training institutions such as Deblin prior to 1939, and the increments from other sources were minimal. Two years was not unusual to complete pilot training and there were few young men. While volunteers were sought in the land forces, eligible young men were overprotected by their superiors loath to see the best of their young cadre leave their units.

A good way of assessing this lack of replacements is the story of the 18th Operational Training Unit (OTU) in Bramcote, Nuneaton. In late 1941 it was officially called by the air ministry the 18 (Polish) OTU and was commanded by a Polish officer. The complement of the Polish OTU in January 1942 was 84 officers and 580 of other ranks. The acme of crews in training was reached in June 1941 when 260 aircrew were being integrated. But by March 1943 the number of new arrivals had diminished to the point that the Polish training base was closed and its functions taken over by a Polish flight in an RAF base at Finningley.

Women in the Polish Air Force

The Poles furthermore, rather belatedly, began to recruit and utilize the many thousands of Polish women who had been liberated from Soviet imprisonment and evacuated to the Middle East in 1942. These women had very quickly been organized by General Anders in the womens auxiliary service. But the Ministry of Defence (the renamed Ministry of Military Affairs) implemented old regulations from February 1940 regarding women in the military which, due to a paucity of Polish women in the West, were in fact moot. The formation of the Polish womens *military* auxiliary finally allowed 6,700 women to serve in the military on the same basis and with close to identical training as the British system. By war's end there were 1,426 Polish women in the Polish Air Force working in many supporting but vital roles, such as drivers, mechanics, medical personnel, communications, meteorological services, military police, and even in one case intelligence debriefing.[37] While the Polish women served in all RAF bases in the United Kingdom, for obvious reasons they were preferentially assigned to Polish units and to RAF bases where the Poles were stationed.

Polish Aircrews in RAF Transport Command

It does not appear that at any time the Poles attempted to form a Polish transport squadron, even though a fair number of Poles were assigned to that command. A total of 257 pilots, 55 navigators, 59 radio operators and 25 plane engineers served in the Royal Air Force's Transport Command, flying between Canada and the British Isles, and between Takoradi (East Africa) and Egypt. Not all this number were flying transport at any given time, but it is not unreasonable to assume that at any time there would have been a sufficient number of complete Polish crews to form a Polish transport squadron of 18 two-engined Dakotas. This would not have been even a scintilla of what was needed for the ambitious plan, but given the circumstances raised by the Poles, namely a complete German collapse, then such a squadron under Polish control, of course undoubtedly with British acquiescence, could have been effective.

The Air War Goes On

In 1943, the Polish Air Force Inspectorate requested that a small number of experienced Polish pilots be seconded to the Desert Air Force in North Africa. This was to get first hand experience of what was going to be the future mission of the squadrons assigned to the 2nd Tactical Air Force. It was again a preparation for the possibility of flying out of primitive bases with minimal radar control. The air ministry readily agreed and 16 Polish fighter pilots were seconded to the RAF 145 Squadron. It probably should be emphasized that this was not a Polish squadron as such, since all the mechanics, armorers, etc. were British. The senior Polish officer was Col. Stanislaw Skalski and the unit was officially referred to as the Polish Fighting Team but inevitably referred to as Skalski's Circus. In a period of two months the Poles scored 25 victories and lost only one pilot who was taken prisoner of war. The most outstanding pilot was the young Horbaczewski. This outstanding success of the Poles led the air ministry to request that some of the Poles be seconded to RAF squadrons. Skalski went on to command the RAF 601 and Horbaczewski to lead a flight in the RAF 43.

Polish fighter squadrons also flew escort missions for American day bombers. The proverbial "little friends" provided over 6,000 hours of escort flying time for the Americans, with 302 (Poznanski) flying the most —1,700 hours. These little friends were like angels for a bomber crew with one or two engines conked out, left behind the tight formation and vulnerable to random enemy fighters.

November 1943 through July 1944

Prologue to Tehran

If 1941 could in retrospect be considered a year of Polish diplomatic success and political building, and 1942 a year of consolidation in which many aspects of the Polish cause still went forward, then 1943 was a year of ever-increasing disasters. This was the year where the relationship with the Soviets on which Sikorski built his hopes (discussed in Chapter 4) failed abjectly. The year of the discovery of the Katyn tragedy was followed by Stalin's breaking off diplomatic relations and capped by Sikorski's death as well as the unfavorable decision from the Combined Chiefs of Staff regarding the Polish underground army.

As 1943 came to an end, the Poles were well aware that the British wanted them to accommodate to Soviet territorial claims. The Polish prime minister, Mr. Mikolajczyk, and a small number of members of his coalition government were inclined to acquiesce to Churchill's pressure. But the British government was far from ready to throw in the towel regarding the future of Poland even though boundary concessions by Poland were expected.

As the Soviet armies approached prewar Polish territories in a successful pursuit of the reeling Germans, the British Foreign Office decided that an attempt should be made to work out the problems. In October 1943, the British secretary of state circulated to the War Cabinet a memorandum on a potential problem which he deemed urgent, namely the question of the Polish underground army, its actual combat role, and the problem of ensuring its equipment as well as British concern regarding its collaboration with the advancing Soviet armies.

Eden was also concerned about the fact that the British till then had discouraged the Polish underground from any combat activities and had supported and endorsed only limited sabotage and intelligence gathering. Were this policy to change there would be the issue of equipping the 65,000 men on active service in the clandestine army. There was a potential reserve of close to 200,000 men who were all unarmed. Eden pointed out that the Combined Chiefs of Staff (see Chapter 5) had rejected such Polish appeals and had apparently made the decision without consulting or even advising the British Foreign Office. Eden felt the whole issue needed to be discussed.

It was, and the War Cabinet with Churchill decided that the Poles should accept modifications in their eastern boundary and the British should intercede on behalf of the Polish military whenever requested by the Polish government. The Polish government at the same time assured the British that the Polish underground would not oppose the Soviets but whenever possible work to assist the Soviet forces.[1]

The historian of British foreign policy, Woodward, has a footnote which could have been easily attributed to a Polish nationalist-romantic historian.

> The Poles — who had a long tradition of underground resistance against desperate odds — had organized not only an underground army known as the Home Army, but a regular apparatus of government. This military and civilian organisation was based on the co-operation of the four principal Polish parties, the Peasant Party, the Socialists, the national Democrats, and the Christian Democrats and was in close and continuous contact and co-operation with the exiled Government in London. If, therefore, the Russians wanted to prevent the revival of Poland as an independent State and to impose, after the liberation of the country, a government under their control, they had to do much more than disown the Government in London. Hence their efforts (while taking temporary advantage of the anti–German activities of the Home Army) to weaken its organisation by attempts to build up a rival underground force — the People's Army — and a rival political organisation. At a suitable time this organisation could be brought into the open, and its legitimate rival liquidated by force. It is not clear from the British documents whether, at all events in the years 1942 and 1943 — and even after the Warsaw revolt — Mr. Churchill fully understood the significance of the Russian attitude towards the non-communist Underground Movement."[2]

Stenton cites SOE estimates that close to 10,000 Soviet armed partisans operated on Polish soil and were supplied by air from Soviet bases.[3] Much of this partisan activity was conducted by a combination of Soviet agents, Soviet military stragglers, and tragic groups of Jews who were hiding in the forests and trying to survive in any way possible. These partisan groups, to survive, had to plunder Polish homesteads and furthermore their indiscriminate anti–German activities brought on brutal German repressions. The AK units were caught in a bind and the Poles fought to protect their communities and found themselves involved in internecine fighting, protecting Polish communities both from the Germans and Soviet partisan groups.

This armed hostility was primarily in the territories east of the Bug, but took place even in occupied central Poland and in the original Generalgouvernment territories. When in 1943 the Polish AK commander attempted to eliminate banditry, his initiative was characterized as an anti–Semitic act.[4] The louder voice carried the day, and the image of alleged Polish AK collaboration with the Germans and anti–Semitic in posture and tradition was accepted in the West in many influential circles.

In turn, the Polish AK Command was distrustful of collaborating with Jewish clandestine groups that were directed by the Soviets, supplied by Soviet air drops, and had shown their happiness at the occupation of Poland by the Soviets in 1939.[5]

There was also the problem of arms. Many Jews have alleged that the Poles were grudging in sharing their arms. There is truth to this argument, but often the underlying facts are ignored. The Polish underground army was woefully lacking in equipment since the supplies from the West were a trickle of the need. The authors of *Destiny*

Can Wait describe the difficulties of moving supplies by air to Poland.[6] Until November 1943 when the Polish Special Duties flight (No. 1586) was moved to Italy, flights from the UK could not be undertaken in the summer during the long days since at least part of the flight would take place in daylight close to German fighter bases. Furthermore, the Halifaxes available to the Poles, at that time, were barely capable of carrying out the mission and because of the heavy extra fuel tanks could take only 2,400 pounds of payload. Of the total of 742 flights from the West to the Polish underground with supplies, only 41 were made prior to the fall of 1943 (i.e., prior to the extermination of the kernel of Jewish resistance in the Warsaw Ghetto)[7] (see Table 1 in Chapter 7). Mackenzie arrives at slightly different figures, but the actual parameters are comparable. He notes a total of nine flights to Poland by April 1942 and a further 41 between September 1942 and April 1943. This delivered a total of 23 tons of material![8] The Poles in the West were unable to satisfy the basic material needs of their countrymen, and the British were not interested in anything more than sabotage and intelligence gathering anyway, hence the supplies were skewed in that direction. At least through early 1944 the Poles moved most of their arms to the eastern Kresy regions where the Polish AK divisions, when fully mobilized, had establishments of about 7,000 officers and men and were in fact well equipped with infantry arms. These arms came from numerous sources, recovered pre–1939 equipment that had been hidden, captured German arms, arms received in air drops and even arms clandestinely manufactured or purchased from sympathizing Hungarian and Italian soldiers.

The American Liberators — and only three of them — were received by the Polish flight in the UK, but only in November 1943. This was after the Combined Chiefs of Staff in Washington accepted the postulate that the Polish underground needed arms, but only for sabotage and not actual military operations. A decision partially strategic, certainly logistical and undoubtedly political.

Tehran

In December 1943, the three major leaders of the anti–Nazi coalition, two democrats and one who had been recently allied with Hitler's Germany and bore the burden of facilitating the onset of the war, met at Tehran. The news of the debate, which began to leak out shortly, was a near-mortal blow to the Poles. The major powers had met, and then decided the Poles' future boundaries.[9] What had been whispered, hinted or implied was now a fact. Poland's ally had to all intents and purposes agreed to the Soviet demand for a large part of eastern Poland.

The news of the Tehran Conference was devastating. The majority of the Poles were undoubtedly depressed, embittered and shell-shocked, but remained committed to their policies of holding fast and planning for the best eventuality. There was a feeling that at worst, the Poles would lose their historic and cherished lands in the east, the Kresy, which had played a long and noble role in Polish history. The possible loss of the city of Lwow was particularly feared and grieved. But many attempted to be optimistic and to see potential gains in the territories to be acquired at the expense of Germany. There was an expectation that at the very least the other city so tied to Polish history, Gdansk, which was denied the Poles by the Western Powers in the post–World War I era, would now, with the rest of Silesia and East Prussia, return to Poland. Some saw in this a satisfactory compensation. This was specially the case for those Poles, like Mr. Mikolajczyk, who were from the west of Poland and had little if any emotional attachment to the historic, legendary marshlands of the Polish-Lithuanian Common-wealth.

On the other hand, the overwhelming majority of the rank and file of the 2 Polish Corps was from the disputed regions. These soldiers were in the process of being moved to Italy. Churchill had been right. Their future situation was indeed tragic.

But the Polish underground state made it clear that there could be no compromise on future Polish boundaries. Their view was that after the years of privation, suffering and bloodletting there could be no loss of Polish territories. There is a confirmatory archival document for this posture with an implied threat. Eden circulated a memo to the War Cabinet which came from an underground courier. Dated February 1943, before the Tehran Conference, it stated simply that the Polish underground recognized the Polish government in exile and that there would be no rival government originating in Poland unless Sikorski decided to cede territory to the Soviets.[10] There was no change in that posture in early 1944. It is probably as a result of that concern that Churchill sent his own emissary — Jozef Retinger (code-named Salamander) — to Poland in April 1944.[11]

The Polish government still had great hopes that with American and British help the rest of Poland would be free and sovereign.

But the climate for the Poles in the United Kingdom had changed. There were still many gestures of real friendship, but the majority of the British press had now completely veered to the side of the Soviets, and not just in the ongoing territorial dispute.

In the House of Commons debate on the Tehran Conference, the British acquiescence to the so-called Curzon Line elicited little disagreement, albeit there was much real sympathy for the Polish side.[12] There were attacks on the Poles in the press and hostile and sarcastic questions in the Parliament, usually from a fringe group of left-wing parliamentarians, such as Mrs. Driberg, Shinwell and Gallagher. Many of these often virulent attacks were based on the fact that many hundreds of Jewish soldiers in the Polish Army in Scotland deserted, alleging anti–Semitism.[13] The British were concerned because this was even further depleting the already scarce manpower resources of the Polish division that was committed to the impending Operation Overlord. The British, after reviewing the very widely bruited charges, wrote in their report.

> The critics have not proved or even sought to prove that anti-semitism is general. Yet by these judicious citations of isolated cases they have succeeded in creating an impression which they are content to leave distant from the truth. Impetuous and sensational exaggerations of the few available facts by the Press almost as a whole, has created a regrettable myth, and has subjected a credulous public to an invidious propaganda.[14]

Frank Savery of the British Foreign Office commented: "It has been the unexpected one-sidedness of the British Press which has most discouraged the average [i.e., Polish] soldier. It is true to say that apart from official Polish announcements, which have naturally been considered biased, the amount of consideration from the purely Polish side of the question has been negligible."[15]

This was now the current anti–Polish climate in the United Kingdom. The issue was not Polish boundaries, though many Britishers still believed that to be the case; the fundamental issue was the structure and composition of the Polish government.

There were some relatively rare exceptions to this general anti–Polish tirade in the British press. The *Scotsman* and the *Catholic Tablet* did the best in this growing flood of anti–Polish invective. The *Daily Telegraph* continued to be objective, and the *Illustrated London News* still remembered that the Poles were allies and fighting on the same side. On February 15, 1944, it carried a piece, captioned —"Poland's Militant Underground Movement Fights On." Four scenes were portrayed of life in Warsaw under occupation. One showed the typical German random roundup on a street, another a court handing a verdict on a German police officer guilty of crimes, and two showed the carrying out of such court decisions. It should be emphasized that the underground courts were convened only after the perpetrator of the crimes had been alerted that he would be tried and if guilty executed.[16]

Churchill's Initiative for the Poles

In early January 1944, the Soviet armies crossed the prewar (Riga Treaty) Polish-Soviet border and this elicited immediate, surprisingly late, concern in British government circles as to the possible consequences of Soviets coming into armed conflict with the Polish underground. It needs to be remembered that these were sparsely populated lands, in which both Polish underground and Soviet partisans were active, but most importantly, territories to which both countries laid claim. Close to 100,000 Polish AK soldiers fought, collaborating with the Soviets. The front-line Soviet officers often acknowledged their appreciation of Polish aid, particularly in Lwow where Soviet tanks were caught without their own infantry support. But once the fighting was over, unless the Poles disappeared they were surrounded and the soldiers given the opportunity to join the Polish People's Communist Army or to go to prison. The officers were not given such an option. In one Polish unit that was surrounded only 440 soldiers out of 7,000 agreed to join the Communist forces, and not a single officer.

It is interesting that in the first instances of such collaboration Soviet commanders referred to the Poles as "home army" units. But then the language changed to conform to the political expediency, and the Poles were disparaged as "so-called home army" or even "white Poles," "illegal formations" and even "bandits."

The Polish government made a number of demarches to the British. Churchill became very proactive in dealing with this looming crisis. The British government made what it considered genuine and even quite strenuous efforts to arrange an accommodation between the Poles and the Soviets. The War Cabinet, with significant attention from Churchill, Eden and Cadogan, worked with the Poles and also through the British ambassador in Moscow, Sir A. Clark Kerr, to arrange a modus vivendi.[17] Stalin was uncompromising and his condition was, in fact, an ultimatum. He demanded that the Polish government had to openly and fully accept the so-called Curzon Line (which the Polish underground refused to endorse) and to reconstruct its London-based government. The Polish prime minister and the coalition government attempted to be as accommodating as possible, facing strong opposition to any form of appeasement from all its constituent groups but did agree that disputed territories east of the Curzon Line be placed under temporary Soviet administration pending a final postwar agreement.

The Polish prime minister's own Peasant Party in Poland, would not allow him any such options. So in a way that was not appreciated, or was conveniently ignored, the "recalcitrant" Polish government was merely legitimately representing its coalition. Furthermore, the majority of the Poles in the West were military. Therefore, there seemed to be a misperception, one which was fueled by the inimical British press, that the Polish government was reactionary and authoritarian and dominated by the military. In fact the majority of the soldiers in the 2 Polish Corps were not career soldiers. The majority of the career elite were dead at places like Katyn or in German prisoner of war camps following the September Campaign. It was also a tragedy of fate that the overwhelming majority of the officers and men of the Polish military in the West, the famous 2 Corps, were from the eastern regions of Poland, the historical Kresy, that were coveted by the Soviets.

The post–Tehran impasse was characterized by Churchill in his speech to the Parliament in February 1944: "I have an intense sympathy with the Poles, that heroic race whose national spirit centuries of misfortune cannot quench, but I have also sympathy with the Russian standpoint. Twice in our lifetime Russia has been assaulted by Germany."[18] It is far from clear as to what German aggression against the Soviets had to do with Poland's boundaries. But at this point logic and historical fact were irrelevant. Churchill did, however, make a strenuous effort to patch relations between the Poles and the Soviets and after prolonged back and forth showed Mikolajczyk a draft of a letter to Stalin which he proposed to send.

This letter guaranteed that were Mikolajczyk and his government allowed to return to a Soviet-controlled Warsaw, then the Poles would agree forthwith to the acceptance of the Curzon Line and would quietly dismiss the Polish commander in chief and the two other members of the Polish Cabinet, including the minister of Defence, General Kukiel, who antagonized the Soviets by calling for an international investigation of the Katyn murders.

In this infamous proposal, Churchill did not include the Polish president. The Polish government balked at this draft and found it unacceptable. But Mikolajczyk agreed tacitly to stipulate to those conditions. Not surprisingly, Stalin refused and demanded the ouster of the Polish president.[19] This was the reason for the complete break between Sosnkowski and Mikolajczyk. The Polish commander in chief now viewed the Polish prime minister as a weak reed and potential traitor while Churchill now knew that Mikolajczyk could be had, which he was in the near future.[20]

It is worth noting that the British ambassador to Poland, Sir Owen O'Malley, minuted the British foreign secretary, Anthony Eden, arguing that Churchill's Polish policy was flawed and contrary not only to British integrity but also to the letter and spirit of the Atlantic Charter. He summarized his view:

The real choice before us seems to me, to put it brutally, to lie between on the one hand selling the corpse of Poland to Russia and finding an alibi to be used in evidence when we are indicted for abetting a murder; and on the other hand putting the points of principle to Stalin in the clearest possible way and warning him that our position might have to be explained publicly with equal clearness. In the second alternative we might indeed fail to deflect him from violent and illegal courses, but it would be on record that we had done our utmost to do so.[21]

There is a handwritten comment from Eden here: "But would it help Poland?"

This was the diplomatic divide; the British sincerely worked toward an independent Poland and were willing to be pragmatic at Poland's territorial expense. To achieve a sovereign Poland they were quite cavalier in disposing of awkward members of the Polish government. The majority of Poles, had they known of O'Malley's memorandum, would have agreed with him. In 1939, Poland chose an ideological route and this was the route which they wished to continue. A pragmatic Poland in 1939 would have followed the Czech, Hungarian or French model, and in retrospect come out as well or badly.

Eden and the British Foreign Office also argued against the dismissal of General Sosnkowski, emphasizing that the underground and the 2 Polish Corps were loyal to the commander in chief. The Foreign Office also commented that Sosnkowski was in the process of ordering a major AK operation which were to cut off German communications between Lwow and Przemysl.[22]

You may know that Operation Jula was conceived and carried out not only because of its tactical military value, but also for the purpose of far greater importance, namely, to prove to the world that the Polish Underground Army is in fact, under the command of general Sosnkowski, and through him of the émigré Polish Government in London. It was hoped that definitely and finally to refute the Soviet claim that the Government had no power in Poland.

Every possible precaution was taken in the methods of disseminating the news of the operation. Propaganda was in the hands of the head of the Polish Section of PWE, Mr. Moray McLaren. PWE control the broadcasts of the European Service of the BBC and on this service , I understand, that the news was given its correct value. Mr. McLaren liaised with the Foreign Office on the political directive to the press to accompany the news. The news was given to the news agencies and was, I understand, given its proper importance by them. The newspapers, however, universally refused to afford it the prominence it so richly deserved. There appears to exist at this time, a very definite ban on anything in the British Press, which could in any way be considered as favorable to the present Polish Government, moreover, at this particular time, it is quite definite that the newspapers and the British public are more interested in the news of anti-semitic incidents which are supposed to have happened in the recent past.[23]

Polish Staff Plans Continue

That was the political and international background. The Poles did not falter, either in their commitment to the war against the Germans, nor to their continued plans for aiding the underground. On December 13, 1943, Maj. Gen. Stanislaw Kopanski, the Polish armed forces chief of staff and hero of Tobruk, issued instructions to the air force staff for further work on the feasibility of aiding the Polish underground. His order, *Plan Wsparcia Powstania. Prace przygotowawcze*[24] (Preparatory plans for the support of the Uprising: Preparatory Plan), in itself a comprehensive document, to the Air Force Staff led in turn to a most comprehensive and elaborate plan for air support of the uprising. In his memorandum, General Kopanski wrote that the Armia Krajowa Command still counted on the arrival of the Polish Air Force to support the uprising. This conviction was allegedly based on prior telegrams and the monthly communiqués from which it was clear that lack of personnel reserves precluded the ability of the Polish Air Force to achieve autonomous combat operations. This memorandum inevitably led to the conclusion that the AK Command had to be advised that the Polish Air Force could not be expected to move its operations to the territory of Poland or give any meaningful support for the Home Army unless the British acquiesced and supported such a move, and even then only if there were significant additions to the Polish Air Force manpower.

Col. Michael Bokalski, of the Polish Air Staff, personally wrote in the margin of the Kopanski memorandum, "Nie bujac Kraju" ("Don't fool the Homeland").[25] But orders are orders and the Section of Operations of the Polish Air Force wrote a brief rejoinder on February 1944, under the very unmilitary title of "Nie Ludzic Kraju!" ("Don't Mislead the Homeland"),[26] and recapitulated all the staff work back to 1942, and again emphasized the crucial importance of the basic condition for such a move and engagement in combat operations: the creation of a Polish Independent Tactical Group; the transfer of more human resources from the land forces to the air force; and the approval for such action by the British Air Ministry, which was equal to a political acquiescence in such Polish plans. This was a very terse and, one might even add, an editorial comment, an impatient memorandum. It concluded that it was vital to send air officers to Poland to clarify the situation.

The officer in charge of this air group that was parachuted into Poland was Col. Jan Bialy. His written instructions came from Major General Izycki and in his postwar debriefing on his mission, Bialy reviewed all of the above issues. He met with Colonels Adamecki (commanding officer of the air section of the AK) and Kurowski (chief of air operations of the AK) and appraised them in detail of the limitations of the Polish Air Force. He was not able to meet with Komorowski.[27] Given the nature of the clandestine situation this was not in itself surprising, but the obvious question remains, how aware were the senior Polish officers of the AK of the real situation? The message conveyed was that the AK could not count on the help of the Polish or Allied Air Forces in event of an uprising, but did it get through to Komorowski?

Colonel Bialy stayed in occupied Poland and his assignment during the Warsaw Uprising was to organize the captured airfield at Okecie near Warsaw. He and his three colleagues, Jerzy Iszkowski, Franciszek Lewkowicz and Edmund Marynowski, had all gone through the highly secret "Enemy Aircraft Circus." This RAF unit, Flight 1426, had numerous German planes and the Poles spent time and even had about five hours of flying time on such planes as the HE-111, ME-110 and JU-88s. The training on German planes postulated that after German airfields had been captured by the Poles, the German planes might be utilized.[28] The reality was that the Germans contained the

Warsaw Uprising quickly (even though it took them 70 days to crush the insurgents) and threw off Polish attempts to capture Okecie and used it to bomb the insurgents (for more on the Warsaw Uprising, see Chapter 7).

One has to come to the conclusion that the realities of the Allied Air Force and in particular of the Polish squadrons were never completely understood by the Home Army commanders. The fact is that even if the British in a moment of complete allied harmony designated all their two-engined Dakotas for transport duties to Poland, the final proverbial bottom line would have been negligible. The British never had sufficient transport planes or crews and as late as 1944 depended on Americans for flying in their Airborne forces in the Arnhem operation. Furthermore, the slow Dakotas would have been annihilated on their flights to Poland.

Polish Wings in 2nd Tactical Air Force

In this series of frustrations, the Poles came closest to the creation of an independent Polish tactical group. This was a result of some serendipity when in the summer of 1943 the Royal Air Force, which was preparing for the invasion of the Continent, formed the Second Tactical Air Force.[29] This RAF command was based on the valuable experiences gleaned from the Desert Air Force, hence called the 2nd, and consisted of two fighter groups (83rd and 84th) and one bomber group.

This was quickly exploited by the Poles, who sought and received British Air Ministry approval for a major Polish tactical group conditioned on a transfer of a further 10,000 men for ground support duties.[30]

The British were, in fact, sympathetic to Polish aspirations for enhanced autonomy. Their staffs in the summer of 1943 minuted:

> In view of the fact that it is the Air Ministry policy to extend to the Polish Air Force every facility, in order that a well balanced nucleus of an Air Force capable of standing on its feet when it returned to Poland, should be available, it is considered that the representations as set out in the attached letter from the P.L.S.O. [Polish Liaison Senior Officer], should be borne in mind when forming this Polish Airfield.[31]

This had to do with the comprehensive staffing of support services for a Polish tactical wing. But following the signing of the new air force pact, which came into effect on April 6, 1944, there is further evidence that the air ministry wished to be helpful and accommodate Polish needs and every evidence that the British Air Ministry lived up to the spirit and the letter of this agreement. But the Poles never had enough personnel to be able to develop such a major air component.

No such transfer occurred since the Polish High Command did not have any human reserves. This would have meant cannibalizing some Polish ground forces and it is unclear whether the British would have allowed that given the fact of their own desperate manpower shortages.[32]

The Poles had not been able to get a tactical group but were able to field the Polish 18th Fighter Group, which consisted of three wings — the First Wing: 302, 308 and

317 Polish Squadrons; the Second Wing: 306 and 317 Polish and 129 RAF; and the Third Wing: 222 RAF, 349 Belgian and 485 New Zealand.

The creation of a women's air service was an attempt to address the personnel deficiencies. The women were assigned to duties in communication, as drivers, military police, meteorologists, mechanics, and medical personnel.

The War Against the Germans Continues Unabated

The Polish air and naval forces continued their fight alongside their allies, primarily the British. In 1943, the Polish 2 Army Corps, under the command of Lt. Gen. Wladyslaw Anders, entered operations in Italy. From now on the Poles, in addition to their own famous syrena (the Warsaw Mermaid), also wore the cross of the crusaders, the insignia of the British Eighth Army.

The Polish Navy continued to take part in all the naval operations. These operations were continuous and were thus described by the first lord of the Admiralty, Alexander, when he opened the exhibition dedicated to the Polish Navy and Merchant Marine in the spring of 1944 in London:

> Whenever in the course of naval operations in this present world conflict at sea a great concourse of ships is gathered together, there is almost always to be seen one or more Polish ensigns, worn either by Polish warships or by vessels of the Polish Mercantile Marine, or by both.
>
> In view of its small size, the number of operations in which the Polish Navy has taken a part is almost incredible, especially bearing in mind that some of them are continuous. Amongst these operations are Narvik, Dunkirk, Lofoten Islands, Tobruk, Dieppe, attacks on shipping in the Channel, Sicily, Italy, Oran and patrols notably in the Mediterranean, and convoy escorting. The recent work of the Polish ships in the Mediterranean has been especially brilliant.

The stirring words, which attest to the actual facts better than anything that could be written by the Poles themselves, and which most Poles would say were well deserved, were in fact directed at a different audience. This was an attempt by the British government to both bolster the Poles and to show the Soviets that the British still regarded the Polish government in London as the constitutional and legitimate authority representing the Polish state. But there is a very interesting archival trail to the behind the scenes of this Polish exhibit and Lord Alexander's laudatory statement.

The British Continue to Support the Polish Cause

The object of the Polish naval exhibit was clearly propagandistic. It had a historical section, a description of the Polish naval war effort and finally a section on future postwar goals. This stated that:

> The Baltic Sea must be an open sea, and German control of the Baltic has to cease. This is indispensable for a lasting World Peace. The Baltic in the hands of one power is a permanent menace to such a Peace.

(b) It is highly desirable to increase the tonnage of the British Mercantile Marine in the Baltic. It played a very small part before the War. For instance, in 1937 it represented only 6.8 per cent of the tonnage that passed through the Kiel Canal.

(c) A larger access to the sea will enable Poland and the Central Eastern European States to be independent of the German transport system."

According to British internal Foreign Office documents:

On receiving from the Polish Minister of Information a short description of the exhibits and aim of the Exhibition, the First Lord is a little shaken.

The advice which has been given to him is that since it is no part of the policy of H.M. Government to ostracise the Poles, there is no reason why he should not fulfill the engagement so long as he keeps his speech to an objective tribute to the part which the Polish Navy and Merchant Marine have played in this war. The First Lord would be grateful to know at the earliest possible moment whether the Foreign Office concur with this view.

Roberts of the Foreign Office indeed concurred with this advice and stated that the Polish aims were in general in line with British policy, "which is directed to giving Poland a good Baltic coastline at the expense of Germany and as compensation for losses to Russia. In view of the considerable service of the Polish Navy and Merchant Marine (including the convoying of supplies to Russia) I can see no reason why the First Lord should not accept this invitation."[33]

In February 1944, the British Vice Chiefs of Staff took up the agenda of a British (SOE) military mission to the Polish underground.[34] This supports the inherent British efforts on Poland's behalf: "I understand that contrary to expectations the question of a British Mission to the Secret army of Poland is to be taken up by the Vice-Chiefs of Staff immediately and will not await the result of the recent approach by Mr. Churchill to marshal Stalin on the major question of Polish/Soviet relations."

The memo discussed the composition of the mission, and the question whether it was to be strictly military in conjunction with Overlord, or a semipolitical mission reporting back to the British on "strength, morale and intentions of the Secret Army, thus enabling HMG to obtain independent evidence with which to answer Soviet allegations of alleged British 'lack of knowledge.'" Finally, it was to be a manifestation of British interest in the question of Polish independence, i.e., in order to convince the Russians and Poles alike that "a complete sell out of Poland to Russia is not the policy of HMG."

This seeming digression illustrates that the official British government posture, particularly that of the Foreign Office, was very supportive of Poland even though the mission took place only in December 1944—a death knell to the Poles.

Meanwhile, in the United Kingdom there continued to be tension within the British ranks. The Poles certainly had a great friend and ally in Lord Selborne, the minister of Economic Warfare; and the air ministry predictably downplayed the military advantages of special duties flights particularly at a time when the bomber offensive appeared to be bringing the long-desired results. It is the British prime minister's position that is both interesting and at least somewhat perplexing given his other acts and speeches.

A case in point is illustrated in the minutes of the Defence Committee section of Special Operations in Poland and Czecho-Slovakia on February 3, 1944:

> Minister of Economic Warfare agreed with the opinion expressed by the Chief of Staffs in their report that the control of special operations in both countries [i.e. Poland and Czechoslovakia] should remain with S.O.E. in London, subject to the direction of the Chiefs of Staff. As regards Poland the position was as follows. Assistance to the Poles had to be provided from the Mediterranean. The German night fighter strength made S.O.E. operations over Poland based in this country impracticable. On the other hand, the Polish Government was established in London. Relations with the Poles involved many difficult political problems which had to be settled here. In the circumstances it would be inconvenient for the control of S.O.E. operations over that country to be centred in the Mediterranean theatre. As regards Czechoslovakia, Lord Selborne said that after the assassination of Heidrich the Germans had conducted a terrible campaign of repression and slaughter which had the effect of stamping out the Secret Army in that country. S.O.E. had made several attempts to encourage the reorganization of resistance, but had met with no success and had received little support or encouragement from the Czechoslovak Government in this country.
>
> Apart from the matters specifically included in the agenda, the Minister wished to raise a few other questions regarding the Polish Resistance Movement. A recent report by the Joint Intelligence Sub-Committee had criticised the degree of autonomy allowed to the Polish authorities in the use of cyphers and in expenditure of money. He reminded the Committee that in 1940, under the authority of the Prime Minister, a credit had been opened for the Polish Government, for the purpose of fostering resistance in Poland, of £600,000, a year. Up to date a total of only £400,000 had been spent. The Poles had recently asked for money to be released from this credit and he had agreed; but in view of the criticism leveled by the Joint Intelligence Sub-Committee, he had thought it desirable to seek confirmation from the Committee.
>
> The Secretary of State for Foreign Affairs stated that he would have liked His Majesty's Government to have had the same control over the Poles as they possessed over our other Allies. He felt, however, that this was not a happy moment to make change, and suggested that the existing arrangements should for the time being, be allowed to continue.[35]
>
> The Minister of Economic Warfare next asked the Committee to give directions for an increase in the assistance to be given to the resistance movement in Poland. A present only 6 aircraft had been allocated for S.O.E. work over Poland and lately only 2 of these were serviceable.
>
> He was satisfied that the Polish Resistance was most vigorous and efficient. The Poles were expert in resistance, and in this respect compared favourably with the people of any other countries occupied by Germany. The Poles themselves claimed that they were containing large German forces. He had heard a figure mentioned of half million men. He urged the Committee to authorise the allocation of 17 aircraft for S.O.E. work over Poland.
>
> The Chief of Air Staff said he felt confident that an increase of supplies to Poland could be achieved were the pool of aircraft for S.O.E. operations in the Mediterranean not restricted as to operations they were permitted to carry out. This pool of 32 aircraft was now available for operations over the Balkans only.

If the pool were "unfrozen" he believed that it would pay great dividend. Weather conditions would at some periods make operations possible in some areas when they were impossible in others.

The Secretary of State for Foreign Affairs stated that the number of aircraft allotted for S.O.E. work over Jugoslavia, Greece and Poland was only 38. It seemed a very small allocation in view of the importance at this stage of the war of encouraging the patriot forces in those countries to resist the enemy and to contain his forces.

The Chief of the Air Staff said our supreme task in the air was to sustain the battle which was being waged by Bomber Command, and which might prove decisive if we did not allow ourselves to be drawn away by less essential calls on our resources. If our Bomber crews felt at this time, when the German defence was increasing its efficiency, that they were not receiving support, their morale was bound to suffer. The large scale bombing of the distant parts of Germany was only possible in the months of February, March, and April, which were the same months which were alone suitable for operations over Poland.

The Prime Minister said that he considered it a matter of high public importance that greater assistance should be given by the Air Staff to resistance movements in occupied Europe, even at some small expense to other responsibilities of the Royal Air Force. Treble the present allocation of aircraft to Poland should be accorded. A diversion of 12 aircraft from the bomber effort over Germany was a small price to pay. There was danger in rigid adherence to overriding priorities. Priorities should only be considered in relation to the assignment to which they referred. An extra 12 aircraft for Poland at this stage might make a considerable difference. Now that the Russians were advancing into Poland it was in our interest that Poland should be strong and well supported. Were she weak and overrun by the advancing Soviet armies, the result might hold great dangers in the future for the English speaking peoples.[36]

This comment by Churchill, not mentioned in his Nobel Prize for Literature–winning memoirs, was made at a highly secret meeting of the highest members of his War Cabinet subcommittee. It was not a propaganda speech delivered to encourage the Poles or, as a British officer said at the time of Yalta, to "jolly them along." It illustrates at least two points: firstly that British policy to Poland was not at this stage of the war completely disinterested, and secondly that the Poles who had intimate dealings with the British must have been subtly encouraged to proceed with their own long-term plans.

Churchill as always took a personal interest in all matters military. He was very invested in the Polish forces, particularly the Polish First Armored, which he had visited with Sikorski in the winter months of 1940–41 when Polish units, however small, were all the allies the British had outside of their commonwealth forces. The following message illustrates Churchill's interest in the division, his concern about the Polish future and finally a tacit recognition of the desperate shortages of men in the British Army. On May 21, 1944, Churchill wrote to the CIGS: "Why are we told that the 1st Polish Armoured Division cannot function because there are not sufficient rear administrative units available to maintain it? Surely a reasonable effort at adjustment could be made to enable this fine division to strengthen our already too slender forces on the Continent."

A week later on May 28, 1944, Churchill followed this point by commenting:

"Please do not on any account let the Polish Division be kept out of the battle-front. Not only is it a magnificent fighting force, but its exploits will help to keep alive the soul of Poland, on which much turns in the future."[37]

On April 4, 1944 Jozef Retinger, Churchill's personal fact finder was parachuted into Poland and was brought back on July 25 by one of the three Mosty (*Wildhorn*) air pickups to Italy. There is every reason to infer from the mission and its secrecy that Churchill was hoping to be able to negotiate on behalf of Mikolajczyk, or even without his approval, a support for a different Polish government. Clearly, what was found in Poland was a strong determination to preserve both the legitimacy of the Polish government in London and the integrity of Polish boundaries.[38]

Retinger's report seemed to suggest that the predominant political element in a liberated Poland would be found in the large Polish Peasant Party. It can also only be inferred that the report confirmed the fact that the Polish underground, both military and its civilian leadership, were in strong support of the Polish government, of the Polish commander in chief, General Sosnkowski, and were adamantly opposed to territorial concessions to the Soviet Union.

The British were still very much committed to Poland. But this was clearly no longer the case for the United States, which gave every indication of wishing to be disengaged from the Polish question. While the Polish ambassador in Washington continued to function and be accorded all pertinent diplomatic privileges, there was no successor following the resignation of the highly respected and pro–Polish U.S. ambassador, Mr. Biddle, in December 1943, shortly before the Tehran Conference. Regarded as a very good friend of the Polish people and of the Polish cause, his resignation in retrospect was ascribed to his disenchantment with his own government's policies.[39] Tony Biddle, as he was known to his many Polish friends, joined the United States military. There was no replacement until mid–1944 when Mr. Bliss Lane was appointed but never arrived in London. He only assumed his duties with the post–Yalta provisional government in Warsaw.[40]

The Polish government continued until late in 1944 to work through its agencies in the United States to attempt to influence the political process on behalf of the cause of Poland by arguing that the issues transcended mere Polish interests, that in fact the cause of Poland was the question of the principles of the Atlantic Charter.

Polish Special Duties Flight in Italy

In late 1943, the Polish Special Duties Flight consisting of six crews plus a small number of reserves was moved to southern Italy. Its establishment was three Liberators and three Halifaxes, and it became part of the Balkans Air Force, flying liaison missions to Poland as well as other neighboring countries. This quickly became a bone of contention between the Royal Air Force authorities and the small but independent-minded unit, which was attempting to implement its own commander's orders. On the first four-plane expedition to Poland from their new Italian base, two of the Polish Liberators crashed with the loss of six airmen, thus reducing the effectiveness of the flight by 33 percent.

There was annoyance at the Olympian heights of the British Air Ministry when the Polish commanding officer, Major Krol, flew to the United Kingdom on an unauthorized flight to report directly to Polish authorities the plight of his unit's situation. The Polish complaint was that the state of the equipment situation was catastrophic and that the Polish flight was not receiving logistical help in the rotation of engines after a mandatory number of hours flown, etc. The British Air Ministry, responding with considerable annoyance, did not refute the facts, but placed the blame on the local Polish flight commander, who failed to follow regular and prescribed RAF policies. The Polish commander in chief was also requested to hold the Polish flight to RAF policies and Air Marshal Slessor was ordered to ensure that the Poles abided by RAF rules. Portal to Sosnkowski on January 28, 1944:

> Thank you for your letter No.96/GNW/44 of the 24th January. I fully understand the difficulties with which the Polish Flight in Italy must be faced in endeavouring to maintain their operational efficiency, and I am sorry to hear from you that the numbers of aircraft in the Flight have been so seriously reduced. At the same time, I feel bound to point out that, owing possibly to a misunderstanding on the part of the Commander of the flight, who has not regarded his unit as being, for operational and administrative purposes, an integral part of the Special Duty Wing formed in Italy for the conduct of Special Operations, neither the Headquarters of the Mediterranean Allied Air Forces nor the Air Ministry have been kept informed of the aircraft state in this Flight. It was only as a result of representations by S.O.E. to the Air Ministry, made, I understand on information received through S.O.E. channels, that we were informed that 2 of your Liberators had crashed and that urgent replacements were required.
>
> My staff were informed by the Flight Commander when he recently visited this country, that in addition to the loss of the 2 Liberators, 2 of the Halifaxes in his Flight were without engines. It transpired, however, that these engines were in fact being provided from M.A.A.F. resources and arrived at Naples on the 14th January. It thus appears that, as a result of the coincidence of normal unserviceability and unfortunate accidents, the strength of the Flight was reduced by about the 13/14th January to a strength of 2 serviceable aircraft.
>
> It is, of course, possible that the remaining Halifax was also temporarily unserviceable, which would have reduced the strength to 1 serviceable aircraft at that particular time.

For Portal to argue with a straight face that senior Royal Air Force commanders were unaware of the loss of two Polish planes and of two crews is not merely unbelievable, but preposterous. Portal acknowledges the importance that the Poles place on their flight, but in his message to Sosnkowski also places the blame for the loss of two Polish planes on the Polish major.

> I must remark that the return of the Flight Commander of No. 1586 Flight to this country apparently to report to you upon matters about which the Air Ministry had not been informed, as they should have been, appears to have been a somewhat irregular proceeding. It is not clear, from my information, that he had been granted permission by the Officer Commanding No. 344 Wing to return, or that there was, from the point of view of the Royal Air Force, any

service technical reason for the visit I have given instruction for the Flight Commander to be informed of the system of higher command of his flight, and for him to be instructed to conform to normal R.A.F. procedure both as regards reporting his aircraft strength and serviceabilty and also the operational control of his unit, and I should be grateful if you would arrange for confirmatory instructions to be sent. I would assure that if this procedure is followed, everything possible will be done to ensure that your operations shall not suffer for lack of provision of the agreed complement of aircraft.[41]

There is evidence that the air ministry sent a scathing message to Mediterranean Allied Air Forces but no evidence that the Polish commander in chief complied with Portal's request for "confirmatory instructions" to be sent. In view of the fact that Krol continued in command and was one of a small handful of officers to be decorated with the Polish Virtuti Militari Gold Cross (Class IV) it does seem that he was complying with Polish policies at the risk of burning his bridges with the British.

But the above exchange illustrates that local Polish requests were being ignored. It is hard to imagine that the Royal Air Force wing commander had no idea that his Polish flight was so short of planes. It was clearly a way of making the Poles toe the line. It also illustrates the generally negative attitudes of the British field commanders to all clandestine activities but in particular those which seemed to be outside of their control. The Cypher telegram, to Mediterranean Allied Air Forces from the air ministry in Whitehall on January 26, 1944, personal for Slessor from Chief of Air Staff, addressed London's unhappiness with the situation in Italy and went on to state:

> I would be grateful if you would arrange for the Flight Commander to be disabused of his wrong ideas since without up-to-date information here we cannot hope to make up the strength of the Polish Flight should casualties occur such as those of the night of 5/6 January. (You will be well aware of the political implications involved.)
>
> More important than the submission of returns however appear to the operational control of the Flight. The Flight Commander Squadron Leader Krol recently arrived in this country in his remaining Liberator on the pretext that the aircraft was in need of overhaul whereas in fact it was due only for a routine inspection which should have been made at the parent airfield or at any rate within the Command.
>
> The real reason for his visit appears to have been to enable the Flight Commander to report to Polish Headquarters in London on a) the low serviceability rate in his unit and b) the circumstances in which two Liberators were lost with their crews on the night of 5/6 January. As a result General Sosnkowski the Polish Commander in Chief has written personally to me about a) and Lord Selborne has written personally to [secretary of state] about b.
>
> The matter of replacement aircraft was already in hand but the second question of Lord Selborne's letter, appears to merit full investigation and although I suspect that the independent attitude of the Polish Flight Commander may have a bearing on the accident I cannot advise S.o S. how to reply until an enquiry has been held.
>
> It is a pity that you must have to be bothered with these matters when your hands must be very full but I must ask you to look into the question of the

control of [Special Duties] Squadrons with particular reference to No. 1586 Flight and ensure that we are not again exposed to criticism of R.A.F. Operational or Administrative arrangements either by the Minister of Economic Warfare or the Polish High Command.

Finally, you should make it absolutely plain to the Polish Flight Commander that his flight is just as much under your command as are all the other R.A.F. units in the Mediterranean. For all operational and administrative purposes, he is under your orders and must deal with nobody but yourself acting through the Commanding Officer of No. 334 S.D. Wing. on all questions other than the reception arrangements in Poland and details of loads to be carried which are dealt with in London between S.O.E. and Polish general Staff. Please confirm that Squadron Leader Krol fully understands the position.[42]

Line officers do not appreciate political interventions. This message speaks a thousand words. It addresses the frustration of Portal in dealing with Lord Selborne and with the Poles, and clearly commiserates with the local RAF commanders in Italy in having to deal with such political issues. The Polish cause could not have been well served by such a message. But that is only part of the problem.

It has often been commented that Poles have an ethnocentric preoccupation with conspiracy theories, inevitably directed at them and to their detriment. But the British had a very elegant manner of always having an alibi for their failures. The RAF Bomber Command is unable or unwilling to commit planes for Poland and seeks to impeach the integrity of the Polish clandestine organization, an integrity which was a model for all. Portal "suspects" that it is the independent attitude of the Polish flight commander that may be responsible for the two crashed Liberators. Apparently the fact that the Polish flight which was to have six four-engined planes on establishment, is down to merely one (!) seems to be a set of circumstances beyond the knowledge or control of any senior RAF command officer.

Later in the war other Polish traits will be alluded to as causes for British incapacity, failure or helplessness at the hands of their more powerful allies, the Americans and the Soviets.

The Poles were not completely satisfied and continued to press their demands for the flight (i.e., six four-engined planes) to be developed into a full squadron of 12 aircraft. This was argued on the merits of the need for that many planes to deliver the requisite supplies to Poland, and also by concern that a loss of one crew and the mechanical impairment of another would leave the Polish effort short, as happened in January 1944 when the two Polish crews which were lost curtailed the establishment of the flight by 33 percent. This added weight to Polish arguments. Understandably, the fact that the Poles had to be supplied by the RAF logistical detail, but were less than completely receptive to being involved in other special duties, must have grated. But it needs to be remembered that the special duties missions enjoyed little sympathy with any of the RAF senior officers, who viewed all such missions, whether flown by RAF or other crews, as a waste of resources and a distraction from other, more important combat flights.

In February 1944, Slessor reported his views of the problem of special duties under his command:

It assumes that the Poles will allow their Halifaxes to be used in the MAAF pool for operations in the Balkans on some nights when operations in Poland are impossible. This is essential and I suggest you put it squarely to the Polish authorities on the following lines. I will do my utmost to see that the effort outlined in para 4 is achieved and will help out on favorable nights with aircraft provided the Poles put their aircraft into MAAF pool. They have not a dog's chance of doing this planned effort without our assistance in view of the weather conditions, and if they do not agree to pooling their aircraft I shall leave them to stew in their own juice and they will be lucky if they get their planned effort.[43]

In Italy, as before in the United Kingdom, the Poles had little choice but to participate in a team effort. In fact, from a purely logical view, the British position was well justified and well argued. Weather conditions varied and at times it made sense for crews to fly to a local target such as northern Italy or the very close Balkans. Such missions also allowed the crews a relative respite from the hazardous and exhausting flights of well over 12 hours to Poland.

But the table shows that the burden was not equitably managed.

This issue of number of flights, Polish unhappiness and at times disingenuous obfuscation led to an interesting British SOE memo which was dated February 21, 1944.[44]

We have on several occasions burnt our fingers badly in mentioning the exact number of flights to Poland. Although these have been mentioned exclusively for the computation of such matters as containers, wireless, reception committees etc., they have always been used by the Poles as a promise, and although we have had the discomfort of denying this promise on many occasions, the mentioning of figures, unless we are one hundred percent sure of fulfillment is dangerous. It is to be remembered that when the Polish flight was moved to Italy the Poles were informed that operations from that theater would be far more favourable than England. As things have turned out the weather there has been so atrocious that for the past eight weeks not one single flight has been possible. We have no certainty that the weather will improve during the period under review and therefore can make no promises whatsoever.

The memo goes on to say that in February there will be no further flights but they should resume in full force in March and April; still, promises as to actual numbers should not be made, since they cannot be guaranteed. The probable number of actual flights will be so much lower than that: "The Poles will undoubtedly look upon this figure as high level sabotage. It should be remembered that from this country under much more difficult conditions during March last year [i.e., 1943] 22 successful flights were carried out to Poland. These were achieved with the Polish flight of 6 aircraft plus a very small number of sorties as a British supplementary effort." The memo goes on to develop this point that while; "hardly conceivable but in actual fact it may turn out that with 18 aircraft plus British extra which the Minister has promised, only 30 successful flights will materialise. There is surely no reason to particularly to draw the Poles' attention to this miserable figure."

The memo then disposes of the argument being made by local RAF commanders about the unreasonableness of the Poles: "It is a complete fallacy that the Poles are unwilling to pool. The one thing they contend is that when there is a chance to fly to Poland those 18 aircraft will fly there whenever the weather is favourable, plus some indefinite assistance from the other aircraft in Brindisi." The memo concludes that the minister should promise only that commitment and not any specific numbers.

But the Polish efforts to help their RAF colleagues to other drop zones were not reciprocated. It was not a question of lack of good will or of courage, it was just that the Poles had a different perception of the importance of flights to Poland, since for them it was a crusade and a symbolic step closer home, while for British crews these flights were strenuous, dangerous and, for their chiefs, less important, hence they were inevitably less invested and less successful. Table 1 illustrates the actual breakdown of the flights to Poland by Polish and other crews, and the role of the Polish crews in carrying out assistance to other targets.

TABLE I

Year	Polish Crews to Poland	Polish Crews to other targets	RAF Crews to Poland
1941	2	0	2
1942	21	93	16
1943	61	130	168
1944	339	604	133
1945	0	95	0
Total	423	922	319

The balance is obvious. There can be no question that the Poles must have often wished to have been left to their own "Polish stew" and not the hard-to-digest English fare!

Final Polish Air Staff Plans on Behalf of the AK

In April 1944, the Poles and the British signed a new air agreement which corrected many of the deficiencies of the prior 1940 agreement and which also changed the Polish Air Force Inspectorate to the Polish Air Force Command. This allowed the Poles to form their own staffs.

The terse rejoinder to the AK must have been thought inadequate and on May 12, 1944, the new Polish Air Force commanding officer, Maj. Gen. Mateusz Izycki, cabled the AK on the crucial question of air support. In a most realistic manner the report stated that to even come close to fulfilling the projected AK needs for air support, more Polish crews, particularly pilots, but also ground support crews, should be trained on British-captured German planes, so that when such planes fell into Polish hands in Poland, pilots and ground crews would be familiar with their flying and maintenance characteristics (RAF Flight 1426 — Enemy Aircraft Circus). Polish officers were given an opportunity to pass through the base, including Colonel Bialy, but the unit was obviously highly secret and the number of planes and trainees limited. The report also identified a number of pre–1939 Polish air bases and newly developed German ones on Polish territory that were to be considered as possible Polish air bases. Further AK reports were requested and the AK was urged to form and train ground units for their capture and defense. The bases identified were Bielany, Bielice, Borowina, Piastow, and Klikawa for fighter squadrons, which had the estimated ability to land 220 planes each day.

The hindsight reaction to this report is that in circumstances analogous to November 11, 1918, the Polish Air Force could be moved to Poland, but that for any meaningful air support of the uprising, Allied intervention was an absolute imperative. Since it was unrealistic to give the AK air support by moving the units to Poland, the memorandum proposed that tactical air support be provided from bases in the West. The plan analyzed air transport needs of moving both the Polish Parachute Brigade and daily tonnage required to support the Polish air units in Poland. The Polish Air Group, which at this point did not yet exist except in a planning stage, but which was to consist of 13 squadrons, would have required 168,784 tons of gasoline and oil, 54,630 tons of munitions plus food, and reserve material. To ensure such a logistical support would have required 339 two-engined transport planes of the DC Dakota type. Since air support to the Home Army had to be coordinated, the importance of improving communications was stressed.

Thus British support was a sine qua non of any Polish endeavor. This scrupulously honest assessment also speculated that an Allied composite group, which could consist of 24 fighter and fighter-bomber squadrons and in which Poles would participate, might be strong enough to give local air support based from Polish-captured and -controlled airfields. This would still have required significant air support by Allied units operating from Western bases. Izycki went on to stress that the Poles had not received any such Allied commitment and reiterated that for the necessary and appropriate number of combat squadrons to be moved to Poland and supplied from Western bases would require an air transport of a size which the Allies did not possess, and that the British lacked actual experience in such operations.

Because of all these points, the support of the uprising by the Polish or Allied-Polish air groups was unrealistic even if a political agreement was reached. The telegram concluded that the London-based staffs had forwarded and would continue to cable numerous instructions and technical specifications to Poland, particularly technical specs of German communication systems and German aircraft but warned that there were only limited possibilities for training on captured German planes in the United Kingdom.

In turn, Izycki requested details of airfields in Poland and the specific targets for eventual bombing from Western bases. For this purpose a questionnaire was developed and cabled regarding details of airfields, with particular emphasis on the number, direction and length of runways, local impediments, guard activities, night flying capability, bunkers, hangars, etc.[45]

Mosty (Wildhorn) Operations

There were no further plans or developments prior to the Warsaw Uprising of August 1, 1944, but during the spring of 1944 there were three successful landings in

Poland. This was the typical technique for inserting and picking up agents in the German-occupied countries of Western Europe and was also practiced by the Soviets in their support of their Communist agents in eastern Poland. But there were two major problems for this to be accomplished between the West and Poland. The long distance required a long-range plane, and that in turn meant a heavy, at least two-engined, aircraft. To land a such a big plane on the primitive fields accessible to the control and protection of the Polish Home Army was difficult.

But on the night of April 15-16, 1944, an RAF two-engined Dakota piloted by Flight Lieutenant E. Harrod with Captain B. Korpowski as second pilot of the 334 Special Duty Wing made the first successful flight. Five Poles were picked up, including Gen. Stanislaw Tatar, who became head of the VI Section of the Polish General Staff. About a month later this was repeated and one of the Poles flown to Poland was Gen. Tadeusz Kossakowski (Krystynek), who had commanded the Polish Engineering Forces in the United Kingdom and was being inserted to organize the Polish clandestine armaments production. A number of individuals were flown out, including Col. Roman Rudkowski, who had been parachuted into Poland in January 1943 as an emissary of the Polish Air Force staff to the Polish underground army. The third and final operation was the most important and most dramatic. On the night of July 25-26, 1944, a Dakota from the same wing, flown by a New Zealander with a Pole as navigator, picked up the parts of a German V rocket and also two important people, namely the British emissary to Poland, Jozef Retinger, and Mr. Tomasz Arciszewski, leader of the Polish Socialist Party, later to be the Polish prime minister. These three flights were codenamed Mosty or Bridges. But by the time the Poles and the Allies had the techniques, the Soviets were in physical control of at least half of prewar Poland.[46]

Mikolajczyk Seeks American Support

The Polish government now embarked on a final political endeavor to seek American support for its policies and took the step of promoting, in a very subtle way, the centralizing of all Polish-American groups to form the Polish-American Congress, whose goal was to exert political pressure on Roosevelt since he was running for his unprecedented fourth term in November 1944.[47]

The Polish prime minister, Mikolajczyk, also solicited an invitation from Roosevelt, which was finally extended and implemented on May 6, 1944.

On his visit to the United States, Mikolajczyk was accompanied by the recently extracted General Tabor who because of his intimate familiarity with conditions in occupied Poland was appointed to head the VI Section of the Polish staff. Mikolajczyk met with the president and other American statesmen and also leaders of the Polish-American community. He also found time at the strong urging of Churchill to meet with Professor Lange, a Polish-born economist, a faculty member at the University of Chicago with strong left leanings who had been granted a visa to the Soviet Union in the middle of the war, and was a very strong advocate of direct dealings with Stalin and the complete remake of the Polish government. (After the war, Professor Lange worked in the Polish Communist diplomatic cadre.) The visit by Mikolajczyk to

Washington achieved nothing for the Polish cause, but possibly strengthened Roosevelt's chances for reelection by firming the overwhelmingly Democratic vote of the Polish-Americans. Roosevelt, as well as Churchill, strongly encouraged Mikolajczyk to travel to Moscow and to attempt to resume diplomatic ties with the Soviets.

While Mikolajczyk was having his meetings, General Tabor was a guest of the Combined Chiefs of Staff in Washington on June 12, 1944, chaired by Admiral W. D. Leahy. In addition to the usual membership, also present was the permanent Polish representative, Colonel L. Mitkiewicz.

> Admiral Leahy welcomed General Tabor on behalf of the CCS and invited him to address the CCS. General Tabor referred to the memorandum previously circulated for consideration by the CCS and said that he wished to emphasize four points in this memorandum:
>
> 1. The necessity for the speediest possible execution of 500 operational flights delivering armament and equipment to the Polish Secret Army, in order to intensify its subversive activities. For this purpose, the monthly allotment of operational flights should be increased to 150–200 per month.
> 2. The need for the allotment of further 1,300 operational flights, to be carried out en masse at the appropriate moment, should the Allied operations be decided upon.
> 3. The necessity for the establishment of an air base in the United Kingdom. The operational flights to Poland are at present carried out from Italy and reach Central and Southern Poland only. From the UK, they will cover northern and north-eastern Poland.
> 4. The vital importance attached to the approval of the requirements submitted to the CCS by Colonel Mitkiewicz under CCS 267 on June 30th 1943. The most urgent needed item at this moment is signals equipment. General Tabor then answered certain questions addressed to him by the CCS. One of these concerned relations between the Polish Secret Army [i.e., AK] and the Red Army.
>
> General Tabor said that in one area of Southern Poland the Soviet Authorities had withdrawn their own partisan units and handed over subversive activities in the areas to the local representative of the Polish Secret Army. This indicated that the Soviet Authorities took a positive view of the value of the Polish Secret Army. Admiral Leahy thanked General Tabor on behalf of the CCS and expressed the hope on behalf of both the CCS and of the American and British nations that Poland would soon be restored to a peaceful and prosperous position.[48]

Mitkiewicz in his postwar memoirs minces no words that Tabor was, to use an American expression, a loose cannon, and having reiterated all the previously argued points, mistook the politeness of Admiral Leahy for approval and tacit promise of support. (General Tabor had just arrived in the West, and had never been to the United States prior to this visit, did not speak English and hence was completely unaware of Anglo-Saxon conventions.) Mitkiewicz was particularly struck by Tabor's positive views on collaboration with the Soviets when the most recent radioed information from Poland was that the Polish AK units were being disarmed or arrested by the Soviets. Mitkiewicz also commented that this particular "fact" of alleged collaboration elicited great enthusiasm among the British representatives.[49]

One of the perplexing things that did happen was that Roosevelt gave Mikolajczyk $10 million in gold and paper money for work by the clandestine groups in Poland.

The Bardsea Plan and Polish Commandos

The episode discussed here, while having its origins much earlier in the war, belongs at this point as an overture to the history of the Polish Parachute Brigade as well as of the Polish commandos who were the first Polish ground forces to return to combat since the Carpathian Brigade was withdrawn from North Africa in 1942.

On August 28, 1942, General Sikorski issued an order to form a Polish commando unit administratively based on the Polish 1st Infantry Brigade which had already given birth to many volunteers for parachuting into Poland. The first independent commando company was intended for integration with the British. The Poles were all volunteers; their first commanding officer was Capt. Wladyslaw Smrokowski. The 100 Polish soldiers were trained on the same lines as their British colleagues. In October 1942, the Polish company arrived in Wales to join the 10th Inter-allied Commando. After Wales, the Poles went to Achnacarry in Scotland, near Fort William, a British training center run by a tough disciplinarian, Col. Charles Vaughan, known to all who went through the camp as "Laird of Achnacarry." After intense training, the Poles entered combat in Italy on the Sangro River in December 1943. After a very bloody series of small firefights, the Poles went on a rest and took further training. But in April 1943 they were seconded, temporarily, to the Polish 2 Corps. This temporary assignment was to become permanent. The company in time evolved into the Polish Motorized Commando Battalion. Their battle honors were to be the same as those of the Polish 2 Corps.

It is possibly because the Poles did such a good job, both in training and subsequent combat, that in late 1942 the British section chief of SOE for Action Continental, Maj. Ronald Hazell, suggested to the Poles, already known to be involved in Action Monica, that there be a joint collaborative effort to stoke the embers of resistance among the Polish migrants in northern France. Thus was borne the Bardsea Plan.[50]

Even in 1943 it was still far from clear where the Allied invasion of the Continent would take place, but the region of Calais was certainly seriously considered. The code name was Roundup. It is also possible that this was a very sophisticated British deception game. But had this been the invasion route it would have brought the Allies into the area known in France as Pas-de-Calais and Nord, which was industrial and had a significant population (thought to be about 150,000) of prewar Polish migrants. The areas in question were Armentieres, Arras, Cambrai.

The Poles were to recruit and train a parachute unit, proficient in both Polish and French, who would organize a large cadre of underground workers able to disrupt German lines of communication and provide the Allies with current intelligence. The Poles were enthusiastic given the fact that the British were to cover the costs.[51] Sikorski, after expressing minor concerns that the Polish unit be dropped only when there was legitimate guarantee that it would be relieved in three days by advancing Allied forces and that only the Polish commander in chief or his designate would authorize such an action, finalized the Polish-British negotiations and signed the contract.

The final "contractual" day was July 14, 1943. It will be noted that this was after Sikorski's accident and death. There was now an embarrassing Polish problem, which stemmed from the fact that Monica had been a ministry project under General Kukiel. As long as Sikorski was both prime minister and commander in chief there was no ambiguity. After his death, the roles were separated and the civilian members of the Polish government balked at signing since it was unclear whether the final authorization was reserved for the commander in chief (Sosnkowski) or the prime minister of the Polish government, now headed by Mr. Mikolajczyk. A very unseemly argument developed in the Polish ranks with the puzzled British guests as spectators. The British pragmatically brought the meeting to a halt by stating that from a military stance the agreement was concluded but the political issue would be decided between the Polish government and Lord Selborne.[52]

It is sad indeed that this internal conflict persisted to May 25, 1944, when it was signed by the Polish government and Lord Selborne. But by this time the British knew where the invasion would occur, and furthermore, Eisenhower, after becoming acquainted with Bardsea, rejected the plan because of the Polish conditions. Also, Eisenhower wished to use the Polish company behind enemy lines, and not as clandestine organizers of larger masses of resistors. This disagreement, quite separate from the nearly analogous negotiations regarding the Polish Parachute Brigade, is not as well known. The Polish government acceded to Allied requests but conditioned the use of the Polish parachute company on collaboration with French resistance and that it would be dropped only into regions controlled by French resistance.

In the meanwhile, the training and recruitment continued. On July 27, 1943, the Polish Ministry of Defense established the Independent Grenadier Company. Its full complement was four staff (senior) officers, 17 junior officers with complete parachute and sabotage training, 53 noncommissioned officers and 66 privates. In January 1944, the Independent Grenadier Company was enlarged to 182 officers and men. The company was being trained with the expectation that the grenadiers would be a cadre of a regiment-sized combat unit after fleshing out with local resistors of Polish background. In June 1944, a number of American officers from the OSS joined the Polish company. Finally, three "fives" of American soldiers of Polish descent joined the Polish company.

The Allied invasion in Normandy put some of the plans on hold. It was still planned that the Polish company would be parachuted when the Allied front reached the proximity of Calais. The Polish company, commanded by Captain Kowalski, now had 12 Polish sections (Adam, Bolek, Cyryl, Dawid, Edek, Felek, Genek, Hanio, Jasiu, Karol, Leon, and Marek), three American sections (Dodford, Dauchet, and Daroves), and most interestingly one British section (Dunchurch) composed of instructors from Special Training Station 63.

The Grenadiers were placed on alert for September 1, 1944, and were in the process of boarding planes as Kukiel came to see them off. At that point Major Hazell informed the Poles that the Allied forces had reached the Belgian border and the operation was cancelled.

On September 9, 1944, the Independent Grenadier Company was dissolved and the Polish personnel assigned to the Polish Parachute Brigade.

The Mission of the Parachute Brigade Is Changed

The Polish Parachute Brigade grew in numbers and by early 1944 had a total of 266 officers and 2,300 of other ranks. However, it was still significantly under strength since there were only a total of 420 riflemen in each of the three parachute battalions. Even so, British interest in that unit began to appear. On March 11, 1944, General Grasset, representing the European section of SHAEF (Supreme Headquarters Allied Expeditionary Force) in a formal letter to the Polish High Command, wished to ascertain whether the Poles would amend existing agreements and release the Polish Parachute Brigade for combat action in Northwest Europe.

> Field Marshal Sir Alan Brooke fully realizes that in accordance with the existing agreement the Polish Parachute Brigade is unreservedly at your disposal for operations in Poland, and is excluded from any operations that are to be undertaken by the Allied Forces. Since this agreement was made the general outlook and requirements of the War have changed and we are now faced with the probability of the most formidable operations of War of all times and one will require the employment of the maximum effort and resources at the disposal of the Allies. In this operation we must not fail.
>
> It was for this reason that the Chief of the Imperial General Staff instructed me to enquire whether you would agree to altering the present agreement concerning the Polish Parachute Brigade and place it at the disposal of the Supreme Allied Commander for operations in Western Europe. Sir Alan Brooke is fully aware of the importance that you and your Government attach to keeping this Brigade intact and available for your own requirements in Poland at a later date. Should you agree to the Brigade taking part in operations in Western Europe, casualties will undoubtedly occur.
>
> On the other hand the prestige and battle experience of the Brigade would be greatly enhanced. It is because the Polish Parachute Brigade is composed of such fine fighting material that the Chief of the Imperial General Staff hopes that it may be available for the critical operations to come.[53]

Grasset's comments are interesting if analyzed. It acknowledges prior agreements but also admits by default the shortages of British forces which makes a small brigade, as was the Polish Parachute unit, worth entering into such a set of negotiations. It encourages and hints that such a bloodied brigade may be of better service in the future. It is also a trifle amusing for a senior British general to be so concerned about Polish "prestige." But possibly the cynicism is not justified. It may be that the British government hoped that an active land participation by Polish forces would revert the mass media anti–Polish attitude.

Furthermore in the letter Grasset suggested that the British would welcome the Polish brigade for one major operation in Northwest Europe and that if losses went over 25 percent the unit would be withdrawn forthwith. The letter also stated: "When

General Kazimierz Sosnkowski, the Polish Commander in Chief, visited the Polish Parachute Brigade in 1944. He is being shown one of the American-produced pack howitzers on the establishment of the brigade. General Sosnkowski (third from left, back row) is wearing the traditional Polish rogatywka (four cornered, garrison cap) and General Sosabowski (second from left, back row) is the commander of the brigade. (Courtesy of the Polish Institute and Sikorski Museum, London.)

an opportunity arises for employing this Brigade in Poland, it will be placed at the disposal of the Polish Commander-in-Chief. It is not possible at this stage to give a definite guarantee on the subject of aircraft, but every effort will be made to release aircraft for the transport of the Brigade to Poland."

The Polish response attempted to outline concerns dealing with inadequate reserves, (the fourth battalion of the brigade had been cannibalized) and attempted to firm up the vague British statement about future opportunities for action in Poland. The Poles agreed with the following reservations: that the brigade would be used as a Polish Airborne Brigade-group, take part in only one major operation or a number of minor ones, and that if casualties exceeded 15 percent it would be withdrawn. Finally, the two most pressing and probably unrealistic conditions:

> The Brigade will be immediately withdrawn from action and placed at the disposal of the Polish C.-in-C. as soon as the possibility or at least probability of its use in Poland will arise. The Polish side will be competent to choose the right moment.
>
>   Field Marshal Sir Alan Brooke to give assurances of providing the means of transporting the Brigade by air/aircraft, gliders, flying personnel and also fighter

escort for [the protection of the Brigade's transportation and that of its supplies] when the Polish Government and the Polish Commander-in-Chief will decided to use the Brigade in Poland.

The memorandum concluded by stating, "I understand that as long as the new agreement is not reached the principals contained in the letter of the C.I.G.S. No. 0175/329/MOI of the 13 June, 1943 are still in force."

On May 21, 1944, Grasset responded to the Polish communiqué. It is fair to say that the original British letter requested Polish acquiescence to the British proposal and made no mention of asking for Polish conditions:

> General Sir Bernard Montgomery does not feel able to accept this Brigade under the conditions mentioned in your above letter. General Montgomery fully realises the shortage of Polish reserves in the United Kingdom and the difficulty which will arise in the replacement of casualties. He also realises the importance which you and your Government attach to this Brigade. But General Montgomery considers that if the Brigade is to be placed under his command he must be given a free hand to employ it in any manner that operations may demand. I am instructed to inform you that the British Chiefs of Staff, whilst unable to give any guarantee regarding the provision of aircraft to transport the Brigade to Poland, or about replacements of equipment, will do their best in the light of the circumstances existing at the time, to meet the requirements of the Polish Authorities in these respects.
>
> I feel sure you will appreciate the position of the British Chiefs of Staff and recognize their inability to commit themselves specifically at this stage of the war.
>
> The Chief of the Imperial General Staff and General Sir Bernard Montgomery[54] both fully understand your wishes regarding the employment of the Polish Parachute Brigade. They consider that this Brigade being composed as it is of such fine fighting material, if available, might make a valuable contribution to the war at some stage in the operations.[55]

The Polish government was consulted by Sosnkowski and in turn the Polish underground leadership. The political pros and cons of acceding or refusing British requests were considered as well as the merits of having a combat-seasoned unit for possible use in Poland. Between March and May 1944 a whole set of meetings occurred, and memoranda were exchanged between the British and Polish High Commands on this issue.[56]

The final consensus was that political issues were vital, that British goodwill needed to be considered and that it might be better to have a smaller but more experienced unit. This was a real dilemma, placing the Poles between the Scylla and Charybidis of losing British support in the future and possibly losing the brigade now.[57] There was no way the Poles could move the brigade to Poland without major British logistical and political support and while the British did not guarantee such cooperation, it did not require much foresight to know that if the British were refused, there would be no assistance in the future. The Polish General Staff had no alternative choice but to plan the best-case scenario and to develop contingency plans and resources accordingly.

It is interesting that Churchill took a different tack from his own generals and minuted General Hollis on June 23, 1944: " I consider that the Polish Parachute Brigade should not be lightly cast away. It may have a value in Poland itself far out of proportion to its actual military power. I trust these views may be conveyed to Generals Eisenhower and Montgomery before the brigade is definitely established in France."[58]

It is again a hint that the British government, and certainly Churchill, looked at all options to save some form of a free Polish state from the rapacious Soviets. Was the reason for the Polish brigade's being spared a part in the French operations due to Churchill? Was there even a British high-level discussion to dissolve the unit and thus to reinforce the badly under strength armored division that landed in France in July? Was there a major shift after the Warsaw Uprising or was the British need for troops so desperate in the Arnhem operations?

The Polish Independent Parachute Brigade was placed unconditionally in the o. de b. of the Allied Airborne Army on June 6, 1944. Grasset wrote a letter of appreciation as did Sir Alan Brooke and even Eisenhower. The Polish Parachute Brigade H.Q. received a cordial telegram: "Delighted you have joined us, will visit you as soon as I can get away. Keep me informed of your difficulties. Originator HQ Airtroops."[59]

The brigade began a grueling and accelerated period of training.

Polish Land Forces Back in Battle

The summer of 1944 was full of exciting and also momentous events for the Western Allies.

The reward of the Polish units of the Home Army, who collaborated with the Soviets in the fight for Wilno and Lwow, was to be surrounded by their short-lived allies, to be disarmed and to see their officers arrested. The men were given the option of sharing their officers' fate or enrolling in the Communist-sponsored so-called Polish Army. But in the West the Poles, through their sacrifice on the field, were able to note certain successes.

The Polish 2 Army Corps opened up the road to Rome by capturing the strongly defended Monte Cairo and Santa Angelo. But the symbolic crown was the Monastery of Monte Cassino, and the Polish commander, Gen. Wladyslaw Anders, cabled his commander in chief, the traditional age-old Polish military message of victory: "God gave us a Victory. The Polish Flag was placed on the ruins of the Monastery at 10.30 of May 18th."[60]

Churchill, after the war in his memoirs, wrote this rather uncharacteristically sympathetic comment:

> The Poles triumphantly hoisted their red and white standard over the ruins
> of the monastery. They greatly distinguished themselves in this their first major
> engagement in Italy. Later, under their thrustful General Anders, himself a
> survivor from Russian imprisonment, they were to win many laurels during
> their long advance to the river Po.[61]

The pro–Polish British press, the *Daily Telegraph* and *Illustrated London News*, carried the picture of the Polish flag flown side by side with the Union Jack. This military success was in reality more of a political success and was accomplished by the loss of

A. V. 20/31/18 (53)

(27)

do. L. S2. 696/11/44
(GWW)

Supreme Headquarters
ALLIED EXPEDITIONARY FORCE
Office of the Supreme Commander

14 June, 1944

My dear General Sosnkowski.

I have just heard from Field Marshal Sir Alan
Brooke that you have placed under my command
the Polish Parachute Brigade.

I write to thank you for making available to
the Allied Expeditionary Force this Brigade
which I know to be composed of fine fighting
material. I can assure you that I greatly
appreciate the efforts which you and your
Government are making towards the war effort
of the United Nations.

Sincerely

Dwight D Eisenhower

General K. Sosnkowski,
Polish Commander-in-Chief,
Rubens Hotel,
Buckingham Palace Road,
London, S.W.1.

A facsimile of the letter sent by General Eisenhower to General Sosnkowski, confirming the Polish agreement to release the Polish Parachute Brigade for action in northwest Europe. (Archives of the Polish Institute and Sikorski Museum, A.V. 20/31/18.)

over 800 dead, and many thousands wounded. The Poles had won their "prestige" and challenged the left-leaning mass media which had insinuated that the Poles did not want to fight the Germans. These scurrilous press attacks ignored the reality that the Polish Navy had been active in operations against the Germans from September 1939 and even on behalf of the Soviets by participating in the Murmansk convoys, and the fact that Polish airmen had already lost well over 1,000 air crew — over 100 percent of the establishment of the bomber squadrons. However contemptible, they had a ready audience.

The Polish corps, which entered operations without any reserves, was indeed hard pressed. But by the middle of June, the Poles had regrouped and entered operations on the Adriatic Coast.

General Anders, who received the Military Order of the Bath from General Alexander for the victory, now to all intentions operated independently with the orders of capturing the port of Ancona, important to the Allies for logistical purposes due to the inadequate Italian roads.[62] The operation was totally carried out by Polish troops, and supported by the Polish 318 City of Gdansk Fighter-Reconnaissance Squadron.

The story of the Gdansk 318 Squadron is important because if there was any Polish Air Force squadron that could have been expected to be based and operate in Poland in support of the Polish AK, then it would have been such a squadron.

With minimal navigational aid, flying out of the most basic fields, and living in tents, the personnel and planes were functioning at the most elementary technical level. It was a clone of the 309 Army Co-operation Squadron that had been specifically reserved by Polish-British agreements to be exclusively under Polish control. It was equipped with the rather outdated Lysanders and the Poles were based in very basic if not actually primitive conditions in various Scottish airfields starting at Renfrew near Glasgow. The squadron consisted of two flights and the routine was to carry out maneuvers with Scottish Command, including Polish troops. The living conditions were basic, the typical temporary huts with no warm water, and the cold and damp Scottish weather. The squadron, without complaints but with pronounced grumbling, saw their colleagues in fighter squadrons win esteem while they flew worn-out and obsolescent aircraft according to a doctrine that had not passed the test in Poland in September 1939.

It was a combination of factors which led to this body of pilots and their gunners-observers being seemingly forgotten since being unreservedly Polish by agreements meant that the RAF authorities could not move it around without a say-so from the Poles. Secondly, the concept of Army Co-operation was being questioned by the RAF and a decision had been arrived at to disband that Command.

In 1942 a new conundrum arose. The Polish HQ decided that they wished to have the squadron moved to the Middle East to join the Polish land forces being evacuated from the Soviet Union. This again led to the British placing the needs of the Polish squadron on a back burner because at best the Poles in the Middle East were not expected to get into operations till late 1943. However, in the spring of 1942, in small batches, pilots of the squadron were seconded to Gatwick to be trained on the newly arriving Mustangs. The officer-pilots also went through the British Army tactical course at Old Sarum. Pilots from Gatwick even got in combat missions over France for reconnaissance purposes. The squadron was partially attached to an RAF Wing (35) and took part in their flights over France.

Finally, in March 1943, as the British implemented their decision to disband the old Army Co-operation Command and were creating the Tactical Air Force, based on their experiences gleaned in North Africa, the 309 Polish Squadron became a fighter-reconnaissance unit and was moved to the 12 RAF Fighter Group. The provenance of the squadron continued to change and an attempt was made to make the squadron a fighter-bomber unit equipped with Hurricanes. The Hurricanes did not work out and finally the whole squadron was equipped with Mustangs and became a fighter unit.

But it cloned the 318 City of Gdansk fighter reconnaissance unit. The most experienced pilots in reconnaissance were seconded to this last-to-be-formed Polish squadron. This was formed on March 20, 1943, at Detling, Kent. The mission was to have the squadron work with the 2 Polish Army Corps. The squadron underwent many months of training in Palestine and in March 1944, having 16 Mk V Spitfires on establishment moved to Italy to join the RAF 285 Reconnaissance Wing. The Polish squadron had 22 officer-pilots, trained in fighter tactics, reconnaissance and artillery spotting. The number of Polish pilots grew well above the RAF establishment. It can only be assumed that the Poles were planning to have a second such squadron working with their ground troops. Because of this excess a number of Polish pilots were loaned to RAF squadrons which were under strength. The squadron was a completely autonomous unit, with its own 70 trucks and ability to move to a new airfield at a moment's notice. The squadron was very much in the front line, at times within German artillery range and on one occasion army engineers had to remove over 1,000 land mines from the airfield and yet only two planes were damaged when taxiing.

The squadron was blessed by luck. Only three pilots were lost and taken prisoner of war. It carried out 3,086 sorties in 1944 and 1,778 sorties in 1945. Sixty percent were artillery spotting, the rest reconnaissance and ground attack.

Invasion of Normandy

The invasion of German-occupied Normandy, codenamed Overlord, was carried out by Allied Forces on June 6, 1944, under the overall command of Gen. Dwight D. Eisenhower. The naval part of the operation was codenamed Neptune.[63]

The Poles did not participate in the first wave that stormed the beaches. But all the Polish air squadrons based in the United Kingdom took part. The Poles flew as many as four missions a day to give their land troops air support.[64] But while all the Polish squadrons took part in the air battle over Normandy only two Polish wings were specifically dedicated to the 2nd Tactical Air Force.

The 18th Fighter Sector, which consisted of three wings and a total of nine fighter squadrons, five Polish (302, 306, 308, 315 and 317), two RAF, one Belgian and one Royal New Zealand Air Force. This fighter sector was formed as early as October 14, 1943. Its original commanding officer was Colonel Rolski but it was Colonel Gabszewicz who led the squadrons in Overlord.

These two Polish wings had an actual establishment of 230 officers, 618 non-commissioned officers and 1,525 airmen, which represented close to 30 percent of the whole strength of the Polish Air Force in mid-1944. The third Polish wing, consisting of 303, 316 and 307 stayed as part of the Royal Air Force's new command — Air Defence of Great Britain — but also flew operations on behalf of the invading forces from bases in south England.

On June 6, 1944 — D-Day — the 18th Fighter Group flew four missions each and the whole group scored 30 victories becoming the top group in the Tactical Air Force. By June 11, the squadrons were operating out of field bases in Normandy.

On July 9, one of the Polish wings returned to the United Kingdom to reinforce the defenses against the attack of the German flying bombs. The 18th Fighter Sector as well as all other sectors were dissolved and all wings were placed directly under the command of 2nd Tactical.

The German flying bomb (V-1) offensive surprised and startled the British public. Coming at a time of victories, when many assumed the war would be over by the end of the year, the new horror seemed unfair and unthinkable. The British threw all their energies into combating this new terror weapon. The launchers were bombed, batteries of anti-aircraft artillery placed in southern England and fast fighter squadrons placed on standing patrols to intercept over the sea. The speed of the flying bombs did not allow for the standard radar interception and fighter squadron scramble. The Polish squadrons which took part in this operation scored a total of 190 successes, which was 10 percent of the total number shot down. Again, the friendly *Illustrated London News* carried a sympathetic story, on August 5, 1944, captioned—"Exit Two Robots. Polish Fighter Pilots in Action over the Channel." It showed one of the Polish-flown Mustangs tipping the wing of the flying bomb to send it out of control into the sea.

The Polish Sector did a good job. On June 6, they gained their first success, shooting down 30 German planes, with 306 (Torunski) and 317 (Wilenski) leading the scorers. By June 11, the squadrons were all based in Normandy. Squadron 315 (Deblin) was not to be outdone and on June 12 jumped seven Focke-Wulfs and shot down four.

Within a very short time the Germans had been swept out of the skies over Normandy. But the German ground forces had potent antiaircraft defenses. Twenty-eight Polish pilots lost their lives between June 6 and August 31, 1944.

One of these losses was Major Horbaczewski who, leading his 315 Deblin boys on a Ranger Rodeo 385 (on August 18) attacked a formation of 20 Focke-Wulfs near Beauvais. Sixteen Germans were shot down, but Horbaczewski was lost.

After the sectors were disbanded, the Polish wing left in the TAF often flew as many as four sorties a day (this was summer and the days were long). Its culminating effort was on August 17 when a total of 157 sorties were flown.

Neptune

All but one (*Garland*) of the Polish surface warships also took part in the invasion. The Polish medium cruiser, *Dragon*, was part of Task Force D and gave the Canadians artillery support while the two small destroyers, *Slazak* and *Krakowiak*, were deployed on the eastern wing of British landings near Ouistreham to cover Allied minesweepers and landing craft. But it was the two fleet destroyers, the *Blyskawica* and *Piorun*, that were involved in the most dramatic sea battle of the Neptune operations. Both Polish warships were part of the Tenth Destroyer Flotilla, which consisted of two divisions— 19th and the 20th — of which *Blyskawica* was the leader. In the famous night encounter off Ushant, the allied navies totally put to rest the German naval effort to interdict the allied landings.

The Allied command issued the following report: "This action, one of the very few which had been fought between large and modern destroyers at night during this war, effected the destruction of half the enemy's force and inflicted damage on at least one of the two who escaped. It was thus a not inconsiderable success and a useful contribution to the safety of our convoys."[65]

The Pierwsza Pancerna Enters Battle

In July 1944, the Polish Armored Division landed in Normandy as part of the Canadian First Army. The division gained battle honors all the way from Normandy though Belgium and Holland, finishing the war with the capture of Wilhemshaven. But in Polish military history it will always be associated with being the cork of the Falaise gap.[66]

Except for the parachute brigade and two training divisions, the Seventh Infantry in Egypt and the Fourth Infantry in Scotland, all other Polish army, air, and naval forces were now fully committed to the Allied cause.

7

July 1944 through December 1944

Political Background to the Warsaw Uprising

A very brief summary of the background is essential to understand the antecedents of the uprising and the Allied and Polish staff response (in London) to this tragic episode that doomed the campaign to assert Polish control in at least a part of the Polish territories.

As long as Sikorski was both commander in chief and prime minister, the London Poles had one voice which urged collaboration between the underground (Armia Krajowa) and the Soviets. At that time, the general officer commanding of the Armia Krajowa, General Rowecki, constantly argued that in view of the inimical Soviet posture to the Poles, there could be no collaboration and while no hostilities would be entered into by the Poles, there would be no attempt to assist them or collaborate with them.

The tragic death of Sikorski, and the still-perplexing betrayal of Rowecki to the Germans a short week later, changed the leadership of the Polish government and of the underground. Furthermore, Mikolajczyk and the new commander in chief, General Sosnkowski, also had different views of possible collaboration with the Soviets. Mikolajczyk, being a pragmatist, based his long-term plans and hopes for Poland on his perceived support from Churchill and was willing to sacrifice some territory for a meaningful resumption of diplomatic relations.[1] Sosnkowski saw no such hope and in his instructions to the head of the AK, General Bor-Komorowski, warned against any collaboration unless there was a prior resumption of political contacts between the Poles and the Soviets and also that it was guaranteed by Poland's only ally — the United Kingdom. In fact, Sosnkowski advanced nearly identical theses as had Rowecki originally. Paradoxically, Komorowski veered 180 degrees and was an advocate of a collaborative stance which was also in line with Mikolajczyk's position but not in line with Sosnkowski's analysis of the political situation.

One of Komorowski's major military advisers was General Tabor, who was also a strong advocate of collaboration with the Soviets and as head of the VI Section in London appeared to play a rather machiavellian role in the unfolding events.

This was all against a background of the Tehran and post–Tehran negotiations between Churchill, the British Foreign Office (they also did not always speak with an identical voice) and the Soviets.[2] For example, Churchill thought that Mikolajczyk

153

ought to dismiss Sosnkowski to please the Soviets. The British Foreign Office did not share that view and what is perplexing is that neither side seemed to realize, or even care, that the post of commander in chief was a constitutional post and could be changed only by the Polish president. Of course, Stalin urged that most of the prominent Poles be dismissed, namely the president (Raczkiewicz); the commander in chief (Sosnkowski); the minister of defence (Kukiel); the minister for foreign affairs (Romer); and even the ambassador to the Court of St. James's (Raczynski). It's an indictment of the British government's posture to their Polish ally that they apparently saw nothing bizarre or outrageous in these demands.

In the summer of 1944 the Soviets had crossed into Polish territory, even into land that they did not claim. Churchill was exerting intense pressure on Mikolajczyk to come to an accommodation with the Soviets. It was quite obvious to all, even to Mikolajczyk, that whenever he conceded a point, new ultimatums were immediately made.

Mikolajczyk was prepared to take a gamble, and on Churchill's urgings and implied promises, to give on the boundary issue to ensure a Polish government in Warsaw. The underground state was psychologically not able to comprehend that Poland's allies had, in fact, already given in on that issue, and were adamantly opposed to any such compromise.

Probably even more importantly, the overwhelming majority of the Polish armed forces were vehemently opposed to territorial concessions under pressure. So was the Polish commander in chief, Sosnkowski. On July 11, Sosnkowski flew to inspect the Polish 2 Corps in Italy. There are no archival documents to prove what is believed by some Polish historians (including the author) that in view of both his constitutional status, as responsible only to the president, and not the prime minister or government, and in view of his senior and respected status, which Mikolajczyk did not posses, Sosnkowski was prepared to dissociate both himself and the Polish 2 Corps from any act by the Polish prime minister during the latter's visit to Moscow. It should be remembered that the overwhelming rank and file of the large Polish 2 Corps in Italy were natives of eastern Poland and had already been through the Soviet gulags. They distrusted the Soviets and were not prepared to accept the loss of their homes.

As Mikolajczyk was flying to Moscow through Cairo, he was advised that the Soviets had formally recognized the Lublin Communist Committee as the provisional government of Poland. Mikolajczyk balked at continuing his trip but was again entreated, cajoled and bullied by Churchill to proceed.

The Warsaw Uprising was a political act masquerading as a military insurrection. It was a heroic effort borne of desperation in a situation which had no answer.[3] It took place after numerous attempts by various units of the AK to collaborate with the advancing Red Army and in every case, after an initial friendly military collaboration and mutual expressions of goodwill, the Poles were surrounded and their soldiers conscripted into the Russian-officered — so-called Polish — army while Polish officers were occasionally also given a choice of joining the so-called Polish People's Army but more often imprisoned in Soviet gulags. If recalcitrant, the soldiers also shared the fate of the majority of their officers. That was the reality which Rowecki had tried to prevent and about which later Sosnkowski tried to warn against.

The Warsaw Uprising, whose outcome, the destruction of the Polish underground state's leadership and complete desolation of the city and its cultural artifacts, was the worst Polish disaster of the war. Even 60 years later there is continued acrimony whether it was justified given the Soviet hostility that was demonstrated at every turn. As the old saying goes, victory has a thousand fathers but defeat is an orphan. It seems on the basis of all current historical research reasonable to state that the decision to initiate the insurrection was local, with tacit support from the Polish government and strong warnings against by General Sosnkowski. Yet, paradoxically, much of the blame is laid on his shoulders for not taking a stronger position against such operations. Critics seem to forget that the Poles were at war with Germany and that a Polish general could not, even if he completely believed the act to be folly, to order his subordinates not to fight Germans.

Just before the uprising, the famed courier from Warsaw, Jan Nowak, made the trip back to Poland with very implicit warnings to the local AK leaders that there was no chance whatsoever of the Poles getting meaningful aid from the West. Prior to leaving London, Nowak met with the Polish ambassador to the Court of St. James's, Edward Raczynski, the British ambassador to the Poles, Sir Owen O'Malley; the head of the Polish Section of SOE, Colonel Perkins; and, of course, with the Polish prime minister, Stanislaw Mikolajczyk. Nowak flew to Italy on the same plane as Sosnkowski, who was flying to hearten the 2 Polish Corps. The trip replicated the tragic trip of Sikorski in reverse, with stops at Gibraltar. But this time the crew were Poles.

After the inevitable period of waiting for good weather and complete synchronization of the receiving committee and local Polish control of a suitable landing field, Nowak was flown into Poland on the third and final Wildhorn (Mosty) operation.[4] He was able to meet with all the senior people of the AK command and the civilian delegates. He conveyed the realities and made it clear that the Poles in Warsaw could not count on support from the parachute brigade, now committed to the Allied o. de b., or any reinforcement by combat planes.

Nowak met with Jan Stanislaw Jankowski, the head of the civilian delegatura of the clandestine Polish state, who responded to the information with the statement that the news was pessimistic if not hopeless, but the underground had no choice since the Burza uprising was part of a long chain of events which started in September 1939. Jankowski opined that fighting in the city would erupt whether it was planned or not, and whether it was desirable or not, and therefore needed to be organized.

Nowak also cites General Pelczynski as stating: "I have no illusion what awaits us after the Russians enter Warsaw and we come into the open, but even if the worst fate should befall me I would prefer that to giving up without a fight. We must do our duty to the end."[5]

Pelczynski spoke like the soldier he was, but did he and did all the other senior officers have a right to gamble with a million civilians and the city?

On July 17, the "imported" Polish Communists formed the Polish Committee of National Liberation which on July 21 was formally recognized as the provisional government of Poland by the Soviets.

On July 20, there was an assassination attempt on Hitler,[6] and the Soviets broke through German defenses on the Bug, and raced for Warsaw. At the same time, the Soviets began to broadcast appeals to the citizens of Warsaw to rise up and throw off the German chains.

In this unpredictable military situation, General Bor-Komorowski, general office commanding of the AK cabled London on July 25, 1944, stating that he wished to be empowered to order an uprising at the best moment. "We are ready to fight for Warsaw at any moment. I will report the date and hour of the beginning of the fight."

On July 26, 1944, the Polish government, without the Polish commander in chief, who was in Italy, sent off a telegram to the AK stating without Sosnkowski's authorization: "At a session of the Government of the Republic, it was unanimously decided to empower you to proclaim the insurrection at a moment which you will decide as most opportune. If possible, let us know beforehand."

In Italy, Sosnkowski became concerned about the situation and cabled the AK through London:

> In the face of Soviet political pressures and known actions, a heroic uprising would be an act lacking in political value — and it could require unnecessary sacrifices. If the aim of the uprising is the occupation of part of Polish territory, it must be taken into account that in this case it will be necessary to defend Poland's sovereignty on recaptured territory, against whatever power questions this sovereignty. Remember, to put this into its proper perspective, that a heroic uprising and cooperation mean nothing in the face of Soviet lack of goodwill.[7]

Given the fact that the Poles possessed such an excellent radio system it has always been questioned why the cable was sent through London, not directly to Poland. In London, the cable was held up for 48 hours by the head of the VI Section, General Tabor. This has been one of the enigmatic issues in the history of the uprising. Presumably, General Tabor strongly identified with Mikolajczyk's desire to arrange a pragmatic relationship with the Soviets and endorsed the Polish government's authorization of July 26. The argument runs that Mikolajczyk wished to impress upon Stalin that the Polish underground was strong and loyal to the Polish government. He may have possibly hoped for that miracle of miracles that having captured Warsaw the Polish underground would be in a position to greet his arrival. Then territorial losses, unfortunate and tragic as they might be, would be compensated for by the presence of a constitutional government in Poland's capital.

There are many opinions that the order cited above is an example of prevarication. But that seems unfair. Sosnkowski could not issue an order forbidding that the Poles rise up against the Germans. That would have been militarily stupid, and politically suicidal. Neither could Sosnkowski issue an outright order for the uprising. He did what any prudent commander in chief has to do, namely outline the parameters of operations and in this case gave a major warning of the political consequences.[8]

That General Bor and his comrades reached a decision to fight seems inevitable given the close to five years of German occupation and bestiality. Perhaps the fairest statement comes from a British historian, MacKenzie, who many years later opined that "The Decision to rise had tragic consequences, but it was not irresponsibly taken."[9]

The Soviet-controlled (so-called Polish) Communist army of General Berling was fighting alongside the Soviets and supposedly helping to liberate Polish territory. For the Poles to refuse to fight would have been a terrible political and public relations defeat, one which would never be easily explained to one's own countrymen, let alone to one's allies. To sit passively while the miniscule but vociferous Communist groups liberated Warsaw and imposed their own authority was just not possible. Without direction, there was also every reason that the populace would go to the streets.

In August 1944, there were no choices. If Smigly-Rydz in early 1939 really said, "With or without ammunition, fight we must and fight we shall," then August 1944 was the time when these words were prophetically true.[10] Having embarked on a military defiance of its enemies, it was in 1944 that the Poles had to prove their resolve and did so heroically!

The issues were not merely political, as to who would get the credit for a liberation of Warsaw, though that was a vital point for the future of the country. The issue was as much the fact that a small struggling uprising would destroy the city while a well-coordinated uprising might save the historic city and its population. It was accepted, and probably correctly, that the kind of tragic arrests perpetrated on the Polish units in Lwow and Wilno would not be repeated in Warsaw, to which even Soviet greed and expansionism made no claim.

The Polish minister of war, General Kukiel, made an official request to Lord Ismay for support and the request was placed on the agenda for August 1.[11] The short memo makes certain points clear: "It looks as though there will be little hope of the Polish requests for the bombing of Warsaw, the employment of their aircraft or of all or part of the Parachute Brigade being agreed to because of the necessity of obtaining Russian approval."

But the memo does suggest a course of action which was never implemented and probably in the long run would have availed the Poles little:

> It seems, therefore, all the more important to get as much material as we can to the Poles in the shortest possible time, because it appears certain that the Poles in the Warsaw area will rise whether or not the British Chiefs of Staff or the Russians approve. I submit that we must therefore give them the best possible chance of success, or at any rate of avoiding being massacred. I feel we should stress this aspect as strongly as possible. In this connection I understand that there are no less than 250 tons of stores for the Poles already packed in containers in Italy which merely await the necessary allocation of aircraft—about 200 sorties.

On August 1, 1944, the Polish underground and the population of the city of Warsaw rose up against the Germans.

The tragedy of Warsaw was that even the most suspicious and skeptical of Soviet intentions and those most pessimistic of British support could not imagine and certainly could never have predicted the unholy alliance of the machiavellian Stalin and the rage of Hitler coupled with British impotence and Roosevelt's disinterest.

The tragedy of Warsaw struck the men of the Polish Parachute Brigade Group especially hard, because only a few months earlier they had received a flag, smuggled out of Poland, embroidered by the women of Warsaw. It was a symbolic expression of the destination of the unit and of the expectation of the citizens of Warsaw that help would come to them from the West.

For the British, the Warsaw Uprising was at best a symbolic question. From a practical point of view it had no consequence for their political or military ends. For the Polish government and the Polish military, it represented one last attempt to place a free Polish leadership in Poland and to restore sovereignty before the yoke of Nazi tyranny was replaced by Communist imperialism. This indeed was the last and final campaign of the war.

Aid to Warsaw

The Polish government and military staff undertook every effort to help Warsaw. The military assistance was directed at efforts to supply the Warsaw insurgents by air and by endeavors to have the Polish Parachute Brigade Group, or part of it, dropped to assist them.

It should also be noted that when on July 31, 1944, the Polish head of Section VI (General Tabor) requested British assistance (for Warsaw) , through his contact, Gubbins, in flying the Polish Parachute Brigade to help the insurgents, "SOE's official response was to support the idea," as well as of "of sending in a British military mission."[12] There was still considerable support, though highly qualified, for aiding the Polish insurgents. In his formal memo to the chiefs of staff, Selborne wrote:

> Two problems military and political. Britain as an ally of Russia could hardly take military action in the Russian theater of war without the concurrence of the Russian Government. In my view the attitude of the Russian Government would largely depend on the outcome of the conversations now taking place between Premier Mikolajczyk and Marshal Stalin. I know that you would wish to do anything possible that would be of assistance to Poland but I thought that you would be anxious to do nothing that would render more difficult a satisfactory outcome of the Mikolajczyk/Stalin conversations.
>
> I need hardly say that I should greatly rejoice if it were found possible to do anything to meet the Polish request. For five years their forces have been fighting alongside ours and have proved good comrades in arms. I do not think it would be militarily very difficult to despatch now to Poland a company of Polish Parachute troops. The air lift is practically within the compass of the aircraft already allocated to SOE for Polish work, and now operating on that work from Italy. The gesture would have a most important effect on the morale of the Polish Secret Army, not only as a signal of British support but also as a demonstration of the identity of the Polish Forces in Italy and England with those in Poland. I also hope that it will be possible to make a declaration concerning the Polish Secret Army analogous to that just made by General Eisenhower concerning the French Secret Army i.e. that we recognize them as an allied fighting force, and combatants under international law. This would give great satisfaction to the Poles and I hope that you will give the matter your sympathetic consideration. Logically it would be very difficult to refuse such a declaration. Our relations with the Polish Secret Army for the last four years have been precisely the same as our relations with the French Secret Army, and of the two the Polish Secret Army is certainly the best organized and most competent.[13]

On August 12, 1944, the Polish commander-in-chief, General K. Sosnkowski, initiated this exchange with a letter to Sir Alan Brooke:

The question of employing part of the Polish Paratroop Brigade in the Battle of Warsaw has not yet been decided upon. The date of the participation of this brigade in the fighting in France is approaching. Therefore, I would be much obliged to you if you would give instructions for one battalion to be diverted from operational duties in France and designated for use in Poland.

Sir Alan Brooke replied the same day:

As General Ismay informed General Kukiel in a letter of August 2nd, we had regretfully to decide against sending part of the Polish Parachute Brigade to Warsaw. It is not possible for us to find the necessary transport aircraft to fly in a unit and maintain it in the Warsaw area. Large numbers of transport aircraft would be required for this purpose and these could not be spared at this critical stage of the campaign in the West.

I would like to assure you that we are doing all that is humanly possible.[14]

On the 13th, the Polish commander in chief responded:

As regards the Polish Parachute Brigade, this unit was formed in accordance with British-Polish understanding, with the aim that their main task would be to give support to the rising in Poland, when the need should occur. It would, therefore, not be easy to explain to these parachutists that they must fight on another front at the time when their brothers are giving their lives in the barricades of Warsaw. I am afraid that a crisis in morale may occur in the ranks of the brigade which could deprive the unit of its fighting value. I fear that acts of desperation may ensue. You, as a soldier, will understand and appreciate my fears.

In the light of the above, I will ask you kindly to reconsider the question of using the brigade for assistance to Warsaw. I suggest the use of one battalion of the unit, or at least one company duly reinforced with heavy weapons. This, I think, would be the minimum capable of dissipating to a certain extent the disquieting adverse atmosphere now prevailing amongst the rank and file of the brigade, which its commander has quite recently reported to me.

I urge, therefore, that in consideration of this situation, as well as in the interests of my suffering country, you would assist the Polish soldier to resolve the anxieties which are besetting him today, and aid me in contriving an honorable way to solve an extremely complicated problem. Would you also find it possible to take into account, while considering your decision, the evidence of good will shown by the Polish Government and myself in having altered the initial arrangements regarding the employment of the brigade and placing it at the disposal of the Supreme Allied Commander.

Last night's flights to Poland, so far as I am informed, were carried out by 11 crews. Of these, I understand only 5 had the task of dropping supplies to Warsaw.

I am sure you will realise the insufficiency of such scale. It is essential that these flights continue. The speediest possible reinforcements of the Polish crews in Italy by sending there the whole of 300 Squadron is, in my view, the only way to meet the existing bitter necessities.[15]

The Poles were appealing to the gentleman's honor. At the same time on August 13, the Polish Parachute Brigade went on a 24-hour fast to protest the lack of help to Warsaw.

The British reply of August 15 was one more polite, but negative, letter. Sosnkowski then wrote a long, impassioned, and bitter letter on August 20 which outlined the issues. Sosnkowski wrote that all interventions on the part of the Poles, and he enumerated them one by one, including the Polish minister of National Defence, the Polish chief of staff, and the various members of the Polish government, had produced "no tangible results." Sosnkowski outlined the Polish postulates: a continuous supply of arms and ammunition to besieged Warsaw, a temporary diversion of Polish crews from 300 Squadron to the Polish Special Duties flight (1586) , the despatch of the Polish Parachute Brigade or at least part of it to Warsaw, the bombing of specific targets in or near Warsaw and the conferment of combatant status on the soldiers of the Home Army. Sosnkowski concluded his letter with a reminder to the British of their obligations to Poland under the provisions of the Polish-United Kingdom Treaty of Mutual Assistance signed in late August 1939:

> The rising of the Polish Underground Army in Warsaw, as an integral part of the Polish Armed Forces fighting side by side with the Allies, is an operation of a military character, directed against the German aggressor and falls clearly under Art. I of the Agreement of Mutual Assistance between the United Kingdom and Poland, signed on 25th August 1939. The two contracting parties are bound, by the provisions of this Article, to afford, one to the other, all the support and assistance in their power. The armed struggle of the Polish Forces, developed since the fall of France and cooperating with Great Britain on land, sea, and in the air, continuously since September 1939, is based primarily on this Alliance.

Sosnkowski then pointed out the fact that the Poles had lost 1,770 air crew or 60 percent of their air personnel in the Allied bomber offensive and had never hesitated in pursuing the common cause. He finished with this admonition:

> The eventual second fall of Warsaw now, in the fifth year of the war, if due to a lack of necessary assistance, would, as I have already mentioned in the previous correspondence, adversely affect not only public opinion in Poland, but also the feelings of all Poles abroad; undoubtedly it will not remain without echo throughout the world, and in Europe in particular.[16]

In this last comment, Sosnkowski was deluding himself or was naive, since the world before, then and since has been singularly impervious to moral issues.

The Polish Special Duties Flight —1586 — was part of the RAF 148 Squadron. Its strength was officially established by RAF regulations at six crews plus three reserve. But the British tolerated a certain increase over the establishment.

The Poles, also by formal agreement, flew missions to other countries and the RAF crews occasionally flew to Poland. The actual track record of successful drops in Poland showed a slant toward the Poles as did the number of planes lost.

A very brief word needs to be said about the focus of Allied air operations based in Italy. The Mediterranean Allied Air Force was obviously supporting the local drive up the Italian peninsula, but preparations were in process for the invasion of the south of France, Dragoon.[17] The special duties squadrons were very active in supporting the anti–German partisan groups in northern Italy and the Tito groups in Yugoslavia. This led to the formation of the so-called Balkan Air Force (Air Vice Marshal W. Elliot in command) which integrated all the activity on behalf of the partisans. The Polish flight at times — too often, the Poles would argue — was assigned to aid the Tito groups rather than the Polish AK. The overall RAF command in the area was held by Air Marshal Sir John Slessor who was subordinate to the American Lieutenant General I.C. Eaker who was general office commanding the Mediterranean Allied Air Force.[18]

On June 14, Major E. Arciuszkewicz took over command of Polish Flight 1586 from Major Krol.

The uprising in Warsaw caught the Polish special duties flight based near Brindisi, Italy, at the end of a long spring and early summer season of very active operations. The official establishment of the flight was a mere six crews. There were six airworthy planes, three Liberators and three used-up Halifaxes; there was nothing in reserve. Not all crews were checked out on both the Halifaxes and the Liberators. This, to some extent, curtailed the flexibility of arranging missions.

This was the actual number of special flights flown by the Poles in June:

> June 21   seven Halifax sorties to Italy and two to Greece
> June 22   six Halifax sorties to Italy and one to Yugoslavia
> June 23   six Halifax sorties to Italy and one to Yugoslavia.

The Polish flight commander, Major Arciuszewicz, refused to fly a fourth day of consecutive operations as contrary to RAF regulations. The RAF station commander, Group Captain Rankink, grounded Arciuszkewicz and attempted to take away his command. But this was no longer 1940 in the United Kingdom, when arbitrary RAF officers ruled the newcomers as was their custom with colonials. The Poles refused to acknowledge this order and all the Polish personnel ignored it. This led to an investigation by Mediterranean Allied Air Force HQ and the Polish Air Force liaison officer, Colonel Brzezina. The authorities upheld the Polish flight commander, but the ill will must have persisted. Ultimately the Poles were more dependent on their RAF infrastructure than the British on the Polish flight.

Anyway, the Poles were given a respite of two nights before sorties resumed:

> June 25   Six Halifaxes and two Liberators, and again
> June 26   same number of sorties.

In the whole of June, the Poles flew 109 missions to Yugoslavia, 55 to northern Italy, three to Bulgaria, and two to Greece. There were no losses but it should be noted there were no flights to Poland even though the SOE archives suggest that there were over 200 tons of containerized material pending dropping in Poland.[19] The usual contents of these containers were a mixture of captured German infantry equipment and ammunition and British antitank weapons (piats), light machine guns (Bren guns) as well as grenades and signals equipment. Whenever possible the containers were also stuffed with medical supplies and even luxury items like chocolates and coffee.

This was not a question of British passivity to the Polish issue, but a reflection that the northern Italian, Yugoslav and Greek fronts were viewed as higher priorities. It can be accepted that the Polish crews, who had all completed their obligatory 25 bomber missions from the United Kingdom in Polish bomber squadrons and had survived a nearly one in three actuarial chance, and had then volunteered for the Polish flight to aid their Polish comrades, were at best disgusted and even angry.

In July, flights to Poland were resumed but the statistics again show the thrust of the Allied effort. Seventy-one flights went to northern Italy, 37 to Poland, 23 to Yugoslavia and three to Greece.

At the end of July 1944, a number of Polish crews had reached that airman's nirvana — a completion of a tour of operational duty, and by regulations, to say nothing of common sense — leave. The Poles had signaled their chief of Sixth Section (responsible for coordinating air drops to Poland) that their official establishment would be down to six crews by August 1 and four by the end of August.

On August 1, even before the flight was aware of the Warsaw Uprising, the flight was further depleted when a Polish plane was shot down on a mission to Hungary. Thus on the first day of the uprising, the Poles had only five crews. To compound the problem, as experienced crews were rotating out, the new crews who had volunteered for this duty came from the Polish Lancaster Squadron and were not familiar or happy with the Halifax aircraft and had problems with the new demands on navigation. The various navigation aids that the RAF Bomber Command now utilized were not available for flights to Poland. This was not a problem for the flights to Warsaw, since the clandestine radio broadcast all day and night and the Allied crews used it as the final radio beacon. But flights to small, out-of-the-way villages where reception committees waited patiently, sometimes for weeks on end, were a navigational challenge even for Polish crews.

Astral navigation was not always of help due to weather conditions and navigator inexperience, and finally, in the last stages of the sortie, the planes had to make visual contact with the reception zone. The weather had to be close to perfect.

The Warsaw Uprising lasted just over 60 days, and during this time 60 nights in theory could have been utilized for flights to Warsaw. Clearly that is an impossibility given bad weather and the many nights when the moon was full. In retrospect, 27 nights were unsuitable due to the above factors.

The following is based on a number of historic accounts and the reports of the RAF Command in the Mediterranean theater of operations.[20]

On August 4, the whole British RAF 148 Squadron of 15 planes, including the Poles, prepared for a flight to Warsaw. At the last moment, Air Marshal Slessor rescinded the order but allowed the mission to territories in Poland but outside of Warsaw itself. But the commander of the flight, Major Arciuszkiewicz, got four crews to volunteer to fly to Warsaw. The Polish mission was successful but the RAF crews attempting to drop supplies into Poland took heavy losses. Four were shot down and one crashed on landing at base.

Not surprisingly, given the Polish "independence" and RAF losses, Slessor ordered all flights to Poland to be placed on hold.

This order was forcefully challenged by the Polish military in London. All efforts were made to get help and to get Slessor to rescind his order. Finally, under intense pressure from the highest political centers of the British government, Slessor, with understandable poor grace, allowed Polish volunteers to fly to Warsaw.[21]

Four Polish crews (Slessor reported only three) flew the mission on August 8 and all returned. Slessor telegrammed on August 9 to Chief of Air Staff:

> Three Poles went to Warsaw last night and dropped supplies on the city. A good many nightfighters were seen and flak experienced at Warsaw, but they got away with it. A gallant show. They will send five more tonight. They are pressing me to send 148 Squadron also. But I intend to adhere to my original decision and not to send any British Halifaxes till last quarter of moon, night of the 11th or 12th of August. A few aircraft on a show like this will sometimes get away with it. Larger numbers will not. Latest effort was a personal signal Sosnkowski to Wilson (which latter has ignored) asking him to order me to continue flights and implying that I am ignorant of the military and moral implications. He probably imagines last night's flights were due to his intervention with Wilson. I gather Sosnkowski has got the sack but I hope further political intervention by Poles in London may be discouraged as much as possible. I am sure it is just as much a nuisance to you as to me.[22]

Slessor must have been aware of the great efforts by the British to get rid of Sosnkowski, who represented a moral force that haunted the British conscience. It is unclear whether the rumors of British pressure on the Polish president to dismiss Sosnkwoski were that rife among the British, or whether Slessor became aware that Raczkiewicz had replaced Sosnskowski with Arciszewski as his presidential successor. This move actually strengthened Sosnkowski's role as commander in chief since the Polish underground parties and the Polish prime minister had for considerable time urged a separation of the two roles. But the die was cast and now British efforts would be directed as much at the Polish general as at aiding the Poles.

On August 11, Churchill visited Naples and met with General Wilson and Air Marshal Slessor. Churchill instructed that all possible aid be given to the insurgents and that bombers of the strategic bomber force, namely, 205 Group, also carry missions to Poland, albeit not always to Warsaw.[23]

On August 23, while still in Italy, Churchill cabled his minister of information, Bracken, as follows:

> Is there any stop on the publicity for the facts about the agony of Warsaw, which seems, from the papers to have been practically suppressed? It is not for us to cast reproaches on the Soviet Government, but surely facts should be allowed to speak for themselves? There is no need to mention the strange and sinister behaviour of the Russians, but is there any reason why the consequences of such behaviour should not be made public?

The British Foreign Office analyzed the situation and came up with this indictment of Churchill as the culprit for this mass media posture:

> Any intelligent Russian reader of the British Press would, I fear, draw the conclusion that Stalin could do almost anything he liked with Mr. Mikolajczyk and the Poles without arousing any unfortunate reactions in this country.
>
> The Prime Minister's remarks about Poland in the debate on August 2nd in fact gave the press very much the line they have been following, that the Russians are reasonable people; that the National Committee and the Polish

Government are to be regarded on the same level, and that a fusion on the terms decided by Marshal Stalin is really our goal. This is not quite the position of His Majesty's Government but it is, I fear, the deduction drawn from the Prime Minister's statement.

These minutes were reviewed by Sargent who added:

I am sure nothing we can say to the press would persuade them to give direct support at the present juncture to the Polish Government. But I should have thought we might have pressed them to publicize the gallant fight which the Polish Army is putting up, especially in Warsaw. At present they are playing this down almost ostentatiously.[24]

Churchill attempted to get Roosevelt to join him in interceding with Stalin for aid on behalf of Warsaw's insurgents. To no avail. Roosevelt responded to Churchill on August 26, 1944, by refusing to join Churchill's rationalizing the "current American conversations on the subject of the subsequent use of other Russian bases." Roosevelt clearly wished to ensure that the Frantic operation not be jeopardized and extended for shuttle bombing against Japan in the future.

Churchill interceded again and Roosevelt responded on September 5:

Replying to your telegrams, I am informed by my Office of Military Intelligence that the fighting Poles have departed Warsaw and that the Germans are now in full control. The problem of relief for the Poles in Warsaw has therefore unfortunately been solved by delay and by German action, and there now appears to be nothing we can do to assist them.[25]

Churchill leaves this absurd message without a comment, because nothing that could be said would do justice. In 1941, Stalin stated that the murdered Polish officers must have escaped to Mongolia. It is unclear to where Roosevelt thought the "fighting Poles" had departed.

On returning to London, at the War Cabinet meeting of September 4 Churchill writes about the meeting that he could not remember "any occasion when such deep anger was shown by all our members." Churchill continues in his memoirs:

I should have liked to say, we are sending our aeroplanes to land in your territory, after delivering supplies to Warsaw. If you do not treat them properly all our convoys will be stopped from this moment by us. But the reader of these pages in after years must realize that everyone always has to keep in mind the fortunes of millions of men fighting in a world wide struggle, and that terrible and even humbling submissions must at times be made to the general aim.[26]

Attempts were made to drop supplies in close proximity to Warsaw and to have Polish AK personnel smuggle the arms into the city. In the first days of the uprising this was actually a very reasonable option, but with each passing day the German blockade of the insurgents became tighter.

Between August 11 and 18, due to favorable weather conditions, the Poles carried out operations each night. To reflect on the stress and wear, each Warsaw flight was an endurance test of nearly 11 hours, in unpressurized planes over enemy-held territory.

An American-built bomber (B-24, Liberator) of the Polish Special Duties Flight, based in Italy (summer 1944). The plane was flown by the crew of Kapitan pilot Zbigniew Szostak. On the night of August 4, 1944, this crew carried out one of the first support flights to the insurgents of Warsaw. On the night of August 14, the crew were lost over occupied Poland after repeated drops to the Home Army. (Courtesy of the Polish Institute and SikorskiMuseum, London.)

After one day's break another eight nights of consecutive flights were carried out. The RAF squadron also attempted to aid the insurgents of Warsaw as did the Royal South African Air Force.[27]

A short list of the initial flights is included here:

8/9 August: 3 Polish aircraft. supplies dropped and all returned.
9/10 August: 4 Polish aircraft. ditto.
10/11/12 August: no operations. adverse weather.
12/13 August: 11 aircraft (mixed British and Polish). 6 successful enthusiastically received by Warsaw's insurgents.
13/14 August: 26 aircraft. successful drops from 8 aircraft.
14/15 August: 26 aircraft (also mixed) 7 crews lost. Eleven drops successful.[28]

On August 15, Air Marshal Slessor reported in his summary that planes from all of his units had the following results:

Twelve successes, six failures, eight missing. In all cases the target was Warsaw. There were no other operations to Poland. Last nights operations to Warsaw.

26 despatched. 11 successful. 8 missing including 6 Liberators of 205 Group. One of 148 Squadron and one Pole. A great deal of flak experienced and night fighters seen. Am going Bari to-day to see Elliott but the two squadrons of 205 Group have lost 25% of their strength in two nights and it is obvious we cannot go on at this rate of loss which fully justifies my misgivings about the whole operation.

I drafted a reply to Polish President which I understand has gone home as chain 42 and 43 to Deputy PM (comment not yet received) and Foreign Secretary, but am told that my last sentence was omitted which was to the effect that: I must warn you that we cannot maintain these arduous operations indefinitely on a large scale.

In view of last night's experience something to that effect must be included. Colonel Kent is away so I cannot consult him. Will signal you further later in the day. Are the Russians doing anything at all? We have now lost 16 heavy bombers and crews trying to help Warsaw which I imagine is about one for every ton of supplies that has reached the Underground Army.[29]

1. Result of operations to Warsaw night 15/15. Nine aircraft despatched to three dropping points in reserve outside Warsaw. Five successful. All returned safely. To-night sixteen are detailed to four dropping zones in same area. Field reports two crews missing night 14/15 baled out and are safe one with Poles and one with Russians.

2. Eaker has heard from Walsh in Moscow that frantic[30] six scheduled for to-day from UK has been cancelled by Russians apparently on grounds that they did not agree with target. I wonder if target was supply Warsaw.

3. You know we are continuing to extend full assistance to Russians in their activities to Jugoslavia. Ten Dakota loads of medical personnel and stores are due to arrive from Russia to-night. We are also helping them shuttle operation with B 25s which I feel would be much better employed supplying Warsaw. Difficult to resist conviction that Russian failure to supply Warsaw is deliberate policy.

On August 17, Slessor cabled:

Eighteen aircraft dispatched, eight successful, six missing including four Liberators of 205 Group and two Poles of 1586. This is a second occasion in three nights in which about 30% of the force despatched has failed to return and our losses in 13 night operations to Poland this month have amounted to 21 lost, three destroyed on landing owing to flak damage, and many damaged out of 113 despatched. I cannot possibly go on at this rate and have instructed Elliot to stop operations to Poland. You will note that this rate of loss was not on Warsaw itself but on woods outside, of which value to the underground can only be rated as better than nothing. The fact must be faced that unless supplies can be sent by say from the UK or by the Russians, the Underground Army is beyond our help. The Prime Minister has been informed, and I understand has accepted the position but this should not be taken from me as he is signaling London himself today.[31]

Kalinowski writes that just in August the Poles carried out 97 flights of which 80 were to Warsaw, three to other drop zones in Poland and 14 to northern Italy. Eight Polish crews were lost, seven on missions to Warsaw.[32]

On September 2, Evill (vice chief of air staff) cabled Slessor from London stating that the British were being "pressured" by Polish authorities to take action and that to alleviate the shortage of aircraft nine Halifaxes had been dispatched and eight more would be withdrawn from Squadron 161. The cable concludes that "We must rely on you however as soon as moon and other conditions permit to try further operations and possibly higher dropping. If these prove successful and you are satisfied that this is a reasonable operation we hope you will again employ British crews."[33]

The British had now developed a barometric parachute opener which allowed air drops from a higher, and thus safer, ceiling, but which alleviated the wide dispersal of air drops. The parachutes were aimed, in some ways, like old-fashioned bombing runs, and opened only at a low altitude, optimizing the reception by the intended recipients.

Slessor, under heavy pressure from his political superiors who in turn were under intense moral pressure from the Polish government, agreed that Polish crews could volunteer for what the British correctly considered to be suicidal missions.

Only a third of the supplies actually fell into the hands of the Poles. On top of that the British were bedeviled by a shortage of suitable planes and the offer of the nine Halifaxes was not well received as Slessor considered them completely unsuitable for such long operations. London also assured Slessor that he was being relieved of any responsibility for losses incurred by the Polish flight.

On September 8, Slessor again cabled the air ministry at Whitehall. He objected to the Halifax fitted with Merlin 20s as unsuitable. He also advised London that all his Halifax planes were due for a major inspection and were deemed dangerous to fly. He further told London that the Halifax situation in squadron 148 and flight 1586 (Polish) was serious and then went on to say:

> Understand from Eaker that Spaatz and Eisenhower are prepared to release U.S. Liberator special duty group to this theater if we can use it. The difficulty and delay in shipping out ground echelons is such that Eaker and I do not think this desirable at this stage of the war. But I suggest this U.S. Group should take over such commitments as may remain at Tempsford, and that you should send out S.D. Halifax II and IIA with experienced crews to build up 148 and 1586. We could take and make good use of 16 at once.

Slessor then recommended that if the war was prolonged beyond the winter, Stirlings would need to be brought into service with special duty squadrons.[34] This cautionary warning was undoubtedly not related to the Polish situation but the British were short of planes and Slessor was being a good staffer and giving his superiors a "heads up."

In return, Slessor was reassured that the Halifax planes being dispatched to Italy had plenty of hours of operation left, and was advised that Tempsford was being equipped with Sterlings (not a happy time for the Tempsford squadron which dreaded flying these planes) and that the Italian theater would just have to accept and do the best they could. In retrospect, it not absolutely clear whether Slessor was in fact convinced that the Halifax planes being sent to him were dangerous and unsuitable, or whether he was to some extent protecting his units, including the Polish flight, from what he perceived to be complete operational folly and near suicide.

There has to be some suspicion of that because Slessor reacts in a very angry and undignified manner to a cable dated September 19 from London, which stated that Rayski "has suggested that the Americans be asked to transfer up to twelve Liberators from Fifteenth Air Force to 1586 Flight. As operations to Warsaw area are purely supply dropping these aircraft may be suitable without modification and would tide over present period." Slessor responded immediately on September 20:

> 1. Your AX 449 19 Sept. Do not agree Rayski's suggestion and am not clear who made it to you. I cannot understand this Warsaw business. Should have thought even a Pole might be capable of hoisting(?) in that it does not make sense to send aircraft from Iceland to drop supplies in Mayfair when the Russians, who now appear to be cooperating, have their forward troops in Southwark and aerodromes in Middlesex.[35]
>
> 2. Fortunately the weather is limiting the extent to which we are able to expend effort and aircrews lives on this folly. But should like to be clear that I continue to exact maximum effort including division of Heavies from Strategic bombing on supply to Warsaw in present conditions in the face of our experience of the very high casualty rate involved.[36]

Slessor was reacting to the one and only American shuttle expedition which took place on September 18, after many discussions and negotiations with the Soviets. That day, 107 Flying Fortresses under the command of Col. Carl Truesdell, USAAF, flew over Warsaw and successfully delivered 388 containers of supplies. The Americans flew on to a Soviet landing base and after a number of days returned through Italian bases to the United Kingdom. As a result of this, the Soviets cancelled all such future shuttle flights, including bombing missions of Germany, alleging that they needed those bases for their own air operations.[37]

In September, the Polish flight managed only 42 operations. Seventeen were to Warsaw, all the others to other countries. Eight crews were lost. The last flight to Warsaw was made on the night of September 20–21.

During the totality of the Warsaw Uprising, the Polish flight lost 17 crews. Only two Polish crews survived the whole period of the uprising. It can be stated categorically that the only reason why the casualty rate among Polish (and also Royal Air Force) crews was not higher was quite simply due to the shortage of suitable and airworthy aircraft. Whether this was due to the actual shortage of suitably engined planes, as the British averred, or whether this problem, which was also confirmed by Polish air experts, was magnified to prevent unnecessary loss of life will probably never be known.

While the Polish and Allied crews were gallantly attempting to do the impossible, the Polish Air Force commander, Gen. Mateusz Izycki, in London did his best to strengthen the Polish flight and its capabilities through a number of contingencies.

It was proposed that the only remaining Polish four-engined (Lancaster) squadron (300) be moved to Italy. It was also urged that seven crews of the Polish Coastal Command Squadron be seconded to the Polish flight and its establishment raised to a squadron. The Polish commander also tried to get permission to move four replacement crews, intended for the 300 Squadron, to reinforce the Polish flight in Italy.

The British Air Ministry denied all these transfers, but eventually, under political pressure, presumably from Churchill, permission was granted. Furthermore a number of staff and liaison as well as training crews were recalled as well as Polish crews of transport command from Canada.

Finally, the Polish flight had a relative plethora of crews but most were not well integrated together and still had to be trained on the Halifaxes.

But the most serious problem was lack of planes. On August 17, the Poles had six planes ready for operations and 37 in various stages of repair. The British 148 Squadron had only three operational planes.

In October, well after the demise of the uprising, the Poles resumed flights to Poland, but obviously not to Warsaw. The Poles also flew missions to Austria, Czechoslovakia, Yugoslavia, Bulgaria and Crete.

Finally, ironically, on November 7 the British Air Ministry acceded to persistent Polish requests and the Polish flight was approved as a squadron and given the old number 301. The final flight mission to Poland took place on December 28, 1944. A total of 55 flights were made to Poland between October and December as well as 222 to other countries between October and February 1945, when the squadron was moved to transport command.

The Polish Special Duties Flight 1586 and its evolving successor, Squadron 301, delivered 292 tons of equipment to the Polish AK. At the same time it delivered 1,284 tons of material to other countries.

During its existence it lost 167 crew members, with 18 missing and 49 taken prisoner of war. This represented 33 full crew complements. Given the fact that for most of the time the official establishment of the unit was six crews with four in reserve this was a 150 percent loss ratio.

Before the Polish tragedy had run its course, on September 15, the commander in chief, General K. Sosnkowski, gave the Polish unit the honour of being called the Defenders of Warsaw.

That may have just about been his last order, because on September 25 the Polish president, under heavy pressure from the British and from the Polish prime minister, requested and reluctantly accepted Sosnkowski's resignation.

On October 2, Warsaw capitulated.

The disaster of the loss of life and cultural artifacts probably will never be remedied. But the destruction of the Warsaw-based AK removed the last, most patriotic segment of the Polish population that would have undoubtedly strongly resisted Communist takeover. Granted military status, the Poles were taken to prisoner of war camps in Germany, where they were subsequently liberated by the Western Allies. Most never returned to Poland.

In view of the plans of Oddzial III for a general uprising in Poland, it is vital to emphasize that the Warsaw Uprising was neither part of this proposed countrywide revolt, nor did its tragic capitulation end the principle of this Polish option. But with the core leadership in German captivity, the plan just faded away like the proverbial old soldier.

The Western world was stunned or embarrassed by Warsaw's tragedy. A debate took place in the House of Commons. Churchill said little, while Eden attempted facile diplomatic acrobatics.[38]

Polish Parachute Brigade in Action

While Warsaw was fighting, the Polish Parachute Brigade, under the command of Major General Sosabowski, originally destined for operations in Poland, took part in the tragic fiasco of the Arnhem drop.[39]

Between June 1944 and September 1944, the Polish Parachute Brigade Group was placed on alert on a number of occasions. The Poles were part of the Allied Airborne Army, commanded by Gen. Lewis H. Brereton.[40] This consisted of two airborne corps. The American corps was commanded by Gen. Mathew B. Ridgway and comprised the 101st and 82nd. The British Corps was commanded by Lt. Gen. Frederick Arthur "Boy" Browning, and consisted of the British 1st Airborne (General Urquhart) and the 6th Airborne Division and the Polish Brigade. The two American and the British 6th Division had both taken part in the invasion of Normandy and were both bloodied. But the Americans were placed in the o. de b. of the Allied Airborne Army, while the British 6th was, in essence, put in reserve. One can only assume that the shortage of men which was to plague the British in the last year of the war may have contributed to this situation.

The Allied Airborne Army was a potential strategic force and was nourished for the one final decisive offensive. With this strategic goal and the existence of such a well-trained force it is not surprising that many plans for its use had been made. For the British of the British Airborne Corps there was a sense that the war was somehow going to end before they had a chance to be at the "party." The speed with which the Germans folded after the battle of Falaise led to each plan being cancelled. Transfigure was to take place near Rambouillet to help liberate Paris; then Linnet in Belgium; and Linnet II to help the Americans bogged down at Aachen. The last was fiercely opposed by Montgomery and also by General Browning, who was relieved of his command by Brereton. Eisenhower, seeking consensus, cancelled Linnet II and then Brereton relented and offered Browning command of Comet. In turn, the operation elicited strong objections from Sosabowski, who demanded written orders from his superior, General Browning. The plan was reconsidered and the two American divisions were added to the next planned operation. The situation became like a Greek tragedy with the inevitability of the airborne troops being used but disagreement about how and where.[41]

There was also the problem between the Poles and their British superior. General Sosabowski stated that his brigade would not be ready for brigade-strength operations until August 1 while Browning demanded readiness to be achieved on July 1, categorically stating that he would be the sole judge of the combat readiness of the Polish brigade. He also offered his opinion (which did not reassure the Poles) to the effect that the Poles were already better prepared than the British at Sicily in 1943, which had been a disaster. As in a Greek tragedy the omens continued to be dark. On July 8, two American transport planes carrying Polish paratroopers on exercise collided and 28 Poles were killed.

The only "party" that the Poles wished for was to fly to Warsaw. One of the diaries has the following poignant comment:

> During the first days of August 1944 the whole brigade took part in brigade strength parachute drop and also participated in other maneuvers to hone the

unit prior to action. It was obvious to all that the brigade would see combat in a short time. We all considered and argued amongst ourselves as to where and when that drop would take place. The wish of us all was that we would go to Warsaw. The heart and minds of all us soldiers, particularly those of the Parachute Brigade, were consumed by Warsaw's tragedy; everybody wanted to help. The privilege of fighting in the ranks of its defenders was our most heartfelt desire.

However, the plans for Market-Garden were not cancelled. The Polish brigade, consisting of just over 2,000 officers and men, was assigned 114 planes and 45 Horsa gliders. The brigade consisted of three paratroop battalions and supporting services. The fourth battalion had been dissolved due to manpower shortages in order to bring the three other battalions up to relative strength. Even so, each battalion only had 565 officers and men, about 60 short of the establishment.

The British plans for the Polish brigade can only be characterized as militarily absurd, but it is possible that the intent was not military but primarily political. This operation took place in the middle of the Warsaw Uprising and there was intense Polish pressure to have at the very least a small, symbolic part of the brigade parachuted into Warsaw or, more reasonably, into its environs. Using the whole brigade and making its importance so vital to Allied success, was the best argument for not considering the Polish request.

There is the possibility of another, very human, reason for this insistence on the Poles as being part of the Allied Airborne Army. The American Corps had two battle-hardened and resolute divisions, the 101st and 82nd, commanded by a parachute veteran — Ridgeway. The British Corps, commanded by Browning, consisted solely of the British 1st Airborne (Urquhart) and the Polish brigade. Without the Poles, the British Corps, commanded by a lieutenant general, would have been a rather anemic and grandiosely termed organization.

The orders for the Poles caused considerable consternation. The whole glider component of the Polish Parachute Brigade Group, carrying all of its anti-tank batteries as well as some component groups of the Polish Brigade Headquarters, particularly Polish liaison officers and signals, was to be flown on the second and third days of the operation and to land north of the Rhine, within the perimeter already held by the British First Airborne Division. Thus, by British staff planning, the Polish Parachute Brigade was being deprived of its anti-tank artillery. The Polish brigade was also deprived of its small American pack howitzers which were sent by the sea train and never took part in the operations.

The orders for the rest of the Polish Parachute Brigade Group, consisting exclusively of riflemen and engineers, were to drop and capture the south end of the Arnhem bridge, whose north end was to be held by the British Parachute Brigade of the First Airborne Division. This drop was planned for the third day of operation. The Poles were then to march over the bridge to reinforce the British perimeter instead of anchoring the south connection until the arrival of the 30th Corps. This was another absurdity. Why air drop infantry south of a bridge merely to have them march over it?

There was a pervasive sense of dismay and impending disaster which greeted these orders in the Polish brigade.

The first Polish glider component, consisting of 10 gliders which took off from Manston, landed on the British-held perimeter, north of the Rhine, without loss on the second day of the operation, September 18. This glider component carried seven anti-tank guns (six pounders), but with only two gunners each. The rest of the artillery personnel were to be parachuted in following days. The guns went straight into action near Oosterbeek, close to the now-famous Hartenstein Hotel.

On September 19, the second Polish glider component, consisting of 35 gliders carrying eight anti-tank guns (this being the full brigade complement of anti-tank artillery) and part of the headquarters of the brigade and of the three infantry battalions, took off and was caught in the air by German fighters. It landed in an area which was only minimally protected on one side by British troops. Five of the guns were lost and casualties among the troops heavy. Those that survived the landing were dispersed to support the defense perimeter of the British Airborne Division. The baptism by fire had begun. Brigadier Urquhart, the British commander, in his intelligence summary writes, "Glider elements of Polish Para Bde landed on LZ (L) but was very heavily opposed from ground and air and suffered severe casualties." Things began to go wrong for the Allies. Bad weather, which delayed the departure of the rest of the Polish Parachute Brigade, also interfered with supply drops to the British Airborne Division and did not allow for Allied air support. The adverse weather and the now-near-legendary ability of German units to counterattack allowed the enemy to keep control of the south end of the Arnhem bridge. This led to a change of orders for the Poles who had been delayed in departure. The new task was to still land south of the river, but closer to Driel and to capture the ferry. The British were unaware that the previous day the ferry had floated down river after damage to its moorings.

On September 21, the Polish paratroopers boarded their planes for take-off at 1400 hours. Sosabowski was very pessimistic about the whole British plan and was not the only one to view Browning's behavior as cavalier. There was a singular shortage of planes and gliders. This shortage forced the British to land their forces in a number of waves, a no-no in airborne operations. Yet, General Browning commandeered 38 gliders just to fly his own corps staff into Holland. These gliders could have been used to inject the Poles on the first day south of the Arnhem bridge. It might have allowed the British division and Poles to actually capture the bridge and hold it until the somewhat leisurely pace of the completely unprepared-for fording British 30th Corps reached it.[42]

At 1635 on September 21, the American planes carrying the Poles reached the projected landing zone, and the Poles landed on a field lightly held by German infantry — not by the British, as was the intelligence summary. The Polish brigade suffered few casualties and proceeded to dig in. The Germans attempted to make sense of this operation and came to the logical but erroneous conclusion that this was an Allied attempt to capture the south end of bridge. Luckily for the Poles, a small German force consisting of regular Wermacht infantry, airmen, sailors and Dutch SS — Sperverrband Harzer — was marched to confront the Poles.

The landing zone was a flat field traversed by drainage ditches which made movement difficult but gave the Germans a good field of fire. The Poles put up smoke grenades. After landing, General Sosabowski realized that most of his First and part of his Third Battalion were missing (these were on the 41 planes recalled due to bad weather). On that first day in the landing zone, General Sosabowski had fewer than 1,000 men under his command with no artillery or anti-tank guns and separated from the rest of the British army. The Poles were unable to establish radio contact with the British Airborne. Also their patrols did not find the ferry in Driel. At 2300 hours, the Polish liaison officer with the headquarters of the Airborne, Lt. Zwolenski, swam the river and gave Sosabowski a summary of the near-tragic situation faced by the British. Zwolenski then swam back to alert the British that the Poles would try to ford the river that very night. Also that day, the forward elements of the British 30 Corps, 5th Battalion of the Duke of Cornwall's Light Infantry, part of the 43 Wessex Division, reached the Poles. The British helped the Poles beat back sporadic German attacks, but had no fording equipment.

The Polish engineers, with great initiative, scrounged among the downed planes and pulled out some of the round aircraft rescue dinghies. These were utilized in addition to some wood rafts, quickly constructed on September 22, to cross the river. All these preparations were made while under continuous harassing fire from German artillery and mortars. When the Poles attempted to cross the river they were met with a hail of mortar and machine gun fire which allowed only one company (8th Company, Third Battalion) to make it across the river. The circular shape of the dinghies and makeshift rafts made from doors etc., as well as the fast current of the river, made ferrying extremely difficult. The ferrying went on till all the dinghies were sunk.

On September 23, the commanding officer of the First Battalion of the Polish Parachute Brigade, still in England, was able to centralize his unit and the remnants of the Third Battalion, whose flight had also been aborted, on one airfield and the 600 or so strong unit was dropped by parachute within the perimeter of the American 82nd Airborne Division.

During the night of September 23, another attempt was made by the Polish troops to aid their British and Polish colleagues on the north side of the river. The British (30th Corps) were now able to provide some larger dinghies, and about 260 Polish paratroopers of the Third Battalion (the 7th and rest of 8th Company) and the parachute component of the anti-tank batteries (i.e., only men without guns) were ferried across. The ferrying again went on till all the large rubber rafts were sunk. The British intelligence reports comment that Polish troops "thickened up all units on the northeast of the perimeter." These new additions never joined up with the original Polish troops of the Third Battalion. Urquhart wrote on September 23, 1147 hours, "1st Airlanding Bde. reports that South Co. 1 Border reinforced by Poles have repelled attacks but Polish casualties 50% of force."

On September 24, the First and remnants of the Third battalions arrived to report to Sosabowski having been transported by American trucks. It is one of the enigmas of this whole operation that trucks with Polish paratroopers were able to get through to the Poles, but major Allied units and river-fording equipment just seemed to be stuck somewhere in the rear echelons. Also, that this was done through a single road corridor that the British armor was reluctant to enter without enabling infantry support.

The British leadership was now in a crisis. Montgomery, in his role as the commander of the Twenty-First Army Group and from his Olympian heights, passed the buck to General Dempsey, the commander of the British 2nd Army. Horrocks, commanding the 30th Corps, is on record as wishing to press forward and make a major river crossing. The British still had the 52st Lowland Division in reserve that was trained and adopted for air movement. Dempsey was more pessimistic and conservative.

Sosabowski's staff officer wrote many years later that Sosabowski was acerbic in his dealings with the British and protested strongly at the decision to withdraw the British Airborne from north of the river. Sosabowski urged strongly that the Allies had enough punch to mount a major river assault and continue the offensive. Sosabowski was astounded to hear that the British army did not have any river-crossing equipment. But the problem was higher up and Sosabowski was not privy to the fact that the word came down from the top that there was inadequate logistical support for continued British offensive in the north.

Each side had a slightly different account of the staff conference and of the tragic events of the night. This began the historic phase of blaming the lower levels. Montgomery dissociated himself from the fiasco, while Brereton claimed a success. Browning took no responsibility but felt that Sosabowski had failed him. The British made one last attempt to ford the river but it is unclear from the literature whether it was a feint to distract German attention from the evacuation of the First Airborne, or a test to determine German defenses. The Dorsets were badly mauled, and those that crossed the river never did join the British Airborne Division, whose own perimeter had shrunk and contracted away from the river.

The war diaries of the Third Battalion Polish Parachute Brigade, which did ford the river, comment on the bitter nature of the fighting and the fact that the unit covered part of the British retreat when evacuation was ordered on September 25. The losses of the battalion were four officers and 12 of other ranks killed and five officers and 45 of other ranks missing. Of 78 men of the Polish anti-tank unit, only 12 made it south of the river.

The best critic of the campaign, Australian reporter Chester Wilmot, in his study analyzed many of the problems. Wilmot highlighted the reluctance of British generals to take casualties and the inability of Eisenhower to concentrate his forces. Having committed his only strategic reserve to Montgomery (the Allied Airborne Army), Eisenhower did not also commit all his logistical resources. In turn, Montgomery had failed to appreciate the vital importance of the port of Antwerp.[43]

On September 27, the first sea train of the brigade joined up with the parachute unit; and on September 29, the second sea train, including all the pack artillery, disembarked at Arromanches in Normandy, hundreds of miles away.

The Polish Parachute Brigade Group was regrouped and ordered to protect bridges near the Dutch town of Neerloon. The effective strength at that point was 1,283 officers and other ranks. On October 7, it left Holland. It also left many Dutch friends. But the controversy over the fiasco was about to begin. Major figures never make mistakes, so a scapegoat had to be found. The worst thing that a subordinate can do is to question orders and to be proved right. Sosabowski's independent attitude, and the fact that he had resisted strongly all British blandishments to have his brigade be part of the British 1st Airborne Division and most importantly that all his original warnings were proved correct made him the obvious target. Sosabowski and his whole brigade became the victims of a very unfortunate scapegoating. "It was a shameful act by the British commanders."[44]

Very shortly after that the British made it clear that they could not work with Sosabowski and insisted on his transfer from the command of the unit which he had created and commanded in battle.

The British assailed the Warsaw Uprising as unplanned and requiring too many planes and incurring too severe losses. The Allied support for the Arnhem operation cost the Allies 35 lost transport planes in a four-day period. But the fiasco of the "bridge too far" was even more deleterious for the Allies and for the British in particular. Londoners continued to see their homes devastated and lives lost by the German terror weapons (V-1 and V-2) based in northern Holland. The war was prolonged for at least six months, and the Allies were forced to ask Stalin for help when the Germans attacked in the Ardennes in December 1944. The whole of the British Airborne Division was lost. The majority of Dutch had to endure one more winter of great privations and many thousands of denizens of German concentration camps, such as Buchenwald and Dachau, did not live to see liberation.

The name of this small, strategically placed Dutch town on the northern branch of the Rhine River estuary is forever linked with the battle honors of the Polish Army from World War II. It joined other exotic places where the army fought: Narvik, Tobruk, Monte Cassino, Ancona, Falaise, Bologna. But all the others were major Polish victories fought by significant bodies of men under Polish command. At Narvik, the Podhalanska Brigade of well close to 6,000 men helped capture the strategic port of Narvik. At Tobruk, the nearly 5,000-man Carpathian Brigade fought off the famed German Afrika Korps for many months, earning renown and proud epithet, with other Allied troops, particularly the Australians, as the "Rats of Tobruk." Monte Cassino, Ancona and the final battle of Bologna marked the march of the nearly 60,000-man Polish 2 Army Corps which, in the words of DeGaulle, "lavished its bravery in the service of its hopes." At Falaise, the Polish First Armored, 17,000 strong contributed by its glorious stand on the Maczuga Hill to the destruction of the German Army Group Center where the Germans suffered their worst defeat, a quarter of a million dead, another quarter million captured. Eleven of their 12 armored divisions were destroyed, and only 21 of the 48 infantry divisions were still in the German o. de b.

Why did Arnhem — a disastrous military operation, flawed from day one, poorly executed and, in the case of the Poles, fought by scattered units of no more than company size — enter this hallowed pantheon of battle honors. At the height of the battle the Polish commander, Maj. Gen. Stanislaw Sosabowski, had a mere 1,000 men under his command, bereft of any artillery. The only answer to this question is that a stand by a small group of men, whether at Thermopylae, Rorke's Drift, or at Westerplatte seems to excite a greater admiration than victorious battles. But there is another reason why it has entered Polish military tradition and symbolism, and that has to do with the fact that the Polish brigade, small as it was, misused as it was, was in fact the only major parachute unit of the Allied armies outside of the British and Americans. Even the Canadians did not have a major airborne unit. Whether it was wise for the Poles to go to such effort to recruit and train such a force is really beside the issue.

The most bitter tragedy for the Polish forces fighting in the West was to realize that their Western friends and allies were at best impotent, or at worst indifferent, concerning the events in Warsaw. The Soviets had placed all kinds of obstacles on shuttle runs for the dropping of supplies from the West and suspended their own operations until January 1945. Even at this late stage in the war the two competing ideologies of Communism and Nazism, locked in a death struggle, still cooperated to put an end to Polish hopes and aspirations for true freedom and sovereignty, just as they had in September 1939.

The battle for Warsaw had been lost, not just on the bloody streets, in the damp and dark cellars and sewers of Warsaw, but in the printing presses of papers published in London, New York and many other cities of Britain and the United States. The more liberal the paper, the more vehemently it took an anti–Polish and pro–Soviet stance. The Poles lost their last campaign, the Warsaw Uprising, not merely because the distance was so long, but because the Western Allies lacked the will to enforce their military prowess and keep their original treaty of August 1939. The Soviets were, in fact, a paper tiger, existing on the profuse Lend-Lease of the United States.

Everything that happened after the Warsaw Uprising was a nightmare and tragedy for the Poles both in the West and also in Poland. Churchill eventually prevailed on Mikolajczyk to espouse a humiliating accommodation to the Soviets and their puppets in the Lublin Committee. He was given a vote of no confidence by the Polish government and resigned his office. The Polish president appointed Mr. Tomasz Arciszewski, leader of the Polish Socialist Party, who had been extracted from Poland in one of the three successful Mosty operations, to the post of prime minister.

Churchill wrote to Stalin:

> A change of Prime Ministers does not affect the formal relations between States. The desire of His Majesty's Government for reconstitution of a strong and independent Poland, friendly to Russia, remains unalterable. We have practical matters to handle with the Polish Government, and more especially the control of the considerable Polish Armed Forces, over 80,000 excellent fighting men, under our operational command. These are now making an appreciable contribution to the United Nations' war effort in Italy, Holland, and elsewhere. Our attitude to any new Polish Government must therefore be correct, though it will certainly be cold.[45]

Churchill accurately reflected the ongoing Polish military effort at the side of the Allies. The events of the last two months of 1944 and the last four months of the war in 1945 were bittersweet for the Poles. Victories for the Allied side were punctuated by Polish feats of arms and tragic irreparable political defeats.

Polish naval units continued to take part in actions and the most notable were the actions of the *Garland* in the Dodecanese, and of the two fleet destroyers, *Blyskawica* and *Piorun* in patrols off the south French coast. The Polish Armored Division started its famous race north on September 1, 1944, the fifth anniversary of the beginning of the war. The Poles covered 470 kilometers in 10 days, captured 40 officers and 3,447 soldiers, took its first breath on September 10, in Ypres. The Poles captured Abbeville, Ghent, Breda, and helped liberate Antwerp. This became tough fighting as the allies had to cross innumerable rivers and canals in the countrysides of Belgium and Holland. The engineers of the division were the unsung heroes.

Operation Freston: The British Military Mission to Poland

December 1944 was the date for the final death throes of the Polish effort. The British informed the Polish government, through the Polish ambassador in London, that henceforth all Polish radio messages to territories occupied by the Soviets (albeit the British used the word "controlled") were to cease, while such cables to the "adherents" of the Polish government in German-occupied Poland were to be cleared by the British authorities.

In this situation of neverending diplomatic defeats and even humiliations, the British suddenly decided to send a military mission to the Polish underground. This had been urged by the Poles for a long time and the Foreign Office consistently turned it down on the bizarre theory that were they to send a mission to the Polish AK, then they would be expected to send one to the Communist forces. When all was lost, Churchill authorized Colonel Hudson and a small group of Englishmen to parachute into Poland. The British had sent such missions to other occupied countries, namely to Yugoslavia, Greece and, of course, France. Churchill initially asked Stalin's permission which was, of course, refused, but finally, in the summer, Churchill personally briefed Colonel Hudson who, with a small group of gallant Englishmen, were parachuted into the southwest corner of Poland on December 26-27, 1944. They landed in a small corner of prewar Poland (which was about to be occupied by the Soviets) and met with General Okulicki, who had succeeded the captured Bor-Komorowski as commander of the AK. Freston was the first of three such missions that were planned, the other two being Fernham and Flamstead. It is really quite unclear as to what Churchill hoped to accomplish; perhaps it was to obtain a first-hand account of what was happening, possibly to give a hint to Stalin that the British were still very much interested in the future of Poland.

But one of the participants (Major Solly-Flood) wrote many years after the war that the mission was to report fully and to keep reporting on all that was seen, to distinguish what was seen from hearsay, to be observers in combat operations but not to undertake any initiatives in such areas, and to hold out no hope (!) of increased supply or help to the Poles and particularly to discourage any possible thought of anti–Soviet military activity. That seems a realistic mission given all that was happening, but why two more such missions?

Solly-Flood wrote in his moving piece, *Pilgrimage to Poland*, that:

> We went to Poland because the Poles wanted, in the face of tendentious accusations of the Russian loud-speaker, impartial official witness of their heroic struggle against Nazi tyranny, and because there were fortunately in the United Kingdom some high-placed persons who did not in the end dissent from this Polish view point. We went too late to be of any public service, and were to see but the death-throe; but this does not detract from the personal experience.[46]

Captured eventually by the Soviets, the British were held incommunicado until after the Yalta Conference, which was the next diplomatic and final blow to Polish hopes.

On January 19, 1945, the Polish president dissolved the Polish Home Army.

January 1945 through VE Day

Bittersweet Victories

The new year found the Polish Fighter Wing in Ghent, warmly welcomed and appreciated by the Belgians who had been liberated by the Polish First Armored Division and who showered the Poles with gratitude.

During 1944, the squadrons of the Polish wing, in the Tactical Air Force, had done sterling work. 308 (Krakowski) had flown 3,824 plane sorties; 317 (Wilenski), 3,412 plane sorties; and 302 (Poznanski), 3,553 plane sorties. From June 1944 to the end of the year, the Poles had flown 7,912 planes sorties (these numbers are included in the above statistics) and dropped 562 tons of bombs, destroyed 30 tanks, 700 vehicles, 30 railway engines, and 60 barges.

But another great victory was to come, to welcome the new year. The Allied armies had hammered the Germans and reached the periphery of German borders by the end of September 1944. The flawed "bridge too far" airborne operation halted the Allies, primarily due to their having extended their supply lines but also because of stiffening German resistance. Then came the German Ardennes offensive and a bloody nose for the Americans, but in the air it was also a bad tactical reversal for the British 2nd Tactical Air Force. The Germans scraped together close to 800 planes from all over Germany and on January 1, 1945, implemented their Bodenplatte, which destroyed 144 planes of the 144 2nd Tactical Air Force. There was also considerable damage inflicted on the air fields.[1]

When the German attack came, the Polish wing was actually in the air carrying out strikes in support of the Allied counteroffensive. As the Polish squadrons were returning they were radio alerted by their home base that it was under heavy attack. The Germans were preoccupied with strafing the base and were unaware that the combat squadrons were in the air. The Poles achieved total surprise. The wing commander radioed his pilots — "They've attacked our base. Save our home." The Poles jumped the unwary Germans and shot down 18. The 308 squadron (Krakowski) was officially credited with 12 and 317 (Wilenski) with six. Only the fact that the Poles were close on "empty" and also had already expended much of their ammunition prior to returning home prevented an even greater "turkey shoot."

The rest of the year was a fight against horrible weather: frost, snow and fog. In the breaks between bad weather the wing supported the Allied offensive against the

Ziegfried Line. The wing also kept changing airfields, always moving up with the advancing land forces.

On April 10, the ground component of the Polish wing crossed into Germany, being the first component of the Polish armed forces to enter enemy soil. Three days later, Polish planes and vehicles ostentatiously flying the white and red Polish colors took over the German air base at Nordhorn.

On May 4, the Polish wing suffered its last casualty of the war. Lieutenant Szczerbinski, leading a section and flying at deck level, attacked a German ship off the German coast. The ensuing explosion of the ship tore off the wing of the Spitfire.

The Polish Mosquito squadron (305) in the Tactical Air Force achieved its most noted episodes when it destroyed with precision bombing a German training post for saboteurs at Chateau-Maulney, and later when it was part of the 9,000 Allied planes which destroyed all German communications in Operation Clarion.

The Polish fighter wing that stayed as part of the Air Defence of Great Britain (ADGB) also took part in the final air battles and interdiction of enemy ground assets. Squadron 315 (Deblinski) was moved to Peterhead in Scotland where it escorted RAF Beaufighters which in turn attacked German shipping off Norway.[2] The Poles on one of these long escort sorties destroyed four Me-109s off the island of Gossen.

In April 1945, a section of the 309 squadron had the first Polish encounter with German jet planes and came out on top, shooting down two Me-262s.

The symbolic finale for the Poles was the Allied bombing of Berchtesgaden on April 25 by 255 Lancasters (including the Polish 300) of the RAF escorted by RAF fighters including the 133 Polish wing (303, 306, 309, 315) The Polish 300 heavy bomber squadron took part in this last operation, achieving the record of having flown more combat missions than any other Allied squadron, British or American.[3] All these operational sorties took place in the psychological shadow of Yalta, which lay on every Polish mind since all were aware that this conference was going to be a terrible blow to Poland. The actual results were even worse![4]

There was not one instance in the Polish Navy, Army or Air Force of refusing to carry out orders, but many were depressed and discouraged and some were bitterly angry. A crew member wrote while flying on a mission to bomb targets in Saxony to aid the Soviet armies that it would be indeed ironic to be killed aiding the Russians.

Yalta

On February 28, 1945, Mr. Petherick in the House of Commons moved that

> remembering that Great Britain took up arms in a war of which the immediate cause was the defense of Poland against German aggression and in which the overriding motive was the prevention of the domination by a strong nation of its weaker neighbours, regrets the decision to transfer to another power the territory of an ally contrary to Article 2 of the Atlantic Charter and furthermore regrets the failure to ensure to those nations which have been liberated from German oppression the full right to choose their own government free from the influence of any other power.[5]

After a very prolonged debate 25 members of the House of Commons voted for this motion and 396 voted against. It is probably fair to say that the degree of sympathy for the Polish cause was much greater than the mere 25 individuals.

The British were very concerned how the Polish military would react to the Yalta communiqué that was published in February 1945. All Polish warships were conveniently in dock for major overhaul. But there were Polish troops on the front line and, of course, in the Polish air units and there was no way the British could rotate the land forces out of the combat zone.

There has to be some speculation that had Churchill's Conservative Party been given a governing majority in the elections of July 25, 1945, the Polish situation may have had some different results. In May 1945, Churchill was already urging the British army to be prepared to rearm the German prisoners and to keep their captured equipment in good condition and finally to ensure that the "128,000 Polish troops should be formed into a Corps of Occupation in some part of the British Zone."[6]

The SOE files for the same month indicate similar optional planning: "It is impolitic to mention the possibility of war with Russia. But, however, remote this may be, if it does take place it will be our duty to contribute to our side. We should surely be negligent if we failed to make every reasonable provision for national defense."

The memorandum develops this point, arguing that in such a dire eventuality the Poles would be very useful and suggesting that possibly they could be based in Italian East Africa, or some similar locality where they would not by virtue of the remoteness of geography be a disturbing influence on "a possible peaceful solution of European differences." The SOE memo states what was often bruited by the Poles in the early days of the war, that some of the Italian colonies ought to be given to the Poles, that such a solution would be most desirable to the Poles themselves; "they envisage the formation of a bilingual colony entering into the structure of the British Commonwealth, with themselves in the role of the French Canadians or the Boers, but without the separatist or anti–British bias."[7]

Churchill continued to be an advocate of the Polish cause, even though with each passing month of the war, the role of the United Kingdom diminished in importance compared to the growing industrial, military and economic might of the United States.

Churchill's concern is well documented in what may have been one of his last letters to Roosevelt of March 3, 1945, when he wrote, "At Yalta we agreed to take the Russian view of the frontier line. Poland has lost her frontier. Is she now to lose her freedom?" Churchill further acquiesced in Britain's relative impotence when he continued in his message: "That is the question which will undoubtedly have to be fought out in Parliament and in public here. I do not wish to reveal a divergence between the British and the United States Governments, but it would certainly be necessary for me to make it clear that we are in presence of a great failure and an utter breakdown of what was settled at Yalta, but that we British have not the necessary strength to carry the matter further and that the limits of our capacity have been reached."[8]

All his attempts to have the United States join with him in a firm stand, or at least get Stalin to agree to enlarging the Communist provisional government to ensure that US and British ambassadors would oversee the elections, were dismissed in Washington.

While Yalta gets the bad name for big power politics, for the trampling of small states' rights, for the complete ignoring of the Atlantic Charter, the fact is that it was in Moscow in 1945 and by Harry Hopkins that the final blow was delivered when he assured Stalin that the United States had no interest or desire in any kind of Polish government that Stalin might propose. Stalin obliged and graciously agreed to expand the Lublin regime by the addition of four of five non–Lublin Poles as long as they were acceptable to Moscow! Hopkins agreed to this. Churchill, rather than possibly negotiate for a real interim government that assured free elections, browbeat Mikolajczyk (no longer prime minister but merely a "non–Lublin Pole) to achieve Stalin's good will.[9] In the words of O'Malley — the Polish corpse was delivered to the Russians and the alibi was believed by the same people who accepted the Soviet explanation for the Katyn murders.

In March 1945, the Soviets invited the Polish underground leadership to a meeting at Pruszkow, near Warsaw, arrested them and flew them to Moscow and placed them on trial for anti–Soviet activities. The fourth and last commander in chief of the Polish underground, Maj. Gen. Leopolod Okulicki, died in a Soviet prison. The arrest of Allied leaders in their own country elicited little negative comment from the Western press or leadership. [10]

After the war, Churchill wrote: "This was in fact the judicial liquidation of the leadership of the Polish Underground which had fought so heroically against Hitler. The rank and file had already died in the ruins of Warsaw."[11]

On VE Day the British celebrated. Hundreds of thousands of Londoners stood in front of Buckingham Palace and expressed their joy. These kinds of enthusiastic celebrations took place in every city, town, hamlet and in every military base and Royal Navy warship. This joy was not experienced by the Poles but in every case the personal bitterness was internalized.

The Polish official and unofficial position is best expressed by the order of the day emanating from Colonel Beill, who was the commanding officer of RAF Faldingworth, an all–Polish base and home of Poland's last bomber command squadron (300). Beill spoke to the assembled Polish officers and other ranks, air and ground crews, and urged them to respect the joy of their hosts and allies. He reminded the Poles that the 300 squadron had won 106 British awards for gallantry and ordered that any comments which could be perceived as derogatory were prohibited.

Discussion and Conclusion

When the achievements are objectively analyzed the only verdict can be that for the Poles luck had run out and that the war was lost because the Soviets were implacable and that possession was nine-tenths of the law, and finally that their devotees commanded the mass media.

What had the Poles succeeded in accomplishing?

A major highly confidential and efficient system of radio communications was implemented and a Polish-controlled system of couriers developed. The amount of material actually transferred to Poland was relatively modest, but not inconsequential. During the war years, between 1941 and 1944, Section VI of the Polish General Staff arranged for 485 drop missions, of which 240 were by Polish; 138 by RAF and South African; and 107 by American crews. Six hundred tons of material were dropped; and $34 million, 1.5 million gold sovereigns and German and Polish occupation money transmitted to the Polish Home Army. The lion's share of this money was for military purposes, the balance for various political, propaganda and charitable goals.

The Poles may be quite correct in blaming the British for insufficient support of the Polish special duties air component. There were more than sufficient Polish crews competent to fly four-engined planes. Had the British released those crews from other activities such as the Ferry Command and 300 Bomber Squadron, and dispatched the number of planes advocated by Lord Selborne, then more supplies would have undoubt-edly been dropped, but the outcome is unlikely to have been significantly altered. Part of that blame has also to be attached to Polish pride. The air ministry actually sug-gested that the 300 Bomber Squadron, rather being "upgraded" to Lancasters, which required more mechanics and crew members, be equipped with Mosquitoes. The Poles turned down this very sensible suggestion. Had this been implemented, then there would have been more aircrew familiar with large four-engined craft available for the Polish special duties flight. But, the availability of suitable long-range planes was always an issue until Churchill ruled in early 1944 that extra planes should be offered the Poles. This was done, but too late for the Polish mission. In late December 1944, the Poles achieved a full squadron complement. Had such been the case for the whole of 1944, one can safely assume that the tonnage dropped to Poland would have been at least double that achieved by the Poles.

The supposed sharing of special duties sorties was heavily stacked against the Poles. One can agree to the point that flights to countries like Yugoslavia, northern Italy or southern France were veritable milk runs compared to flights to Poland. But the energy level, the utilization of planes, especially engines, took a heavy tool on crews that had volunteered for aiding Poland and not Italian Communists or Titoist partisans.

The actualization of a Polish parachute training center was a highly desirable suc-cess, but the efforts to expand the cadre unit to a full brigade group were a gross mis-judgment of reality. The blame can only be attached to the Polish General Staff which failed to heed the very obvious British warnings that air transport was not available for such a major unit. In fact, Paszkiewicz was right in 1942 when he cautioned at Siko-rski's planning conference that expanding the cadre unit to a full brigade would make it a very tempting morsel for the British. He urged that it stay a cadre unit.

Had there been a possibility of a drop of a company-sized unit in Poland, then the symbolic value would have been as significant as the dropping of a whole brigade. In retrospect, the cadre training base should have trained some small company-sized units available for special commando-type missions and a large number of cichociemny officers (in fact, well over 2,000 volunteered for such service) trained to lead locally recruited groups increased and were dropped into Poland.

It made little sense to train a rifle carrying paratrooper so that he could parachute into Poland when there were thousands of eager young men able to carry a rifle and familiar with the surroundings. It was a different situation for the senior officer mate-rial and specialists. Well over 2,000 volunteered for such service .

The Polish government can probably be correctly criticized for not placing more effort into the air force, particularly the single-engined fighter ground support squadrons. But not all the men available to the Poles were suitable for service in such a specialized and highly technical service.

Of course. the single most severe blow to Polish efforts was the refusal of the Combined Chiefs of Staff to integrate the Polish Home Army with Western strategy. That decision was certainly based on both the close-to-insurmountable logistical issues, but also political problems between the Poles and the Soviets.

There is a tendency to see the Polish-British situation in rather radical black and white. Many denigrate the Poles for their unrealistic, romantic view of world politics; and many a Pole is convinced that the British practiced duplicity and exploited the Polish resolve to fight. Firstly, the administrative effort which went into the creation of the underground army and its support is anything but romantic. Hard work and that factor too often scorned — bravery — contributed to the Polish success. That the Poles failed had as much to do with the long distance and the problem of Polish-Soviet and Western Allied-Soviet relations as any factor. That the Poles continued to try to implement their policies surely cannot be held against them. But even though the British more often than not honestly stated their inability or possibly their unwillingness to assist the Poles in their very ambitious endeavors, it should be remembered that there were often hints of indirect support.

Two British services went out of their way to show a gesture of courtesy and collegial warmth in their official victory celebrations. The Royal Navy in its parade in Plymouth invited Polish participation and the Royal Air Force appointed a special historical committee to publish the story of the Polish Air Force in the United Kingdom, aptly named in the circumstances: *Destiny Can Wait*. In a dignified ceremony which only the British are capable of putting on, a Polish Air Force memorial at Northolt was unveiled in 1949. Every year, in September, Polish Air Force veterans and British Air Ministry and subsequently Defence Ministry representatives attended to pay tribute to the heroes and allies of the war.

In the official Royal Air Force history, the tribute to the Polish Air Force was also generous and warm:

> All these allied contingents gave something unique; and if we mention especially the Polish airmen, it is not only that their contribution was the greatest in size — with fourteen squadrons and some fifteen thousand men, including their own ground staff, besides many pilots in the British squadrons — and that their fighting record in all Home Commands and Europe and the Mediterranean was unsurpassed, but also that victory brought them no reward only further exile from home and loved ones they had fought so long and bravely to regain.[12]

Yet, in the same three-volume history, the Polish Squadrons are simply listed as RAF squadrons.[13]

Appendix I

AGREEMENT BETWEEN THE GOVERNMENT OF THE UNITED KINGDOM AND THE POLISH GOVERNMENT REGARDING MUTUAL ASSISTANCE (WITH PROTOCOL) LONDON, AUGUST 25, 1939

The Government of the United Kingdom of Great Britain and Northern Ireland and the Polish Government:

Desiring to place on a permanent basis the collaboration between their respective countries resulting from the assurances of mutual assistance of a defensive character which they have already exchanged:

Have resolved to conclude an Agreement for that purpose and have agreed on the following provisions:

Article 1.

Should one of the Contracting Parties become engaged in hostilities with a European Power in consequence of aggression by the latter against that Contracting Power, the other Contracting Power will at once give the Contracting Power engaged in hostilities all the support and assistance in its power.

Article 2.

i. The provisions of Article 1. will also apply in the event of any action by a European Power which clearly threatened directly or indirectly, the independence of one of the Contracting Powers, and was of such a nature that the Party in question considered it vital to resist with its armed forces.

ii. Should one of the Contracting Powers become engaged in hostilities with a European Power in consequence of action by that Power which threatened the independence or neutrality of another European State in such a way as to constitute a clear menace to the security of that Contracting Party, the Provisions of Article 1. will apply, without prejudice, however, to the right of the other European State concerned.

Article 3.

Should a European Power attempt to undermine the independence of one of the Contracting Powers by a process of economic penetration or in any other way, the Contracting Powers will support each other in resistance to such attempts. Should the European Power concerned thereupon embark on hostilities against one of the Contracting Parties, the provisions of Article 1. will apply.

Article 4.

The methods of applying the undertakings of mutual assistance provided for by the present Agreement are established between competent naval, military and air authorities of the Contracting Parties.

Article 5.

Without prejudice to the foregoing undertakings of the Contracting Parties to give each other mutual support and assistance immediately on the outbreak of hostilities, they will exchange complete and speedy information concerning any development which might threaten their independence and, in particular, concerning any development which threatened to call the said undertakings into operations.

Article 6.

i. The Contracting Parties will communicate to each other the terms of any undertaking of assistance against aggression which they have already given or may in future give to other States.

ii. Should either of the Contracting Parties intend to give such an undertaking after the coming into force of the present Agreement, the other Contracting Party shall, in order to ensure the proper function of the Agreement, be informed thereof.

iii. Any new undertaking which the Contracting Parties may enter into in future shall neither limit their obligations under the present Agreement nor indirectly create new obligations between the Contracting Party not participating in these undertakings and the third State concerned.

Article 7.

Should the Contracting Parties be engaged in hostilities in consequence of the application of the present Agreement, they will not conclude an armistice or treaty of peace except by mutual agreement.

Article 8.

i. The present Agreement shall remain in force for a period five years,

ii. Unless denounced six months before the expiry of this period it shall continue in force, each Contracting Party having the Right to denounce it at any time by giving six months notice to that effect.

iii. The present Agreement shall come into force on signature.

Halifax

Raczynski

Protocol

The Polish Government and the Government of the United Kingdom and Northern Ireland are agreed upon the following interpretation of the Agreement of Mutual Assistance signed this day as alone authentic and binding:

1. (a) By the expression of "a European Power" employed in the Agreement is to be understood Germany.

(b) In the event of action within the meaning of Article 1 or 2 of the Agreement by a European Power other than Germany, the Contracting Parties will consult together on the measures to be taken in common.

2. (a) The two Governments will from time to time determine the hypothetical cases of action by Germany coming within the ambit of Article 2 of the Agreement.

(b) Until such time as the two Governments have agreed to modify the following provisions of this paragraph, they will consider: that the case of contemplated by paragraph (1) of Article 2 of the Agreement is that of the Free City of Danzig; and that the cases contemplated by paragraph (2) of Article 2 are Belgium, Holland, Lithuania.

(c) Latvia and Estonia shall be regarded by the two Governments as included in the list of countries contemplated by paragraph (2) of Article 2 from the moment that an undertaking of mutual assistance between the United Kingdom and a third State covering those two countries enters into force.

(d) As regards Roumania, the Government of the United Kingdom refers to the guarantee which it had given to that country; and the Polish Government refers to the reciprocal undertakings of the Roumano-Polish alliance which Poland has never regarded as incompatible with her traditional friendship for Hungary.

3. The Undertakings mentioned in Article 6 of the Agreement, should they be entered into by one of the Contracting Parties with a third State, would of necessity be so framed that their execution should at no time prejudice either the sovereignty or territorial inviolability of the other Contracting Party.

4. The present protocol constitutes an integral part of the Agreement signed this day, the scope of which it does not exceed.

    Halifax

    Raczynski

One of the original English-language copies of this treaty is in the Polish Institute and Sikorski Museum, London. A. II. 76/1. and A.II. 76/2. Both are graced with the respective family seals of the signers.

In March 1944, the secretary of state for Foreign Affairs, Mr. Anthony Eden, responded to a question in the House of Commons: "Article 8 of the Anglo-Polish Agreement regarding mutual Assistance, signed in London on August 25, 1939, provides that the agreement shall remain in force for a period of five years from the date of signature, and that, unless denounced six months before the expiry of the of this period, it shall continue in force, each contracting party having thereafter the right to denounce it at any given time by giving six months notice to that effect. There is, therefore, no question of this Agreement expiring in August, 1944, and no need for any extension of the Agreement at this time." Jedrzejewicz, *Poland in the British Parliament, 1939–1945*, p. 418.

Appendix II

FIRST POLISH–UNITED KINGDOM AGREEMENT (1940) PERTAINING TO THE POLISH AIR FORCE

The Government of the Polish Republic and the Government of the United Kingdom of Great Britain and Northern Ireland, reaffirming their determination to prosecute the war to a successful conclusion,

Recognizing the importance in their common interest of maintaining the armed forces of Poland,

Desiring to establish the principles on which those forces, under the Supreme Command of the Polish Commander-in-Chief, shall be organized for co-operation with the Allied Armed Forces, and recalling the Agreement and Protocol signed in London on the 18th November, 1939 providing for the co-operation of certain units of the Polish naval Forces with those of the United Kingdom, have agreed as follows:

Article 1.

The Polish Armed Forces (comprising Land, Sea and Air Forces) shall be organised and employed under British command, in its character as the Allied High Command, as the Armed Forces of the Republic of Poland allied with the United Kingdom.

Article 2.

Units of the Polish Air Force referred to in Article 1 shall be organised to operate with the Royal Air Force. The organisation of the Polish Air Force in the United Kingdom shall be extended, in accordance with the provisions of Appendix I of the present agreement, so as to utilise such Polish Air Force personnel now in the United Kingdom as maybe necessary for the execution of those provisions.

Article 3.

The Government of the United Kingdom shall afford their assistance in the reconstitution of the Polish Land Forces, in accordance with the conditions laid down in Appendix II of the present agreement.

Article 4.

Any costs incurred by or on behalf of any Department of the Government of the United Kingdom in connection with the application of the present agreement shall be refunded out of the credit granted by His Majesty's Government to the Polish Government to finance the cost of maintaining the Polish military effort.

In witness whereof the undersigned, duly authorised thereto by their respective Governments, have signed the present agreement and have affixed their seals.

Done in London, in duplicate, in the English language the fifth day of August, 1940. A Polish text shall be agreed upon between the Contracting Governments, and both texts shall then be equally authentic.

> Winston S. Churchill
>
> Halifax
>
> Wladyslaw Sikorski
>
> August Zalesky*

Appendix I (Relating to the Polish Air Force)

Article 1.

Constitution

1. The Polish Air Force will be reorganised from those officers and men of the Polish Air Force arriving in British territory who are selected for service by a joint board or boards composed of Polish and British representatives. The personnel selected will be required to pass a medical examination according to the normal Royal Air Force standard. This will be carried out by an Anglo-Polish medical commission.

2. Four bomber squadrons, two fighter squadrons and one army co-operation squadron will be formed as soon as possible, with about 200 per cent. reserves of flying personnel and about 50 per cent. reserves of other personnel. Three or more additional squadrons with the same reserves will be formed as facilities become available.

3. (i) All the trained personnel of the Polish Air Force who are not required for the squadrons now forming will be utilised as soon as possible individually, or in groups in appropriate units or establishments of the Royal Air Force, or in the British aircraft industry until it becomes possible to absorb them in Polish Air Force units. It is understood that Polish flying personnel not required for the squadrons now forming and for the reserves of about 200 per cent. allotted to these squadrons will be employed for operational service in units other than those of the Polish Air Force only during the present critical period and with the specific consent of the Polish Commander-in-chief. If so employed, they will operate only from bases in the territory of the United Kingdom.

(ii) All possible assistance will be given by the Royal Air Force in the expansion of the Polish Air Force and in forming further reserves for the squadrons of the Polish Air Force.

*Zalesky's name is misspelled — should be Zaleski.

Partly trained personnel, in particular pilots, will be given every opportunity to complete their training in the appropriate Royal Air Force establishments. Until training facilities are available, they will be retained with the Polish Air Force and will be given employment on ground defence duties or other work in connection with the Polish Air Force units.

(iii) Untrained personnel who are not required for service with the Royal Air Force will be at the disposal of the Polish authorities for employment with the Polish Army or otherwise.

(iv) Arrangements will be made as soon as circumstances permit to train more pilots for service with the Polish Air Force.

4. An Inspectorate of the Polish Air Force will be formed whose duty it will be to inspect the units of the Polish Air Force. The Inspectorate will communicate with the British Air Ministry on all matters relating to the work of these units. The Inspectorate will also maintain liaison, if necessary through special liaison officers, with the Headquarters of Royal Air Force Commands in which Polish Air Force units are placed. The channel of communication between the Inspectorate and formations of the Royal Air Force will be the Directorate of Allied Air Co-operation in the Air Ministry.

Article 2. Employment.

1. With regard to duties, rights and amenities, Polish Air Force personnel will be treated on the same footing as Royal Air Force personnel.

2. The units of the Polish Air Force will be used in the same manner as the units of the Royal Air Force, but when circumstances permit, the units of the Polish Air Force will operate together. One Polish Army Co-operation Squadron when formed will be attached to the Polish Army while operating under British Command in its character as the Allied High Command, and will be entirely under the operational control of the Commander of the appropriate Polish military formation, subject to the normal flying regulations and restrictions laid down by the Royal Air Force. Other squadrons of the Polish Air Force may be used in support of the Polish Army when necessary.

Article 3. Organisation.

1. Except as provided in Article 2 for the employment of a Polish Army Co-operation Squadron, operational control of the Polish Air Force units will rest entirely with the Royal Air Force Command to which they are attached.

2. The stations at which units of the Polish Air Force are based will be commanded by British officers. Where a station is used solely or primarily for the accommodation of units of the Polish Air Force there will be a Polish commanding officer who will co-operate with the British Station Commander, the latter being senior. Circumstances may arise in connection with the employment of Polish Army Co-operation Squadrons which may require variations in the application of the present paragraph.

3. Polish Air Force units will be provided with equipment of a similar kind and on the same scales as the corresponding units of the Royal Air Force.

4. The supply, maintenance and training of all units of the Polish Air Force serving with the Royal Air Force will be organised through the normal Royal Air Force channels.

5. The numbers and gradings of the officers and men to be authorised for units of the Polish Air Force serving with the Royal Air Force will be those which would be allowed in

accordance with normal Royal Air Force practice, and Royal Air Force regulations as to the qualifications of the personnel will be applied. In special circumstances Royal Air Force practice may be varied where it is in the interests of effective co-operation that this should be done. Where it is necessary for administrative convenience, certain posts may be duplicated to enable British as well as Polish personnel to be borne against them. Where it is found that suitable Polish personnel are not available to fill posts in the establishments of the Polish Air Force units, British personnel may be appointed to fill them.

6. All promotions within the approved establishment of the Polish Air Force units serving with the Royal Air Force will be made on the authority of the Commander-in-chief of the Polish Forces.

(i) Recommendations for the promotion of officers will be forwarded to him through the normal Royal Air Force channels and will be subject to the concurrence of the appropriate Royal Air Force authorities.

(ii) Responsibility for the promotion of airmen will belong, in the first instance, to the holder of the post to which the responsibility would normally attach under Royal Air Force regulations. If such post is held by a Polish Officer, the promotion will be effected forthwith. If it is held by a British Officer, the recommendation for promotion will be forwarded to the Commander-in-chief of the Polish Forces or to an officer nominated by him, in order that effect may be given to it without delay.

Article 4. Discipline.

1. Personnel of the Polish Air Force serving with the Royal Air Force, whether in Polish units or individually, will be subject to Royal Air Force discipline and to Royal Air Force law, as if they were commissioned or enlisted in the Royal Air Force, so long as they are serving with the Royal Air Force. They will be subject also to Polish Military Law, but where the terms of Polish Military Law and British Air Force Law differ, the latter will prevail.

2. Where a military court is constituted for the trial of an officer or airman of the Polish Air Force serving with the Royal Air Force, it will consist of an equal number of British and Polish officers as judges, with, in addition, a British officer as president of the court.

3. Officers and airmen of the Polish Air Force serving with the Royal Air Force will, however, be liable to be tried and punished in accordance with the laws for the time being in force of the United Kingdom or of any territory outside the United Kingdom under the authority of His Majesty's Government in the United Kingdom for offences committed by them against such laws.

Article 5. Pay and Allowances.

A detailed scale of pay and allowances for officers and men of the Polish Air Force serving with the Royal Air Force will be drawn up and agreed as soon as possible. So far as possible the rates will be based on those in force in the Royal Air Force, after allowance has been made for taxation to which British personnel are liable.

Article 6. Miscellaneous.

1. The personnel of the Polish Air Force serving with the Royal Air Force will take an oath of allegiance to the Polish Republic.

2. The uniform of the Royal Air Force will be adopted as the uniform of the Polish Air Force with such distinctive Polish symbols or other badges as the Polish authorities desire. On grounds of security, rank-badges of the Royal Air Force pattern will be worn and will correspond to the posts held under Royal Air Force establishment.

3. Aircraft used by the Polish Air Force while serving with the Royal Air Force will bear British military markings with a distinctive Polish marking on the fuselage.

4. The Polish Air Force ensign will be flown with the Royal Air Force ensign at all Royal Air Force stations at which units of the Polish Air Force are based.

Article 7.

Any difficulties arising out of the preceding articles, and any matters not covered by them will be settled, so far as possible, by direct discussion between the appropriate Polish and British authorities.

Appendix III

POLISH-BRITISH LAND FORCES AGREEMENT (1940)

Article 1.

1. Polish Land Forces will be organised out of the Polish troops now in the territory of the United Kingdom and the Polish troops now in the Middle East.

2. The following articles refer to these Land Forces and their composition will be as follows:

(i) The necessary Headquarters Staffs and a certain number of formations (possible motorised) together with the necessary ancillary services.

(ii) The number of these formations will depend on the Polish possibilities, especially as to personnel.

Article 2.

The Polish Land Forces will be completed by the following means:

(i) A mobilisation of Polish citizens living in the United Kingdom.

(ii) The drafting of volunteers who may come from Poland, the British Commonwealth of Nations or other countries.

Article 3.

1. The Polish Land Forces form the Army of the Sovereign Polish Republic.

2. In principle all the units of the Polish Land Forces will be used so as to form one operational formation in any one theatre of operations under the Command of the Polish Commander in that theatre or of a Commander appointed by him. These forces will be under British Command, in its character as the Allied High Command, which may delegate the Command to a British Commander of appropriate rank. Nevertheless, in exceptional cases, Polish units or formations may be placed under different British Commanders provided that the consent of the Polish Commander is given in each case.

3. Polish units and formations will be commanded by Polish Officers. Polish organisation, Polish regimental colours and all distinctions of rank and badges of the Polish Army will be retained.

Article 4.

The soldiers of the Polish Land Forces will take an oath of allegiance to the Polish Republic.

Article 5.

The Government of the United Kingdom agree to arm and equip the Polish Land Forces.

Article 6.

The British Military Authorities will detach a suitable number of officers and non-commissioned officers of the British Army as instructors to other Polish Land Forces for the period of their instruction and to facilitate the familiarising of the Polish cadres with British material. Officers of the Polish Staffs and of the various Services of the Polish Land Forces will be attached by the British Military Authorities to units of the British Army for short periods of training.

Article 7.

1. All officers and other ranks of the Polish Land Forces will be subject to Polish military law and disciplinary ruling, and they will be tried by Polish Military Courts.

2. They will, however, be liable to be tried and punished in accordance with the laws for the time being in force of the United Kingdom or of any territory outside the United Kingdom under the authority of His Majesty's Government in the United Kingdom for offences committed by them against such laws.

3. A separate agreement will define the method of application of the present article.

Article 8.

At least one field hospital will be organised on the territory of the United Kingdom for wounded and sick Polish personnel. Accommodation will also be provided in stationary hospitals. These medical installations will be manned by Polish Staffs and Polish personnel.

Article 9.

Officers and other ranks of the Polish Land Forces will be remunerated in accordance with a separate agreement to be negotiated between the two Governments.

PROTOCOL.

The Government of the United Kingdom shall lend to the Polish Government such assistance as is in their power, with a view to the negotiation of an agreement between the Polish Government and the Government of Canada concerning the establishment in Canada of a recruiting and organising base for the Polish Armed Forces. The method of negotiation of such an agreement will be a matter for settlement between the Polish and Canadian Governments, but if the United Kingdom Government are invited by those Governments to assist in the negotiations, they will be happy to do so.

Done in London in duplicate the fifth day of August, 1940, in the English language.

A Polish text shall subsequently be agreed upon between the Contracting Governments, and both texts shall then be equally authentic.

Winston S. Churchill

Halifax.

Wladyslaw Sikorski

August Zalesky.

[This was accompanied by a letter from Winston S. Churchill to his excellency, Gen. Wladyslaw Sikorski, G.B.E., on August 5, 1940:]

Your Excellency,
    With reference to Article 4 of Appendix I and Article 7 of Appendix II to the agreement which we have signed to-day concerning the organisation and employment of the Polish Forces,
I have the honour to inform your Excellency that his Majesty's Government in the United kingdom intend to invite Parliament to pass as soon as possible the necessary legislation to empower the competent Polish authorities and courts to exercise the jurisdiction over the Polish air and land forces for which provision is made respectively in the above mentioned articles, and to authorise the British civil and military authorities concerned to extend the necessary measures of assistance to the Polish authorities to enforce that jurisdiction. You will appreciate that until these powers have been obtained from Parliament, it will not constitutionally be possible for the provisions in question concerning the jurisdiction of the Polish authorities and courts to be enforced by the authorities of the United Kingdom. I can, however, assure your Excellency that His Majesty's Government will do their utmost to regularise the position as soon as possible.

I have the honour to be,
    With the highest consideration
Your Excellency's obedient Servant,
        Winston S. Churchill.

Appendix IV

REVISED POLISH-BRITISH
AIR FORCE AGREEMENT (1944)

Protocol

The Government of the Polish Republic and the Government of the United Kingdom of Great Britain and Northern Ireland,

Desiring to make fresh provision for the organisation and employment of the Polish Air Force in association with the Royal Air Force, as well as for the exercise of jurisdiction over members of the Polish Air Force in the United Kingdom or in any territory outside the United Kingdom which is under the authority of the Government of the United Kingdom,

Have decided to conclude a Protocol for the purpose of amending as required the provisions of the Agreement concluded between the two Governments in London on the 5th August, 1940, respecting the Polish Land and Air Forces, and of the Protocol concluded between the two Governments in London on the 22nd November, 1940, concerning jurisdiction over the Polish Armed Forces, and have agreed as follows:

Article 1

From the date of the signature of this Protocol the provisions of Article 2 of the aforesaid Agreement of the 5th August, 1940, and the provisions of Appendix I to that Agreement to which the same Article 2 relates, shall cease to have effect, and personnel of the Polish Air Force shall be organised and employed in accordance with the conditions laid down in the Annex to this Protocol.

Article 2

(i) From the date of signature of this Protocol the provisions of Article 2 of the aforesaid Protocol of the 22nd November, 1940, shall cease to have effect, and the reference in Article 1 of the aforesaid Protocol to Article 2 thereof shall be read as a reference to this Article.

(ii) From the date of signature of this Protocol jurisdiction over members of the Polish Air Force shall be exercised in accordance with the remaining Articles of the Protocol of the 22nd November, 1940, except in so far as is specifically provided to the contrary in Article 6 of the Annex to the present Protocol.

In witness thereof the undersigned, duly authorised for this purpose by their respective Governments, have signed the present Agreement and have affixed thereto their seals.

Done in London, in duplicate, the 6th day of April, 1944.

Edward Raczynski

Alexander Cadogan

ANNEX

Article 1

Constitution of the Polish Air Force

1. The Polish Air Force in the United Kingdom, which constitutes a part of the sovereign Polish Armed Forces, shall be composed of—
    i) The General Headquarters of the Polish Air Force.
    ii) Appropriate staffs of their cadres.
    iii) Operational units of various types.
    iv) Non-operational units and services of various types or their cadres — in particular, Training, Maintenance and Signals units.
    v) Trained reserves of personnel for the above-mentioned General Headquarters, Staffs, and other units.

2. In addition to the establishments already authorised or subsequently amended by mutual agreement, the Polish Air Force shall possess, where practicable, all the other institutions and organisational elements required for the future development of a modern Air Force in accordance with establishments to be agreed between the Air Ministry of the United Kingdom (hereinafter referred to as the Air Ministry) and the General Headquarters of the Polish Air Force.

3. The existing number and types of squadrons shall only be changed as a result of direct discussions between the appropriate Polish and British authorities.

4. An establishment shall be worked out in each Royal Air Force Command to be spread through Command, Group and Station Headquarters to ensure the provision of training facilities for Polish Staff officers in each branch of the Staff and their appropriate employment.

5. (i) At the head of the Polish Air Force shall be an Air Officer Commanding-in-Chief, appointed by the Polish Commander-in-Chief of the Polish Armed Forces.
    (ii) The Air Officer Commanding-in-Chief of the Polish Air Force shall have at his disposal a Staff called the General Headquarters of the Polish Air Force.
    (iii) The Air Officer Commanding-in-Chief of the Polish Air Force shall possess the power of a Commanding Officer, but in the operational sphere the powers of the appropriate British Air Officers Commanding-in-Chief shall be safeguarded in accordance with Article 2 of this Appendix.
    The General Headquarters of the Polish Air Force shall communicate with the Air Ministry and with the Headquarters of the Royal Air Force Commands through the Directorate of Allied Co-operation and Foreign Liaison of the Air Ministry.

Article 2

Command of the Polish Air Force

The following principles shall be accepted to secure the Command of the Polish Air Force:

i) The operational control of units of the Polish Air Force shall remain vested in the Air Officer Commanding-in-Chief of the Royal Air Force Command concerned.

ii) (a) Where a station is used solely or primarily for the accommodation of units of the Polish Air Force, there shall be a British Station Commander.
At such Stations a Polish Commanding Officer shall also be appointed in the same rank but subordinate to the British Commanding Officer. Consideration shall be given by Air Officers Commanding-in-Chief to the possibility of Polish officers taking over command of Stations used solely or primarily for the accommodation of units of the Polish Air Force.

(b) At Stations other than those specified in sub-paragraph (ii) (a) of this Article, where Polish units or comparable bodies specifically organised for Polish personnel are accommodated, a Polish Commanding Officer shall be appointed.

(c) For detachments of Polish personnel, other than those specified in sub-paragraphs (ii) (a) and (b) of this Article, a Senior Polish Officer may be appointed by agreement with the Air Ministry.

(d) The British Station Commander shall exercise his command over Polish Air Force units or personnel exclusively through the Polish Commanding Officer or the Senior Polish Officer. The Polish Commanding Officer or the Senior Polish Officer shall be responsible to the British Station Commander for all the matters relating to Polish units or personnel at a given Station.

(e) The Polish Commanding Officer or Senior Polish Officer on a Royal Air Force Station shall be entitled to communicate directly with his superior Polish authorities.

Article 3

Organisation and Employment

1. With regard to duties, rights and amenities, personnel of the Polish Air Force shall be treated on the same footing as personnel of the Royal Air Force, if not otherwise provided by this Appendix.

2. Units of the Polish Air Force shall be used in the same manner as units of the Royal Air Force, but when circumstances permit, units of the Polish Air Force shall operate together.

3. The Polish Air Force shall conform to the organisation at Royal Air Force Stations as laid down by the Royal Air Force Air Officers Commanding-in-Chief. A deviation from this principle may be admissible by mutual agreement.

4. The Polish Air Force shall continue to make use of certain Royal Air Force Organisations in so far as this may be necessary in order to avoid duplication and ensure administrative economy.

5. Squadrons and units of the Polish Air Force shall be commanded exclusively by Polish officers and shall be subordinated to the Royal Air Force for operational duties. Royal Air Force control over operational and non-operational units shall be exercised through the Polish Commanding Officer or Senior Polish Officer at the Station.

6. Units of the Polish Air Force shall be provided with equipment of a similar kind and on the same scales as the corresponding units of the Royal Air Force.

7. The supply, maintenance and training of all units of the Polish Air Force shall be organised through the normal channels of the Royal Air Force.

8. In special cases where it is necessary for administrative convenience, certain posts may be duplicated to enable British as well as Polish personnel to be borne against them. Where it is found that suitable Polish personnel are not available to fill posts in the establishments of units of the Polish Air Force, British personnel may be appointed to fill them and Polish personnel may similarly be appointed to fill posts in the establishments of units of the Royal Air Force.

Article 4

Training

1. Subject to the Agreement of the British Air Ministry Polish Flying and Ground Personnel and Instructors shall be trained in numbers considered necessary by the Air Officer Commanding-in-Chief, Polish Air Force, to fill the establishment requirements of the squadrons, organisational units and reserves specified in paragraphs 2 and 3 of Article 1 of this Appendix.

2. Conditions, methods and syllabi of training, duties and rights of Polish personnel in training shall normally be based upon Royal Air Force regulations.

3. Personnel for the Polish Air Force shall normally be trained in Polish Training Schools. When this is not possible, they shall be trained in groups or singly in Royal Air Force Training Schools.

4. Where these are not provided under British regulations, the General Headquarters of the Polish Air Force shall be entitled, subject to the agreement of the Air Ministry, to organise such special Schools and Courses as are obligatory under Polish regulations and are considered necessary for the future development of the Polish Air Force.

Article 5

Personnel

Within the limits of the agreed establishments the General Headquarters of the Polish Air Force shall be responsible for the posting, commissioning and promotion of the personnel of the Polish Air Force and other related matters, provided that —

   i) the machinery for actually effecting the above shall remain as at present;

   ii) The General Headquarters of the Polish Air Force shall conform generally to Royal Air Force procedure and regulations;

   iii) The posting by the General Headquarters of the Polish Air Force of officers above the rank of Flight Lieutenant shall be subject to prior consultation with the Royal Air Force Command concerned, or with the Air Ministry, as may be necessary;

   iv) Polish Air Force personnel shall remain subject to the same conditions as regards operational tours, and tours of duty overseas, as personnel of the Royal Air Force. In special circumstances, exceptions to this principle may be permitted, but they shall be subject to consultation between the Air Ministry and the General Headquarters of the Polish Air Force.

v) Personnel accepted for service in the Polish Air Force shall be required to pass a medical examination according to the normal standards of the Royal Air Force. This examination shall be carried out by an Anglo-Polish Medical Board.

Article 6

Discipline

1. In accordance with Article 2 of the present Protocol, of which this Annex forms a part, members of the Polish Air Force shall, except as provided in Paragraph 2 of this Article, be subject to the jurisdiction of the Polish Military courts and authorities, applying Polish Military Law, under the conditions laid down in the Protocol of the 22nd November, 1940, consigning jurisdiction over the Polish Air Force as amended by the aforesaid Article 2.

2. For practical reasons, individuals and small detachments of Polish Air Force personnel serving within units of the Royal Air Force and not under the immediate command of a Polish Commanding Officer or a Senior Polish Officer shall continue to be subject to Royal Air Force Law in so far as breaches of discipline are concerned which can be dealt with summarily under Royal Air Force law until such time as they are formed into Polish units or comparable bodies specifically established for Polish personnel, or until a Polish Commanding Officer or a Senior Polish Officer is appointed to command them by agreement with the Air Ministry. Personnel of the Polish Air Force alleged to have committed offences against discipline which cannot be dealt with summarily under Royal Air Force Law, shall be handed over to the competent Polish authorities for disposal. The Air Ministry and the General Headquarters of the Polish Air Force shall agree upon the particular Polish detachments to which this exceptional arrangement shall from time to time apply.

3. In order to avoid any risk of confusion and misunderstanding at Stations where units or personnel of the Polish Air Force are serving, the General Headquarters of the Polish Air Force shall arrange for the necessary instructions to be issued to all personnel of the Polish Air Force who are serving at Royal Air Force Stations to comply strictly with all flying regulations, station orders and similar regulations for the safety and security of the Stations.

4. Officers of the Royal Air Force commanding Stations at which units or personnel of the Polish Air Force are serving shall have the power, if necessary, to order the arrest of members of the Polish Air Force for any breaches of discipline on the Station and to retain them in custody until they have been disposed of summarily or until they can be handed over to the appropriate Polish authorities for disciplinary action under the Polish Military Law.

Article 7

Pay and Allowances

1. So far as possible the rates of pay and allowances for officers and men of the Polish Air Force shall be based upon those in force in the Royal Air Force, after allowance has been made for taxation to which personnel of the Royal Air Force are liable.

2. Except as may hereafter be agreed between the Air Ministry and the General Headquarters of the Polish Air Force, the existing rates shall continue in force, as shall also the arrangements under which such pay and allowances are issued through Air Ministry channels.

Article 8

Formation of Ancillary Sections

1. It is agreed in principle that ancillary sections shall be formed as soon as sufficient Polish personnel become available.

2. In order to allow Polish officers to gain general experience in all branches of modern aviation, the Air Ministry shall endeavor, when opportunity occurs, to introduce individual Poles into Air Ministry departments and branches and into ancillary sections, including those concerned with civil aviation and the supply and maintenance of aircraft.

Article 9

Miscellaneous

1. The uniform of the Polish Air Force shall be Royal Air Force blue with such distinctive Polish symbols or other badges as the Polish authorities desire. The rank badges of the Royal Air Force pattern shall be worn and shall correspond to the posts held under Royal Air Force establishment.

2. Aircraft used by the Polish Air Force while serving with the Royal Air Force shall bear British Military markings with a distinctive Polish marking on the fuselage.

3. The Polish Air Force ensign shall be flown with the Royal Air Force ensign at all Royal Air Force Stations at which there is a Polish Commanding Officer.

4. At Royal Air Force Stations where a Polish Commanding Officer has been appointed, the internal organisation of squadrons and units shall be governed in so far as possible by Polish rules and regulations.

Article 10

1. The provisions of this Annex apply equally to personnel, units and other organisational groups of the Polish Air Force serving outside the United Kingdom as a result of mutual agreement between the British and Polish authorities.

2. Any difficulties arising out of the preceding articles, and any matters not covered by them shall be settled so far as possible by direct discussions between the appropriate Polish and British authorities.

Appendix V

COSTS OF THE POLISH FORCES
WHILE BASED IN THE UNITED KINGDOM

Due to the British decision to rescind the recognition of the Polish government based in London on July 5, 1945, and to grant it to the Communist regime, it was to the latter that the British presented the account for all expenditures for the civilian and military aspects of the Polish government and its employees and military personnel.

The total sum was:

Armament and Equipment	£ 75 million;
Pay and allowances for the military	£ 47 million;
Civilian and diplomatic missions	£ 32 million.

The British agreed that the sum of £ 75 would be wiped out but that the Poles would be expected to pay the £ 79 for salaries. The Polish communists objected and stated that the Soviets did not expect repayment for the military and that they would not pay those expenses, but would consider the civilian debt as reasonable.

It is not exactly clear how much of that amount was ever paid to the British. The various trade and financial negotiations that occurred in the postwar years would require a chartered accountant to figure this out. But it is unlikely that even much of the civilian debt was ever paid back to the British. The Polish gold went back to Poland and its fate is unknown.

For the best account of the story or odyssey of the Polish gold, see Wojciech Rojek, *Odyseja Skarbu Rzeczypospolitej: Losy zlota Banku Polskiego, 1939–1950*. For a short English account of how the Polish gold was evacuated and saved in 1939, see Robert Westerby and R.M. Low, *Polish Gold*. For discussion of the internal Polish repercussions of failure to ensure its safety in 1940 after the French armistice, see p. 68 above. There are a number of scattered references to Polish gold deposits in historical literature. Churchill, in *Their Finest Hour* (p. 422), mentions Polish and Belgian gold recovery as a significant secondary gain of the unsuccessful Dakar operation of 1941. He writes, "The Poles and Belgians would also have their gold, which was moved before the armistice to Africa by the French Government for safety, recovered by them." Since the Dakar operation was a failure, the gold stayed in Vichy French control. The

Poles owe the French a debt of gratitude for not handing these Polish assets to the Germans.

In *The Complete War Memoirs of Charles de Gaulle,* on pp. 538 and 539, de Gaulle refers to the gold that had been entrusted by the State Bank of Poland to the Bank of France in September 1939 and which in 1940 had been stored at Bamako in French Africa. In spite of strong protests from the Soviet government, de Gaulle writes that in March 1944 that he placed the gold in Polish possession. The British Foreign Office archives also have the following references: FO 688 29/13 and FO 371-39505. In 1942, a Polish agent — Kowalski — finds the Polish gold in French Africa, near Kayes. It is then shipped to Dakar and Casablanca. The Polish gold comprises a total of 153 crates of gold bars and 471 crates of gold coins, weighing 62 tons. In 1944, permission is obtained for the Royal Navy to begin shipping the gold to the Bank of England for deposit on behalf of the Bank Polski. Only 3 and half tons per warship are carried to obviate risk to gold were any of the warships sunk. All gold was finally moved.

Appendix VI

STRENGTH OF THE POLISH FORCES IN EXILE AT WAR'S END

Total Polish Air Force manpower (and including women's service of 1,602): 19,400.

Losses: 1803 killed.

Total Polish Armed Forces in Exile in May 1945:

Ground forces	171,220
Air force	19,400
Navy	3,840
Total	194,460

Appendix VII

MILITARY SYMBOLISM: OCCUPIED HOMELAND SENDS TWO FLAGS TO ITS WARRIORS IN EXILE

Finally, in every society symbolic acts have a very important meaning and serve to inspire and remind of individual responsibility and of belonging to a group and shared common values. In the military, from Roman times, it has been the standard of the unit which serves as a cohesive symbol of allegiance. It is again a commentary on the close connection of the Polish Air Force and the Polish Parachute Brigade with occupied Poland and its clandestine Home Army that the standards of both were embroidered in Poland and smuggled out. The first of the two was the standard of the Polish Air Force which was embroidered by the Polish women of Wilno in 1940 (prior to the Soviets taking over this unfortunate country), and smuggled out in the most unusual situation, namely through the Japanese Embassy in Berlin, to Japan and then to the UK. Of course, this was before Pearl Harbor. It was presented, at a very moving drumhead service, to the first of the Polish squadrons, the 300, on July 16, 1941, at Swinderby, England, by General Sikorski.

The standard of the Parachute Brigade was embroidered by the women of Warsaw and brought out by a *Mosty* (Wildhorn) mission in 1944. This flag, a classic Polish amaranth Maltese cross on a field of white has a stylized Archangel Michael in the middle and the words *Surge Polonia*. On the other side, in the middle is the traditional Polish eagle, with the Madonna of Czestochowa, or symbolic queen of Poland on the top aspect of the cross and the words God and Country on the bottom. It was accompanied by a letter written by the women of German-occupied and brutally crucified Warsaw, which was yet to endure its most horrible calvary. "Loved Ones (kochani). We send you a flag which will accompany you to victory. The flag is a missive to all of you from your loved ones. The parchment is a cardinal's coat, treasured by his ancestors for many generations, the ink is silk, silver and gold thread, purchased by universal contributions. Your Mothers and Fathers want you know that you are their pride and love." This illustrate the bonds between the crucified country and its military in exile and was presented to the parachute brigade by the president of Poland, Wladyslaw Raczkiewicz, on June 15, 1944, at Cupar in Scotland.

Appendix VIII

Chronology of Important Events

1/22/1917: Wilson calls for an independent Poland. Later this becomes his 13th point.

6/4/1917: France decrees the organization of an autonomous Polish army composed of volunteers from France and the United States, and from Poles conscripted into service by the Germans and Austrians and taken prisoner of war by Western coalition forces.

9/20/1917: France formally recognizes the Dmowski Committee as representing Polish interests.

3/3/1918: Treaty of Brest-Litovsk. Russia leaves the allied anti–German coalition. The first postulate of Pilsudski's political program is met and one of the partitioning powers is knocked out of the war.

6/3/1918: Declaration of Versailles. The question of a united and independent Polish state, with free access to the sea, constitutes one of the conditions for a just and durable peace and rule of rights in Europe.

12/11/1918: Poland regains independence after more than a century of partitions. Pilsudski and Sosnkowski, released from German prison, arrive in Warsaw. The German-appointed Regency Council appoints Pilsudski head of state and itself resigns.

5/3/1920: Outbreak of the Polish-Soviet War.

8/18/1920: Battle of Warsaw won.

10/18/1920: Conclusion of hostilities between Poland and the Soviet Union.

2/19–21/1921: Polish-French political and military agreement signed in Paris by Pilsudski and Sosnkowski. Poland agrees to a standing army of 30 infantry divisions to aid France in event of war with Germany, while France agrees to keep the sea lanes open in event of war with the Soviet Union. This treaty was the keystone of Polish foreign policy and was in force in 1939.

3/3/1921: Polish-Romanian treaty of mutual assistance in event of danger from the Soviet Union.

3/18/1921:	The Treaty of Riga between Poland and the Soviet Union finalizes the Polish-Soviet boundary and leads to restoration of normal relations.
4/16/1922:	Rapallo. A German-Soviet treaty of collaboration. Poland viewed this as aimed at her interests.
1/11/1923:	Belgian and French troops occupy the Ruhr. Britain and the United States dissociate themselves from this act. Marshal Foch visits Warsaw.
4/26/1925:	The Polish prime minister, General Sikorski, visits Paris and signs a protocol to the 1921 Polish-French Treaty. It provides for significant financial aid to the modernizing of the Polish armed forces and for major French capital investment in such industrial projects as the construction of the port of Gdynia.
10/16/1925:	Locarno Pact. Signatories were Germany and Western coalition partners. Germany agreed never to seek a revision of her western boundaries.
5/12/1926:	Pilsudski's coup d'état.
6/25/1932:	Polish-Soviet Non-aggression Treaty signed in Moscow.
1/30/1933:	Hitler becomes chancellor of Germany.
1/26/1934:	Polish-German Declaration of Non-Aggression.
4/23/1935:	New constitution enacted, which gives the president considerable authority and power.
5/11/1935:	Pilsudski dies.
3/7/1936:	Germans march into the Rhineland. Openly break the Versailles Treaty obligation.
9/6/1936:	Marshal Edward Smigly-Rydz visits France and negotiates an agreement for the modernization of the Polish armed forces, known as the Rambouillet agreement.
3/15/1939:	German troops enter Prague.
3/31/1939:	The United Kingdom guarantees Polish sovereignty.
4/28/1939:	Germany breaks off the Polish-German declaration of nonaggression and also the German-British treaty on warship tonnage limitation.
8/23/1939:	Molotov-Ribbentrop Pact.
8/25/1939:	Polish-United Kingdom treaty of mutual aid.
8/25/1939:	Polish Aviation Service placed on secret mobilization. Polish merchant marine instructed to stay out of the Baltic and if in the Baltic to leave immediately.
9/1/1939:	Germany invades Poland.
3/3/1939:	The United Kingdom and France honor their treaty obligations and declare war on Germany.

9/17/1939:   The Soviet Union implements the secret protocol of the MolotovRibbentrop pact and invades Poland.

9/18/1939:   The Polish government crosses the Romanian boundary and is interned.

9/27/1939:   Warsaw receives orders carried by a plane from Romania to capitulate.

9/30/1939:   Raczkiewicz appointed to the presidency.

10/1/1939:   Hel capitulates.

10/4/1939:   General Kleeberg capitulates at Kock.

10/14/1939:   ORP *Orzel* sails into a British port. Longest operating combat unit of the Polish armed forces in September 1939.

11/18/1939:   Polish-United Kingdom Naval Agreement signed in London.

1/4/1940:   Polish-French Military Agreement.

5/8/1940 to 6/8/1940: The Podhalanska Brigade participates in Allied operations at Narvik.

6/5/1940:   The chief of staff of the Polish Army, Col. Aleksander Kedzior, resigns in protest over Sikorski's agreement to dispatch the Polish Grenadier Division without its antitank guns and not as part of a Polish corps to the front line. Replaced by Col. Tadeusz Klimecki.

6/17/1940:   France, through its Madrid embassy, seeks an armistice.

6/18/1940:   Polish troops begin to evacuate to the United Kingdom.

6/22/1940:   France capitulates.

8/5/1940:   Polish-United Kingdom military agreement.

8/31/1940:   Polish 303 (Kosciuszko) Squadron enters operations in the Battle of Britain.

4/3/1941:   Sikorski embarks on his first trip to the United States.

6/21/1941:   Germany attacks the Soviet Union.

8/30/1941:   Sikorski and Maiski sign an agreement establishing diplomatic relations and the Soviet Union agrees to allow a Polish army to be formed on Soviet soil.

9/9/1941:   The Atlantic Charter signed by President Franklin D. Roosevelt and Prime Minister Winston S. Churchill.

12/7/1941:   Pearl Harbor.

12/30/1941:   Sikorski visits the Soviet Union and inspects Polish troops. On his way to the Soviet Union, visits the beleaguered garrison at Tobruk and inspects the Polish Carpathian Brigade.

2/15/1942:   Singapore falls to the Japanese. Churchill describes this as the greatest defeat ever suffered by British armies.

3/20/1942:   Sikorski's second visit to the U.S.

The presentation of the Polish Air Force Standard embroidered under Soviet occupation by the women of Wilno in July 1941. General Sikorski (front right) is seen with Air Chief Marshall Sir Charles Portal, Chief of the (British) Air Staff. The standard has just been received and is held by General Ujejski, Inspector of the Polish Air Force. (Courtesy of the Polish Institute and Sikorski Museum, London.)

4/1/1942:   Sikorski hosts a major military and strategic planning conference of all his senior generals.

7/1/1942:   Poland is officially included by the United States as a recipient of the Lend-Lease Act of March 11, 1941.

7/4/1942:   All Polish troops evacuated from the Soviet Union to the Middle East.

8/19/1942:   Allied landings in Dieppe.

October 1942: British defeat the Germans at El Alamein. First British land victory of the Second World War over the Germans.

11/29/1942:   Sikorski's third visit to the U.S.

4/13/1943:   Berlin radio announces the discovery at Katyn of the bodies of over 4,000 missing Polish officers captured by the Soviets in 1939.

4/25/1943:   After the Polish government requests that the International Red Cross investigate the cause and date of death of the Polish officers, the Soviet Union breaks diplomatic relations with the Polish government in London.

The Color party of the Polish Parachute Brigade, with the brigade standard embroidered by the women of Warsaw, 1944, under German occupation. (Courtesy of the Polish Institute and Sikorski Museum, London.)

5/24/1943 to 7/4/1943: Sikorski visits Polish troops in the Middle East and on his way back is killed in a plane accident at Gibraltar. The post of Prime Minister went to Stanislaw Mikolajczyk, while General Sosnkowski became the Commander in Chief.

9/8/1943: Italy surrenders.

November 1943: Teheran Conference.

1/31/1944: The first elements of the 2 Polish Army Corps arrive in Italy.

4/4/1994: Jozef Retinger (Salamander), Churchill's personal representative, is parachuted in to Poland and is extracted by the third Mosty (Wildhorn) operation on 7/25/44.

5/6/1944: Mikolajczyk flies to Washington for a 10-day visit which includes three meetings with Roosevelt.

5/18/1944: Polish 2 Army Corps troops capture Monte Cassino.

6/6/1944: Allies land in Normandy.

7/29/1944: The Polish First Armored Division enters combat in Normandy.

8/1/1944: Warsaw Uprising begins.

9/18/1944: Polish Parachute Brigade participates in the Arnhem operation.

9/30/1944:   Gen. Kazimierz Sosnkowski is dismissed from his function as the Polish commander in chief. Gen. Tadeusz Bor-Komorowski, the GOC Polish Home Army, appointed to that now-symbolic post.

10/2/1944:   Warsaw Capitulates.

12/27/1944:   British military mission (Freston) to Poland. Meets with Okulicki and is shortly captured by Soviets.

12/28/1944:   Last flight to Poland by Squadron 301.

1/19/1945:   Polish underground army dissolved by presidential decree.

February 1945: Yalta Conference.

3/31/1945:   Polish underground leaders accept an invitation to meet with the Soviet representatives, and are all arrested and flown to Moscow and placed on trial. General Okulicki last GOC of the Polish Army in Poland dies in Soviet hands of unknown cause.

5/8/1945:   Victory in Europe Day.

7/5/1945:   Allies rescind their recognition of the Polish government in London.

1946:   Polish armed forces in the West begin to be demobilized.

1945–1947:   Civil war in Poland.

6/6/1947:   President Wladyslaw Raczkiewicz dies. He is buried at the Polish Military Cemetery, Newark, England.

12/19/1990:   First free elections in Poland and Lech Walesa elected president.

12/22/1990:   Ryszard Kaczorowski, last president of the exiled Polish government, flies to Warsaw and is greeted as a head of state and at Walesa's inaugural hands over the presidential insignia. The 1935 Constitution had survived 50 years.

Chapter Notes

Preface

1. (NA) PRO AIR 19/815 80530 (October 1943)
2. Mackenzie, *The Secret History of SOE*, p. 311.
3. For a brief English-language study, see Bor-Komorowski, *The Secret Army*. For a comprehensive study of the Home Army, see Czarnocka, ed. *Armia Krajowa w Dokumentach, 1939–1945*, in five volumes.
4. Ney-Krwawicz, *Powstanie Powszechne w Koncepciach i Pracach Sztabu Naczelnego Wodza i Komendy Glownej Armii Krajowej* (the concept of a general uprising in the plans and work of the staff of the commander in chief and of the Headquarters of the Home Army), Warsaw, 1999.
5. Kacewicz, *Great Britain, the Soviet Union and the Polish Government in Exile, 1939–1945*. Prazmowska, *Britain, Poland and the Eastern Front, 1939*. As well as, *Britain and Poland 1939–1943: The Betrayed Ally*; Karski, *The Great Powers and Poland, 1919–1945. From Versailles to Yalta*; and Meiklejohn Terry, *Poland's Place in Europe*.
6. The first and by many considered to be the most significant actually occurred before the outbreak of the war, namely the sharing of Polish cryptographic successes with the French and British that took place on July 25, 1939. See Ronald Lewin, *Ultra Goes to War*, pp. 25–50. Kozaczuk in his study, *Enigma*, describes not just the relatively well-known contribution of the Poles to Bletchley Park, but the fact that the Poles continued to work in France, even in disguise in Vichy France, and were part of the network Bruno.

This was a continued interception of German radio communications and their deciphering. The Poles in Bruno (Rozycki, Rejewski and Zygalski) were also tied into the Polish intelligence network that had a monopoly at that time on intelligence gathering from France for the UK. They also collaborated with Slowikowski's Polish intelligence services in North Africa. It is a relatively little-known fact that the Poles used their own ciphering machine, Lacida, built before the war and sent to France. (Lacida was the name given to the machine that was actually called LCD for Langer, Ciezki and Danilewicz, the men who designed and built it at the Polish AVA facilites.) Other contributions were the development of the Polish land mine detector, which contributed to the British victory at El Alamein. Polish engineers in the UK also developed the Polstein gun. There were a number of aviation-related inventions, such as the Rudlicki fragmentation bomb dropper for B-17s, and one by Swiatecki for Vickers-Armstrong. Two Polish officers, Tadeusz Lesser and Roman Lubienski, developed the FIDO (Fog Investigation and Dispersion Operation) system, which undoubtedly saved many Allied lives as the planes came home at night into the typical British fog. A total of 257 pilots, 55 navigators, 59 radio operators and 25 plane engineers served in the Royal Air Force's Transport Command, flying between Canada and the British Isles, and between Takoradi (East Africa) and Egypt. There were 55 officers working at the Royal Aircraft Establishment, Farnborough, and smaller numbers at Aeroplane and Armament Experimental Establishment, Boscombe Down. One of the outstanding pilots who worked at AAEE was Maj. Janusz Zurakowski, a famed test pilot for DeHavilland and later for the Canadians. A number of aircraft designers also found work in British and Canadian industry, including Jakimiuk, and Prauss, to name the best known. There were also major combat contributions, such as in the Battle of Britain and the fact that the seemingly miniscule contribution of three fleet destroyers in 1939 had to be confronted with Churchill's concern documented in his *The Gathering Storm*, p. 465: "Destroyers were our most urgent need. None had been included in the 1939 program, but sixteen had been ordered in 1939." The Polish armored division in Northwest Europe in 1944 was in reality one-fifth of all armored divisions under British command. See Dwight E. Eisenhower, *Crusade in Europe*, p. 514. Finally, when in August 1944 French and other troops were moved from the Italian front to the invasion of southern France (Operation Dragoon), it is not a stretch to assert that without the 2 Polish Army Corps the whole allied campaign would have bogged down.

7. Some of these areas were quite exotic. Tobruk, Narvik on land, and sea operations as far south as Freetown, as far north as Murmansk and most of the Mediterranean.

8. (NA) PRO AIR 19/815 805330.

9. Archives of the Polish Institute and General Sikorski Museum, London, (hence cited as APISM) LOT AVII/1b.

10. See Chapter 1 for details (APISM LOT A. I 3/1e).

11. Merrick, *Flights of the Forgotten: Special Duties in World War Two*, p. 16.

12. Nekrich, *German-Soviet Relations, 1922–1941: Pariahs, Partners, Predators*. Also, Roberts, *The Unholly Alliance: Stalin's Pact with Hitler*.

13. Paret and Moran, *Carl von Clausewitz: Historical and Political Writings*.

14. Glantz and House, *When Titans Clashed: How the Red Army Stopped Hitler*.

15. Bell, *John Bull and the Bear: British Public Opinion, Foreign Policy and the Soviet Union, 1941–1945*. See also, Melvin Small, "How we Learned to Love the Russians: American Media and the Soviet Union During World War II," *Historian,* (1974) 36: 455–478.

16. Bohlen writes that during the San Francisco conference, Harriman opined that the goals of the United States and the Soviet Union were so opposed that future collaboration was unrealistic. A number of prominent Americans were outraged and one even stated in a broadcast that "diplomats who lost their belief in the ultimate purpose of our diplomacy in relation to the Soviet Union were expendable." Bohlen concludes in his chapter "Ashes of Victory" that "liberals in academia and the media clung to faith in a future that would reconcile American liberty and Soviet totalitarianism. ... This postwar refusal to face reality inflicted wounds on American liberalism that still fester." *Witness to History, 1929–1969*, pp. 224, 556–557.

17. As late as 1948, Joseph Tenenbaum (president of the World Federation of Polish Jews, living in New York during the war) condemned the Polish government for seeking an impartial investigation of the murders but also enthused about the new Polish Communist government as "for the first time in its history, Poland has a government free from bias and bigotry." *In Search of a People: The Old and New Poland*, pp. 209–229.

18. *The Memoirs of General Lord Ismay*, Viking Press, NY, 1960, p. 392.

19. On April 17, 2003 (page A8) *New York Times* correspondent Frank Bruni wrote from Athens the European Union had "extended its reach to a broad swath of Europe once allied with the former Soviet Union." Thus, through carelessness historical myths are propagated. On 4/9/2004 the New York Times reported that Frank Bruni, who had been their Rome Bureau Chief was named "the newspaper's restaurant critic."

20. The *Baltimore Sun* on May 21, 1999, reported that U.S. federal prosecutors were claiming that John D. was a "guard at four Polish death camps." Professor Deborah Lipstadt, who has fought her own war on the Holocaust deniers, and is considered an expert on the Second World War experience of the Jewish people, wrote in the *Baltimore Sun* on August 22, 1992, about the tragedy of the Bosnians and the ethnic cleansing: "These detention camps are horrible but they are not the equivalent of the death camps in Poland with their gas chambers." On July 10, 2003, Douglas Martin in the *New York Times* wrote "Sobibor, a secret death camp in Eastern Poland." These hurtful, misleading and libelous innuendos have been brought to the attention of responsible individuals, with no palpable remedy. The *New York Times* and *Wall Street Journal* frequently write of "Polish concentration camps."

21. An exception is the magisterial study by a young Polish historian, Ney-Krwawicz, *Powstanie Powszechne w Koncepciach i Pracach Sztabu Naczelnego Wodza i Komendy Glownej Armii Krajowej*.

22. Kahn, *Seizing the Enigma: The Race to Break the German U-Boat Codes, 1939–1943*. Lewin, *Ultra Goes to War:* Keegan, *Six Armies in Normandy*; Middlebrook, *Arnhem, 1944*; Divine, *Navies in Exile*; Urquhart, *Arnhem*; Majdalany, *The Battle of Cassino*.

23. *Destiny Can Wait: The Polish Air Force in the Second World War*; Anders, *An Army in Exile*; Sosabowski, *Freely I Served*; Cynk, *The Polish Air Force at War, 1939–1945*; Cholewczynski, *Poles Apart*; Peszke, *Poland's Navy 1918–1945*; Belcarz and Peczkowski, *White Eagles: The Aircraft, Men and Operations of the Polish Air Force, 1918–1939*; Garlinski, *Poland, S.O.E. and the Allies*; Kozaczuk, *Enigma*; Bor-Komorowski, *The Secret Army*; Kukiel, *Six Years of Struggle for Independence*; Kleczkowski, *Poland's First Hundred Thousand*; Hempel, *Poland in World War II*; Filipow and Wawer, *Passerby, Tell Poland ...*, *Narvik, Tobruk, Monte Cassino, Falaise*; Baluk, *Poles on the Fronts of World War II*.

24. (NA) PRO AIR 19/815 80530.

25. Churchill, *Hinge of Fate*, p. 269.

26. Buckingham, *Arnhem, 1944: A Reappraisal*, pp. 43–48. See also Chapter 7.

27. Charmley, *Churchill's Grand Alliance*, p. 80.

28. W. Averell Harriman and Elie Abel, *Special Envoy to Churchill and Stalin, 1941–1946*, p. 291. The Polish prime minister, Stanislaw Mikolajczyk, the head of the Polish Peasant Party, had no estates, no title, not even formal education. The overwhelming number of the other rank of the

70,000 Polish 2 Corps fighting in Italy at the side of the Allies, were from Eastern Poland, the Polish "*Kresy.*" These soldiers, deeply attached to their small holdings, were far from aristocrats or feudal landlords.

29. Charmley, *Churchill's Grand Alliance*, p. 139.

30. Mayers, *The Ambassadors and America's Foreign Soviet Policy*; Romerstein and Breindel, *The Venona Secrets: Exposing Soviet Espionage and America's Traitors*; Bishop, *FDR's Last Year, April 1944–April 1945*; Weinstein, *The Haunted Wood: Soviet Espionage in America—The Stalin Era.*

31. Harbutt, *The Iron Curtain: Churchill, America, and the Origins of the Cold War*, pp. 105–107. Also see Sherwood, *Roosevelt and Hopkins: An Intimate History*, pp. 897–910.

32. Charmley, *Churchill's Grand Alliance*, p. 79.

33. Woodward, *British Foreign Policy in the Second World War*, Vol. 1, pp. 22–30, 33–80. See also Howard, *The Mediterranean Strategy in the Second World War.*

34. Piszczkowski, *Miedzy Lizbona a Londynem*, published by the Polish Institute and General Sikorski Museum, London, 1979. Based on archives in the Polish Institute and comprising the papers of Polish foreign ministry staff and intelligence officers in Lisbon with representatives of Romania and Hungary.

35. Rogers, *Churchill's Folly: Leros and the Aegean—The Last British Defeat of World War II.*

36. Howard, *The Mediterranean Strategy in the Second World War.*

1. The Interwar Period, 1919–1939

1. MacMillan, *Peacemakers: The Paris Conference of 1919 and Its Attempt to End War.*

2. Wandycz, *Lands of Partitioned Poland, 1795–1918.*

3. Wandycz, *Soviet-Polish Relations, 1917–1921.*

4. Zamoyski, *The Battle for the Marchlands.* Also, see D'Abernon, *The Eighteenth Most Decisive Battle of the World, Warsaw 1920.* Also, Dziewanowski, *Joseph Pilsudski. A European Federalist, 1918–1922.*

5. Latawski, ed. *The Reconstruction of Poland, 1914–1923.* Specifically Chapter 5, "The Battle of Danzig and the Polish Corridor at the Paris Peace Conference of 1919," by Anna M. Cienciala, and Chapter 7, "Dmowski's Policy at the Paris Peace Conference: Success of Failure," by Piotr Wandycz.

6. Hehn, *A Low Dishonest Decade*, pp. 68–69.

7. Wandycz, *France and her Eastern Allies, 1919–1925.*

8. For a superb account of the heavy international squabbling and petty rivalries at the peace conference which either decided the future of nations or the very least attempted to set boundaries, see Macmillan, *Paris, 1919: The Six Months that Changed the World.* Also, for a more personal account, see Carton de Wiart, *Happy Odyssey.* De Wiart, who headed the British military mission during the early days of Poland's struggles and again in 1939, wrote: "I cannot remember our government [i.e., UK] agreeing with the Poles over any question, and there were many: Danzig, that first nail in Poland's coffin; Vilna, Eastern Galicia, Teschen; the demarcation of the Russian-Polish frontier; and Upper Silesia," p. 119. Also, "Britain with her usual anti–Polish policy was definitively opposed to giving it [i.e., Eastern Galicia] to the Poles. I went to Paris to see Mr. Lloyd George on the matter and to try to persuade him either to give Eastern Galicia outright to the Poles, or at any rate to use his influence to that end. He refused point-blank and he never spoke to me again," p. 112.

9. Citino, *The Evolution of Blitzkrieg Tactics: Germany Defends Itself Against Poland, 1918–1933.*

10. Mueller, "Rapallo Reexamined: A New Look at Germany's Secret Military Collaboration with Russia in 1922," *Military Affairs*, 40 (1976): 109–117.

11. Korbel, *Poland Between East and West: Soviet and German Diplomacy toward Poland*; Debicki, *Foreign Policy of Poland, 1919–1939*; Riekhoff, *German-Polish Relations 1918–1933.*

12. (NA) PRO FO 371/19221.

13. "We must cut our losses in central and eastern Europe — let Germany, if she can, find her 'lebensraum,' and establish herself, if she can as a powerful economic unit." From *The Diaries of Sir Alexander Cadogan, 1938–1945*, p. 119.

14. Cienciala and Komarnicki, *From Versailles to Locarno: Keys to Polish Foreign Policy, 1919–1925.*

15. Polonsky, *Politics in Independent Poland, 1919–1939.* For a very unique and excellent account of the economic aspects of the interwar politics, see Kaiser, *Economic Diplomacy and the Origins of the Second World War.*

16. Rothschild, *Pilsudski's Coup D'État.*

17. Jedrzejewicz, "The Polish Plan for a Preventive War against Germany in 1933," *Polish Review*, XI (1966): 62–91. Also see *The Diplomats, 1919–1939*, pp. 612–614.

18. The French foreign minister is reported to have assured Ribbentrop that Germany would have its long-sought "free hand in the East." See Hehn, op.cit., p. 92.

19. The following monographs address the Polish prewar military planning and budgets: Kozlowski, *Wojsko Polskie, 1936–1939*, and Krzyzanowski, *Wydatki Wojskowe Polski w Latach, 1918–1939*; Stachiewicz, ed. *Waclaw Stachieiwcz: General Szef*

Sztabu Glownego, 1935–1939; Kurowski, *Lotnictwo Polskie w 1939 roku*; Bartel, Chojnacki, Krolikiewicz, Kurowski, *Z Historii Polskiego Lotnictwa Wojskowego, 1918–1939. Wojna Obronna Polski, 1939. Wybor Zrodel, Przygotowania wojenne w Polsce 1935 oraz kampania 1939 w relacjach i rozwazaniach szefa Sztabu Glownego i szefa sztabu Naczelnego Wodza.*

20. Cienciala, *Poland and the Western Powers, 1938–1939.*

21. Newman, *March 1939: The British Guarantee to Poland*, pp. 156, 194.

22. *The Polish White Book: Official Documents concerning Polish-German and Polish Soviet Relations, 1933–1939*, p. 78.

23. Richard A. Woytak, "The Promethean Movement in Interwar Poland," *East European Quarterly* (1984) 18: 273–278. A number of officers from the Soviet enslaved countries were employed by the Polish armed forces under a contract. One of these was the father of a future chief of staff of the American forces, General Shalikashvili.

24. Komorowski, "Doswiadczenia wojskowe polskiej konspiracji" in Panecki, ed., *Polski Wysilek Zbrojny w Drugiej Wojnie Swiatowej*, pp. 70–71.

25. Marcin Kwiecien and Grzegorz Mazur, "Dzialalnosc prometejska i dywersia na Wschodzie. (Relacia majora Wlodzimierza Dabrowskiego)," *Zeszyty Historyczne* (2002) 140: 102–116.

26. Grzywacz, Kwiecien and Mazur, op. cit.

27. Waclaw Malinowski, "O Organizacji Oddzialow Spadochronowych w Wojsku Polskim przed 1939." *Wojskowy Przglad Historyczny*, 1961; 2:162–174

28. AISM LOT A.I. 2/11 On August 8, 1939, a French Amiot E bomber landed at Okecie. In turn the Poles mobilized a group of experts and prepared landing fields for the French in western Poland. Colonel Karpinski, a very experienced officer and well acquainted with Polish aviation matters, was moved to what turned out to be a complete dead end.

29. Jedrzejewicz, ed. *Diplomat in Paris, 1936–1939: Memoirs of Juliusz Lukasiewicz, Ambassador of Poland*, pp. 202–290, specifically 290. Also, *The Polish White Book: Official Documents Concerning Polish-German and Polish-Soviet Relations 1933–1939*, pp. 137–138.

30. McLeod and Kelly, eds. *Time Unguarded: The Ironside Diaries, 1937–1940*, p. 85.

31. Turnbull and Suchcitz, eds. *The Diary and Despatches of a Military Attache in Warsaw, 1938–1939*, p. 47.

32. McLeod and Kelly op. cit., pp. 81–82. Also Kaiser, *Economic Diplomacy and the Origins of Second World War: Germany, Britain, France and Eastern Europe*, p. 307. In April 1939, Beck, on a visit to London, asked for a loan. The British ambassador in Warsaw, the FO and all UK military ministries supported the Polish request but the UK Treasury refused. Poles requested 60 million pounds and since the UK had little to offer Poland the Poles wanted the money to be spent primarily in the USA. In June 1939, the representatives of the Polish treasury again requested an unrestricted loan of 24 million pounds sterling. On June 28, Simon agreed to 5 million to be spent in the UK conditioned on France doing the same (France did).

33. Lewin, *Ultra Goes to War.*

34. The construction and existence of Polish bunkers and set field defenses is relatively unknown. There is an excellent chapter on the Polish "schrony" in Kaufmann and Jurga, *Fortress Europe: European Fortifications of World War II.* p. 305.

35. Meehan, *The Unnecessary War. Whitehall and the German Resistance to Hitler.*

36. There is a short article in English which describes the travails of the Polish military mission in London. It specifically deals with the attempt to obtain modern British fighter planes. Wojtek Matusiak, "The First Polish Spitfire," *Air-Britain Aeromilitaria* 29, no. 116 (2003): 169–172.

37. Grzywacz, Kwiecien, Mazur, *Zbior dokumentow pplk. Edmunda Charaszkiewicza.*

38. Wilkinson and Astley, *Gubbins and SOE.* Also, Wilkinson, *Foreign Fields: The Story of an SOE Operative.*

39. The British and the French were convinced throughout the 1943's — with considerable justification — that oil was going to be the keystone to the outcome of the war. See Butler, *Grand Strategy*, Volume II, HMSO, London, 1957, pp. 213–214.

40. Grzywacz, Kwiecien, Mazur, op. cit., pp. 131–134.

41. Wikinson and Astley, op. cit., pp. 38–40. Also, the Polish pilot, Aleksander Onoszko, confirms this story in a short article in *Skrzydla*, December 1994, pp. 25–27, a periodical of the Polish Air Force Association in London. Onoszko became a pilot in the Polish Air Force, flew in the 304 Bomber Squadron and at war's end was a major. After the war he flew for British Airways.

42. *Happy Odyssey: The Memoirs of Lieutenant-General Sir Adrian Carton de Wiart.*

43. Nekrich, *Pariahs, Partners, Predators: German-Soviet Relations, 1921–1941*, pp. 114–122.

44. The Polish merchant marine sailed as part of the Commission Interalliee des Transportes Maritimes. Finally it became part of the Allied merchant navy pool. See Peszke, *Poland's Navy 1918–1945*, pp. 199–202.

45. Peszke, op. cit., pp. 31–32.

46. Cieplewicz and Zgornik, *Przygotowania Niemieckie do agresji na Polske in 11939 roku w swietle Sprawozdan odzialu II sztabu glownego Wojska Polskiego.*

47. *The British War Blue Book: Documents Concerning German-Polish Relations and the Outbreak of Hostilities between Great Britain and Germany on September 3rd, 1939.*

Cannistraro, Wynot Jr. and Kovaleff, *Poland and the Coming of the Second World War: The Diplomatic papers of A. J. Drexel Biddle, Jr., United States Ambassador to Poland, 1937–1939.*

48. APISM LOT A.I.3/1e. Riess made it to the United Kingdom where he was assigned to the RAF testing and experimental base at Boscombe Down. He was killed in an accident in 1942 while testing a Halifax bomber. The date of September 27 was voted by the Polish Parliament in 2001 as the official commemorative holiday of the Secret State.

49. Strzembosz, *Rzespospolita Podziemna*, pp. 18–37.

50. Keegan in his *Battle for History* wrote "the Polish army—almost completely unmechanized, almost without air support, almost surrounded by the Germans from the outset and, shortly, completely surrounded when the Red Army joined the aggression—fought more effectively than it has been given credit for," p. 67.

51. Zaloga, *Poland 1939: The Birth of the Bliztkrieg.*

52. The number of English-language studies of September 1939 is small. The only ones which merit any mention are as follows. Neugebauer, *The Defense of Poland, September 1939.* This was the first semi-official Polish report. A good and very readable study is by Zaloga and Madej, *The Polish Campaign, 1939.* Baldwin, *The Crucial Years, 1939–1941*, pp. 64–72. Maier, Stegeman and Umbreit, eds. *Germany and the Second World War, Vol. II Germany's Initial Conquests in Europe*, pp. 69–150.

53. Kennedy, *The German Campaign in Poland, 1939.* See also Zaloga and Madej, *The Polish Campaign, 1939.*

54. Maier, Rohde, Stegeman and Umbreit, eds. op. cit., pp. 125–126.

55. See also Rossino, *Hitler Strikes Poland: Bliztkrieg, Ideology, and Atrocity.*

56. Weinberg, *The Foreign Policy of Hitler's Germany: Starting World War II, 1937–1939.* Also, Rossino, op. cit.

57. Gross, *Revolution from Abroad: The Soviet Conquest of Poland's Western Ukraine and Western Belorussia.* Also Piotrowski, *Poland's Holocaust.*

2. The Fight Continues: October 1939 through June 1940

1. *Reprint of the Konstytucja Rzeczypospolitej Polskiej*, Jozef Pilsudski of America, New York, 1944, pp. 36–40.

2. The actual sequence of events was far more complex but irrelevant to the topic; see Pestkowska, *Za Kulisami Rzadu Polskiego na Emigracji*, pp. 11–32. Sikorski, who had good contacts with the

French going back to his days as prime minister in the 1920s and was a member of Front Morges (an opposition group to the Polish government), traveled from Romania to France in the company of the French ambassador, Noel. For a succinct English account of these changes, see Polonsky, *Politics in Independent Poland*, pp. 502–505.

3. Jedrzejewicz, ed., *Julian Lukasiewicz, Diplomat in Paris*; Raczynski, *In Allied London.*

4. Pestkowska, *Kazimierz Sosnkowski.*

5. Sword, ed., *Sikorski: Soldier and Statesman.*

6. The Rada Narodowa was a Polish parliament in exile in which all the various political parties except for the Communists were represented. It had no executive authority over the government but did have a major moral sway in the process of its discussions and decrees. Within weeks the name *Rada Narodowa* was changed to *Rada Narodowa Rzeczypospolitej Polskiej.* All war time Polish government decrees may be found in Kunert. ed. *Rzeczpospolita Polska Cazu Wojny. Dziennik Ustaw i Monitor Polski, 1939–1945.*

7. *Polskie Sily Zbrojne w Drugiej Wojnie Swiatowej, Kampania na Obczyznie.* Tom II Czesc 1, pp. 19–31. This number represented about 80 percent of the mobilized military aviation on September 1, 1939.

8. Alexander Statiev, "Antonescu's Eagles Against Stalin's Falcons: The Romanian Air Force, 1920–1941," *Journal of Military History* 66 (2002): 1085–1113.

9. Kurcz, *The Black Brigade.*

10. Peplonski, *Wywiad Polskich Sil Zbrojnych na Zachodzie, 1939–1945*, pp. 30–33.

11. Colonel Jozef Jaklicz, the 1939 assistant chief of staff of the Polish Army, wrote a very succinct and dramatic account of the last three days of the work of the Polish staff just prior to crossing the Romanian boundary. He states that on September 16, Smigly-Rydz met one on one with Major Galinat. The inference from subsequent events was that as early as the 16th Galinat was being instructed to begin clandestine activities in occupied Poland modeled on the work of the 1917–1918 Polska Organizacja Wojskowa. *Zeszyty Historyczne* 12 (1967): 140–162.

12. Grzywacz, Kwiecien and Mazur, op. cit.

13. Tarczynski, *Organizacja Zrzutow Materialowych dla Armii Krajowej*, p. 1.

14. (NA) PRO ADM 199/1393 80530. A formal British internal memo states: "In view of General Sikorski's statement that the Polish Government has good means of communicating with their people in Poland through neutral countries, the need for sending agents by air was not apparent."

15. (NA) PRO HS4/321.

16. *Ibid.*

17. *Ibid.*

18. Unlike the majority of the officers of the

Polish clandestine forces, Colonel Fieldorf started his odyssey in the United Kingdom. Later in the war, hundreds of relatively junior officers were parachuted to Poland from bases in the UK and Italy. For a biography of this hero, see Zachuta, *General "NIL": August Emil Fieldorf.*

19. Ney-Krwawicz, *Powstanie Powszechne w koncepcjach i pracach Sztabu Naczelngego Wodza i Komendy Glownej Armii Krajowe*j, pp. 24–30. Also see Garlinski, *Poland, SOE and the Allies*, pp. 30–38.

20. Medlicott, *The Economic Blockade.*

21. While there are a number of excellent English-language studies of the Polish situation in World War II in which inevitably the Poles are presented as passive objects, often victims of the foreign policies of the big powers, there is a lack of any monograph which would show Polish foreign policy attempts, however modest, except for the Polish policy toward their southern neighbor. Wandycz, *Czechoslovak-Polish Confederation and the Great Powers, 1940–1943.* But for a good study of the British policies in the Balkans region, see Woodward, *British Foreign Policy in the Second World War*, Vol. 1, pp. 22–30, 33–80.

22. In fact, General Sikorski's wife left occupied Poland as a result of the intervention of the Italian officials. She traveled through Italy and joined her husband.

23. The Polish estimate turned out to be close to the mark. At war's end, in spite of heavy losses, the Polish Air Force in the West had 14 squadrons and many air crew in transport command.

24. About 1,500 aviation personnel were in Lithuania and due to the far stricter oversight by the Lithuanians and a very effective sea blockade to prevent smuggling of Poles to Sweden, they were eventually captured by the Soviets when the Baltic countries were taken over. They avoided the fate of their colleagues captured in Poland in September 1939 and were in the long run given amnesty in 1941 and moved to the UK to rejoin the main body of the Polish Air Force.

25. For an excellent discussion of the Polish Air Force in France, see Belcarz, *Lotnictwo Polskie we Francji.*

26. Slizewski, *The Lost Hopes: Polish Fighters over France in 1940.*

27. Jackson, *France, The Dark Days, 1940–1945.* It may be added that when the Third Republic negotiated an armistice with Germany in June 1940, its demise was not mourned by many. On July 9, 1940, the French Parliament met in Vichy and by a close to unanimous vote abolished the post of president and voted Petain as head of state. The Third Republic was dead and Vichy France had been born.

28. Belcarz, *GC 1/145 in France, 1940.*

29. I have always been intrigued as to the origin of the often-repeated allegation that Poland's Military Aviation was destroyed on the ground in the first day(s) of the war. The opening of the SOE files recently may throw some light on this. These contain the report of General Carton de Wiart, head of the British mission to Poland, NA PRO HS4/223 and /225. de Wiart makes that statement (while Wilkinson in his book; *Foreign Fields: The Story of an SOE Operative*, p. 75 confirms) that on September 10 the British Mission met with General Rayski of the Polish Military Aviation and he assured them that the Polish planes had been destroyed on the ground. Now the question that can not be answered is whether the British misunderstood Rayski, (presumably the conversation was in the lingua franca of Eastern Europe, namely French; or whether Rayski was attempting to make a dramatic point to urge the British to speed up their deliveries or initiate bombing operations.

30. Report of Flight-Lieutenant Landau, NA PRO AIR 2/4213.

31. NA PRO FO 371/124465.

32. Brown, *Airmen in Exile: The Allied Air Forces in the Second World War.*

33. For the British thinking on this strategic and economic issue, see Woodward, *British Foreign Policy in the Second World War*, Vol. I, pp. 58–91.

34. Kersaudy, *Norway, 1940.*

35. Sopocko, *Orzel's Patrol: The Story of the Polish Submarine.* There is only one English-language monograph dedicated to the Polish Navy in World War II: see, Peszke *Poland's Navy, 1918–1945.*

36. Ney-Krwawicz, op. cit., p. 38.

37. Belcarz, *Polskie Lotnictwo we Francji.* Author mentions the following planes flown by the Poles: Loire LO-46, Potez 63-11, Potez 540, Potez 25 TOE, North American A 57, Marcel Bloch MB 152, Koolhoven FK 58, Caudron C 714, Morane Saulnier MS 406, Liore et Olivier LeO 451, Bloch MB 210, Bloch MB 174 A3, Bloch MB 131, Amiot 143, Loire 46, Dewoitine D520, Curtiss Hawk H 75 A2. See also Belcarz, *GC 1/145 in France.*

38. Kukiel, *General Sikorski: Zolnierz i Maz Stanu Polski Walczacej.*

39. Benoist-Mechin, *Sixty Days that Shook the World: The Fall of France, 1940.* Spears, Vol. 1, *Assignment to Catastrophe: Prelude to Dunkirk*, and Vol. 2, *Assignment to Catastrophe: The Fall of France.*

40. Roskill, *The War at Sea, 1939–1945*, Vol. I, p. 239.

3. June 1940 through June 1941

1. The situation of the Polish airmen was finessed by the British by their insistence on

enrolling all of them as members of the Royal Air Force Volunteer Reserve. See Chapter II for the background to this issue.

2. (NA) PRO PREM 7/2 83781.

3. *Ibid.*

4. From what I have been able to research, the "French" Poles were also initially all enrolled in the RAFVR pending the new agreement of August 5, 1940. While I have not seen any archival evidence, I am basing my opinion on the fact that my father, who arrived in the United Kingdom on *Arrandora Star* in June 1940 from France, was also enrolled in the RAF Volunteer Reserve.

5. For example, in the RAFVR the holder of Poland's highest decoration, the Virtuti Militari, could not have worn the brevet unless authorized by RAF superiors. After this the Virtuti Militari was highest in order of precedence.

6. (NA) PRO AIR 8/ 370 83781.

7. (NA) PRO AIR 2/ 5153.

8. (NA) PRO AIR 8/295.

9. For details of the pertinent military agreements, see Appendix II.

10. Garlinski, *Poland in the Second World War.*

11. Woodward, *British Foreign Policy in the Second World War*, Vol. II, pp. 502–551. Also, Howard, *The Mediterranean Strategy in the Second World War.*

12. Anna M. Cienciala, "The Question of the Polish-Soviet Frontier in 1939–1940: the Litauer Memorandum," *Polish Review* 33, No. 3: 295–323. Also see "Dwa Memorialy Sztabowe na temat Zwiazku Sowieckiego z polowy 1940 roku," *Bellona* (1960) No. 1: 36–40.

13. Deighton and Hastings, *Battle of Britain*, and Mason, *Battle Over Britain*, give a complete list of all participants and their confirmed victories. The Poles of 303 came in first. Robinson, *RAF Fighter Squadrons in the Battle of Britain*, writes about the Polish 303: "In four and half weeks in combat it had been credited with 126 enemy aircraft destroyed, for the loss of eight of its own pilots killed. It was an achievement unequalled by any other RAF fighter squadron."

14. Wegrzecki, *Kosynierzy Warszawscy: Historia 303 Dywizionu Mysliwskiego Warszawskiego Imienia Tadeusza Kosciuszki*, Londyn, 1968. This compilation of the squadron diaries contains the photographs of all the luminaries who came to pay their compliments.

15. Cisek, *Kosciuszko, We are Here! American Pilots of the Kosciuszko Squadron in Defense of Poland, 1919–1921.*

16. Wegrzecki, op. cit., p. 53.

17. Churchill, *Their Finest Hour*, p. 182.

18. The RAF Museum at Hendon, a suburb of London, has a Defiant in the markings of the 307 Polish Squadron.

19. o. de b. of all Polish squadrons and their equipment, see Appendix IV.

20. Gretzyngier, *Poles in the Defence of Britain (July 1940–June 1941).*

21. Enough has been written to suggest that the Jerzy network was the only Allied group until Donovan came on the scene in 1943. Also the Poles had a major clandestine system in Northeast France built around the prewar Polish migration. See also Peplonski, *Wywiad Polskich Sil Zbrojnych na Zachodzie, 1939–1945.*

22. Foot, *SOE: The Special Operations Executive*, p.195

23. Wilkinson, *Foreign Fields: The Story of an SOE Operative*, p. 122. For a sympathetic picture of this glamorous figure, see Binney, *The Women who Lived for Danger: The Agents of SOE.*

24. I have been unable to research this question, but it seems intuitive that given the prewar close relations between the Hungarians and the Poles, there must have been active assistance from certain elements of the Hungarian military in arranging this "escape."

25. Siemaszko, *Radiotelegrafia i Radiowywiad (1939–1946)*, pp. 9–13. I am deeply indebted to Mr. Siemaszko for providing both published as well as personal information of the depth and richness of the Polish military wireless services.

26. Siemaszko, *Lacznosc i Polityka*, and *Radiotelegrafia i Radiowywiad (1939–1946)*. The British SOE report dated December 24, 1941, confirms the essentials of the significant Polish accomplishment. See (NA) PRO HS4/136 27181.

27. Taken from Foot, op.cit., p. 109.

28. See Stenton, *Radio London and Resistance in Occupied Poland*, pp. 278–311. This is an outstanding book and gives an excellent background on many of the diplomatic issues between the Poles, British and the Soviets. But it does not seem to give a clear differentiation between the BBC Service from London and radio Swit. Also see Garnett, *The Secret History of PWE: The Political Warfare Executive, 1939–1945.*

29. Churchill, *The Grand Alliance*, p. 686.

30. Balfour, *The Armoured Train: Its Development and Usage.*

31. Pienkos, *For Your Freedom Through Ours: Polish-American Efforts on Poland's Behalf, 1863–1991.*

32. Richards, *Secret Flotillas: Clandestine Sea Lines to France and French North Africa, 1940–1944.*

33. Slowikowski, *In the Secret Service: The Lighting of the Torch.*

34. Tadeusz Piszczkowski, *Miedzy Lizbona a Londynem*, published by the Polish Institute and General Sikorski Museum, London, 1979. Based on archives in the Polish Institute and comprising the papers of Polish Foreign Ministry staff and intelligence officers in Lisbon with representatives of Romania and Hungary.

35. Foot, op.cit.

36. *Ibid.*, p. 30.

37. NA PRO HS4/185 23532.

38. Ney-Krwawicz, op. cit., p. 79. Also, see *Armia Krajowa w Dokumentach, 1939–1945*. Tom I, pp. 301–303.

39. (NA) PRO AIR 8/295 80530.

40. For a comprehensive account of the structure of the Polish General Staff and Ministry of War, see J. Lunkiewicz, (colonel, Polish Army) "Naczelne Wladze Polskich Sil Zbrojnych na Obczyznie w latach, 1939–1945," *Bellona*, Number II (1957): pp. 42–56, and Nos. II–V: pp. 3–11.

41. Ney-Krwawicz, op. cit., p. 81.

42. Mackenzie, *The Secret History of SOE*, p. 311.

43. In his memoirs, Sosabowski does more than just leave an impression that the whole idea of the Parachute Brigade and entre to Ringway was his own sole initiative and his role in its formation is a matter of historical legend. See Sosabowski, *Freely I Served*. This version is also accepted by Cholewczynski in his excellent book, *Poles Apart: The Polish Airborne at the Battle of Arnhem*.

44. (NA) PRO HS4/185 23532.

45. *Ibid.*

46. Garlinski, op. cit., pp. 55–62, gives a full account of the early beginning and the Polish officers in the training of Poles and in some case of British SOE officers (e.g. Captain Strawinski, an expert in mining, killed later in Italy in 1944).

47. Jackson, *The Secret Squadrons: Special Duty Units of the RAF and USAAF in the Second World War.*

48. (NA) PRO AIR 19/818 80530.

49. Tadeusz Kmiecik, "Dzialalnosc Wydzialu Lotniczego KG AK w Czasie II Wojny Swiatowej," *Wojskowy Przeglad Historyczny* No. 3–4 (1990): 143–157.

50. Ney-Krwawicz has unearthed an interesting fact, that in July 1941 Sikorski communicated with the Polish Air Force Inspectorate to remedy the current personnel situation and assignments, with the words, "czas w ktorym musieliscie sie wyslugiwac RAF skonczyl sie." Op. cit., p. 156.

51. APISM LOT AV II/1a.

52. *Ibid.*

53. (NA) PRO HS4/155. I first reported this finding in *Polish Review*, Vol. 42 (1997): 401–416.

54. Pimlott, ed., *The Second World War Diaries of Hugh Dalton*, p. 142.

55. *Ibid.*, p. 133.

56. NA PRO HS4/149 31884.

57. Churchill, *The Unrelenting Struggle: War Speeches by the Right Hon. Winston S. Churchill, C.H. M.P.*

58. Ney-Krwawicz, op. cit., p. 185.

4. June 1941 through December 1942

1. Gorodetsky, *Stafford Cripps' Mission to Moscow, 1940-1942.*

2. Gorodetsky, *Grand Delusion: Stalin and the German Invasion of Russia.*

3. Gross, *Revolution from Abroad: The Soviet Conquest of Poland's Western Ukraine and Western Belorussia.* Compare with Gross, *Polish Society Under German Occupation: The Generalgouvernement, 1939–1944.*

4. Cholawski describes his experiences in the east of Poland and writes; "At the end of August, 1942, the Soviet Command appointed Gilchik commander of the Jewish Unit. Gilchik was a Russian Jew from Kopy and the Soviet Command which was directed by the Communist Party, placed more faith in persons from the East." *Soldiers from the Ghetto. The First Uprising Against the Nazis*, p.95. Also Pinchuk, *Shtetl Jews under Soviet Rule. Eastern Poland on the Eve of the Holocaust*, pp. 20-27.

5. Churchill, *The Grand Alliance*, p. 378.

6. *Ibid.*, p. 391.

7. Anna M. Cienciala, "General Sikorski and the Conclusion of the Polish-Soviet Agreement of July 30th, 1941: A Reassessment," *Polish Review* 41 (1996): 401-434.

8. *Documents on Polish-Soviet Relations, 1939-1945*, Vol. I. pp. 392-393, and Jedrzejewicz ed., *Poland in the British Parliament*, Vol. 1, pp. 469-480.

9. (NA) PRO HS4/218.

10. Pomian, *Joseph Retinger: Memoirs of an Eminence Grise.*

11. *Destiny Can Wait: The Polish Air Force in the Second World War*, pp. 28-29.

12. The following is only one example of the pro–Soviet propaganda that was endemic in the United States. Joseph E. Davies in an article in *Life* (March 29, 1943) wrote: "The Soviet Government is not a predatory power like Germany or Japan," while the editors of *Life* compared the Soviet Union favorably to the United States: "Like the USA the USSR is a huge melting pot only in a different way. They don't mix as much as our ethnic groups do; yet the system by which all these people are held runs parallel to ours in that it is a federation." If these people did not mix, then how was it a melting pot? But in those days any critique of the Soviets was regarded as an antiwar sabotage.

13. (NA) PRO WO 216/19 38026.

14. *Documents on Polish-Soviet Relations*, p. 68.

15. Churchill, *Hinge of Fate*, p. 499.

16. Churchill, *Their Finest Hour*, p. 598.

17. Churchill, *The Hinge of Fate*, p. 279. Also,

Hastings, *Bomber Offensive: The Myths and Reality of the Strategic Bombing Offensive, 1939-1945.*

18. (NA) PRO AIR 8/295 80530.

19. Kalinowski, *Lotnictwo Polskie w Wielkiej Brytanii*, pp. 250-254.

20. Tarczynski, *Organizacja Zrzutow Materialowych dla Armii Krajowej*, pp. 53-57.

21. The issue of dropping leaflets over Poland was disputed by the Poles who felt that there was no need for propaganda aimed at the Germans. Also, possession of such leaflets was tantamount to a death sentence and would alert the Germans that such flights were taking place. For this discussion see, NA PRO HS 4/ 149 31884.

22. Bieniecki, *Lotnicze Wsparcie Armii Krajowej*, pp. 32-34.

23. (NA) PRO AIR 19/818 80530.

24. *Ibid.*

25. (NA) PRO AIR 19/815 80530.

26. (NA) PRO AIR 19/815 80530.

27. NA PRO HS4/149 31884.

28. Tarczynski, op. cit.

29. Allanbrooke in his diaries for that time writes: 23 April 1942, "There are two opposed camps in the Poles now. Sikorski and those in England wish to transfer a large contingent home to form forces here, the others wish to form Polish forces in the Middle East. Personally I am in favour of the latter. Any forces in the Middle East this summer will be a Godsend to us." On 24 April, 1942, Alanbrooke writes: "Long talk with Anders. Luckily he is a strong supporter of leaving as many Poles as possible in the Middle East." *War Diaries, 1939-1945 of Field Marshal Lord Alanbrooke*, p. 252.

30. APISM A.XII.1/129.

31. Quoted in *Documents on Polish Soviet-Soviet Relations, 1939-1945*, pp. 344-347.

32. Regulski to Klimecki, quoted in *Documents on Polish-Soviet Relations, 1939-1945*, p. 373.

33. *Ibid.*, p. 344.

34. Churchill, *Hinge of Fate*, p. 269. For an excellent discussion of Anders' role in this see, Meiklejohn Terry, *Poland's Place in Europe*, Chapter "Retreat from Rapprochement, pp. 199-244.

35. *Ibid.*, p. 496.

36. *Ibid.*, p. 919.

37. Patton, *War as I Knew It.*

38. APISM A.V. 20/31 18.

39. (NA) PRO WO 193/42 80751.

40. *Ibid.*

41. APISM A.V. 20/31 18.4

42. Iranek-Osmecki, *The Unseen and Silent.* Garlinski's Polish edition of Poland SOE and the Allies, *Politycy i Zolnierze*, has a complete record of all the couriers parachuted or flown into Poland in the three Wildhorn missions.

43. Peplonski, *Wywiad Polskich Sil Zbrojnych na Zachodzie, 1939-1945*, p. 261.

44. Iranek-Osmecki, op. cit. Exactly 100 were killed, either in combat, or after capture by the Germans or Soviets, often after torture.

45. Laquer, *The Terrible Secret*, pp. 119-122.

46. Karski, *Story of a Secret State.*

47. Lerski, *Poland's Secret Envoy, 1939-1945.*

48. Foot, *SOE: The Special Operations Executive*, op.cit., p. 131.

49. APISM LOT A.V. II/1b.

50. Mitkiewicz, *Z Generalem Sikorskim na Obczyznie* and *W Najwyzszym Sztabie Zachodnich Aliantow, 1943-1945*

51. (NA) PRO AIR 19/815 80530.

52. (NA) PRO ADM 199/1393 80530.

53. *Ibid.*

54. *Destiny Can Wait*, op. cit., p. 142.

55. Franks, *The Greatest Air Battle, 19th August, 1942.*

5. January 1943 through November 1943

1. Kmiecik, "Dzialalnosc Wydzialu Lotniczego KG AK w Czasie II Wojny Swiatowej Opracowania plk. Pil. Bernarda Adameckiego," *Wojskowy Przeglad Historyczny* (1990), Numer 3–4, pp. 143–157.

2. Lerski, *Poland's Secret Envoy, 1939–1945*, p. 75.

3. APISM LOT A.V. II /1b.

4. *Ibid.*

5. Stenton, *Radio London and Resistance in Occupied Europe*, . p. 280.

6. *Ibid.*, p. 290.

7. *Ibid.*, p. 291.

8. Stenton, *Radio London and Resistance in Occupied Europe*, Chapter 26, "Katyn: A gift for Goebbels," pp. 297–311.

9. Stenton, *ibid.*, p. 311.

10. Churchill, *Hinge of Fate*, p. 760, and Zawodny, *Death in the Forest.*

11. Karski, *The Great Powers and Poland, 1919–1945. From Versailles to Yalta.* Also, Polonsky, *The Great Powers and the Polish Question, 1941–1945*; and *Documents on Polish-Soviet Relations, 1939–1945.*

12. The museum combined with the Polish Institute in London and is located at 20 Princes Gate, very near Albert Hall.

13. This cemetery also contains the bodies of nearly 400 Polish airmen who died in plane accidents, or whose battle-damaged craft failed them over Britain. In 1947, the president of Poland, His Excellency Wladyslaw Raczkiewicz, was also interred with his soldiers.

14. This speech is not included in Churchill's memoirs, nor is there even a mention of Sikorski's

accident. It is filed in the National Archives at Kew Gardens, (NA) PRO FO 371/ 7863, as a rough draft and was published in the *Daily Telegraph* July 15, 1943. There is a peculiar silence on this, akin to the famous comment that the "dog didn't bark."

15. Jedrzejewski, ed., *Poland in the British Parliament*, Vol. II, pp. 202–228.

16. (NA) PRO AIR 2/9234. There is also an excellent account, in the form of detailed transcripts of the proceedings in Sword, *Sikorski: Soldier and Statesman*, pp. 167–209.

17. *Ibid.*

18. The other Cambridge traitors were David Maclean, Guy Burgess, James Cairncross, and Anthony Blunt, in Newman, *The Cambridgea Spies.* Norman Davies writes about the corrosion of British political life by avowed Soviet spies and thousands of sympathizers. Christpher Hill (a Soviet mole and card-carrying Communist Party member) ran the Soviet desk at the Foreign Office; Peter Smollet held an analogous position at the Ministry of Information and duly defected; and Kim Philby in the Soviet Section of counterintelligence of MI6. In '*Rising 44: The Battle for Warsaw*, p. 159. Also see O'Malley, *The Phantom Caravan*, wrote shortly after the war, before Davies' views became politically acceptable: "Nearly all newspapers, the BBC, the Army Bureau of Current Affairs, the Army Educational Department, the Political Warfare Executive" all indulged in unapologetic pro–Soviet and anti–Polish stance. O'Malley concludes "persons who had changed their names, or were of mulitple allegiance, self appointed saviours of society, bitter little Messiahs, do-gooders, cranky professors, recognizable fellow travellers, and numberless cam followers from among frustrated and ambitious intellectual proletariat — all burrowing like wood beetles, corrupting the oaken heart of England," p. 251–252.

19. Mitkiewicz, *Z Generalem Sikorskim na Obczyznie*, pp. 238–239. Col. Leon Mitkiewicz was involved in many senior functions of the Polish General Staff in London, including being head of the II (Intelligence Section) of the Polish staff and then Polish delegate to the Combined Chiefs of Staff in Washington, D.C.

20. "Thursday April 9, 1942 : Went to see CIGS about various things…. Found him rather impatient with our attitude of giving everything Russians ask and getting nothing in return, Of course the Russians are fighting — but for themselves and not for us. Meeting with AS [i.e., Eden, Cadogan's political boss] and many others about the form of our Treaties with Russia. A [i.e., Eden] determined to go ahead, gallops gaily over the ground, which will give way under him one of theses days. We're selling the Poles down the river." " Thursday 23 April 1942. Message from Joe [i.e., Stalin] about our visitor from Moscow who may … give us a

rough passage over the Treaty (which I hear is beginning to cause a stink amongst MP's egged on by Victor Cazalet." From *The Diaries of Sir Alexander Cadogan, 1938–1945*, edited by David Dilks, pp. 446–448. The opposition was in fact quite strong among the Anglican and Roman Catholic Church leaders and in the ranks of the Conservative Party with Duff Cooper and Harold Nicolson egged on by Cazalet writing to Eden against boundary changes under the pressures of war.

21. Kunert and Szymer, *Stefan Rowecki*.

22. After the war he authored one of the few and by far the best of studies of the Polish underground army, *The Secret Army*. For his biography, see Kunert, *General Tadeusz Bor-Komorowski w relaciach i dokumentach*.

23. Churchill, *Closing the Ring*, p. 653.

24. The Poles were relatively sympathetic to the desertion of close to 2,000 Polish Jews from Polish forces in the Middle East. But as is often the case in these disputes, Polish archives are challenged so it is pertinent to cite what Jewish authors remember. See Silver, *Begin, the Haunted Prophet*. Begin himself wrote in *White Nights* that he only enrolled in the Polish Army after it became obvious that they were being evacuated to the Middle East. Hirschler and Eckman in their biography of Begin, *From Freedom Fighter to Statesman*, wrote correctly that Begin did not desert, but that he was released from service by the Poles. But they add "most other Jewish refuges from Poland who had come to Palestine with the Anders Army shed their uniforms almost immediately after their arrival without the formality of an official discharge." Also see Dear and Foot, *The Oxford Companion to World War II*: " Some 3,000 Poles who deserted from Anders' Army when it arrived in Palestine subsequently joined Jewish resistance organizations which fought the British," p. 297.

25. National Archives, College Park, CCS 334 218.

26. (NA) PRO WO 193/41 80751.

27. National Archives, College Park, MD. CCS 334 218.

28. APISM LOT AV II/1b.

29. (NA) PRO WO 193/42 80751.

30. *Ibid.*

31. *Ibid.*

32. *Ibid.*

33. (NA) PRO AIR 19/815 80530. The reference to the Polish eastern border reflects that by the middle of 1943 the British had caved in to Soviet demands for Polish territory. See also a cable to the British ambassador in Washington, D.C., from the foreign office. (July 17, 1943, two weeks after Sikorski's accident). "Your Excellency will appreciate that in advocating such a settlement [i.e., the FO was urging the Curzon Line with Poland keeping Lwow and getting Danzig and all of East Prussia]

of Russia's western frontier we should be driving a coach and horses through the Atlantic Charter. We should hope that the President would be prepared to join us on the box." (NA) PRO FO 371/37045. This is cited in Kitchen, *British Policy towards the Soviet Union during the Second World War*, p. 165.

34. APISM LOT AV II/1a.

35. *Ibid.*

36. J. Rostowski, "Polish School of Medicine. University of Edinburgh, 1941–1945," *British Medical Journal* (1966): 1394–1351.

37. APISM LOTA.V. II/ 1a.

6. November 1943 through July 1944

1. Woodward, *British Foreign Policy in the Second World War*, Vol. 2, pp. 635–657.

2. Woodward, *ibid.*, Vol II., p. 641 (October 1943).

3. Stenton, *Radio London and Resistance in Occupied Europe*, p. 291. (NA) PRO file cited—HS4/ 137.

4. For a discussion of this controversial order, see John Lowell Armstrong, "The Polish Underground and the Jews: A Reassessment of Home Army Commander Tadeusz Bor-Komorowski's Order 116 against Banditry," *Slavonic and East European Review* 72 (1994): 259–276. An excellent and as objective a discussion of the ethnic strife in eastern Poland may be found in Snyder, *The Reconstruction of Nations*, pp. 154–201.

5. Cholawski, "When the Russians first came [i.e., in 1939] everyone was happy," p. 33. That can be very well understood in the situation that Soviets seemed more acceptable to local Jewish populations than being occupied by the Germans. What was more difficult to for the Poles to accept was the degree of enthusiastic collaboration with the Soviet Communist authorities. See (NA) PRO FO 371/39534 which objectively confirms this charge. Pinchuk, *Shtetl Jews under Soviet Rule: Eastern Poland on the Eve of the Holocaust*, who thus describes these tragic days: "Polish and independent Jewish sources stress the large scale Jewish expression of enthusiasm towards the Red Army," p.23, and describes the prominent role of Jews in the revolutionary committees that took over the administration of the territories with "expressions of suppressed grudges and hatreds against the haughty Polish officials," pp. 25–26. Kurzman, *The Bravest Battle*, wrote that following the formation of the Jewish secret military there ensued negotiations between the Polish Home Army and the Jewish group regarding their allegiance to the Polish government. The Poles were clearly concerned about the proclivity of the Jewish groups to the Communist cause. Kurzman writes: "Mordechai finally authorized Arie to tell the Home Army with diplomatic ambivalence, since we are citizens of Poland, the decisions of the Polish Government binding upon us." The Polish Home Army was aware of the ambivalence. Yet it was the Polish underground and the Polish government that attempted to arouse Western concern about the Jewish tragedy. See Laquer, *The Terrible Secret: Suppression of the Truth about Hitler's Final Solution*, Chapter 4: "News from Poland," pp. 101–122.

6. *Destiny Can Wait: The History of the Polish Air Force in Great Britain*, pp. 214–217.

7. McLean, *The Ghetto Men: The SS Destruction of the Jewish Warsaw Ghetto, April–May, 1943*. Pelczynski (chief of staff and deputy commanding officer of the AK) writes that the Poles gave the Jewish organization planning resistance all the military equipment in the district of Wola. Seventy pistols, 10 rifles, two light machine guns with ammunition as well as 600 grenades. This help is often either scorned as woefully inadequate or even ignored. The Polish AK also turned over dynamite, and helped the Jewish group with advice regarding the construction of bunkers, etc. The Jewish military groups commanded by Mordechai Anielewicz also attempted to get help from the Communist People's Guard (Gwardia Ludowa) but the extent of such assistance, if any, has not been established. Tadeusz Pelczynski (major general, Polish Army) "Opor Zbrojny w Ghetcie Warszawskim 1943 roku," *Bellona*, Numbers 1 and 2 (1963): 42–49. Piotrowski, *Poland's Holocaust*, p. 108, writes that only one in ten of the Polish soldiers in the AK had a revolver or a rifle and even a year later, at the time of the Warsaw Uprising, only 20 percent of the Polish soldiers were armed.

8. Mackenzie, *The Secret History of SOE*, p. 517.

9. Eubank, *Summit at Tehran: The Untold Story*.

10. (NA) PRO CAB 66134/108655.

11. See Zbigniew Siemaszko, "Retinger w Polsce w 1944r.," *Zeszyty Historyczne* 12 (1967): 56–115.

12. Jedrzejewicz, *Poland in the British Parliament, 1939–1945*, Vol. 2, pp. 286–407.

13. Jedrzejewicz, *ibid.*, pp. 422–494.

14. (NA) PRO WO 371/39481.

15. (NA) PRO FO 371/139484 118894.

16. Babinski, W., "Prasa angielska w sprawach Polskich na przelomie lat 1943–1944," *Zeszyty Historyczne* 20 (1971).

17. Dilks, ed., *The Diaries of Sir Alexander Cadogan, 1938–1945*, pp. 592–608.

18. Jedrzejewicz, op.cit., p. 341.

19. Woodward, *ibid.*, Vol. 3, pp. 161–196. Also, see Jedrzejewicz, op. cit., pp. 311–407.

20. The Soviets were by and large getting what

they wanted. A demand was made to have an American foreign office officer, Loy Henderson, fired for his less than starry-eyed enthusiasm about the Soviets. Litvinov made his ultimatum to Sumner Welles. The criticism was made in the context of the Soviets not appreciating the billions of dollars in lend-lease. Henderson was sent to Iraq. It is not surprising that the Soviets expected to get their way. Fleming, *The New Dealer's War*, pp. 294–296. Also, De Santis, *The Diplomacy of Silence: The American Foreign Service, the Soviet Union, and the Cold War, 1933–1947*, p. 85.

21. (NA) PRO FO 954/20.

22. Woodward, ibid., p. 187. Also (NA) PRO HS4/167. Report re Operation Jula.

23. (NA) PRO HS4/167 (April 1944). There is nothing regarding this issue in Garnett, *The Secret History of PWE, the Political Warfare Executive, 1939–1945*. Engel, *Facing a Holocaust: The Polish Government-in-Exile and the Jews, 1943–1945*, p.173: "For reasons that have yet to be fathomed, it proved much easier to exercise British and American public opinion about allegations that several hundred Jewish soldiers were being taunted and abused in the Polish army, [Engel assumes the charges to be true, which was not a conclusion drawn by the British Foreign Office] than about reports that German forces were systematically murdering millions of Jewish civilians in centers especially designed for that purpose." Engel then answered his own question: "Jewish leaders on the other hand calculated that their own collective interests, and those of the Jewish people as a whole, demanded that they maintain good relations with the Soviet Union...." It is striking that Jewish members of the House of Commons were more concerned about alleged Polish anti–Semitism than by the restrictions placed by their own government on the immigration of Jews from Europe to Palestine, a policy which undoubtedly cost many thousands of Jewish lives. See Offer, *Escaping the Holocaust*.

24. APISM LOT AV II/1a.

25. *Ibid*.

26. *Ibid*.

27. Postwar report by Colonel Bialy. APISM LOT A.V. II/1m.

28. (NA) PRO AIR 29/868.

29. Shores, 2nd Tactical Air Force.

30. (NA) PRO AIR 37/90 96925.

31. (NA) PRO AIR 37/90 9625.

32. The British Army was experiencing a severe shortage of men, particularly infantry. In September, Montgomery was asked to provide an army headquarters for Mountbatten in Burma, to provide a corps headquarters also for Burma, and to give up the 52nd Airborne and two infantry divisions, also for Burma. Hamilton, *Final Years of the Field Marshal, 1944–1974*, p. 102. In March 1944, the British

infantry in Italy was in a critical state. Many antiartillery units were disbanded to augment infantry where battalions were reduced from four to three companies. Two infantry brigades were reduced to cadre strength and the 1st Armoured Division was broken up. John Peaty, "The Desertion Crisis in Italy, 1944," *RUSI* 147, No. 3 (2002): 76–83.

33. (NA) P.R.O. FO 371/39506).

34. NA PRO HS4/147 27181.

35. This came up again in late 1944 and Lord Selborne and his staff urged to "leave well alone." He also pointed that if the Poles were pushed they would figure out a way of bypassing the British censors. Lord Selborne also wrote that in this field (i.e., sabotage and intelligence) "we are indebted to the Poles; their contribution to the war effort has been greater than ours in this field." (NA) PRO HS4/144.

36. (NA) PRO AIR 19/815 80530.

37. Churchill, *Closing the Ring*, p. 711

38. Pomian, *Memoirs of an Eminece Grise*. Also see Nowak, *Courier from Warsaw*, op.cit., p. 388.

39. Ciechanowski (Polish ambassador in Washington, D.C.), *Defeat in Victory*, pp. 272–273.

40. Lane, *I Saw Poland Betrayed*.

41. (NA) PRO AIR 19/816 80530.

42. *Ibid.*

43. (NA) PRO AIR 19/815 80530.

44. NA PRO HS4/ 317.

45. APISM. LOT A.V. II/1a.

46. Garlinski, *Poland, S.O.E. and the Allies*.

47. The best English-language account of Mikolajczyk's visit to the United States is Ciechanowski, op. cit., pp. 305–330. But also see a doctoral dissertation from the University of Kansas, Bradley E. Fels, "That Poland Might Be Free: Polish-American and Polish Efforts to gain American Support for Poland during the Second World War" (2001).

48. National Archives and Records Adminsitration (US) College Park, MD. 334 CCS.

49. Mitkiewicz, *W Najwyzszym Sztabie Zachodnich Aliantow* (*In the Supreme Staff of the Western Allies*), London, 1971.

50. The best account of this combined Polish-British effort can be found in Tadeusz Panecki, "Plan Bardsea w Wykonaniu Wydzialu Spraw Specialnych MON (W. Brytania 1942–144), *Wojskowy Przeglad Historyczny*, pp. 128–138.

51. It should be emphasized that all costs of salary, equipment, gasoline and ammunition, just to mention the most obvious, were the responsibility of the Polish government. The cost of this venture was over £100,000. See Appendix V re final accounting.

52. British perception of this "internecine strife" is to be found in (NA) PRO HS4/136 2718.

53. APISM A.V. 20/31 18.

54. "We have got difficult problems ahead, and to employ the forces of those Allies circumscribed by various restrictions is militarily unsound, and

appears to me politically unwise. Some of those countries who did very little to help us fight the enemy, e.g. France, now appear to be laying down conditions because they see the end in sight. I consider that nations that have been under the heel of Germany must do as we tell them until the war is over and Germany defeated. They will probably have to do as we tell them even after that. I would rather not have them at all." Hamilton, *Master of the Battlefield. Monty's War Years, 1940–1944*, p. 558.

55. APISM. AX II/32/72.

56. APISM. A.V. 20/31 18.

57. APISM. PRM –K 102/70f.

58. Churchill, *Triumph and Tragedy*, p. 592.

59. APISM. A.XII 23/72.

60. This priceless relic hangs in the Polish Institute and General Sikorski Museum, London. See, Denfeld, *World War Two Museums and Relics of Europe*.

61. Churchill, *Closing the Ring*, p. 600. Parker, *Monte Cassino*.

62. Brooks, *The War North of Rome, June 1944–May 1945*, pp. 152–370.

63. Eisenhower, *Crusade in Europe*.

64. A short excellent account of one of these bases is in Moor, *Mustang Wing: RAF Brenzett Advanced Landing Ground—Romney Marsh, 1942–1944*.

65. There are a number of accounts of this night battle. But in my own writings (see *Poland's Navy*) I have used the (NA) PRO ADM 199/1644 . Also see Roskill, *The War at Sea, 1939–1945*, Vol. 3, pp. 56–57.

66. Keegan, *Six Armies in Normandy*.

7. July 1944 through December 1944

1. Paczkowski, *Stanislaw Mikolajczyk: Czyli Kleska Realisty*.

2. Woodward, *British Foreign Policy in the Second World War*, Vol. 2, pp. 612–662, and Vol. 3, pp. 154–277.

3. Ciechanowski, *The Warsaw Rising of 1944*. Also, Zawodny, *Nothing but Honor: The Story of the Warsaw Uprising, 1944*. Davies, *Rising '44. The Battle for Warsaw*.

4. (NA) PRO HS4/156 has a comment from Lord Selborne to the chiefs of staffs: "A fresh instance of their efficiency has just occurred. The aerodromes in Poland from which the parts of the German secret rockets were brought back last week by SOE were seized and held by a Brigade of the Polish Secret Army for the purchase of this operation. Up to that morning the aerodrome had been in use by the Germans." This was also the landing field which received Nowak.

5. Nowak, *Courier from Warsaw*, pp. 291–342. The citation from Pelczynski is on page 335.

6. The British Foreign Office papers regarding British involvement, if any, in the von Weizsacker peace overtures are closed until the year 2018! See Gilbert, *Winston S. Churchill*, p. 868.

7. Translated from the original Polish. Telegram # Ldz. 6213/tj. Quoted in *Polskie Sily Zbrojne w Drugiej Wojnie Swiatowej*, Vol. 3, *Armia Krajowa*. Edited by the Historical Commission of the Polish General Staff, London, 1950, p. 665.

8. My analysis of the available archival and published material is in line with Davies' categorical statement "anyone who believes that the Commander in Chief can be counted on among the instigators of the Rising is plain wrong." Davies, op. cit., p. 211.

9. MacKenzie, *The Secret History of SOE*, p. 523.

10. Michael Peszke, "Poland's Preparation for World War Two," *Military Affairs* 43 (1979): 18–24.

11. NA PRO HS 4/147 28181. (31 July, 1944) File captioned: General Rising by the Polish Secret Army in Warsaw Area. Brief for CD.

12. David Stafford, *Britain and European Resistance, 1940–1945: A Survey of the Special Operations Executive with Documents*, University of Toronto Press, Toronto, 1980.

13. (NA) PRO HS4/156.

14. (NA) PRO WO 216/98 3802.

15. *Ibid*.

16. *Ibid*.

17. Breuer, *Operation Dragoon: The Allied Invasion of the South of France*.

18. Saunders, *Royal Air Force, 1939–1945*. Vol. 3. *The Fight is Won*, pp. 236–243.

19. (NA) PRO HS4/148.

20. (NA) PRO AIR 8/1170 15969. Also, *Destiny Can Wait*, op. cit., pp. 218–228, and two excellent Polish monographs: by Bieniecki, *Lotnicze Wsparcie Armii Krajowej* (Air Assistance to the Underground Army), and Kalinowski, *Lotnictwo Polskie w Wielkiej Brytanni, 1940–1945* (Polish Air Force in Great Britain, 1940–1945).

21. Slessor, *The Central Blue*, pp. 610–622.

22. (NA) PRO AIR 8/1170 15969.

23. Churchill, Vol. 6, *Triumph and Tragedy*, op. cit. Churchill confirms that he was installed in Villa Rivalta, p. 79. Churchill does not mention his meeting with Slessor re Warsaw, but has a whole chapter, "The Martyrdom of Warsaw," where he enumerates the undoubtedly sincere and great efforts to get Roosevelt and Stalin to aid the Polish insurgents, pp. 113–128.

24. (NA) PRO FO 371/39408. The allusion to Churchill can be found in Waclaw Jedrzejewicz, *Poland in the British Parliament, 1939–1945*, Vol. 3, pp. 1–33. This section also includes the heated discussion in the House of Commons on the Warsaw

Uprising, and the Soviet failure to assist the insurgents.

25. Churchill, *Triumph and Tragedy*, op. cit., pp. 113–128. Also, Kimball ed., *Churchill and Roosevelt: The Complete Correspondence*, in three volumes, Vol. 3, pp. 259–365.

26. Churchill, *Triumph and Tragedy*, Chapter IX, "Martyrdom of Warsaw," pp. 113–128.

27. Orpen, *Airlift to Warsaw: The Rising of 1944.* Orpen gives a very good account of the airlift with special attention to the South African squadron and its crews who did their best to aid a cause that they barely understood.

28. (NA) PRO AIR 8/1170 15969. Also, *Destiny Can Wait*, op. cit., pp. 218–228, and two excellent Polish monographs: by Bieniecki, *Lotnicze Wsparcie Armii Krajowej* (Air Assistance to the Underground Army), and Kalinowski, *Lotnictwo Polskie w Wielkiej Brytanni, 1940–1945* (Polish Air Force in Great Britain, 1940–1945).

29. (NA) PRO AIR 8/1170 15969.

30. *Frantic* was the American code name for shuttle bombing. Heavy bombers from Italy or the UK landed at American-staffed bases in the Soviet Ukraine. Also, Conversino, *Fighting with the Soviets: The Failure of Operation Frantic, 1944–1945.*

31. (NA) PRO AIR 8/1170 15969.

32. Kalinowski, op. cit. p. 270.

33. (NA) PRO AIR 8/1170 15969.

34. *Ibid.*

35. Slessor's rude remark about Poles may be forgiven. He was undoubtedly heartsick about the loss of his crews, including the Polish personnel. It is much more difficult to explain his remark in his autobiography, *The Central Blue*, p. 611: "The Poles may have been tactless and often stupid, but they were indomitably brave." Were they tactless because they inopportuned their allies for assistance, or were they tactless because they wished to know who murdered over 10,000 of their officers? Were they stupid, as the German historian suggests, because "The inadequacy of Polish political judgment was reflected in the belief of effective support from Britain and France"? Maier, Rhode, Stegeman and Umbreit, eds., *Germany and the Second World War, Vol. 2, Germany's Initial Conquests in Europe*, pp. 125–126.

36. *Ibid.*

37. Julian, "The Role of the United States Army air Force in the Warsaw Uprising, August–September 1944," *Air Power History* 42 (1995): 22–35.

38. Jedrzejewicz, op. cit., Vol. 3, pp. 5–33.

39. (NA) PRO WO 171/3933784 and Polish Institute London Archives, A.V. 20/31/26; 20/31/31; 20/31/34; 20/31/36; 20/31/38; 20/31/38; 20/31/40; 20/31/42. Also Cholewczynski, *Poles Apart*; Mid-

dlebrook, *Arnhem, 1944: The Airborne Battle*; Urquhart, *Arnhem*; Buckingham, *Arnhem, 1944*; and Swiecicki, *With the Red Devils at Arnhem.*

40. Brereton, *The Brereton Diaries.*

41. Buckingham, *Arnhem, 1944*, pp. 55–56.

42. Buckingham, op.cit., pp. 68–73.

43. Wilmot, *The Struggle for Europe*, pp. 555–601. A slightly different analysis is presented by B. H. Liddell Hart, *History of the Second World War*, pp. 560–567.

44. Buckingham, *Arnhem, 1944*, pp. 198–199. Also, Middlebrook, *Arnhem, 1944: The Airborne Battle*, pp. 447–449.

45. *Documents on Polish-Soviet Relations*, pp. 485–486.

46. Peter Solly-Flood, "Pilgrimage to Poland," *Blackwood's Magazine* 269 (May 1951). Also see Bines, *Operation Freston. The British Military Mission to Poland, 1944.*

8. January 1945 through VE Day

1. Saunders, *Royal Air Force, 1939–1945*. Vol. 3, pp. 208–210. Also, Franks, *Battle of the Airfields: Operation Bodenplatte, 1 January, 1945.*

2. For a general history of these shipping strikes, see Nesbit, *The Strike Wings: Special Anti-Shipping Squadrons, 1942–1945.*

3. Middlebrook and Everitt, *The Bomber Command War Diaries: An Operational Reference Book, 1939–1945.*

4. Harbutt, *The Iron Curtain*, pp. 52–116.

5. Jedrzejewicz, *Poland in the British Parliament*, pp. 334–594.

6. Churchill, *Triumph and Tragedy*, p. 649.

7. NA PRO HS4/291 31896.

8. Kimball, *Churchill and Roosevelt*, p. 565. Also, Churchill, *Triumph and Tragedy*. p. 374.

9. Harbutt, op. cit., pp. 105–107.

10. Woodward, *British Foreign Policy in the Second World War*, Vol. III, p. 548. Also see the report of Sir A. Clark Kerr (British ambassador in Moscow) to the Foreign Office, pp. 556–558.

11. Churchill, *Triumph and Tragedy*, p. 435.

12. Saunders, op. cit., p. 370.

13. Ibid., p. 414. No. 84 Group lists a number of constituent wings, including No. 131 Wing comprised of Squadrons 302, 308 and 317. There is nothing to alert the reader that the wing was an all–Polish unit consisting of three Polish fighter squadrons: 302 (Poznanski), 308 (Krakowski) and 317 (Wilenski).

Bibliography

General Remarks on the Bibliography and Archival Background

This study of the British and Polish strategic goals for the Polish armed forces is based on the Polish archives in London at the Polish Institute and General Sikorski Memorial Museum (cited as **APISM**) and the National Archives in Kew Garden, cited as (NA) PRO. The most important holdings in the National Archives (PRO) are the War Cabinet (CAB), War Office (WAR), Air Force (AIR) and Admiralty (ADM). The recently opened files of the Special Operations Executive (HS4) offer relatively new information.

Since this monograph is directed at the English-reading public, I have tried to limit my notes to English language sources and use Polish historical works only if they are especially valuable or if there is no English-language study whatsoever to document my point. Having said that, it is important to note that much of my work is based on the six volumes of the *Polskie Sily Zbrojne w Drugiej Wojnie Swiatowej — Kampanie na Obczyznie.* (Polish Armed Forces in World War Two — Campaigns in Exile), and *Armia Krajowa* (Home Army), both edited by the historical commission of the Polish General Staff in London and published by the Polish Institute and General Sikorski Museum in London in 1950, 1959 and 1975.

The foundation of all published works on the Polish Air Force, both before the war and during the war, is the final report of the Committee of the Historical Section of the Polish Air Force, chaired by Col. Olgierd Tuskiewicz. This was finalized in 1947 but never published probably because of lack of financial resources. All subsequent published books are based on these findings. The ones which are noteworthy are Franciszek Kalinowski, *Lotnictwo Polskie w Wielkiej Brytanii*, Paris, 1969, and Adam Kurowski, *Lotnictwo Polskie w 1939 roku*, Warsaw, 1962, and, surprisingly free of Communist polemics, Ryszard Bartel, Jan Chojnacki, Tadeusz Krolikiewcz, and Adam Kurows's *Z Historii Polskiego Lotnictwa Wojskowego 1918–1939* (Warsaw, 1978).

There are a number of very specific works which require and absolutely deserve special mention. I need to emphasize the importance of Jan Tarczynski's study of Polish Institute archives regarding the efforts to sustain the AK by air drops — *Organizacja Zrzutow Materialowych dla Armii Krajowej*; also Marek Ney-Krwawicz, *Powstanie Powszechne w Koncepcjach i Pracach Sztabu Naczelnego Wodza i Komendy Glownej Armii*

Krajowej. This monograph is undoubtedly one of the most meticulous and detailed accounts of the efforts of the Polish staff in the West and the staff of the Polish underground army to prepare for a general uprising against the Germans.

Every book cited in footnotes is also listed fully in the bibliography, hence in the endnotes and footnotes I have only given the last name of the author and title.

To help the reader navigate through the complexities of events I included a brief, probably somewhat ethnocentric, chronology in the present work. But for a comprehensive almanac see Robert Goralski, *World War II Almanac, 1931–1945*.

Abella, Irving, and Harold Troper. *None Is Too Many: Canada and the Jews of Europe, 1933–1948.* New York: Random House, 1982.

Addison, Paul, and Jeremy A. Crang. *The Burning Blue: A New History of the Battle of Britain.* London: Pimloco, 2000.

Ambrose, Stephen E. *D-Day: June 6, 1944, The Climactic Battle of World War II.* New York: Simon & Schuster, 1994.

Anders, Wladyslaw. *An Army in Exile.* London: Macmillan, 1949. Reprinted, Nashville, TX: Battery Press, 1981.

Andrew, Christopher. *Her Majesty's Secret Service: The Making of the British Intelligence Community.* New York: Viking, 1986.

_____. *The Sword and the Shield: The Mitrokhin Archive and the Secret History of the KGB.* New York: Basic Books, 1999.

_____, and David Dilks, eds. *The Missing Dimension: Governments and Intelligence Communities in the Twentieth Century.* London: Macmillan,1994.

_____ and Vasili Mitrokhin. *The Mitrokhin Archives: The KGB in Europe and the West.* London: Allen Lane/Penguin, 1999.

Aster, Sidney. *1939: The Making of the Second World War.* New York: Simon and Schuster, 1973.

Baginski, Henryk. *Poland and the Baltic: The Problem of Poland's Access to the Sea.* London: Oliver and Boyd, 1942.

_____. *Poland's Freedom of the Sea.* Kirkcaldy, UK: Allen, 1942.

Balfour, G. *The Armoured Train: Its Development and Usage.* London: Batsford, 1981.

Baldwin, Hanson W. *Battles Lost and Won.* New York: Harper and Row, 1966.

_____. *The Crucial Years, 1939–1941.* New York: Harper and Row, 1976.

Baluk, Stefan, and Marian Michalowski. *Poland at Arms, 1939–1945.* Warsaw: Polonia, 1990.

Baluk, Stefan Starba. *Poles on the Fronts of World War II, 1939–1945.* Warsaw: ARS, 1995.

Barbarski, Krzysztof. *Polish Armour, 1939–1945.* London: Osprey, 1982.

Badsey, Stephen. *Arnhem 1944: Operation Market Garden.* London: Osprey, 1993.

Batowski, Henryk, ed. *17 Wrzesnia 1939.* Proceedings of a conference held in Kracow 25th and 26th October 1993. Polska Akademia Umiejetnosci, Krakow, 1994.

Bauer, Piotr, and Boguslaw Polak. *Armia Poznan w Wojnie Obronnej*, Warsaw: MON, 1983.

Beaumont, Joan. *Comrades in Arms: British Aid to Russia, 1941–1945.* London: Davis-Poynter, 1980.

Beck, Jozef. *Final Report.* New York: Speller, 1957.

Beesley, Patrick. *Very Special Intelligence: The Story of the Admiralty's Operational Intelligence Centre, 1939–1945.* New York: Doubleday, 1978.

Beevor, J. G. *S.O.E. Recollection and Reflexions, 1940–1945.* London: Bodley Head, 1981.

Bekker, Cajus. *The Luftwaffe War Diaries.* Ballantine: New York, 1969.

Belcarz, Bartlomiej. *GC 1/145 in France, 1949.* Sandomierz: Stratus, 2002.

_____. *Polskie Lotnictwo we Francji.* Sandomierz: Stratus, 2002.

_____, and Robert Peczkowski. *White Eagles: The Aircraft, Men and Operations of the Polish Air Force, 1918–1939.* Ottringham, UK: Hilcoki, 2001.

_____, and Tomasz J. Kopanski. *PZL, P. 11c.* Sandomierz: Stratus, 2003.

Bell, P. M. H. *John Bull and the Bear: British Public Opinion, Foreign Policy and the Soviet Union, 1941–1945.* London: Edward Arnold, 1990.

_____. *The Origins of the Second World War in Europe*. London: Longman, 1986.

Benoist-Mechin, Jacques. *Sixty Days that Shook the World: The Fall of France, 1940*. New York: Putnam, 1963.

Bethell, Nicholas. *The War Hitler Won: The Fall of Poland, 1939*. New York: Rinehart & Winston, 1972.

Bickers, Richard Townshend. *The Battle of Britain*. London: Salamander Books, 1990.

Bines, Jeffery. *Operation Freston: The British Military Mission to Poland*. Private printing, 1999.

Binney, Marcus. *The Women Who Lived for Danger: The Agents of SOE*. New York: Harper Collins, 2002.

Bishop, Jim. *FDR'S Last Year: April 1944–April 1945*. New York: Pocket Books, 1975..

Bohlen, Charles E. *Witness to History, 1929–1969*. New York: Norton, 1973.

Bond, Brian. *France and Belgium, 1939–1940*. Newark: University of Delaware Press, 1975.

Bor-Komorowski, Tadeusz. *The Secret Army*. Nashville: Battery, 1984.

Breitman, Richard, and Walter Laquer. *Breaking the Silence*. New York: Simon and Schuster, 1986.

Brereton, Lewis H. *The Brereton Diaries: The War in the Air in the Pacific, Middle East and Europe, 3 October 1941–8 May 1945*. New York: Morrow, 1946.

Breuer, William B. *Operation Dragoon: The Allied Invasion of the South of France*. Novato, CA: Presidio, 1987.

British War Blue Book. Documents Concerning German-Polish Relations and the Outbreak of Hostilities between Great Britain and Germany on September 3, 1939. London: His Majesty's Stationery Office, 1939.

British Bombing Survey Unit. *The Strategic Air War Against Germany, 1939–1945*. London: Cass, 1997.

Brooks, Timothy R. *The War North of Rome, June 1944–May 1945*. Edison, NJ: Castle Books, 2001.

Brown, Alan. *Airmen in Exile: The Allied Air Forces in the Second World War*. Gloucester, UK: Sutton Publishing, 2000.

Buckingham, William F. *Arnhem, 1944*. London: Tempus, 2002.

Budiansky, Stephen. *Battle of Wits: The Complete Story of Codebreaking in World War II*. New York: Free Press, 2000.

Burrin, Phillipe. *France Under the Germans: Collaboration and Compromise*. New York: New Press, 1997.

Butler, James Ramsay Montagu, ed. *Grand Strategy, Volume II, September 1939–June 1941*. London: Her Majesty's Stationery Office, 1957.

_____, ed. *Grand Strategy, Volume III, June 1941–August, 1942*. London: Her Majesty's Stationery Office, 1964.

Cannistraro, Philip V., Edward D. Wynot, Jr., and Theodore P. Kovaleff. *Poland and the Coming of the Second World War: The Diplomatic Papers of A.J. Drexel Biddle Jr., United States Ambassador to Poland, 1937–1939*. Columbus: Ohio State University Press, 1976.

Cazalet, Victor A. *With Sikorski to Russia*. London: Curwen, 1942.

Chamberlain, Neville. *In Search of Peace*. 1939. Reprint, Freeport, NY: Books for Libraries, 1971.

Charmley, John. *Churchill's Grand Alliance: The Anglo-American Special Relationship, 1940–1957*. New York: Harcourt Brace, 1995.

Chodakiewicz, Marek Jan. *Between Nazis and Soviets: Occupation Politics in Poland, 1939–1947*. Lexington, MA: Lexington Books, 2004.

Cholawski, Shalom. *Soldiers from the Ghetto: The First Uprising Against Nazis*. New York: Herzl Press, 1980.

Cholewczynski, George. *Poles Apart: The Polish Airborne at the Battle of Arnhem*. New York: Sarpedon, 1993.

Churchill, Winston S. *The Second World War*. In six volumes: *The Gathering Storm, Their Finest Hour, The Grand Alliance, The Hinge of Fate, Closing the Ring, Triumph and Tragedy*. London: Cassell, 1948, 1949, 1950, 1951, 1952 and 1954 respectively. The American edition is different in some points, but the citations are to the British edition unless otherwise noted.

_____. *The Unrelenting Struggle: War Speeches by the Right Hon. Winston S. Churchill*. London: Ayer, 1942.

Ciechanowski, Jan. *Defeat in Victory*. London: Odnowa, 1947.

Ciechanowski, Jan M. *The Warsaw Rising of 1944*. New York: Cambridge University Press, 1974.

Ciechanowski, Konrad. *Armia Pomorze*. Warsaw: MON, 1982.

Cienciala, Anna M. *Poland and the Western Powers, 1938–1939*. Toronto: University of Toronto Press, 1968.

_____, and Titus Komarnicki. *From Versailles to Locarno*. Lawrence: University of Kansas Press, 1984,

Cieplewicz, Mieczyslaw. *Obrona Warszawy we Wspomnieniach*. Warsaw: MON, 1984.

Cisek, Janusz. *Kosciuszko, We are Here! American Pilots of the Kosciuszko Squadron in Defense of Poland, 1919–1921*. Jefferson, NC: McFarland, 2002.

Citino, Robert M. *The Evolution of Blitzkrieg Tactics: Germany Defends Itself against Poland, 1918–1933*. New York: Greenwood, 1987.

Clemens, Diane Shaver. *Yalta*. London: Oxford University Press, 1972.

Colvin, Ian. *The Chamberlain Cabinet: How the Meetings in 10 Downing Street, 1937–1939, Led to the Second World War: Told for the First Time from the Cabinet Papers*. London: Taplinger, 1971.

Conversino, Mark J. *Fighting with the Soviets: The Failure of Operation Frantic, 1944–1945*. Lawrence: University of Kansas Press, 1997.

Copp, Terry, and Robert Vogel. *Maple Leaf Route: Falaise*. Alma, ON: Maple Leaf Road, 1983.

Corum, James S. *The Roots of Blitzkrieg: Hans von Seekt and German Military Reform*. Lawrence: University of Kansas Press, 1992.

Courtois, Stephane, ed. *The Black Book of Communism: Crimes, Terror, Repression*. Cambridge, MA: Harvard University Press, 1999.

Coutouvidis, John, and Jaime Reynolds. *Poland, 1939–1947*. London: Leicester University Press, 1986.

Cumft, Olgierd, and Hubert Kazimierz Kujawa. *Ksiega Lotnikow Polskich. Poleglych, Zmarlych i Zaginionych, 1939–1945*. Warsaw: MON, 1989.

Cynk, Jerzy B. *The Polish Air Force at War, 1939–1945*, in two volumes. Atglen, PA: Schiffer, 1998.

_____. *Polish Aircraft, 1893–1939*. London: Putnam, 1971.

Czarnocka, Halina, ed. *Armia Krajowa w Dokumentach 1939–1945*, in five volumes. London: Gryf, 1970, 1973, 1976, 1977 and 1981.

Czarnomski, F.B., ed. *They Fight for Poland: The War in the First Person*. London: Allen and Unwin, 1941.

D'Abernon, Lord Edgar V. *The Eighteenth Decisive Battle of the World, Warsaw, 1920*. London: Hodder and Stoughton, 1931.

_____. *Versailles to Rapallo*. Garden City, NY: Doubleday, 1929.

Dalecki, Ryszard. *Armia Karpaty*. Warsaw: MON, 1979.

Dalton, Hugh. *The Second World War Diary, 1940–45*. Edited by Ben Pimlott. London: Cape, 1986.

Danchev, Alex and Daniel Todman. *War Diaries (of Field Marshal Lord Alanbrooke) 1939–1945*. Berkeley: University of California Press, 2001.

Davies, Joseph E. *Mission to Moscow*. New York: Simon and Schuster, 1941.

Davies, Norman. *God's Playground: A History of Poland*, New York: Columbia University Press, 1984.

_____. *Rising '44: The Battle for Warsaw*. New York: Macmillan, 2003.

_____. *White Eagle — Red Star: The Polish-Soviet War 1919–1920*. London: Pimlico, 1972.

Deane, John R. *The Strange Alliance*. New York: Viking Press, 1947.

Dear, I. C. B., ed. *The Oxford Companion to World War II*. Oxford: Oxford University Press, 1995.

Debicki, Roman. *Foreign Policy of Poland, 1919–1939*. New York: Praeger, 1962.

Deighton, Len, and Max Hastings. *Battle of Britain*. New York: Michael Joseph, 1990.

Deist, Wilhem, Manfred Messerschmidt, Hans-Erich Volkman, and Wolfram Wette. *Germany and the Second World War*, Vol. I. Oxford: Oxford University Press, 1991.

Denfeld, D. *World War Two Museums and Relics of Europe*. Manhattan, KS: Military Affairs/Aerospace Historian, 1980.

DeSantis, Hugh. *The Diplomacy of Silence: The American Foreign Service, the Soviet Union and the Cold War, 1933–1947*. Chicago: University of Chicago Press, 1980.

Derecki, Miroslaw. *Na Sciezkach Polskich Komandosow*. Lublin, Poland: Wydawnictwo Lubeslskie, 1980.

Dilks, David, ed. *The Diaries of Sir Alexander Cadogan*. London: Cassell, 1971.

Divine, A.D. *Navies in Exile*. New York: Dutton, 1944.

Divine, Robert A., ed. *Causes and Consequences of World War Two*. Chicago: University of Chicago Press, 1969.

Documents on Polish-Soviet Relations 1939–1945, in two volumes. London: Heinemann, 1961–1967.

Drozdowski, Marian Mark, ed. *Mocarstwa Wobec Powstania*. Warsaw: Wydawnictwo Bellona, 1994.

Duffy, Peter. *The Bielski Brothers*. New York: Harper Collins, 2003.

Duraczynki, Eugeniusz. *Rzad Polski na uchodzstwie, 1939–1945: Organizacja, personalia, polityka*. Warsaw: Wydawnictwo Ksigzkai Wiedza, 1993.

_____, and Romuald Turkowski. *O Polsce na uchodzstwie: Rada Narodowa Rzeczyspospolitej Polskiej, 1939–1945*. Warsaw: Wydawnictwo Sejmowe, 1997.

Dymarski, Miroslaw. *Stosunki wewnetrzne wsrod polskieho wychodztwa politycznego i wojskowego we Francji i w Wielkiej Brytanii, 1939–1945*. Wroclaw: Wroclaw University Press, 1999.

Dziewanowski, M.K. *Joseph Pilsudski: A European Federalist, 1918–1922*. Stanford, CA: Hoover Institution Press, 1969.

Eden, Anthony. *The Reckoning: The Memoirs of Anthony Eden, Earl of Avon*. Boston: Houghton Mifflin, 1965.

Ehrman, John. *Grand Strategy: August 1943–September 1944*. Edited by James Ramsay Montagu Butler. London: Her Majesty's Stationery Office, 1956.

Eisenhower, Dwight D. *Crusade in Europe*. Garden City, NY: Doubleday, 1949.

Ellis, L.F. *Victory in the West. Vol. I, The Battle of Normandy*. London: Her Majesty's Stationery Office, 1962.

_____. *Victory in the West. Vol. II, The Defeat of Germany*. London: Her Majesty's Stationery Office, 1968.

Emmerson, James Thomas. *The Rhineland Crisis. 7 March, 1936: A Study in Multilateral Diplomacy*. Ames: Iowa State University Press, 1977.

Engel, David. *Facing a Holocaust: The Polish Government-in-Exile and the Jews, 1943–1945*. Chapel Hill: University of North Carolina Press, 1993.

Eubank, Keith. *Summit at Tehran: The Untold Story*. New York: Morrow, 1985.

Feis, Herbert. *Between War and Peace: The Potsdam Conference*. Princeton, NJ: Princeton University Press, 1960.

Fiedler, Arkady. *Squadron 303*. Letchworth, UK: Letchworth, 1942. This book saw two editions in London, two in New York, French and Portuguese translations, and three underground editions in occupied Poland.

Fieldorf, Maria, and Leszek Zachuta. *General "NIL": August Emil Fieldorf*. Warszawa, Poland: Pax, 1993.

Filipow, Krzysztof, and Zbigniew Wawer: *Passerby, Tell Poland....* Warsaw: Arkedy, 1991.

Fleming, Thomas. *The New Dealer's War: FDR and the War within World War II*. New York: Basic Books, 2001.

Foot, M. R. D. *SOE: The Special Operations Executive, 1940–1946*. Frederick, MD: University Publications of America, 1984.

Franks, Norman. *The Battle of the Airfields: Operation Bodenplatte, 1 January 1945*. London: Grub Street, 2002.

_____. *The Greatest Air Battle: Dieppe, 19th August, 1942*. London: Grub Street, 1992.

French Yellow Book. *Diplomatic Documents (1938–1939)*, New York: Reynal & Hitchcock, 1940.

Fuller, J. F. C. *The Second World War, 1939–1945*. New York: Meredith, 1968.

Garlinski, Jozef. *Intercept: Secrets of the Enigma War*. London: Dent, 1979.

_____. *Poland in the Second World War*. London: Macmillan, 1985.

_____. *Poland, S.O.E. and the Allies*. London: George Allen and Unwin, 1969.

Garnett, David. *The Secret History of PWE: The Political Warfare Executive, 1939–1945*. London: St. Ermin's, 2002.

Gates, Eleanor M. *End of the Affair: The Collapse of the Anglo-French Alliance, 1939–1940*. Berkeley: University of California Press, 1981

Gatzke, Hans W. *Stresemann and the Rearmament of Germany*. Baltimore: Johns Hopkins Press, 1954.

Gibbs, N. H. Edited by James Ramsay Montagu Butler. *Grand Strategy. Vol. I, Rearmament Policy*. Her Majesty's Stationery Office: London, 1976.

Gildea, Robert. *Marianne in Chains: In Search of the German Occupation, 1940–1945*. London: Macmillan, 2002.

Glantz, David M., and Jonathan M. House. *When Titans Clashed: How the Red Army Stopped Hitler*. Lawrence: University of Kansas Press, 2003.

Glees, Anthony. *The Secrets of the Service: A Story of Subversion of Western Intelligence*. New York: Carroll and Graf, 1987

Glowacki, Ludwik. *Obrona Warszawy i Modlina, 1939*. Warsaw: MON, 1985.

Gnys, Wladek. *First Kill: A Fighter Pilot's Autobiography*. London: Kimber, 1981.

Godlewski, Jerzy. *Bitwa nad Bzura*. Warsaw: MON, 1973.

Gooderson, Ian. *Air Power at the Battlefront: Allied Close Air Support in North-West Europe, 1943–1945*. London: Cass, 1997.

Goralski, Robert. *World War II Almanac, 1931–1945: A Political and Military Record*. New York: Putnam, 1981.

Gorodetsky, Gabriel. *Grand Delusion: Stalin and the German Invasion of Russia*. New Haven, CT: Yale University Press, 1999.

_____. *Stafford Cripps' Mission to Moscow, 1940–1942*. New York: Cambridge University Press, 1984.

Goulding, A.G. *Uncommon Valour: The Story of RAF Bomber Command, 1939–1945*. London: Goodall, 1996.

Goulter, Christina J. M. *A Forgotten Offensive: Royal Air Force Coastal Command's Anti-Shipping Campaign, 1940–1945*. London: Cass, 1995.

Graham, Dominick, and Shelford Bidwell. *Tug of War: The Battle for Italy, 1943–1945*. New York: St. Martin's Press, 1986.

Gross, Jan T. *Polish Society Under German Occupation: The Generalgouvernement, 1939–1944*. Princeton, NJ: Princeton University Press, 1979.

_____. *Revolution from Abroad: The Soviet Conquest of Poland's Western Ukraine and Western Belorussia*. Princeton, NJ: Princeton University Press, 1988.

Grzywacz, Andrzej, Marcin Kwiecien and Grzegorz Mazur. *Zbior Dokumentnow pplk. Edmunda Charaszkiewicza*. Krakow: Ksiegarnia Akademicka, 2000.

Hamilton, Nigel. *Master of the Battlefield: Monty's War Years, 1942–1944*. New York: McGraw-Hill, 1983.

_____. *Monty: Final Years of the Field-Marshal, 1944–1974*. New York: McGraw-Hill, 1986.

Harbutt, Fraser J. *The Iron Curtain: Churchill, America and the Origins of the Cold War*. Oxford: Oxford University Press, 1986.

Harriman, W. Averell, and Elie Abel. *Special Envoy to Churchill and Stalin, 1941–1946*. New York: Random House, 1975.

Harris, Arthur. *Bomber Offensive*. New York: Macmillan, 1947.

Hart, B. H. Liddell. *History of the Second World War*. New York: Putnam, 1970.

Harvey, A.D. *Arnhem*. London: Cassell, 2001.

Harvey, Maurice. *Scandinavian Misadventure: The Campaign in Norway, 1940*. New York: Hyperion Books, 1990.

Hastings, Max. *Bomber Command: The Myths and Reality of the Bombing Offensive, 1939–1945*. New York: Dial, 1979.

_____. *Overlord: D-Day and the Battle for Normandy*. New York: Simon and Schuster, 1984.

Haynes, John Earl, and E. Harvey Klehr. *Venona: Decoding Soviet Espionage in America*. New Haven, CT: Yale University Press, 1999.

Hehn, Paul N. *A Low Dishonest Decade: The Great Powers, Eastern Europe, and the Economic Origins of World War II, 1930–1941*. New York: Continuum International, 2002.

Hempel, Andrew. *Poland in World War II: An Illustrated Military History*. New York: Hippocrene Books, 2000.

Henderson, Neville. *Failure of a Mission: Berlin, 1937–1939*. New York: Putnam, 1940.

Hibbert, Christopher. *Arnhem*. London: Windrush Press, 2003.

Higham, Robin. *Air Power: A Concise History*. New York: Macdonald, 1972.

Hinsley, F. Harry, and Alan Stripp. *Code Breakers: The Inside Story of Bletchley Park*. Oxford: Oxford University Press, 1994.

Hough, Richard, and Denis Richards. *The Battle of Britain: The Greatest Air Battle of World War II.* New York: Norton, 1989.

Howard, Michael. *Grand Strategy. Vol. IV, August 1942–September 1943.* Edited by James Ramsay Montagu Butler. London: Her Majesty's Stationery Office, 1972.

_____. *The Mediterranean Strategy in the Second World War.* London: Weidenfeld and Nicolson, 1968.

Hughes, Thomas. *Overlord: Pete Quesada and the Triumph of Tactical Air Power in World War II.* New York: Simon and Schuster, 1995.

Iranek-Osmecki, George, editor and translator. *The Unseen and Silent.* London: Sheed and Ward, 1954.

Ismay, Hastings. *The Memoirs of General Lord Ismay.* New York: Viking, 1960.

Jackson, Julian. *France: The Dark Years, 1940–1944.* Oxford: Oxford University Press, 2001.

Jackson, Robert. *The Secret Squadrons: Special Duty Units of the RAF and USAAF in the Second World War.* London: Robson Books, 1983.

James, Robert Rhodes. *Victor Cazalet: A Portrait.* London: Hamilton, 1976.

Jaworzyn, J. F. *No Place to Land: A Pilot in Coastal Command.* London: Kimber, 1984.

Jedrzejewicz, Waclaw, ed. *Jozef Lipski: Diplomat in Berlin, 1933–1939.* New York: Columbia University Press, 1968.

_____. *Julian Lukasiewicz: Diplomat in Paris.* New York: Columbia University Press, 1970.

_____. *Pilsudski: A Life for Poland.* New York: Hippocrene Books, 1982.

_____. *Poland in the British Parliament, 1939–1945.* 3 vols. New York: Pilsudski, 1946–1962.

Jordan, Peter. *Aviation in Poland: A Brief Historical Outline.* London: Maxlove Publishing Co., Ltd., 1946.

Jurga, Tadeusz, and Wladyslaw Korbowski. *Armia Modlin.* Warsaw: MON, 1990.

Kacewicz, George. *Great Britain, the Soviet Union and the Polish Government in Exile, 1939–1945.* The Hague: Nijhoff, 1979.

Kahn, David. *Seizing the Enigma: The Race to Break the German U-Boat Codes, 1939–1943.* Boston: Houghton Mifflin, 1991.

Kaiser, David E. *Economic Diplomacy and the Origins of the Second World War: Germany, Britain France and Eastern Europe, 1930–1939.* Princeton, NJ: Princeton University Press, 1980.

Kalinowski, Franciszek. *Lotnictwo Polskie w Wielkiej Brytanii, 1940–1945.* Paris: Literary Institute, 1969.

Karski, Jan. *The Great Powers and Poland, 1919–1945: From Versailles to Yalta.* Lanham, MD: University Press of America, 1985.

_____. *Story of a Secret State.* Boston: Houghton Mifflin Company, 1944.

Karolevitz, Robert F., and Ross S. Fenn. *Flight of Eagles: The Story of the American Kosciuszko Squadron in the Polish-Russian War, 1919–1920.* Sioux Falls, SD: Brevet Press, 1974.

Kaufmann, J. E., and R. M. Jurga. *Fortress Europe: European fortifications of W.W. II.* Conshohacken, PA: Combined Publishing, 1999.

Keegan, John. *The Battle for History: Re-fighting World War II.* New York: Vantage Books, 1996.

_____. *The Second World War.* New York: Penguin, 1990.

_____. *Six Armies in Normandy.* New York: Viking, 1982.

Kemp, Anthony. *The Maginot Line: Myth and Reality.* New York: Stein and Day, 1982.

Kemp, Peter. *No Colours or Crest.* London: Casell, 1958.

Kennan, George F. *Memoirs, 1925–1950.* Boston: Little, Brown, 1967.

Kennedy, John. *The Business of War.* London: Hutchinson, 1957.

Kennedy, Robert M. *The German Campaign in Poland, 1939.* Washington: U.S. Government Printing Office, 1956.

Kersaudy, Francis. *Norway 1940.* New York: Harper Collins, 1990.

Kersten, Krystyna. *The Establishment of Communist Rule in Poland, 1943–1948.* Berkeley: University of California Press, 1991.

Kitchen, Martin. *British Policy Towards the Soviet Union during the Second World War.* New York: St. Martin's, 1986.

Kleczkowski, Stefan. *Poland's First Thousand.* London: Hutchinson, 1944.

Kimball, Warren F., ed. *Churchill and Roosevelt: The Complete Correspondence.* 3 vols., *Alliance Emerging, Alliance Forged* and *Alliance Declining.* Princeton, NJ: Princeton University Press, 1984.

Koniarek, Jan. *Polish Air Force, 1939–1945*. Carrollton, TX: Squadron/Signal, 1994.

Kopanski, Stanislaw. *Wspomnienia Wojenne, 1939–1946*. London: Veritas, 1961.

Korbel, Jozef. *Poland Between East and West: Soviet and German Diplomacy Toward Poland, 1918–1933*. Princeton, NJ: Princeton University Press, 1963.

Kot, Stanislaw. *Conversations with the Kremlin*. Oxford: Oxford University Press, 1963.

Kozaczuk, Wladyslaw. *Enigma*. Translated and edited by Wladyslaw Kasparek. Lanham, MD: University Publications of America, 1984.

_____, and Jerzy Straszak. *Enigma: How the Poles Broke the Nazi Code*. New York: Hippocrene Books, 2004.

Kukiel, Marian. *Six Years of Struggle for Independence: A Review of Poland's Military Contribution to Allied Victory*. Newtown, Wales: Montgomeryshire Printing Co., Ltd., 1947.

Kunert, Andrzej Krzysztof. *General Tadeusz Bor-Komorowski w relacjach i dokumentach*. Warszawa: Rytm, 2000.

_____, ed. *Rzeczpospolita Polska Czasu Wojny. Dziennik Ustaw RP i Monitor Polski, 1939–1945*. Warszawa: Wydawnictwo Kopia, 1995.

_____, ed. *Rzeczpospolita Polska Czasu Wojny. Rozkazy Naczelnego Wodza do zolnierzy, 1939–1945*. Warszawa: Wydawnictwo Kopia , 1997.

Kunert, Andrzej Krzysztof, and Jozef Szyrmer. *Stefan Rowecki: Wspomnienia I Notatki Autobiograficzne (1906–1939)*. Warszawa: Czytelnik, 1988.

Kurcz, F.S. [Wartime pseudonym of Skibinski, Franciszek]. *The Black Brigade*. London: Atlantis, 1943.

Kurowski, Adam. *Lotnictwo Polskie w 1939 roku*. Warsaw: MON, 1962.

Kurzman, Dan. *The Bravest Battle: The Twenty-Eight Days of the Warsaw Ghetto Uprising*. New York: Putnam, 1976.

Kutz, C.R. *War on Wheels: The Evolution of an Idea*. Harrisburg, PA: Military Service, 1940.

Lamb, Richard. *The Drift to War, 1922–1939*. New York: St. Martin's, 1989.

Lane, Bliss A. *I saw Poland Betrayed: An American Ambassador Reports to the American People*. Indianapolis: Bobbs-Merrill, 1948.

Laquer, Walter. *The Terrible Secret: Suppression of the Truth About Hitler's Final Solution*. Boston: Little, Brown, 1980.

Latawski, Paul, ed. *The Reconstruction of Poland, 1914–1923*. New York: St. Martin's Press, 1992.

Leasor, James. *War at the Top: Based on the Experiences of General Sir Leslie Hollis*. London: Michael Joseph, 1959.

Leitgeber, Witold. *It Speaks for Itself*. London: Polish Forces Press Bureau, 1946.

Lerski, George Jur. *Poland's Secret Envoy, 1939–1943*. New York: Bicentennial, 1988.

Leslie, R. F., ed. *The History of Poland Since 1863*. New York: Cambridge University Press, 1980.

Lewin, Ronald. *Ultra Goes to War*. New York: McGraw-Hill, 1979.

Lewis, Julian. *Changing Direction: British Military Planning for Postwar Strategic Defence, 1942–1947*. London: Sherbrook Press, 1988.

Lisiewicz, M., et al. *Destiny Can Wait: The Polish Air Force in the Second World War*. 1949. Reprint, Nashville, TX: Battery, 1988.

Lukacs, John. *Five Days in London, May, 1940*. New Haven, CT: Yale University Press, 1999.

_____. *George F. Kennan and the Origins of Containment, 1944–46*. Columbia: University of Missouri Press, 1997.

Lukas, Richard C. *Forgotten Holocaust: The Poles under German Occupation*. Lexington: University of Kentucky Press, 1986.

_____. *The Strange Allies: United States and Poland, 1941–1945*. Knoxville: University of Tennessee Press, 1978.

Mackenzie, William. *The Secret History of SOE: The Special Operations Executive 1940–1945*. London: St. Ermin's Press, 2000.

MacLeod, R., and Dennis Kelly, eds. *Time Unguarded: The Ironside Diaries, 1937–1940*. New York: Greenwood, 1962.

Macmillan, Harold. *The Blast of War*. New York: Pan Macmillan, 1968.

MacMillan, Margaret. *Paris 1919: Six Months that Changed the World*. New York: Random House, 2001.

_____. *Peacemakers: The Paris Conference of 1919 and its Attempt to End War*. New York: John Murray, 2003.

Macnab, Roy. *For Honour Alone: The Cadets of Saumur in the Defence of the Cavalry School, France, June 1940*. London: Robert Hale, 1988.

Maczek, Stanislaw. *Od Podwody do Czolga*. Edinurgh: Tomar, 1961.

Madeja, Witold, ed. *The Polish 2nd Corps and the Italian Campaign*. Allentown, PA: Game Book Marketing, 1984.

Maier, Klaus, Horst Rohde, Bernd Stegeman, and Hans Umbreit. *Germany and the Second World War*, Vol. 2. Oxford: Oxford University Press, 1991.

Majdalany, Fred. *The Battle of Cassino*. Boston: Houghton Mifflin, 1957.

Mason, Francis K. *Battle Over Britain*. London: McWhirter Twins, 1969.

Marsh, L. G. *Polish Wings Over Britain*. London: MaxLove, 1943.

Mayers, David. *The Ambassadors and America's Soviet Policy*. Oxford: Oxford University Press, 1995.

McLaren, Anna. *Poland at Arms*. London: John Murray, 1942. (Foreword by Sikorski.)

McLean, French. *The Ghetto Men: The SS Destruction of the Jewish Warsaw Ghetto, April–May 1943*. New York: Schiffer, 2001.

Medlicott, W.N. *The Economic Blockade*, Vols. I and II. London: Her Majesty's Stationery Office, 1952 and 1959.

Meehan, Patricia. *The Unnecessary War: Whitehall and the German Resistance to Hitler*. London: Sinclair-Stevenson, 1992.

Merrick, K.A. *Flights of the Forgotten: Special Duties in World War Two*. New York: Orion, 1989.

Middlebrook, Martin. *Arnhem, 1944: The Airborne Battle*. Boulder, CO: Westview Press, 1994.

_____, and Chris Everitt. *The Bomber Command War Diaries: An Operational Reference Book, 1939–1945*. London: Penguin Books, 1985.

Mitkiewicz, Leon. *W Najwyzszym Sztabie Zachodnich Aliantow, 1943–1945*. London: Veritas, 1971.

_____. *Z Generalem Sikorskim na Obczyznie*. Paris: Kultura, 1968.

Montgomery, Bernard L. *A History of Warfare*, New York: Collins, 1968.

Moor, Anthony John. *Mustang Wing: RAF Brenzett Advanced Landing Ground, Romney Marsh, Kent, 1942–1944*. St. Leonards-on-Sea: HPC, 1999.

Moulton, J. L. *Battle for Antwerp: The Liberation of the City and the Opening of the Scheldt, 1944*. New York: Allan, 1978.

Murray, G. E. Patrick. *Eisenhower Versus Montgomery: The Continuing Debate*. Westport, CT: Praeger, 1996.

Murray, Kenneth Malcom. *Wings Over Poland: The Story of the 7th (Kosciuszko) Squadron of the Polish Air Service, 1919, 1920, 1921*. New York: Appleton, 1932.

Murray, Willamson, and Allan R. Millett. *A War to be Won: Fighting the Second World War*. Cambridge, MA: Harvard University Press, 2000.

Nadeau, Remi. *Stalin, Churchill and Roosevelt Divide Europe*. New York: Praeger, 1990.

Nekrich, Aleksandr M. *Pariahs, Partners, Predators: German-Soviet Relations, 1922–1941*. New York: Columbia University Press, 1997.

Nesbit, Roy Conyers. *The Strike Wings: Special Anti-Shipping Squadrons, 1942–1945*. London: Her Majesty's Stationery Office, 1995.

Neugebauer, Norwid M. *The Defense of Poland (September 1939)*. London: Kolin, 1942.

Newman, Simon. *March 1939: The British Guarantee Poland*. Oxford: Oxford University Press, 1976.

Newman, Verne W. *The Cambridge Spies: The Untold Story of Maclean, Philby, and Burgess in America*. New York: Madison Books, 1991.

Ney-Krwawicz, Marek. *Powstanie Powszechne w Koncepciach i Pracach Sztabu Naczelnego Wodza i Komendy Glownej Armii Krajowej*. Warsaw: Wydawnictwo Naukowe Semper, 1999.

Nowak, Jan. *Courier from Warsaw*. Detroit: Wayne State University Press, 1982.

Offer, Dalia. *Escaping the Holocaust: Illegal Immigration to the Land of Israel, 1939–1945*. Oxford: Oxford University Press, 1990.

Olson, Lynne, and Stanley Cloud. *A Question of Honor: The Kosciuszko Squadron. Forgotten Heroes of World War II*. New York: Knopf, 2003.

O'Malley, Sir Owen. *The Phantom Caravan*. London: Murray, 1954.

O'Neill, William L. *A Better World: The Great Schism, Stalinism and the American Intellectuals.* New York: Simon and Schuster, 1982.

Orpen, Neil. *Airlift to Warsaw: The Rising of 1944.* Norman: University of Oklahoma Press, 1984.

Overy, Richard. *The Battle of Britain: The Myth and the Reality.* New York: Norton, 2000.

Paczkowski, Andrzej. *Stanislaw Mikolajczyk: Czyli Kleska Realisty.* Warsaw: Omnipress, 1991.

Panecki, Tadeusz. *Polski Wy silek Zbrojny w Drugiej Wojnie Swiatowej.* Warsaw: Wojskowy Instytut Historyczny Akademii Obrony Narodowej, 1999.

Paret, Peter, and Daniel Moran. *Carl von Clausewitz: Historical and Political Writings.* Princeton, NJ: Princeton University Press, 1992.

Parker, Mathew. *Monte Cassino: The Hardest-Fought Battle of World War II.* New York: Doubleday, 2004.

Patton, George. *War as I Knew It.* Boston: Houghton Mifflin, 1947.

Paulsson, Gunnar S. *The Secret City: The Hidden Jews of Warsaw, 1940–1945.* New Haven, CT: Yale University Press, 2002.

Pease, Neal. *Poland, the United States and the Stabilization of Europe, 1919–1933.* Oxford: Oxford University Press, 1986.

Peplonski, Andrzej. *Wywiad Polskich Sil Zbrojnych na Zachodzie, 1939–1945.* Warsaw: Morex, 1995.

Perlmutter, Amos. *FDR and Stalin: A Not so Grand Alliance, 1943–1945.* Columbia: University of Missouri Press, 1993.

Pestkowska, Maria. *Kazimierz Sosnkowski.* Wroclaw: Ossolineum, 1995.

_____. *Za Kulisami Rzadu Polskiego na Emigracji.* Warsaw: Oficyna Wydawnicza Rytm, 2000.

Peszke, Michael Alfred. *Poland's Navy, 1918–1945.* New York: Hippocrene Books, 1999.

Petrow, Richard. *The Bitter Years: The Invasion and Occupation of Denmark and Norway, April 1940– May 1945.* New York: Morrow, 1974.

Piekalkiewicz, Janusz. *Arnhem, 1944.* New York: Stalling, 1976.

_____. *Cassino: Anatomy of the Battle.* London: Orbis, 1980.

_____. *The Cavalry of World War II.* London: Orbis, 1979.

Pienkos, Donald. *For Your Freedom Through Ours: Polish American Efforts on Poland's Behalf, 1863–1991.* New York: East European Monographs, 1991.

Pinchuk, Ben-Cion. *Shtetl Jews Under Soviet Rule: Eastern Poland on the Eve of the Holocaust.* Oxford: Oxford University Press, 1990.

Polish Ministry of Information, London. *Polish Troops in Norway.* 1943.

Polish White Book: Official Documents Concerning Polish-German and Polish-Soviet Relations, 1933–1939. New York: Roy, 1940.

Polonsky, Anton. *The Great Powers and the Polish Question, 1941–1945.* London: London School of Economics, 1976.

_____. *Politics in Independent Poland, 1921–1939.* Oxford: Clarendon, 1972.

Pomian, Jan. *Joseph Retinger: Memoirs of an Eminence Grise.* Brighton, England: Sussex University Press, 1972.

Ponting, Clive. *1940: Myth and Reality.* Chicago: Ivan R. Dee, 1991.

Prazmowska, Anita. *Britain and Poland, 1939–1945: The Betrayed Ally.* New York: Cambridge University Press, 1995.

_____. *Britain, Poland and the Eastern Front, 1939.* New York: Cambridge University Press, 1987.

Pruszynski, Ksawery. *Poland Fights Back.* London: Hodder and Stoughton, 1941.

Raczynski, Edward. *In Allied London.* London: Weidenfeld and Nicolson, 1962.

Ray, John Philip. *The Battle of Britain: New Perspectives: Behind the Scenes of the Great Air War.* London: Arms and Armour, 1994.

Reddaway, W. F., J. H. Penson, O. Halecki, and R. Dyboski, ed. *Cambridge History of Poland.* 2 vols. 1941. Reprint, New York: Cambridge University Press, 1971.

Richards, Brooks. *Secret Flotillas: Clandestine Sea Lanes to France and French North Africa, 1940–1944.* London: Her Majesty's Stationery Office, 1996.

Riekhoff, Harald von. *German-Polish Relations, 1918–1933.* Baltimore: Johns Hopkins University Press, 1971.

Roberts, Geoffrey. *The Unholy Alliance: Stalin's Pact with Hitler.* Bloomington: Indiana University Press, 1989.

Robinson, Anthony. *R.A.F. Fighter Squadrons in the Battle of Britain*. London: Arms and Armour, 1987.

Rogers, Anthony. *Churchill's Folly: Leros and the Aegean—The Last British Defeat of World War Two*. London: Weidenfeld and Nicolson, 2003.

Rojek, Wojciech. *Odyseja Skarbu Rzeczypospolitej: Losy zlota Banku Polskiego, 1939–1950*. Krakow: Wydawnictwo Literackie, 2000.

Romerstein, Herbert, and Eric Breindel. *The Venona Secrets: Exposing Soviet Espionage and America's Traitors*. Washington: Regnery, 2000.

Roos, Hans. *A History of Modern Poland*. New York: Knopf, 1966.

Roskill, Stephen W. *The War at Sea, 1939–1945*, Vol. 3. London: Her Majesty's Stationery Office, 1960.

Ross, Graham, ed. *The Foreign Office and the Kremlin: British Documents on Anglo-Soviet Relations, 1941–1945*. New York: Cambridge University Press, 1984.

Rossino, Alexander B. *Hitler Strikes Poland: Bliztkrieg, Ideology, and Atrocity*. Lawrence: University of Kansas Press, 2003.

Rothschild, Joseph. *Pilsudski's Coup d'État*. New York: Columbia University Press, 1966.

Rozek, Edward J. *Allied Wartime Diplomacy: A Pattern in Poland*. New York: Wiley, 1958.

Ryan, Cornelius. *A Bridge Too Far*. New York: Simon and Schuster, 1974.

_____. *The Longest Day*. New York: Popular Library, 1959.

Rzepniewski, Andrzej. *Obrona Wybrzeza w 1939 roku*. Warsaw: MON, 1970.

_____. *Wojna Powietrzna w Polsce, 1939*. Warsaw: MON, 1970.

Saunders, Hilary St. George. *Royal Air Force*, Vol. III, *The Fight Is Won*. London: Her Majesty's Stationery Office, 1954.

Scholfield, Brian B. *Operation Neptune*. Annapolis: Dell, 1974.

Segal, Simon. *The New Order in Poland*. New York: Knopf, 1942.

Shephard, Ben. *A War of Nerves*. Cambridge, MA: Harvard University Press, 2001.

Sherwood, Robert E. *Roosevelt and Hopkins: An Intimate History*. New York: Harper and Brothers, 1948.

Shores, Christopher F. *2nd Tactical Air Force*. Reading, England: Osprey, 1970.

Siemaszko, Zbigniew S. *Dzialanosc Generala Tatara*, London: Polska Fundacja Kulturalna, 1999.

_____. *Lacznosc i Polityka*. London: Polska Fundacja Kulturalna, 1992.

_____. *Radiotelegrafia i Radiowywiad (1939–1946)*. London: Polska Fundacja Kulturalna, 2003.

Sikorski, Wladyslaw. *Modern Warfare*. New York: Roy, 1943.

Slessor, Sir John. *Central Blue*. London: Cassell, 1956.

Slizewski, Grzegorz. *The Lost Hopes: Stracone Zludzenia*. Koszalin: Panda, 2000.

Slowikowski, Rygor. *In the Secret Service: The Lighting of the Torch*. London: Windrush, 1988.

Smith, Bradley F. *Sharing Secrets with Stalin: How the Allies Traded Intelligence, 1941–1945*. Lawrence: University of Kansas Press, 1996.

Smith, E. D. *The Battles for Cassino*. New York: Scribner, 1975.

Snyder, Timothy. *The Reconstruction of Nations: Poland, Ukraine, Lithuania, Belarus, 1569–1999*. New Haven, CT: Yale University Press, 2003.

Sopocko, Eryk. *Orzel's Patrol. The Story of the Polish Submarine*. London: Methuen, 1942.

Sosabowski, Stanislaw. *Freely I Served*. Nashville: Battery, 1982.

Spears, Major-General Sir Edward. *Assignment to Catastrophe*. Vol. 1, *Prelude to Dunkirk*. New York: Wynn, 1954.

_____. *Assignment to Catastrophe*. Vol. 2, *The Fall of France*. New York: Wynn, 1955.

Stachiewicz, Bogdan, ed. *Waclaw Stachieiwcz: General Szef Sztabu Glownego, 1935–1939*. Warsaw: Rytm, 1998.

Stachura, Peter D., ed. *The Poles in Britain, 1940–2000: From Betrayal to Assimilation*. London: Cass, 2004.

Stafford, David: *Britain and European Resistance 1940–1945*. Toronto: University of Toronto Press, 1983.

_____. *Churchill and Secret Service*. New York: Overlook, 1998.

Steer, Frank. *Arnhem: The Fight to Sustain: The Untold Story of the Airborne Logisticians*. Barnsley, UK: Pen and Sword Books, 2000.

Stettinius, Edward R., Jr. *Roosevelt and the Russians: The Yalta Conference*. New York: Doubleday, 1949.

Stoler, Mark. *Allies and Adversaries: The Joint Chiefs of Staff, the Grand Alliance and U.S. Strategy in World War II*. Chapel Hill: University of North Carolina Press, 2000.

Strzembosz, Tomasz. *Rzeczpospolita Podziemna*. Warszawa: Wydawnictwo Krupski, 2000.

Suchcitz, Andrzej. *See* Turnbull.

Swiecicki, Marek. *Seven Rivers to Bologna*. London: J. Rolls Books, 1946.

_____. *With the Red Devils at Arnhem*. London: MaxLove, 1945.

Sword, Keith ed. *Deportation and Exile. Poles in the Soviet Union*. New York: St. Martin's, 1994.

_____. *Sikorski: Soldier and Statesman*. London: Orbis Books, 1990.

_____, ed. *The Soviet Takeover of the Polish Eastern Provinces, 1939–1941*. New York: St. Martin's, 1991.

Szarota, Tomasz. *Stefan Rowecki, "GROT."* Warszawa: Panstwowe Wydawnictwo Naukowe, 1983.

Tarczynski, Jan. *Organizacja Zrzutow Materialowych Dla Armii Krajowej*. London: Polish Underground Movement Study Trust, 2001.

Taylor, A. J. P. *The Origins of the Second World War*. New York: Atheneum, 1985.

Taylor, John W. R., and Kenneth Munson. *Military Air Power*. London: New English Library, 1975.

Taylor, Telford. *The March of Conquest: The German Victories in Western Europe, 1940*. New York: Simon and Schuster, 1958.

_____. *Munich: The Price of Peace*. New York: Doubleday, 1979.

Tebinka, Jacek. *Polityka Brytyjska wobec problemu granicy Polsko-Radzieckiej, 1939–1945*. Warsaw: Uniwersytet Gdanski, Instytut Historii, 1998.

Tedder, Lord. *With Prejudice*. Boston: Little, Brown, 1966.

Tennenbaum, Joseph. *In Search of a Lost People: The Old and the New Poland*. New York: Beechhurst, 1948.

Tent, James Foster. *E-Boat Alert: Defending the Normandy Invasion Fleet*. Ramsbury, UK: Airlife, 1996.

Terry, Sarah Meiklejohn. *Poland's Place in Europe*. Princeton, NJ: Princeton University Press, 1983.

Toland, John. *The Last 100 days*. New York: Bantam, 1966.

Turnbull, Elizabeth, and Andrzej Suchcitz, eds. *Edward Roland Sword: The Diary and Despatches of a Military Attache in Warsaw, 1938–1939*. London: Polish Cultural Foundation, 2001.

Turner, Henry Ashby. *Stresemann and the Politics of the Weimar Republic*. Princeton, NJ: Princeton University Press, 1963.

Ulam, Adam B. *Expansion and Coexistence: The History of Soviet Foreign Policy 1917–1967*. New York: Praeger, 1968.

Umiastowski, Roman. *Poland, Russia and Great Britain, 1941–1945*. London: Hollis and Carter, 1946.

_____. *Russia and the Polish Republic*. London: Aquafondata, 1944.

Urquhart, R. E. *Arnhem*. New York: Norton, 1958.

Van Dyke, Carl. *The Soviet Invasion of Finland, 1939–1940*. London: Cass, 1997.

Wandycz, Piotr S. *Czechoslovak-Polish Confederation and the Great Powers, 1940–1943*. Bloomington: Indiana University Press, 1956.

_____. *France and Her Eastern Allies 1919–1925*. Minneapolis: Minnesota University Press, 1961.

_____. *Lands of Partitioned Poland, 1795–1921*. Cambridge, MA: Harvard University Press, 1969.

_____. *Polish Diplomacy: Aims and Achievements 1919–1945*. London: Orbis, 1988.

_____. *Soviet-Polish Relations 1917–1921*. Cambridge, MA: Harvard University Press, 1969.

_____. *Twilight of French Eastern Alliance, 1926–1936*. Princeton, NJ: Princeton University Press, 1988.

_____. *The United States and Poland*. Cambridge, MA: Harvard University Press, 1980.

Watt, Donald Cameron. *How War Came: The Immediate Origins of the Second World War, 1938–1939*. New York: Pantheon Books, 1989.

Wedemeyer, Robert. *Wedemeyer Reports*. New York: Holt, 1958.

Wegrzecki, Kazimierz. *Kosynierzy Warszawscy*. London: Veritas Foundation, 1968.

Weinberg, Gerhard L. *The Foreign Policy of Hitler's Germany: Starting World War II, 1937–1939*. Chicago: University of Chicago Press, 1980.

_____. *A World at Arms: A Global History of World War II*. New York: Cambridge University Press, 1994.

Weinstein, Allen, and Alexander Vassiliev. *The Haunted Wood: Soviet Espionage in America—The Stalin Era*. New York: Random House, 1998.

West, Nigel [Rupert Allason]. *The Sigint Secrets: The Signals Intelligence War, 1900 to Today*. New York: Morrow, 1986.

_____, and Joan Bright Astley. *Gubbins and SOE*. London: Perseus, 1993.

West, William J. *The Betrayal of MI5*. New York: Wynwood, 1990.

Wilkinson, Peter. *Foreign Fields: The Story of an SOE Operative*. London and New York: Tauris, 1997.

Wilmot, Chester. *The Struggle for Europe*. London, 1954.

Willmott, H.P. *The Great Crusade: A New Complete History of the Second World War*. London: Joseph, 1989.

Wilt, Alan F. *War From the Top*. Bloomington: Indiana University Press, 1990.

Woodward, Llewellyn. *British Foreign Policy in the Second World War*. London: Her Majesty's Stationery Office, 1962.

Woytak, Richard A. *On the Border of War and Peace*. New York: Columbia University Press, 1979.

_____. *Werble Historii*. Bydgoszcz: SP. Sprint, 1999.

Wroblewski, Jan. *Armia Lodz, 1939*. Warsaw: MON. 1975.

_____. *Armia Prusy, 1939*. Warsaw: MON, 1986.

_____. *Samodzielna Ggrupa Operacyjna—Polesie, 1939*. Warsaw: MON, 1989.

Wynn, Humphrey, and Susan Young. *Prelude to Overlord*, Novato, CA: Airlife, 1983.

Wynot, Edward D. *Polish Politics in Transition: The Camp of National Unity and the Struggle for Power, 1935–1939*. Athens: University of Georgia Press, 1974.

Young, Peter. *World War, 1939–1945: A Short History*. New York: Crowell, 1966.

Zagorski, Waclaw. *Seventy Days: A Diary of the Warsaw Insurrection 1944*. London: Muller, 1957.

Zajac, Jozef. *Dwie Wojny, 1914–1939*. London: Veritas, 1964.

Zaloga, Steve, and Victor Madej. *The Polish Campaign, 1939*. New York: Hippocrene, 1985.

Zaloga, Steve J. *Poland 1939: The Birth of Bliztkrieg*. Botley, UK: Osprey, 2002.

_____. *The Polish Army 1939–1945*. London: Osprey, 1982.

Zamoyski, Adam. *The Battle for the Marchlands*. New York: Columbia University Press, 1981.

_____. *The Forgotten Few: The Polish Air Force in the Second World War*. New York: Hippocrene Books, 1995.

_____. *The Polish Way: A Thousand Year History of the Poles and their Culture*. New York: Franklin Watts, 1988.

Zawodny, J. K. *Death in the Forest: The Story of the Katyn Forest Massacre*. South Bend, IN: University of Notre Dame Press, 1962.

_____. *Nothing but Honor: The Story of the Warsaw Uprising 1944*. Stanford, CA: Hoover Institution Press, 1978.

Zoltowski, Adam. *Border of Europe*. London: Hollis and Carter, 1950.

Index